Gwen Verdon

ALSO BY PETER SHELLEY
AND FROM McFARLAND

*Neil Simon on Screen: Adaptations and
Original Scripts for Film and Television* (2015)

Sandy Dennis: The Life and Films (2014)

Australian Horror Films, 1973–2010 (2012)

Jules Dassin: The Life and Films (2011)

Frances Farmer: The Life and Films of a Troubled Star (2011)

*Grande Dame Guignol Cinema: A History of
Hag Horror from* Baby Jane *to* Mother (2009)

Gwen Verdon
A Life on Stage and Screen

Peter Shelley

McFarland & Company, Inc., Publishers
Jefferson, North Carolina

Acknowledgments: Special thanks are offered to Barry Lowe and Kath Perry. Additional thanks are given to Rick McKay, Catherine Porter, Michael Schnurr, Stewart South, and Photofest.

LIBRARY OF CONGRESS CATALOGUING-IN-PUBLICATION DATA [new form]

   Names: Shelley, Peter.
   Title: Gwen Verdon : a life on stage and screen / Peter Shelley.
   Description: Jefferson, North Carolina : McFarland & Company, Inc., Publishers, 2015. | Includes bibliographical references and index.
   Identifiers: LCCN 2015036738| ISBN 9780786497362 (softcover : acid free paper) | ISBN 9781476621036 (ebook)
   Subjects: LCSH: Dancers—United States—Biography. | Actresses—United States—Biography.
   Classification: LCC GV1785.V467 S54 2015 | DDC 792.8092—dc23
   LC record available at http://lccn.loc.gov/2015036738

BRITISH LIBRARY CATALOGUING DATA ARE AVAILABLE

© 2015 Peter Shelley. All rights reserved

No part of this book may be reproduced or transmitted in any form or by any means, electronic or mechanical, including photocopying or recording, or by any information storage and retrieval system, without permission in writing from the publisher.

Front cover: Gwen Verdon as Lola in the 1958 film *Damn Yankees* (Warner Bros./Photofest)

Printed in the United States of America

McFarland & Company, Inc., Publishers
  Box 611, Jefferson, North Carolina 28640
    www.mcfarlandpub.com

Table of Contents

Acknowledgments — iv
Preface — 1

1. Beginning and Jack Cole — 5
2. Working with Jack Cole in Films — 20
3. *Can-Can* — 35
4. *Damn Yankees,* Bob Fosse and *New Girl in Town* — 46
5. *Damn Yankees* on Film and *Redhead* — 65
6. Semi-Retirement and Motherhood — 81
7. *Sweet Charity* — 93
8. *Sweet Charity* on Film — 121
9. *Children! Children!* — 135
10. *Chicago* — 151
11. *All That Jazz* — 169
12. The Mature Actress — 182
13. Fosse Dies — 202
14. Charity One Last Time and *Fosse* — 221

Appendix: Performances on Stage, Film, Television and Record — 237
Bibliography — 243
Index — 263

Preface

I first became aware of Gwen Verdon in the film version of *Damn Yankees* (1958) so it was fascinating for me to discover that her association with choreographer Bob Fosse had been preceded by an earlier phase of her career. This made writing the book a journey of discovery. Verdon had a remarkable career and her life can be seen as having five separate acts, since her work in show business was interrupted by two temporary retirements. Her career can be divided into two periods when she worked with two choreographers who changed its direction. They were Fosse and Jack Cole; Verdon acted as dance assistant and muse to their choreographic ambitions. Fosse in particular was responsible for giving Verdon two of her five acts, by creating the stage show *Sweet Charity* for her and bringing her out of her second retirement.

But for someone to have had five acts in her life, she needs to be special, and Verdon certainly was that. She was an extraordinary dancer, and though her singing voice was ordinary, her dramatic abilities made up for them. Verdon's gifts as an actor would later be displayed in dramatic roles that defined the last act of her life. In his review of her Broadway show *Redhead*, Brooks Atkinson wrote that she did everything that anyone could expect of a musical performer, and more. "She can portray character like a fully licensed dramatic actress. She can sing in a russet-colored voice that is mighty pleasant to hear ... and she can dance with so much grace and gaiety that her other accomplishments seem to be frosting on the cake."

Verdon's persona was a combination of sexiness and innocence, qualities that have been described as Chaplinesque. She was a great admirer of Chaplin, who she called an art nouveau ballet dancer. Verdon came across as someone who was naughty but nice, a hard-luck bad girl who wore her heart on her sleeve. This paradox was embodied in her Charity Hope Valentine from the stage show *Sweet Charity*, the prostitute with a heart of gold whose need for the love of a man made her naïve and pure.

More street-wise than bright, Charity was masochistic and pathetic but lovable. Verdon never got the chance to commit her stage performance to film for the ages, though we have glimpses of it in her television guest appearances. What makes some of these performances even more heartbreaking is the suspicion that she may have known at the time she did them that she was not to do the film.

There is, in fact, a sadness about Verdon's career. Being allowed to do the film version of *Damn Yankees* after she had done the stage role did not lead her immediately to more films. She returned to the stage and would later make more films and television appearances, but the forces needed to capitalize on her triumph in *Damn Yankees* did not converge for her. This is not so unusual for performers who are mostly associated with their work in theater. Think of the limited film careers of Ethel Merman and Carol Channing. But the fact that this happened to Verdon, who already had a film career as a Jack Cole dancer, seems even more frustrating. Perhaps if Bob Fosse had decided to begin his career as film director earlier than he did, things may have been different. But this was not to be, and even when he did begin making films, he never cast Verdon.

Her golden period on stage is deemed to be a relatively brief one, from *Can-Can* in 1953 to *Redhead* in 1959. It was considered golden because Verdon enjoyed four hot shows in a row and won Tony awards for each of them, a record unequalled by any other musical actress. Her string of hits was broken after her comeback role in *Sweet Charity* in 1966. Although the show was a box office winner, it failed to earn her the Tony Award. Her disappointment must have been worsened by the fact that Fosse, *her own husband*, overlooked her for the movie version. Verdon considered that acting in musical comedies, which had been her forte, was still acting. However, her desire to do "straight" parts was not satisfied. The one attempt she made, the 1972 thriller *Children! Children!*, was a flop that closed on its opening night. Although Verdon wanted to try again, the few offers she received were badly timed, and then they dried up. Perhaps she became pigeonholed by the industry because of her own success. Even when she presented at the Tony Awards multiple times, it was nearly always for musical comedy awards. Verdon resurfaced after she decided that she was now too old to dance on stage and she transitioned to working in supporting roles in film and making television guest appearances. While it is wonderful to see her in these, there is still a sadness in the limitations of these opportunities.

This biography is the first full-length book on Verdon. She had been given a chapter in Roy Harris' 1997 book *Eight Women of the American*

Stage, but it was a small one. Verdon was also sporadically mentioned in biographies and studies of Fosse. These were Kevin Boyd Grubb's 1989 *Razzle Dazzle: The Life And Work of Bob Fosse*, Martin Gottfried's 1990 *All His Jazz: The Life And Death of Bob Fosse*, Margery Beddow's 1996 *Bob Fosse's Broadway*, and Sam Wasson's 2013 *Fosse*. Additionally, she was featured in Glenn Loney's 1984 *Unsung Genius: The Passion of Dancer-Choreographer Jack Cole*. However, none of these books provides a satisfactory look out Verdon's life and career as an individual. This book attempts to do so, although since some of her work for television in particular remains unavailable for viewing, it regrettably cannot be considered a definitive study.

Accessing the aforementioned sources and any associated biographies and books on Verdon's co-workers allowed me to consider differing views of some of the events in her life and to highlight any apparent inaccuracies. My research also had me review interviews that Verdon gave to newspapers and magazines. Since not all of her work is available on DVD or video, I viewed some of her film and television guest appearances via rare collectors' prints, and was pleased to find that some could also be seen on YouTube. Where a title could not be viewed, I have provided as much information as I could obtain. One I especially regret not being able to get was Verdon's 1973 made-for-TV movie *Deadly Visitor*.

The book is written as a biography, with Verdon's career presented in the context of her life. I have not made new chapters for each of the stage shows or films or television appearances or recordings. Rather they are mixed into the biography, although I have given an analysis of the work when possible. For what I have viewed and heard, I have commented specifically on Verdon's appearance and performance, as well as provided any relevant notes on the title's narrative. I have also discussed the critical reaction that the work received. To complement the text, I have supplied photographic portraits and stills from some of her film, television, and stage work. Additionally the book comes with a brief appendix of the star's work and a bibliography of reference sources.

1

Beginning and Jack Cole

Gwyneth Evelyn Verdon was born in Culver City, at the California Lutheran Church Hospital, but the date differs according to sources. Some give it as January 13, 1925, others January 16. Her surname rhymes with "stirred-in" and not "spurred on" as *Time* magazine said in its 1955 cover story on her. Verdon said the confusion probably came from her trying to explain that the name wasn't Vernon and then it was thought to be pronounced that way. Her name would be often spelled Vernon. People also put two ns in her first name.

She was the second child of Joseph William Verdon (December 31, 1896–June 23, 1978) and Gertrude Lillian Verdon nee Standring (October 24, 1896–October 16, 1956). The Verdons also had a son, William O'Farrell Verdon (August 1, 1923–June 10, 1991), nicknamed "Red" because of his red hair. Her parents were English immigrants who had come to America via Canada. They were show people though Joseph also worked as a gardener. Verdon's great-grandfather was an actor in Shakespearean repertory, touring the British provinces, and her grandfather was an English step dancer. Gertrude told newspapermen that her parents were strolling players in England, which Verdon said her mother made up to deflect the press attention given to Verdon. It had the opposite effect, which led Gertrude to tell a bigger, crazier lie: that Verdon was born in the shadow of MGM studios. That too failed though Verdon herself would perpetuate the myth by using it in her own theater program biographies. She also said that she was born in between MGM and 20th Century-Fox, between the back gate of one and the front gate of the other. The family lived in a $12-a-month bungalow on Keystone Avenue near the MGM studios. The location made Verdon say that she always felt like a Keystone Cop.

Gertrude was a dancer and a veteran of Denishawn, the modern dance company founded by Ruth St. Denis and Ted Shawn. She ran a dancing school in Culver City. Joseph was also in the industry, being a second best boy electrician at MGM. It is said that he worked on nine or ten Garbo films, partially because she liked having the familiar faces of the same crew members around her. Verdon would say that when she was three, he would come home and tell her about all the big stars he had lit that day but all she ever wanted to hear about was the monkey in the Tarzan movies. Rather than ask to watch any of the MGM musical dance numbers being filmed, or Garbo, Verdon only wanted to see the Tarzans. She was intrigued with the intelligence of the monkey, and thought that he was far brighter than any human.

A series of infantile diseases afflicted Verdon at the age of two. She had measles, chicken pox, mumps, and whooping cough. She required a hernia operation and then suffered a severe case of rickets which left her in bed for months. Verdon would say that rickets was a disease of the poor and that she was born with them because of bad nutrition. Her knees were so badly knocked that they crossed over each other and gave her big sores. For a time she had to be carried from one place to another because she couldn't walk. Also the muscles on the inside of the leg were too long for the muscles on the outside. Because of her misshapen legs, Verdon was nicknamed "Gimpy" by other children. A doctor suggested that Verdon's legs be broken so that they could be reset and straightened but her mother disagreed. Gertrude is said to have torn up the letter with this recommendation. At first she thought of taking her daughter to an orthopedic hospital in Los Angeles, but then had a more experimental idea. Since Verdon's problem was muscular rather than crippling, her mother insisted that that the exercise of dancing was a better therapy; a natural corrective for body defects. Gertrude is quoted as saying, "That child is like wild sunset! She *will* dance!" The dance of Ruth St. Denis had exercises that would not stretch the inside muscles because you didn't have to turn out or use those particular muscles.

For nearly ten years the girl's legs were encased in ugly high-topped corrective shoes laced up to her knees and rigid leg braces which earned her the nickname "Boots" Verdon. Later she would claim that this was a refrain she still heard in her sleep. She only wore them in her off-hours but they gave the girl a sense of shame and a fear of discovery and recrimination. Verdon said that people would look at her and she would think that she was pretty but still a cripple. Even after she was able to take them off, she was afraid that something give her away to be the cripple she knew people saw her as. To hide her deformity, Verdon would stand with her right leg turned; Bob Fosse would later make it one of his signature looks. The leg positioning came from incorrect dancing. Ballet training had the dancers' feet turned out for a stand but Gertrude had learned that the muscle used to turn out was the wrong one to use for her daughter. Therefore Verdon learned ballet with her toes turned in. Her legs were not her only problem since she was also cross-eyed, freckled, bespectacled, and pathetically skinny. Verdon would say that she had to learn to accept herself as an ugly duckling and to hope that people would learn to like her a little in spite of the way she looked. As dance was prescribed for her legs, eye exercises were given to correct her squint and ballet would keep her eyes busy rolling up into her head to focus together on images which were never there.

She said that she didn't remember exactly when she started dancing. Since her mother was a dancer, she thought everybody and their mother danced. At Gertrude's school, Verdon studied under the instruction of Ernest Belcher. Known as the dancing teacher to the stars, he was the father of Marge Champion, who also attended the same classes, as did Tula Ellice Finklea who would become Cyd Charisse. Marge Champion tells that she met Verdon when she was eleven and Verdon was seven. Verdon learned ballet, buck-and-wing, soft shoe and the waltz clog. Belcher would tell her that any contortionist can learn to stick their leg up in the air, but only a rare person can do it the right way and become a dancer. That's the kind of person that Verdon wanted to be. Belcher demanded perfection but he was not the kind of teacher who fired one to great heights. Rather, he saw that an unemotional technique should be thoroughly planted. Verdon was grateful for his influence.

At the age of three, Verdon had entertained at an MGM Christmas party thrown by Marion Davies. The first time when she was in front of an audience was when she was three and a half. Gertrude worked at the Los Angeles Cotton Club as a dancer, doing ethnic pseudo–Oriental numbers. The dinner show audience members were all white, the night show audience members all black, and at 2 a.m. it was mixed. One night Verdon's father drove her and her brother to the club and, upon arriving, told Verdon to get Gertrude. In her pajamas, she walked up the red carpet that led into the candlelit club and onto the stage where Willie Covan, a black tap dancer, was performing. He asked her what he could do for her and Verdon told him, "I want my mother!" The audience laughed when they heard it. Verdon would later study acting with Covan, although she felt his approach was old-fashioned. She said that she also appeared in her first act with Covan and his wife Flo, who was beige with red hair and freckles. It was known as Covan and Family, and Verdon played their daughter.

At four she appeared with Gertrude in a dance act called the Two

Flying D'Arcys at the Los Angeles Biltmore Hotel. She also was taught the Hawaiian hula dance by her mother and performed at Loyola University in Los Angeles. The sight caused a priest to come running down the aisle to tell her that she was lewd. Verdon didn't know what the word meant but she still ran off stage in response. Verdon was billed as Baby Alice, "the fastest tapper in the world," at the Shrine Auditorium. She claimed that this was a title that didn't mean anything because that's what everybody called themselves, and you were only considered good if you were fast. You could really be terrible but if you were fast, that was all that mattered. Some sources claim that the Baby Alice credit was when Verdon was six although she said she was five and in an act with four-year-old June Brady. Brady imitated Fanny Brice, Sophie Tucker and Mae West while Verdon tap-danced, told the corniest jokes, and did pratfalls. She and Brice also ended up together doing a pseudo–Hawaiian dance. She also danced at Loew's State and the Million Dollar Theatre.

At nine Verdon was in a ballet at the Hollywood Bowl, and also performed as a hula dancer, acrobat and clown in the circus. According to Marge Champion, one ballet at the Bowl was called Carnival in Venice and all the dancers had specialty acts to help give the illusion of a painting come to life. Champion did "The Spirit of the Night" in a Grecian outfit. Verdon and Gertrude and a little dog were people wandering through the streets. During the June rehearsal, it was very hot, which made the dog vomit. Belcher's assistant Maria stripped Verdon down to a leotard and put poms poms on her and a little tail and a leash around her neck and she became the dog.

Dancing toughened Verdon's muscles, straightened her legs and developed her body. The eye exercises corrected the squint. But she sometimes rebelled against the discipline imposed on her. She says it was at the age of ten that she first tried to break away from dancing when she discovered boys and baseball. Her mother discouraged her from a career in baseball by pointing out that dancing gave her grace and poise. Verdon didn't want to hear that and threatened to run away from home, packing greasepaint in her suitcase rather than a tube of toothpaste. But soon she would learn that Gertrude was right. Poise would bring boys faster than a .300 batting average. When she wasn't working, Verdon attended at a school for professional children. She also began to accumulate elements that she would incorporate in her dancing, such as learning sign language from a deaf mute girl in school. Learning to sign gave Verdon a greater facility with hands and fingers. Verdon said that she wasn't really interested in dance and she didn't know she was dancing until she saw a Fred Astaire film and became enamored with him. In the fourth grade when she was about eight, she began signing her homework Ginger Verdon, after seeing an Astaire–Ginger Rogers movie. When the teacher asked "Why Ginger?" the girl told her, "Because I can't be Fred."

At eleven Verdon made her uncredited film debut as a solo ballerina in the musical romance *The King Steps Out* (1936). Directed by Josef von Sternberg for Columbia Pictures, the film starred Grace Moore as Bavarian Princess Elizabeth, who goes to the Viennese Hellbrunn summer palace to prevent her sister Helena from marrying their cousin, the Austrian Emperor Franz Josef Habsburg, to whom Helen is betrothed. The screenplay is said to be based on the 1932 German operetta *Sissy*, also known as *Lisa*, by Hubert and Ernst Marischka and composed by Fritz Kreisler, which in turn was based on the play *Sissy's Brautfahrt* by Ernst Decsey and Gustav Holm. The film was made between January 6 and February 26, 1936.

Verdon only appears in one scene. At first she is amongst a group of what is said to be sixty Viennese Imperial ballerinas who have been summoned to perform for the emperor's birthday. The girls are seen wearing tutus and dancing in a rehearsal room that would seem too small for them to move in. Verdon is given her own medium shot for a few seconds as she twirls in circles. In a scene where the dancers are addressed by Colonel Von Kempen, Verdon is not visible.

The film was released on May 28, 1936, and was lambasted by Frank Nugent in the *New York Times* (who made no mention of von Sternberg) and later by Pauline Kael. The director would repudiate the film and ask that it not be included in retrospectives of his work. However it proved to be a box office hit.

Verdon went on to perform at American Legion and Canadian Legion meetings and Boy Scout jamborees, and attended Hamilton High School where her classes included drawing and sewing. The class clown, she got into trouble for imitating her teachers. Verdon's future championing of causes is said to have been stimulated by a school sit-down strike on behalf of Japanese-American neighbors herded into detention camps in World War II. Gertrude tried to imbue the same theatrical ambitions in her son William, though she found that he had not been bitten with the same show biz bug as his older sister. She dressed him up when he was fourteen in a trenchcoat to make him look the required sixteen to audition for the part of Huck Finn, but he didn't get the part.

At twelve, Verdon was part of a group that did gypsy dances for Shriner's conventions and the like. At thirteen, she had developed a 36-

inch bust, 24 inch waist and 36- inch hips, and with the right makeup she could project the image of a young adult. Some sources claim that at this time Verdon lied about her age, claiming to be sixteen, and was cast as one of the Broadbent Dancers in a revival of *Show Boat* at the Los Angeles Civic Light Opera Association. The production was part of the Third Annual Light Opera Festival at the Auditorium Theatre. A program for the show with Verdon listed in the cast is dated 1940, which puts her age at fifteen. Her casting came about after she had been taking classes with choreographer Aida Broadbent, and thereafter she would be cast in Broadbent's opera dance group for seven summers. These included "nature dances" in productions like *Gypsy Baron* and *The Red Mill*. The shows also played San Francisco and all the dancers lived together. Gertrude traveled with her daughter.

Verdon said that the ballet company also appeared in the MGM musical comedy *Presenting Lily Mars* (1943). The film was in production from August 3 to late October, 1942 with reshoots done in March 1943 and it was released on April 29, 1943. It is possible that she is amongst the chorus dancers in the number "Is It Really Love (Or the Gypsy in Me?)," in the rehearsal for "Kulebiaka (Russian Rhapsody)" which is later headed by Judy Garland, observing Martha Eggerth rehearsing "When I Look at You," in the boarding house crowd scenes, in the opening night show performance of "Kulebiaka" headed by Eggerth, and in the finale behind Garland in "Where's There Music." In the "Kulebiaka" opening night scene one girl resembles Verdon, standing behind Eggerth in one shot as the star sings, but it cannot be confirmed that it is in fact her.

At fourteen Verdon was chosen "Miss California" by the Catalina bathing suit company, and posed for ads on Venice beach. When she decided to learn to ice skate, she took her lunch with her every day to the rink and glided around getting to know all the instructors. They taught her enough that she was offered a skating job the first time she auditioned. Verdon said that her skating was uncontrolled and that she did a figure eight in squares. At this time she also picked up the ability to sing, although at her age it was considered comparatively late in life to begin to use it in a professional capacity.

At fifteen Verdon appeared at a San Diego club as half of a ballroom team called Verdon and Del Velle. She also frequented burlesque houses because she felt that burlesque was the real folk dancing of the United States: "It grew up here. And the stripper is a natural, spontaneous growth from the hoochy-cooch of the carnivals and country fairs." Verdon watched with admiration and with the seriousness of a Ph.D. candidate the gyrations and controlled torso sinuosities of Georgia Sothern and Charmaine, and found sermons in their bumps and grinds. Her study would pay off in her later Eve in "The Garden of Eden Ballet" of *Can-Can*. She was also drawn to the burlesque clowns in baggy pants and became fascinated by Chaplin's Little Tramp character. Verdon's interest in the comic but sad persona would later develop so that her characters would be indebted to the French clown Pierrot and to Harlequin, the sixteenth-century *commedia dell'arte* figure who was the prototype for many circus clowns and burlesque comedians. She also won a part in a water ballet although she had no previous experience in swimming.

At sixteen Verdon was the specialty act "Girl in Gold," wearing a rubber bra and panties and with her entire body painted by Gertrude in shimmering gold powder and glycerine, presented before a house of loud and hungry men, in a review at the Hollywood nightclub N.T. Granlund's Florentine Gardens. The choreography is credited to Dave Gould, the show headlined Sugar Geise, and the chorus included Marie McDonald, Yvonne De Carlo, and Carol Haney. There is footage of Verdon supposedly at sixteen dancing on film on YouTube, although it is not known what the occasion was. Wearing a black tutu and a black feather in her hair, she dances en pointe in front of stationary ladies wearing fashion wear before a man enters singing. Regrettably the clip ends before the man can be seen properly.

Also when she was sixteen, she was in a repertory group. She played in *Pygmalion* and in the comedy *Biography*. However Verdon's burgeoning theatrical career soon came to a halt when she got married.

Sources differ as to how old Verdon was when she met the man she would marry. Some say it occurred in 1942 when she was seventeen, others say she was only sixteen. However old she was, this man would prompt her to give up her professional career and elope with him. He was James Archibald Henaghan, sometimes spelled as Heneghan. Blonde, brash and fun-loving, he was twice her age. He was also a divorced sometime-screenwriter, gossip columnist on Louella Parsons' staff, literary agent for Mickey Spillane, promoter and general man-about-Hollywood. Verdon had only known Henaghan for six months when she agreed to marry him, and she is said to have lied to the Orange County judge that she was twenty-two.

Exactly nine months later, on March 9, 1943, Verdon bore him a son, Jimmy O'Farrell Henaghan. Henaghan said that Verdon's father, who reportedly hated Henaghan, was waiting with a shotgun to make sure that the baby didn't arrive a day before it was due. Leaving her child in the care of her parents, Verdon followed her husband into journalism and reviewed movies and nightclub acts for *The Hollywood Reporter*. She also served occasionally as her husband's "leg woman" or news chaser. Verdon said that she had to use fake by-line names because she was underage. Some of these were Phyllis Taylor and Glynda O'Farrell. She once got close to being sued for two million dollars for libel, which highly flattered her. At a burlesque house in Los Angeles, Verdon studied the strippers and learned some of the techniques that she would later use in *Damn Yankees*.

She also made one more film appearance. Some sources claim that she appeared uncredited as a cheerleader in the Republic B musical *Hoosier Holiday* (1943). However the available print does not feature Verdon, and the only cheerleaders on screen are said to be played by Nancy Brinckman and Jane Allen. The film had an original running time of 72 minutes, and since the viewed print is only 63 minutes it is possible that Verdon was edited out.

Verdon *can* be seen as a girl in a nightclub in Columbia's B musical comedy *Blonde from Brooklyn* (1945). Again uncredited, she only appears in one scene where she has an exchange with the film's leading man, Robert Stanton. After having planned to meet a jukebox girl at La Cucaracha at quarter to nine, he sees Verdon sitting at alone at the bar. Wearing a mink coat, she is looking for someone. He tells her the time is a quarter to nine, thinking she might be the jukebox girl. In response, Verdon says, "It is? And Jack said he'd be here at eight. Some nerve!" and then she exits. Directed by Del Lord, the film was in production from February 12 to 28, 1945. It was released on June 21 with the taglines "Brooklyn Beauty Turns Southern Cutie!" and "A 20 Whistle Salute!"

One source claims that Verdon auditioned for Jack Cole to play a chorus girl in *Blonde from Brooklyn*. There are chorus girls in the film but they sing, not dance, which puts this claim into question. Another question is whether Cole was in a position to have offered Verdon such a part at the time. Although he is not credited for the film's musical numbers, Cole had come to Columbia to become the studio's resident choreographer in February 1944, while the film was in production. Verdon knew Cole since he was an alumnus of the Denishawn school. She is quoted as saying that she had auditioned for Cole when she was seventeen, which would have been in 1942. Verdon admitted that she had lied about her age and when she was found out, she was fired. In the *New York Times* obituary for Cole (February 20, 1974), Anna Kisselgoff wrote that Verdon became Cole's student in 1944.

Verdon claimed that she worked for Cole on the Columbia musical *Tars and Spars*, which was in production from July 26 to September 17, 1945. She said that she rehearsed one number but when it was discovered that she didn't belong to the film chorus union she was fired. Verdon claimed that she didn't remember if the number was shot before she was let go. Sid Caesar, who was in the film, confirms in his book *Caesar's Hours, My Life in Comedy with Love and Laugher* that Verdon was Cole's assistant on it. Cole himself is not credited on the film, which was directed by Alfred Green and released on January 10, 1946.

The star said that she was hired by Cole later and spent a brief time as one of his Columbia dance troupe, but this is presumed to have happened in 1947 when she had an assignment to review Cole's nightclub act at Los Angeles' Slapsie Maxie's. Verdon claimed that when she went backstage to see Cole, she told him that she hadn't danced in three years. Cole apparently advised her to get in condition and to come back to see him. Verdon got in shape, auditioned for him at Columbia, and got the job. She would later say that before she saw the show she had never heard of Cole, which contradicts the story of her auditioning for *Blonde from Brooklyn* and her supposed earlier stint in his Columbia Pictures troupe. She also said that she never wrote a review of the show.

Although Cole's Columbia contract was supposed to last until 1948, he found that he was no longer being given films at the studio. A major strike had affected production and resulted in cutbacks. Another reason may have been that he was not called upon to work on Rita Hayworth's films, as he had been in the past. Cole got the contracts for himself and his dancers suspended so that they could work elsewhere, and he reactivated his club act in places like Ciro's and Slapsie Maxie's. After seeing his show, Verdon went backstage and again told him that she wanted to join his group. Another source writes about Verdon's audition, though it is not known whether this refers to her first audition for Cole or one she did for him to return to his group. It is claimed that when Verdon went backstage to see Cole, she wore a dress so tight that she could hardly sit down, which amused the choreographer. At the audition, Cole gave her a few ballet sequences to do, calling them out in an esoteric dialect that the Culver City girl could not understand. She supposedly responded by saying, "If you say it in English, I'll do it." Cole translated and she did the dances beautifully, and her assured sensuality supposedly shocked the both of them. She had experience but he thought Verdon had no real training, and this was something that he thought he could give her. He also thought she needed style and she was prepared to do whatever he asked so that she could become one of his nightclub dancers. Verdon could see his strength and vision and intelligence; he was more powerful than any choreographer she had yet met. She also knew that he could wreck her if he wanted to, but she vowed, "I won't let him beat me."

Some sources claim that Verdon's decision to work with Cole led to the end of her marriage: She filed for divorce in June 1947. Others say she met with Cole after she had started divorce proceedings. Verdon had supposedly left Henaghan on New Year's Eve 1943. Her decision was also made due to his alleged alcoholism, which saw him behave in a violent and domineering fashion. Henaghan claimed that Verdon was happy just to be a housewife, but other sources say that it made her miserable. Being a Cole student both fulfilled her renewed desire to dance and also enabled her to provide financially for her son. She sold everything she owned except for books and records, and was now known as "Gwenneth" Verdon.

In Chicago, Cole had previewed a seven-minute number to the Benny Goodman Big Band recording of the Louis Prima song "Sing, Sing, Sing (With a Swing)." It was originally performed by Cole and three men; some sources claim that he created it for Verdon. If he was going to use a female dancer in the number, it would have been Florence Lessing, his dance partner at the time. The song would later be used in the 1978 Broadway show *Dancin'* which Bob Fosse choreographed and directed. Lessing was replaced by Carol Haney as Cole's leading dancer, but after more nightclub appearances in Los Angeles and New York, Haney decided to leave the group to become Gene Kelly's new assistant. For an engagement at the Colonial Inn in Florida, Cole replaced Haney with Verdon. Next came an appearance at Ciro's in Hollywood where Verdon did a clown number. The applause and the demand for encores made her feel sure of herself for the first time on stage, although she dismissed the role as a paint-and-costume one. She may have been accepted as an artist but she still felt that when people stared at her offstage, it was because she was funny-looking.

It was reported that Cole had to provide Verdon with a chaperone because of her age, although she was twenty-two at the time. Cole apparently insisted that she earn a high school diploma through a correspondence course, since it is assumed that her education had been halted by her work as a professional dancer. Verdon says that when they were in Chicago, Cole would give her classes before the performance and, in the daytime, his friend Jack Gray took her to museums and libraries. The correspondence course had Verdon studying typing and shorthand to be a secretary, an occupation she never needed to pursue. Cole and Gray also had her read all of the Claudine books by Colette, which would later help her with her role in *Can-Can* on stage.

It was Gray who noticed Verdon's talent for mimicry. She had done imitations of her schoolteachers, other's people's parents and other people she met when she was a kid just for the fun of it, and Gray thought that she could use this for musical comedy. Verdon also studied choreography, music, drama, costume design, history, anatomy, physiology, sociology, and poetry. She learned the East Indian dances that Cole specialized in. Ruth St. Denis had incorporated Indian Dance at Denishawn, but Cole did not agree with her idea of what it should be. Verdon said that Denis' idea of East Indian dance was to go around "goosing angels." He had studied with La Meri, as Verdon would do, although he superimposed his own variations and deliberate distortions. Cole had also studied with Uday Shankar and read the Bhagavad Gita to understand all the stories and characters, and he made his dancers do the same. His work created a unique Eastern variation on jazz dancing. Verdon described him as a pioneer in incorporating jazz into musical theater.

She also had heard that Cole was admired by the Chicago and New York club gangsters. They thought he was extraordinary and loved his act. They also had an odd fear of him because he was so weird-looking. She was told that they wouldn't want to meet Cole in a dark alley, but she felt that that the more you knew him, the more beautiful he became. Cole was also known to be a strict disciplinarian and his perfectionist frustrations often resulted in temperament. As his new lead dancer, Verdon is said to have borne the brunt of it, since Cole would act out against her as a lesson to the others. While he is said to have admired Verdon's "insane drive and Scottish-Irish streak of belligerence," she reportedly took his abuse without objection. It was only after he had retreated that she would react, once reportedly flinging a chair against the wall of her dressing room in anger. Perhaps Verdon knew better than to fight Cole because she knew her position and also that she was getting an education from a master. Her relationship with him was the first of two times in her life where she served a choreographer, with the second being her later partnership with Bob Fosse. Verdon was presumably happy to serve as the instrument of these two men because she also benefited from the dynamic. They were deemed to be creative geniuses and she was the definitive interpreter of their work. However, the men were different and what Verdon did for each was different too. Legend has it that Verdon became Cole's associate choreographer. She said that she was a helper and that's all. She didn't contribute a thing. He worked out the dances, gave them to her and she just passed them along.

A three-months-plus return engagement at Slapsie Maxie's saw Cole and Verdon billed with Marie Groscup, Patricia Toun, Carl Ratcliff, and Richard D'Arch. Cole was contracted to choreograph a new musical called *Bonanza Bound!* and he presumably arranged to have her cast with him. They went to New York for rehearsals. Verdon attended the Broadway play *Galileo* which ran at the Maxine Elliott Theatre from December 7 to 14, 1947. She is said to have admired the performance of Joan McCracken in the part of Virginia since she was the first dancer Verdon had seen who had done a play and not danced. McCracken would later be one of the dance partners and wives of Bob Fosse.

Bonanza Bound! had music by Saul Chaplin and book and lyrics by Betty Comden and Adolph Green. Directed by Charles Friedman, the show was set during the Alaskan Klondike gold rush of 1898. Cole hoped to include an authentic Eskimo number which the dancers executed naked. Talked out it, he substituted a Totem Pole Dance, exchanging nudity for Freudian phallic symbolism. However the choreographer felt that his rehearsal time was unacceptably limited. He had Verdon and Dick Reed of Ballet Theatre, who knew his Cole technique, but he had to spend time training the others so that they could pick up his cues as he gave them. As a result it is claimed that dances were unfinished. Verdon said that Cole didn't want dancers doing a ballet; he wanted them to be townspeople who belonged in the place and the time of the musical and who danced. They couldn't look like ballerinas waiting for their moment to perform. Verdon is said to have played the part of a gypsy, but was refused the job of understudy to the lead Allyn McLerie by the producers.

The show didn't make it to Broadway, only enjoying a brief season in tryouts in Philadelphia from December 26, 1947, to January 3, 1948. Some sources say the show was on at the Shubert; others at the Forrest Theatre. The show was also recorded on December 28 for a Broadway cast album by RCA Records but the record was never released. Verdon said that the closing notice went up between the acts of the first preview on Christmas Eve, 1947.

In the *On Stage* article on Verdon in the edition of *People Weekly* dated June 23, 1975, author Clarke Taylor claims that she was in the chorus of the MGM musical *Easter Parade*, directed by Charles Walters. The film was in production from November 19, 1947, to mid–February, 1948, and shot at the MGM studios and backlot. Verdon is not credited in the film. In John Reid's book *Memorable Films of the Forties* he lists Verdon as one of the chorus dancers in the number "Stepping Out with My Baby." She said that you can see her dash by in one number wearing a black wig (all the female dancers in the number have dark hair to match their tropical makeup). It is possible that one girl seen is Verdon, wearing a yellow dress, a green boa and a yellow feather in her hair.

Cole was next engaged to choreograph for director Jules Dassin the musical *Magdalena*, also known as *Magdalena: A Musical Adventure*. It had music by Brazilian composer Heitor Villa-Lobos, book by Frederick Hazlitt Brennan and Homer Curran and lyrics by Robert Wright and George Forrest. The show was set in Colombia in 1912 and centred on the clash between Roman Catholicism and the native Indian religion among South American emerald miners. Dassin attempted to evoke a sense of period and place by having the actors portraying the Indian principals speak in a strange, unidentifiable accent. The production cost a then unheard of sum for a musical of between $250,000 and $300,000. It was first performed on July 26, 1948, at the Los Angeles Civic Light Opera. A season from August 16, 1948, at the San Francisco Curran Theatre (San Francisco Light Opera) gained good reviews, with John Hobart in the *San Francisco Chronicle* describing it as an evening of "unrelieved magnificence." However, when the show moved to the Ziegfeld Theatre on Broadway, it was lambasted. Brooks Atkinson wrote in the *New York Times* that it was one of the most overpoweringly dull musical dramas of all time and that "watching the slow process of the plot is like being hit over the head with a sledge hammer repeatedly all evening." Atkinson made no mention of Cole's dances, and only commented that the production was elaborately old-fashioned and the direction ponderous. However, the

Portrait of Gwen Verdon in the stage show *Alive and Kicking* (1950). Photograph by Talbot.

show enjoyed a decent run from September 20 to December 4, 1948, no doubt buoyed by articles and photo-essays in *Life* and *Colliers* magazines. Plans for a Broadway cast recording were abandoned because of a musicians' strike. However, the show was revived in a concert performance on November 24, 1987, at Alice Tully Hall in New York's Lincoln Center, and this led to a complete cast recording with Evans Haile conducting for the Orchestra New England issued by CBS (Sony) on October 10, 1989. Verdon would say that the dances in the original show were truly extraordinary and described how one had all the men as trees and all the women were birds, which she found fantastic. There was also a very formal Spanish numer with fans, Castilian Spanish, and a "Pianolita" sequence. She claims these numbers influenced *Man of La Mancha*, the Broadway musical for which Cole later staged the dances.

By the end of 1948 Cole's contract at Columbia Pictures had expired. He announced that his next Broadway show would be the revue *Alive and Kicking* which he would choreograph and dance in as well. He did not start on it till 1949 in New York. It was to be a Ziegfeld Follies–style show in which Verdon as Cole's assistant would also make her Broadway debut as a dancer. (Bob Fosse with his then dance partner Mary-Ann Niles had unsuccessfully auditioned for the show.) Directed by Robert H. Gordon, it was described as a musical "dedicated to youth, laughter, melody, color, and motion." It featured comic sketches involving the way a newspaper is run, military higher-ups, psychiatrists, and the popularity of the Edith Piaf style of singing. There were also songs written by Hal Borne and Irma Jurist and lyrics by Paul Francis Webster and Ray Golden. Cole's dances were his trademark smorgasbord of ethnic styles. It had tryouts at the Shubert Theatre in Boston (beginning on December 8, 1949) for two and a half weeks, and in Hershey, Pennsylvania, in January 1950. The show then moved to Broadway but only enjoyed a brief run at the Winter Garden Theatre (January 17 to February 25, 1950).

Credited in the cast as Abou's wife in the Hindu-influenced number "Abou Ben Adhem," Gwen played opposite Cole who was Abou Ben Adhem. She danced with him in the number, as well as in "I Didn't Want Him," "Love It Hurts So Good," "Propinquity" and "Cole Scuttle Blues." Verdon also danced in "One Two Three," which featured her and Marie Groscup as kids, dressed up in mother's old clothes, who fought and made fun of the young lovers who sang the song. Cole had the women upstage the singers by walking on a fence, since he hated the song and felt he needed to provide something to take the curse off it. The idea of kids dressed up in adult clothes would be reworked for the number "I Feel Like

Dancing" in the film *Meet Me After the Show* (1951), in which Verdon would also appear.

In the *New York Times*, Brooks Atkinson described the show as mediocre but praised Cole's work without mentioning Verdon. She felt that she had been critically ignored when Atkinson commented that the easiest way to remain invisible was to dance with Cole on the same stage. Later writing on dance in the Broadway musical season for the *New York Times*, John Martin did mention her, saying that a good word should be said for the stunning Verdon. She said that she thought Jack Gilford was extraordinary in a sketch about trying to quit smoking and that the show would have run longer than forty-six performances if Ed Sullivan's show wasn't so popular on television. This is because Verdon felt that people could see the same type of thing at home.

She continued to study Oriental and Eastern dance with Le Meri while she worked with Cole. Verdon also began teaching with Cole when he gave lessons at Eugene Loring's American School of Dance in Hollywood, taking beginners to prepare them to dance for him. He would soon quit the classes because he felt the students were lazy and solely interested in the jobs he could get them in film. She stayed, taking over the classes. Cole's concern became a non-issue because nobody expected to get a job from her. One night a week Verdon also taught non-paying students who couldn't afford the school's courses. In order to know the source of movement and its emotional impact, she studied anatomy and got a skeleton to find out just what movement the body was capable of. Verdon found out how far the hip socket could turn and where it couldn't go. She also discovered how much she could demand of a student: to find the limit and then stretch for that.

In 1950 Verdon was part of Cole's troupe performing "Harlequin's Odyssey" at Caro's. In the act Cole played an anguished Harlequin who was the clown as symbol of all people leading a wonderful and brave existence. Verdon was the "Golden Woman" garbed in lengths of cheesecloth who represented Fate. The act included a whorehouse ballet which reportedly got them thrown out of the nightclub, though Cole doubted that the patrons were the ones who were offended because they didn't know what it was. Cole and Verdon were photographed in costume for *Parade* and *Dance Magazine*, surrounded by a religious holy image called a Santo and giant tarot cards.

2

Working with Jack Cole in Films

Gwen Verdon's film career resumed when she became Jack Cole's dance assistant on film. From September 18 to December 1950 Cole and Verdon were in Paris for the musical sequences on the musical comedy *On the Riviera* (1951), which marked a new association he had with 20th Century–Fox. The film was a remake of their musical comedies *Folies Bergere de Paris* (1935) and *That Night in Rio* (1941). They were adaptations of the German play, "The Red Cat" by Rudolph Lothar and Hans Adler, which had been produced on Broadway in 1934. The film was directed by Walter Lang and the new songs were by Sylvia Fine, wife of its star, Danny Kaye. The screenplay by Valentine Davies and Phoebe and Henry Ephron involved New York impressionist Jack Martin, who is working at the Cote d'Azur nightclub on the French Riviera. Jack is the spitting image of French aviator Henri Duval and impersonates him.

Verdon's duties included teaching Kaye's co-star Corinne Calvet how to walk up stairs. She had supposedly never even walked to music, let alone danced, so Verdon taught her with the help of a piano player. The teacher also appeared in three of the musical numbers in the film. Verdon is the lead showgirl in a chorus for the "Rhythm of a New Romance" number. In it she wears a cancan black dress with blue feathers, feathered headdress, and black gloves as opposed to the other chorus girls who wear Moulin Rouge blue dresses with black feathers. Verdon leads the girls doing the cancan, speaks in French and says "Gesundheit" in response to Kaye's "sarcophagus" lyric, and rubs noses with him. Speaking to Mike Douglas on his TV show on January 19, 1969, Verdon said that it wasn't her voice used for the lines—she mouthed the words for someone else to say. She said the moment was rehearsed with Kaye and Verdon but then two six-foot-two showgirls were brought in for the filming. Kaye asked why he couldn't do it with Verdon and was told that dancers can't talk.

Kaye refused to do the scene with the showgirls, only with Verdon. She got the job but she lip-synched.

For the number, she resisted doing the cancan because she told Cole that she thought it vulgar. To persuade her to do it, he told her to think of the dance as that of a female athlete. The number features a set with one of Cole's favored staircases and the international locations include India and Spain with a geographical outline of the country labelled on a back curtain. For India, Verdon dances barefoot and is dressed in blonde wig with green headpiece, orange pants and a sheer outfit to suggest torso nudity with gold bangles around her breasts, arms and feet. She was also one of the chorus clowns in the *commedia dell'arte* "Popo the Puppet" number, suspended by blue ribbon strings, dancing and singing. Verdon wears a blue wig and gloves, red hat and slippers, and a red, white and blue dress. Her third appearance in the film is as one of the back-up

Verdon (right) with an unidentified dancer and Danny Kaye in the "Popo the Puppet" number in *On the Riviera* (1951).

dancers in the "Happy Ending" finale, wearing a black bejewelled cap with a green feather, and a dress with green and black horizontal stripes. Verdon has a moment where she dances alone, then is joined by George Martin who wears a black suit and green shirt. At one point her underwear is seen because of her movement in the knee-length dress that is split on the sides to her thighs.

The film was released in New York on May 23, 1951, and Los Angeles on May 25, 1951, with the taglines "You Never Saw So Much Before! It's Oomph-la-la when you go gay the Riviera way, with song and dance and gals-galore!," "The Whole World of Entertainment Is Yours in the Most Kaye-Lossal Musical of the Year!" and "The World's Most Exciting Entertainer in the Year's Most Wonderful Musical Show." It was praised by *Variety* but received a mixed review from Bosley Crowther in the *New York Times*. A box office hit, it received Academy Award nominations for Best Art Direction and Set Decoration, and Best Music Score.

In his biography *The Lives of Danny Kaye: Nobody's Fool*, Martin Gottfried revealed that Verdon and Kaye had an off-stage liaison. The writer claims that the sexual magnetism between the two is apparent in the "Rhythm of a New Romance" number and their almost-kiss. The relationship reportedly lasted until Kaye's next film, the family musical *Hans Christian Andersen* (1952), which was in production from January 21 to May 26, 1952. The intimate friendship between Verdon and Kaye is said to have come about because of his supposed marital crisis of the time with wife Sylvia Fine. Verdon would say that she loved the way Kaye always dismissed the talk by saying that he had a very good head on Fine's shoulders.

In Paris, Verdon studied mime with Jean-Louis Barrault; acting without words but with body movement. Verdon was also part of the floor show at the Lido. Donn Arden and Ronn Fletcher, whom she had met while working with Cole, did a steady stint in Paris every year. Fletcher was invited to do choreography for the Copacabana in Florida, and asked Verdon if she wanted to play his part in Paris. She agreed but was concerned because she couldn't speak French. Fletcher told her that to teach French girls, all you had to do was play charades. Verdon went to Paris with Arden, who took care of costuming and parading the women. She worked at dance ideas and found it a perfect laboratory because Paris was without the American prudery over nudity. Verdon first experimented with the mambo, which she introduced to France. However she found that the French were not as liberated as she had hoped. They would allow her to have naked girls but they had to stand still and the dancers had to wear clothes. They also demanded that the dancers had to have white skin, since it was claimed that Parisians were less interested in Indians. Verdon compromised but she wasn't happy about it. The dancers, whom she had wanted to be nude, were in conservative costumes that could have been worn at a ball at Buckingham Palace. They tripped over the naked showgirls who stood stolidly in the way. Verdon summed up the experience with the quip that it was an easy job: When in doubt, just bring on the nudes.

She and Cole were back in Hollywood for their next assignment for 20th Century-Fox, the Biblical romantic drama *David and Bathsheba* (1951). It was filmed on location in Nogales, Arizona, and at the Fox studios from November 24, 1950, to January 1951. Verdon was an uncredited specialty dancer and only appears in one scene: She performs a number of Near Eastern parentage with sinuous, erotic overtones at a banquet for King David of Israel (Gregory Peck). Director Henry King cuts away twice from Verdon's dance to David, who sits with his military leader Uriah (Kieron Moore). The cutaways are presumably done as a narrative choice, since the focus of the performance is not the dancer as much as David's preoccupation with Uriah.

Verdon begins on a staircase and runs down to the floor level accompanied by the music of an unseen orchestra. She is dressed similarly to the way she was in the Indian sequence of the "Rhythm of a New Romance" number in *On the Riviera*. She is barefoot and has a bare midriff with gold fringed pants, and has gold bracelets around her arms. Here she also wears a black headdress and a bra that shows cleavage. Verdon holds what look like two tennis racquets and wears a black and red cape that she discards, and red veils that she uses in the dance. She also writhes on a red carpet.

The film was released on August 10, 1951, with the taglines "Mighty as Goliath! Fiery as their Love!" and "For this woman ... he broke God's own commandment!" It was praised by *Variety*, the *New York Times*, and Tony Thomas and Aubrey Solomon in *The Films of 20th Century Fox*. A box office hit, it was nominated for Academy Awards for Best Screenplay, Best Cinematography, Best Art Direction and Set Decoration, Best Costume Design and Best Music. Verdon reported that in some cities her dance sequence was cut; it was only allowed in the larger cities "where there was progressive education." She said that it was cut particularly in the South because she was an Egyptian Negress dancing for a white man. "It was the Bible, what could I do?" She is quoted as saying the following about the film. "David wanted to go to war but he was supposed to go home to Bathsheba, and my dance was supposed to put him in the mood

A black-wigged Verdon as a specialty dancer gets paid by King David of Israel (Gregory Peck) as Uriah (Kieron Moore) watches in a lobby card for *David and Bathsheba* (1951).

to go home to her. Well, I guess it was too much, because everybody who saw it got the same idea."

Cole and Verdon's next Fox assignment was the musical *Meet Me After the Show* (1951). Directed by Richard Sale, the film was in production from December 14, 1950, to February 21, 1951, with the dance sequences shot from March 8 to April 1951. The film was a remake of the comedy *He Married His Wife* (1940) with new songs by Jule Styne and Leo Robin. The story centered on the relationship between Broadway star Delilah Lee (Betty Grable) and her husband, producer-director Jeffrey Ames (Macdonald Carey). Verdon was again uncredited and appears in three scenes, with the finale of "I Feel Like Dancing" having her credited with her real name in the movie's show program. The credit also separates her from the dancers for the number, since it reads "Delilah Lee and Dancers with Gwen Verdon."

For the "Bettin' on a Man" number she is said to be the woman in silhouette with the man (who is said to be Cole) also in silhouette. Verdon wears a long-sleeved black dress with a black head scarf, black fishnet stockings and black high heels. She and Cole appear on an upper level and dance wearing long horsetails, while Betty Grable sings the song on the lower level by a garishly styled piano and a chorus of clapping male dancers. During the number, as Verdon and Cole move to simulate a race, Grable and the chorus look out with racing binoculars. She is Sapho in the "No Talent Joe" number, one of two back-up dancers for Grable. The women both sing and speak the introduction as they hold an urn on their shoulders with their right hands and gold fronds in their left. They wear black diaphanous low-cut long-sleeved and short-skirted dresses, seamed stockings, gold shoes and necklaces and headdresses, and sculptured hairdos.

For "I Feel Like Dancing" Verdon accompanies Grable as one of two female dancers with a male chorus who are all presented as children in dress-up. The two women are dressed like men, in trousers and horizontal-striped sweaters and with their hair covered by feathered hats, which adds androgyny to the moment when they dance together like a romantic couple and hug. Verdon also speaks in the number when she yells, "Beat me. Tyrone Power beat me." One's eye goes more to Verdon than Grable when the two dance together. The first half of the number presents Grable and Verdon as slum kids holding off the marauding boys who wear buckets on their heads like helmets and wield cap pistols. Scaring the boys away, the girls find boxing gloves and a piece of material in a garbage can. Verdon is more tomboyish and, taking the gloves, wants to fight whereas Grable prefers the material and strikes toreador poses. Then they climb a tree, hitch a ride across the backlot on a clothesline, and land on a rooftop.

The film was released in New York on August 15, 1951, and in Los Angeles on August 21, 1951, with the tagline "It's America's Big Date for a Great Time...!" It was praised by *Variety* and by Tony Thomas and Aubrey Solomon in *The Films of 20th Century Fox*. The film became a box office hit.

The team of Cole and Verdon was back for the Fox musical *The I Don't Care Girl* (1953). Directed by Lloyd Bacon, the film was shot from October to November 1951 with additional dance sequences shot in December and then in February and March 1952. The long time between the film being in production and its release suggests that Fox lacked confidence in it, and reportedly half of the footage originally shot was scrapped. The screenplay by Walter Bullock is about the vaudeville performer Eva Tanquay (Mitzi Gaynor) who was nicknamed "The I Don't Care Girl" after the song she made famous. Verdon, again uncredited, only

Betty Grable (left) and Verdon dressed in male drag for the "I Feel Like Dancing" number in *Meet Me After the Show* (1951).

appears in the "Beale Street Blues" number as the lead back-up dancer. She has a long red hairpiece, a long pink ruffled dress and pink fedora, and uses a red sash which she also wears as a shawl. Verdon opens the number, and after Eva enters, takes her parasol and moves around her as Eva sings. The number ends with a split level effect. Verdon is on the top level with boy dancers, and Eva and Larry are on the floor level, and the back-up dancers do an identical dance to those on the top. There is a story that either Gaynor or Fox didn't want Verdon to dance the same step next to Gaynor. Cole overcame this problem with the use of the split-level when both women do the same step.

Sources differ as to when the film was released. Some say it was December 24, 1952; others January 14, 1953. The tagline was "The Wild and Wonderful Musical About the BAD Girl of Show Business!" It was lambasted by *Variety*, and received a mixed reaction from Tony Thomas and Aubrey Solomon in *The Films of 20th Century Fox*. The film was not a box office hit.

2. Working with Jack Cole in Films

Verdon was next seen on screen, uncredited, in the Fox comedy *Dreamboat* (1952) without Cole being attached to the film. Directed by Claude Binyon, it was in production from December 27, 1951, to February 2, 1952, with additional sequences shot in late March and early May 1952. Clifton Webb stars as Underhill College English literature professor, Thornton Sayre, who used to be the silent movie actor Bruce Blair, with the nickname of "Dream Boat." Threatened with losing his job, Thornton goes to New York to stop his movies from being broadcast on the television show of his former acting partner, Gloria Marlowe (Ginger Rogers).

Verdon appears only once as the female dancer with two male dancers in long shot in a television commercial for the prune juice Prunecta. She wears a long black sequined strapless dress with long black gloves. Regrettably, the dancers are shown within the frame of the television screen as the point of view of the watchers. Verdon is given a medium close-up for the end of the commercial, holding a glass of the product.

The film was released in New York on July 25, 1952, and in Los Angeles on August 22, 1952, with the tagline "Fresh! Wonderful! And Loaded with Laughter!" It received a mixed review by Bosley Crowther in the *New York Times* but was praised by Tony Thomas and Aubrey Solomon in *The Films of 20th Century Fox* and Laura Wagner in *Anne Francis: The Life and Career*. The film was a box office disappointment. In her autobiography *Ginger: My Story*, Rogers writes that Verdon helped to choreograph the harem dance that she did in one of the silent movies. There is no choreographer credited for the film.

It is reported that Verdon did post-production work on the MGM musical comedy *Singin' in the Rain* (1952) which took place from January 1952 with the film being released in New York on March 27 and in Los Angeles on April 9. Carol Haney and Jeanne Coyne were the uncredited assistant dance directors to Gene Kelly and Stanley Donen. Verdon is said to have aided Haney and Coyne in dubbing the sound of Kelly's taps and splashing noises for the film's famous title sequence which was shot on July 17 and 18, 1951. The ladies had to stand ankle-deep in a drum full of water to match the soggy on-screen action. Kelly had gone to Germany in January 1952 to make his next film, the romantic thriller *The Devil Makes Three*, so he was apparently unavailable for the post-synching. Verdon said that it was Haney who dubbed Kelly and she did the swashing of the water. In her 1977 television interview with Dick Cavett, she said that she and Haney put on Kelly's tap shoes after the film was made and dubbed his taps as they danced in pans of water. She said that Haney called her in to help because she was a friend, and also because the job was fun.

While doing it, the women laughed hysterically. However other sources claim that Kelly did dub all his own taps and that extra sloshing sounds were dubbed in after them, although there is no evidence of this activity in the MGM archives. The claim that recordings were made in ankle-deep water has also been questioned since it is thought that it is impossible for anyone to make a recording of taps in these conditions.

Cole and Verdon reunited at MGM for their next film, the musical *The Merry Widow* (1952), which was in production from September 12 to December 1951, and directed by Curtis Bernhardt. MGM had previously made the film in 1925 as a drama directed by Erich von Stroheim and 1934 as a musical directed by Ernst Lubitsch and starring Jeanette MacDonald and Maurice Chevalier. The musical was based on the German operetta of the same title with music by Franz Lehar and book and lyrics by Victor Leon and Leo Stein. The new version starred Lana Turner in the title role. The screenplay by Sonya Levien and William Ludwig changed the plot so

Verdon (right) as one of the lead chorus girls doing the cancan at Maxim's in *The Merry Widow* **(1952).**

that now the widow is the American Crystal Radek, whose fortune is needed by the country of Marshovia to pay their national debt. Verdon appears in only one scene, uncredited, as one of the two leading cancan dancers in the chorus at Maxim's (the other dancer is Ellen Ray). She wears a large black hat, a black slip and tights and pink underwear and holds a scarf as she dances. Verdon sings and screams for the number, and also winks and points to the camera after she bends over backwards. She also speaks after the number is over, calling out to Danilo simultaneously with the other lead dancer.

Released on September 5, 1952, *The Merry Widow* was praised by Bosley Crowther in the *New York Times* and in Jeanine Basinger's book on Lana Turner, but not by John Douglas Eames in his book *The MGM Story*. A box office hit, it was nominated for the Best Costume Design and Best Art Direction and Set Decoration Academy Awards.

Back at Fox, Cole and Verdon reunited with Betty Grable for the musical comedy *The Farmer Takes a Wife* (1953), a remake of Fox's 1935 romantic comedy of the same name. The new film was directed by Henry Levin and in production from May 28 to August 5, 1952, with additional sequences shot in December 1952. The screenplay was by Walter Bullock, Sally Benson and Joseph Fields, and based on a play of the same name by Frank B. Elser and Marc Connelly and the novel *Rome Haul* by Walter D. Edmonds. The story is set in the shipping town of Rome, New York, in 1850 and centers on the boat of Jotham Klore (John Carroll), *The Old Hickory*, his cook Molly Larkins (Grable), and their new driver Dan Harrow (Dale Robertson).

Verdon appeared in two scenes. She is in the opening scene and has two lines of dialogue as she asks questions of Molly. She also appears for the number "We're in Business," first in a white dress with red trim as part of the chorus who falls into the canal. Later she reappears to sing and dance with Grable. Both women wear plaid shirts, potato sacks dresses, white pantaloons, black stockings, black caps and metal plates as shoes. They dance on the deck of a boat as "native women from Utica" and bang more metal plates in their hands. Cole has the number continue in the water, as Dan throws semi-naked boys over his shoulder, and Grable and Verdon jump into the canal.

The film was released on June 12, 1953, in New York and July 24, 1953 in Los Angeles. The taglines were "The Musical That's Bustin' Out All Over!," "The Full of Fun Musical Joy!," and "The Happiest Wedding of Song and Dance in Many a Honeymoon!" It was lambasted by *Variety* and Tony Thomas and Aubrey Solomon in *The Films of 20th Century Fox*, and received a mixed reaction from Bosley Crowther in the *New York Times*. The film was not a box office hit.

During the making of this film, Verdon went solo again for Universal-International's romantic adventure *The Mississippi Gambler* (1953), directed by Rudolph Mate. Shot on location at the Corrigan Ranch in Simi Valley, California, and the Park Lake on the Universal Studios backlot, it was in production from June 10 to July 1952. The original screenplay by Seton I. Miller centers on Mark Fallon (Tyrone Power), a riverboat gambler in Mississippi of the 1850s who yearns for New Orleans plantation heiress Angelique Dureau (Piper Laurie). Uncredited again as a performer (Verdon played a voodoo dancer), she did receive her first screen credit for choreography for the film. However it is not known whether she also choreographed the waltz at the Governor's Ball, since Hal Belfer was an uncredited dance director.

Verdon appeared in only one scene where she performs a Creole dance to the "Haitian Devil Song." She wears tropical makeup on her face and arms and her hair is black. She dances with four male black dancers who are bare-chested. Her makeup may now be politically incorrect. Her costume is a white layered dress topped with a yellow apron and she has ribbons in her ponytailed hair. She initially uses a hand fan which she discards and then a dead chicken. They are presumably part of the voodoo of the dance that her character uses to aid the romance of Mark and Angelique, since she throws the bird at him. Maté employs cutaways to the observers to demonstrate the effect of the dance, with the

Verdon in tropical makeup as a voodoo dancer in *The Mississippi Gambler* (1953).

couple being separated increasing the dance's supposed hypnotic power. The cutaways also suggest that the effect of the dance is more important than us seeing the dance itself, which is apparent since at one point Maté obscures the view of Verdon by framing her between the back of Mark and another man. Additionally, the number does not have a natural conclusion since its music continues under dialogue.

The film had its world premiere in St. Louis, Missouri, on January 13, 1953, and then opened in New York on January 29, 1953, and in Los Angeles on February 6, 1953. The tagline was "Meet the Fabulous Mark Fallon…. His Game Is Fancy Women…. And His Fate Is Lady Luck!" It received a mixed reaction by *Variety*, A.H. Weiler in the *New York Times*, and Clive Hirschhorn in *The Universal Story*. The film was a box office hit and received an Academy Award nomination for Best Sound Recording.

In her memoir, *Learning to Live Out Loud*, Piper Laurie writes about Verdon's appearance as the lead native dancer in the scene, which was designed to show the awakening of the hidden passion in Angelique as she watches the dancing. She says that she thought that Verdon's dancing and the music were so terrific that it was easy to get into what Angelique was feeling. Her cheeks became so flushed that, when the rushes were seen, the front office and makeup department accused her of secretly adding to her rouge and ruining the footage.

From November 17, 1952, to January 1953, Verdon assisted Jack Cole on the musical numbers of *Gentlemen Prefer Blondes*. Cole created the dances for Jane Russell and Marilyn Monroe first with Verdon. He worked out movements that he knew the two actresses could manager as Verdon watched and memorized what he did. Then she would do them and Cole would watch her to plan the camera angles. Then Monroe and Russell would be brought in and Verdon would teach them the moves. Since Monroe didn't have dancing ability, Cole had to be very patient with her as she rehearsed the numbers endlessly. Verdon had fond memories of coaching her and said that she worked very hard. "She was so conscientious—and not stupid, by any means." Verdon felt that Monroe could do anything you asked her to do if you could show it you her, and she taught the actress how to simultaneously look sexy and to *satirize* looking sexy. Monroe would say of Verdon, "If Gwen can't teach you a routine you're rhythm bankrupt with incompatible feet." In her book *Marilyn Monroe: Private and Undisclosed*, Michelle Morgan quoted Verdon's son Jim, who said that he visited the set. He said Monroe had trouble remembering steps and moves from one day to the next but she always behaved in a professional manner. Jim would also claim that his mother became very fond of her and would always defend Monroe from attacks on her lack of will. Verdon said that the actress had a good sense of humor, something which she felt nobody ever talked about. Also she thought that if Monroe had as many friends as people who *claimed* they were, then she would still be alive—although Verdon thought she would have hated becoming older. It was said that Verdon also coached Russell and Monroe in their walks so that Monroe had less sex and Russell more. It is also rumored that at one point in the film, Verdon dubs both actresses' swaying bottoms. However Verdon wouldn't take credit for Monroe's famous wiggle-walk. She thought that the actress was a sort of genius in that department who would have found out how to do it regardless.

Studio publicity announced that Verdon would appear in the "Diamonds Are a Girl's Best Friend" production number "performing a 'washwoman dance,' scrubbing 'Lorelei's' diamonds and hanging them out on a line to dry." This dance does not appear in the number, and Verdon is not in the film. A January 1953 *Hollywood Reporter* news item stated that Verdon was working with Monroe and Jane Russell on a "cancan number with a 'Three Musketeers' dueling motif," but that number also does not appear. The film had its world premiere on July 1, 1953, in Atlantic City, New Jersey, opened July 15 in New York and July 31 in Los Angeles. It was praised by William Brogdon in *Variety* and Gordon Gow in his book *Hollywood in the Fifties*, but received a mixed reaction from Bosley Crowther in the *New York Times*. The film was a box office hit.

It was during the dance rehearsals, for the film's "Two Little Girls from Little Rock" that Verdon was invited to audition for the show *Can-Can* in New York. Some sources say that she was approached by choreographer Michael Kidd who was working on a Fox soundstage simultaneously and was to be the choreographer for the show. This source is questionable since Kidd was apparently working at MGM on the dances for *The Band Wagon* (1953) at this time. Others say it was co-producer Cy Feuer who approached her. When she told Cole about the opportunity, he supposedly encouraged her with the comment, "Sometimes in your life, you've got to be on trial. It's good for you."

Verdon was happy to leave Hollywood because she had found the work there a grind and there was little acknowledgment of her contribution. She was particularly peeved when she had reportedly substituted for one star in long shots performing difficult dance moves while the star took the close-ups and got the acclaim. This idea was given further detail in Verdon's February 6, 1966, *New York Times* interview with Rex Reed. He wrote that she had doubled for Monroe's torso, Rita Hayworth's feet, and Betty Grable's rear view. In her 1977 Dick Cavett television interview she denied that she ever appeared on film as parts of other people. Verdon told Cavett that she did dub the sound of the dancing feet of Grable, Dan Dailey, June Haver, Danny Kaye and Sammy Davis, Jr., which was part of her job as a dance assistant. The Dailey and Haver job would appear to be for the Fox musical *The Girl Next Door* (1953), with the credited choreographer as Richard Barstow although it is rumored that Michael Kidd also worked on the film. It was in production from October to December 1951 with additional filming in 1952. Verdon was at Fox on other films at these times and therefore could have performed the post-production dubbing.

She is said to have left for New York with her Siamese cat and her dog to take advantage of the paid weekend she had been given to audition. Although Verdon was confident in performing the cancan dance, she believed she still had little chance of getting the part because she was a relative unknown on Broadway. The audition was held at the Warwick Hotel. Verdon was apparently so afraid of singing in front of the show's composer, Cole Porter, that she asked to dance first because she was more confident in that ability. When she had to sing, Verdon said, "I was so scared that my legs wouldn't hold me," so she asked if she could sit as she sang. Some sources say that she sang "Pennies from Heaven," others the Porter song from the score, "If You Loved Me Truly." Verdon supposedly saw Porter wincing, and she assumed that he hated her. She didn't know that he was actually wincing from the pain of his legs that had been crippled in a horse-riding accident. Verdon didn't know about his legs but learned that something was amiss when Porter made his way to the stage with the aid of two canes, and she noticed that he was wearing spats. When he told her that he liked her breathless voice, she responded, "I'm not breathless—I'm scared." Verdon danced the cancan, and then read for the part of Claudine. She says she read the scene with the stage manager and she found it silly. Verdon was told that she was meant to be an ingénue; someone her mother had told her was always the young, unknowing girl in a play or musical. However she asked, "Isn't an ingénue something that was back at the turn of the century?" Verdon was told that that was when the play took place.

Her audition lasted an unusually long time, just under an hour. When she was finished, Abe Burrows, director and writer of the musical's book, addressed her as Claudine. She had the part.

Verdon offered to dye her red hair black for it. Some sources say that

Michael Kidd had asked her to do so when he first approached her but Burrows didn't think that necessary and hired her just as she was. When she returned to the hotel she ordered room service for herself, because she had always wondered what it would be like to do so. When Verdon returned to *Gentlemen Prefer Blondes* and told Cole that she got the part, Cole is said to have punched her. Apparently the punch came from his anger at the idea of losing her as his assistant although he was also glad for her. He would go to the show's opening night and gave Verdon a pair of earrings that she would wear in every single show after. But this would not be the last time she would work with Cole.

Before leaving for Broadway, Verdon met Bob Fosse at a party hosted by Kidd. They knew each other from when she had worked on *The Merry Widow* and he was under contract but had yet to make a film. Another source claims that they met later when Verdon was working on *The Farmer Takes a Wife*. Although they were at different studios, it is said that dancers who worked regularly were familiar with their competition even at rival companies. Verdon would say that the dancers all came together to cook and eat. At the party, Verdon supposedly talked about how she felt that movies weren't showing her off at her best. She cited how some of her screen dances had been cut, apparently at the behest of Hollywood's Production Code. It amused her that she was considered too sexy to be on-screen because she didn't believe it to be true. Verdon never thought of herself as sexy, since when she had to be, she just kidded it. She believed that she could get away with more on stage where there were no censors and that's what appealed to her about the upcoming show. This was despite the fact that doing the cancan was old hat to her, since she had already performed it in *On the Riviera* and *The Merry Widow*.

3

Can-Can

In *Can-Can*, showgirls in Paris at the Montmartre dance halls of 1893 introduce the scandalous dance of the title, and are charged with (and acquitted of) obscenity for performing it. Of the musical numbers, Claudine had a duet with the sculptor Boris, "If You Loved Me Truly," and danced in "Quadrille," "The Garden of Eden Ballet" and "The Apaches." Verdon thought of the character as Colette's Claudine with LaGoulue's hair, but approached it from the dance rather than acting standpoint. She admitted that she gave Michael Kidd a hard time because she felt he wasn't giving her enough good things to do. She also objected to his athletic dancing style which she found more jumping around rather than emotionally based, an indication of the different dance backgrounds the dancers had come from. Verdon felt that she had to act to do Jack Cole's dances because in order to be a good dancer, you had to know how to act. She felt that dancing was the expression of a life and emotions. Verdon also suggested to Kidd that she do something like Ruth St. Denis for "The Garden of Eden Ballet," beginning when Eve was supposed to be innocent. This idea was based on a dance her mother had done with St. Denis, a "hell-bent-for-beauty"–type dance that was very Isadora Duncan-ish. However, Eve's costume, which gave the impression that Verdon was nude with a few strategically placed fig leaves, presented her as more sexy than innocent. Her cold relationship with Kidd was observed by Cy Feuer who thought that she didn't like him because he was a lesser talent than her present Svengali, Jack Cole. She did what Kidd told her to do but without showing any sign of respect or real appreciation. Verdon would later change her opinion of him when she worked with Fosse who set her straight. Fosse, claimed that Kidd had transformed her life with his choreography and he even forced her to apologize for the way she had treated him.

It is said that Verdon's part was cut down to keep the peace since it was felt that she outshone the show's star, Lilo. Verdon knew just enough French to understand Lilo's husband who was also her manager when he complained that she was in too many scenes. Her dialogue was cut, some say, until she had none left. Other sources claimed that Verdon was left with only eight lines. Verdon remembers that when the show opened, her only lines were "Oh, Boris!" which she said eight times, and "What's on the menu?" Her numbers were reduced from seven to four and she only had two featured dances. Verdon said that they took her out of one dance before it ended and had Lilo come on. In the "Garden of Eden" number, she finished upstage and the star came out dressed like a peacock. Lilo also had Verdon offstage at the end of three of her dances so that there would be no applause, and Verdon's stage name of "Gwenyth" was truncated to "Gwen" to take up less room on the theater marquee. Even her one song, the duet with Boris, initially had her vocal supplemented by seven others before she proved to Cole Porter that she could sing.

Shelah Hackett, who was one of the chorus dancers (and would later marry Kidd), reported that Verdon had threatened to leave the show in tryouts because of the reduction of her part. In his book on Cole Porter, William McBrien reports that at one point in the staging she was asked to duck behind a piece of furniture in order to make room for Lilo, something that Verdon refused to do. She gave her notice and arranged to leave after a four-week run. The producers supposedly accepted it and said she could leave once they had found a replacement. When the show came to New York, Verdon was looking forward only to getting out, but the reception she received changed the producer's minds.

Tryouts were held in Philadelphia for six weeks before the show opened on May 7 at Broadway's Shubert Theatre. In the *New York Times* Brooks Atkinson wrote that the spectacular dancing was the best thing in the show. He said that Verdon led the dancing "with impudence, recklessness and humor," and that her spinning and grinning portrait of Eve in the "Garden of Eden Ballet" was brilliant. In a later article on the show, Atkinson wrote that Verdon's "dancing and comic acting capture the spirit of festivity admirably. What she has to do is pertinent and uproarious."

Verdon reportedly made no great impression with the "Quadrille" and "Garden of Eden Ballet" in the tryouts, and presumably not on opening night. But after "The Apaches," the theater rocked with applause. The audience demanded her reappearance, and would not allow the show to continue otherwise. Verdon apparently was in her dressing room, having taken off her costume, and now only wore a robe. This is supposedly how she walked back onto the stage, led by Feuer. One source reverses the appearance of the Apache number and the ballet in the show's running order, writing that "The Apaches" is in the show's first act and not the second as otherwise described. The error implies that the audience would have been rewarded with Verdon's return performing in the ballet, as opposed to just having her appear on stage to receive the applause before the show continued with its three final numbers.

According to another source, the applause came for Verdon after "The Garden of Eden Ballet," which is somewhat more believable. The ovation for Verdon is said to have lasted for seven minutes, and had the audience chanting "We want Verdon! We want Verdon!" Shelah Hackett says that Verdon was in her bra and panties after she had finished "The Apache" and that it was Kidd who told Verdon that she had to go back onstage for another bow. Verdon apparently told him that she couldn't go back because "I'm naked." He threw a towel over her and led her out onto the stage. Verdon said that she was in her dressing room wearing opera-lengths with a zipper that didn't work. When she was called to come on stage to answer the applause, she said she held her costume in front of her. She also apologized to the two actors whose act she had interrupted and claimed to have spoiled.

Portrait of Verdon in the stage show *Can-Can* **(1953).**

Verdon thought that the audience had determined that she was the underdog and reacted like that because they had initially been denied the opportunity to applaud. Verdon later told dancer Harry Evan that she hated getting standing ovations. The reason was that once, when her son Jimmy came to visit her when he was a boy, she sent him to a matinee of an Ethel Merman show. When he came back, Verdon asked him what he thought. He told her that he thought it was very strange that this old woman came out onto the stage and people stood up and she hadn't even done anything. *Time* magazine also reported that Verdon's experience only made her more humble, not allowing personal success to give her a swelled head. Her memory of being a girl in corrective boots made her self-conscious about attention and uncomfortable in public. It was said that she would rather walk through fish markets than sign autographs at Sardi's, and was happy to remain backstage as part of the show.

The applause supposedly irked star Lilo since she had the first act's final number, "Allez-Vous En." In William McBrien's book on Cole Porter, he wrote about Lilo's jealousy of Verdon receiving the applause. Making her Broadway debut, the French star had been brought over from Paris by Cy Feuer, and Porter wrote the song "I Love Paris" specifically for her to sing in the show. Assuming that the leading lady should be treated like the star, Lilo reacted to what she saw as the misplaced reception as "The battle of Verdon." In his review, Brooks Atkinson had praised Lilo but apparently this was not enough for her. As a result she had her costume in the show's finale changed from what she saw as an inappropriate old calico dress to a beautiful white evening gown. Verdon was diplomatic enough to comment that Lilo was an extraordinary performer "who made some mistakes on opening night." She would also comment that she didn't really blame Lilo for her behavior when she was afraid that Verdon was stealing the show, since she *was* its star; "In the theater, that's like another woman in a marriage triangle." She would also comment that part of the problem was that Lilo came out of the French music hall where the star never had anybody around who was better than second-rate.

The new star was reportedly mobbed by fans when she left the theater and had to ride with a policeman on the back of his horse to get to the Hotel Astor opening night party. *Can-Can* was a huge hit, running for over two years on Broadway, up until June 25, 1955, with Verdon replaced in the role by Joan Holloway and Ronnie Cunningham for some performances. An original Broadway cast recording, released by EMI Records in 1990, includes "If You Loved Me Truly" as performed by Verdon, Hans Conried and chorus.

The show was Verdon's big break, making her a Broadway star at twenty-eight; it was a little older than usual for a dancer to do so. She partly attributed her success to the fact of her few appearances in the show but those were enough to win her the Tony Award for Best Featured Actress in a Musical. Another Tony was given to Michael Kidd for Best Choreography. Verdon's success raised her salary from $175 a week to $500 and she stayed with it for over a year. However she continued to feel uncomfortable with the situation and offered to resign. The producers wanted her to stay, promising her better billing, but she refused because she felt the part didn't warrant it. Instead, she asked for, and got, more money. Verdon said that she wasn't planning a star career and just wanted to survive. She was uncomfortable with the idea of stardom, which saw the street where she was living blocked off to traffic after the paparazzi discovered her location. In the beginning she said that it scared her and it landed her in analysis. "I knew something was expected of me, but if you've come from the wrong side of the tracks, you think, 'I ain't got it.'"

Verdon's interview with Murray Schumach of the *New York Times* appeared on May 31, 1953. He described how for the interview that took place in her hotel room she wore a gray-tailored suit with a yellow rose beneath her collar. Verdon commented that the poise she gained from dancing protected her from the public stares she received, particularly from women, after *Can-Can*. They looked at her goulou hair that she said had the cruller look that belonged on a Toulouse-Lautrec poster. Verdon felt they thought her hair must be phony because it was unbelievably red. Then when they saw her freckles, they weren't so sure. The article reported that Verdon had received offers for movies, television, and other stage musicals, none of which she had accepted. She was apparently concerned about what she thought was a neglect of her dancing. She recalled some advice she received when she was younger: Never be so active that you look unattractive. Schumach wrote that her legwork in the show seemed to call for a new definition of active and he ended with the comment, "She seems to have done for dancing what the jet did for flying."

The *Life* magazine edition of June 1, 1953, featured an article on the show entitled "The Old Oo-La-La in *Can-Can*," with pictures in its theater section. It called the show a dancing triumph and claimed that Verdon was the best thing in it. Accompanying photographs showed Verdon dancing as Eve, doing the cancan for a chorus of laundresses, and in the background of the finale with the chorus dancers.

While she was performing in *Can-Can*, Verdon went back to Cole. She briefly assisted him in New York on the dances and musical numbers for the stage musical *Kismet* before its Broadway opening on December 3, 1953, at the Ziegfeld Theatre. For its story with a Middle Eastern setting, Verdon is said to have reminded Cole of the things he had done with East Indian dance. On October 8, 1953, she appeared in a color-TV CBS special shot at the Waldorf Astoria Hotel, "Eye Opener." It involved a demonstration of a new color picture tube, developed by CBS, that could be received on sets as black-and-white pictures.

Verdon made the first of seven appearances on the comedy-musical variety show *Toast of the Town* (aka *The Ed Sullivan Show*) on October 11, 1953. She was presumably on to promote *Can-Can*, but not known if she performed. In his book *Right Here on Our Stage Tonight!: Ed Sullivan's America*, Gerald Nachman writes that Verdon was banned from again appearing on the show after this episode. Apparently Sullivan had been displeased by her blasting New York columnists like himself when she spoke on a Walter Winchell newscast at the Friars Club that year. As a result Verdon would not be seen on Sullivan's show again until 1966 to promote the stage version of *Sweet Charity*.

She was interviewed by Earl Wilson in an article entitled "The Girl Who Showed 'Em How'" published in the February 1954 *Silver Screen* magazine. The interview took place at New York's Sardi's and Verdon talked about *Can-Can* and Hollywood. She described the famous title dance of the show as "the way you can see how much underwear you can show in the hardest way." Of her experience in Hollywood, Verdon was cynical, saying that all you could make there was money. She preferred the Broadway life. "I know the race out there that they call their life, and it's a life I couldn't live and a race I couldn't run." Verdon reported that she had made eight films and even now, when she got a call from Hollywood, she didn't get too excited. She said, for one thing, it was probably Mother calling. And if it was somebody trying to get Verdon to come to Hollywood, she still wasn't excited. That's because she was born there. In three photographs, Verdon was in her *Can-Can* costume. She had her skirt alternately over her head with one leg raised, being held up with her legs spread, and being held up as her left leg rests on her right upper thigh. The fourth photo showed Verdon in a black sleeveless top and tied pants, barefoot. In a dance pose, her hands were held at an angle from her arms and her left leg was on toes while her right was flat.

Verdon appeared as Shirley Kochendorf in a drama on NBC's *Goodyear Television Playhouse* entitled "Native Dancer." It was filmed in New York and broadcast on March 28, 1954. Directed by Vincent J. Donehue, it was the story of an undiscovered, talented ballerina whose agent cooks up a hoax which backfires. But eventually the dancer's luck changes. Verdon next starred as Cathy, a dancing glow-worm, in the CBS made-for-TV production of the musical *Once Upon an Eastertime* (1954), broadcast on April 18, 1954. It had songs by Victor Young and choreography by Eugene Loring. Directed by Byron Paul, the film centered on a small town boy named Pell who eats a forbidden Easter egg and is transported into a magical kingdom where he learns the difference between good and evil.

The cast of the made-for-TV musical *Once Upon an Eastertime* (1954): (from left) Verdon, Bobby Clark, and Doretta Morrow.

A *Variety* review praised the "dancing, singing and clowning" but said that the story fell apart and described the program overall as "a miserable failure."

In the March 1954 edition of *Esquire* magazine was the article "Gwen Verdon: The Anatomy of Glamour" by Robert W. Marks. She appeared in four photographs by Eve Arnold in dance class, in bare feet wearing black-laced pants, a bra and bare midriff, and a black string necklace. Marks described Verdon offstage as "all alertness, sensitivity, freshness" and quoted a telegram she received from Darryl F. Zanuck: "This is to apologize for not having noticed you before." The article also described a recent day when Verdon was sitting in the window of a 59th Street Longchamps, having lunch and watching the people pass. Suddenly she noticed that they were no longer passing. A crowd had gathered and were watching her and she became terrified. They might have seen her as the theater's newest glamour star, a target for hungry stares and the longing looks of those who needed symbols with which to feed their fantasies. Verdon could not accept the idea that she had such a special beauty which could impress or console others. In her mind she was still the stumbling, squint-eyed, undesirable little girl and the crowd had come to yell "There is 'Boot's Verdon!" She also told Marks about the happiest moment of her career: She walked along a Florida beach wearing a scanty bikini and there were no crowds or a need for her to be rescued by lifeguards. Nobody yelled "skinny" or "Boots." Nobody even looked at her twice. She at last felt she could be herself and that she had arrived.

It was at this time that a friend suggested she try to get producer Robert Fryer to help her obtain the rights to a play by Maurine (sometimes spelled Maureen) Dallas Watkins entitled *Chicago* which had been directed on Broadway by George Abbott in 1926. The play had also been adapted into two Hollywood films, one a silent comic crime drama of the same title in 1927 and the second a romantic comedy called *Roxie Hart* (1942) starring Ginger Rogers. Roxie was based on the real-life Beulah Sheriff Annan, who had been charged with murdering her lover in 1924 and found not guilty. Verdon had supposedly seen the Rogers version on television one day while she was flipping between it and coverage of the Army-McCarthy hearings in Washington and knew that something about Roxie interested her. "She's a nobody of a character whose life is passing her by [and] she doesn't like that. She wants desperately to *do* something. Her way of judging her life is whether or not it's had importance for others." The film presented Roxie as innocent of the crime, which was not true of the play or the silent film version. Verdon became obsessed with one day playing Roxie, and did her own research into the murder. Producers had told her that they would back any project that she wanted to do. However they balked at this one. They couldn't understand why she wanted to play such a "bum." Verdon would have to wait to try again.

The *New York Times* of May 6, 1954, reported that Verdon had renewed her contract to continue in *Can-Can*. Bob Fosse is said to have gone out with her after the show on May 13, 1954, which was also the opening night for his Broadway show *The Pajama Game*. On June 13, 1954, the *New York Times* reported that Verdon would leave *Can-Can* on September 4 to play the role of Gladys in Columbia Pictures's *Pal Joey*. She was to co-star with Marlon Brando and the film was to begin production in October. After that, Verdon was said to have three movie offers from Britain to choose from. *Pal Joey* was going to be directed by George Cukor and also star Barbara Stanwyck as Vera. Another proposed arrangement had Billy Wilder directing Brando and either Marlene Dietrich or Mae West as Vera. The Brando-Verdon production of *Pal Joey* was not to be. Columbia would eventually make their version of the Broadway musical in 1957 with Barbara Nichols as Gladys and Frank Sinatra in the title role. It is not known what happened to the three British films.

The *New York Times* on August 27, 1954, reported that Verdon was now scheduled to leave *Can-Can* on September 6 to make a movie (its title is not mentioned). This date was confirmed in the *New York Times* on September 5. It had been announced in the *Los Angeles Times* in August 1954 that Fox had purchased the film rights to *Can-Can* and they intended to cast the French ballerina Jeanmarie and Verdon. But after this announcement came the news that it was delayed until 1956. In April 1955 *Variety* reported that Nunnally Johnson was to direct and Cary Grant and Jeanmarie were to star. Then in March 1956 Dick Powell was to direct and the film was to be shot in Paris. In April 1956 Henry King replaced Powell. By October 1958 Vincente Minnelli was negotiating to direct with Marilyn Monroe to star.

The film finally went into production with Walter Lang directing from August to October 1959 with Frank Sinatra and Shirley MacLaine cast in the lead roles. Verdon was overlooked for the part of Claudine in favor of Juliet Prowse, with Claudine's Broadway song "If You Loved Me Truly" cut from the soundtrack. Hermes Pan staged the dances, and it is said that Verdon agreed to coach Prowse in her numbers. Prowse had played an uncredited dancer in the United Artists musical comedy *Gentlemen Marry Brunettes* (1955) which was the next film project for Jack Cole and Verdon. It is thought that the women had met on this film which led to Prowse getting Verdon to help her on *Can-Can*.

Released in March 1960, *Can-Can* received some notoriety after Nikita Khrushchev, the Soviet premier who was on a trip to the United States, was brought to the film's set to view a special performance. *Can-Can* was not a box office hit.

Gentlemen Marry Brunettes, directed by Richard Sale, was shot from

September 8, 1954, to early January 1955 at the Shepperton and MGM Studios in England and Paris Studio Cinema in France. Based on the novella "But Gentlemen Marry Brunettes" by Anita Loos, it was a sequel to *Gentlemen Prefer Blondes*. Fox had considered protesting the production of the film because they felt that it would infringe upon their rights to make a sequel. So in order to avoid any complications, screenwriters Sale and Mary Loos (the niece of Anita) changed the names of the characters and much of the plot, retaining only the title and the idea of two American singers going to Paris.

Connie (Jeanne Crain) and Bonnie Jones (Jane Russell), sisters and nightclub performers, work in Paris. Verdon appeared in a flashback to 1926 with Rudy Vallee at a party. She has two lines, "She's disenchanted? We're all disenchanted" before she dances and disappears into the crowd. Verdon wears a sparkly brown sleeveless flapper dress with waist sash, black bonnet and red beads, and has a long cigarette holder. However she cannot be spotted as a backup dancer in the scene once Russell and Crain appear in sparkly silver dresses to dance on a table as Mimi and Mitzi Jones to "Miss Annabelle Lee."

The film had its world premiere in Chicago on September 22, 1955, and opened in New York on October 29 with the tagline "See 'em sizzle in the big, buxom, beautiful musical!" The film was lambasted by A.H. Weiler in the *New York Times* and Ronald Bergan in his book *The United Artists Story*.

Playing a maid, Verdon had an additional dance sequence filmed in the Jones sisters' hotel room but it was cut. The *New York Times* (June 5, 1955) reported that the British Board of Film Censors supported the American Production Code Administration decision to cut Verdon's dance sequence. The British censors found both her dance and costume objectionable, though it was said that the sequence would be retained for the American release. However the dance is missing from prints available in America *and* Britain. On the same date in *Daily Variety* it was reported that the dance was cut because Verdon wore a garter high on her thigh, which wasn't acceptable. Other sources claim that in the number she was a Dior model who sheds her garments one by one, and that the number was deemed obscene for dancing that was too sexy in a costume too brief. In the September 23, 1955, *Hollywood Reporter* it was suggested that the reason for the cut was that she wore a rose in the wrong place. A still exists of Verdon's burlesque costume for the number: a brief one-piece with flowers on the top and in her crotch, a garter linked to suspenders and black stockings, a big "chocolate box" bow at her back, black high heels, long black gloves and a feathered picture hat, and she holds a white parasol. Verdon herself would describe the cut dance as "just humorous and kind of athletic."

While she was in Paris, Verdon was asked by Robert Griffith, Fred Brisson, and Harold Prince to be in their next Broadway show *Damn Yankees*. The female lead was Lola, who was the Devil's right hand, and the part required someone to dance but also sing and act. Carol Haney may have seemed like the producers' obvious choice for the part and it may have become a career advance for her, but she was presumably contracted to stay in *The Pajama Game* in the part of secretary Gladys Hotchkiss, which was then running on Broadway. Haney's connection with Verdon also had the women look similar, though Haney at 5'6" was taller than Verdon's 5'4" and she had a deeper speaking voice. The producers had approached Mitzi Gaynor and the French ballet dancer Jeanmarie, but both had rejected the part. Verdon said that Marilyn Monroe wanted the part but other sources say she turned it down. Apparently the show's choreographer, Bob Fosse wanted Verdon. Although she had limited singing experience, the producers were willing to take a chance on her because of her spectacular dancing talents.

But Verdon initially turned them down. She preferred to stay with Cole rather than return to Broadway. Cole was unimpressed with the offer and believed that playing such a part would be debasing Verdon's talent. But the producers persisted because they wanted her, and eventually she agreed and they got her. So once again Verdon said goodbye to Cole and hello to Fosse.

4

Damn Yankees, Bob Fosse and *New Girl in Town*

Director George Abbott had helped author Douglass Wallop adapt his book *The Year the Yankees Lost the Pennant* into a musical for Broadway with songs by Richard Adler and Jerry Ross who had done the same for Abbott's previous show, *The Pajama Game. Damn Yankees*, a retelling of the Faust legend, was set during the 1950s in Washington when the New York Yankees dominated major league baseball. There was a feeling that musicals about baseball were jinxed because you couldn't show the game on stage, and those that had tried in the past were failures. However the producers Fred Brisson, Robert Griffith and Harold Prince moved ahead. Verdon said that after she had been cast she nearly lost the job when she went dancing with Abbott. They were doing the merengue at Roseland and he was on the wrong beat. Verdon started to count for him and Abbott was not pleased.

Fosse was as leery about working with Verdon as she with him. Although she had not been asked to audition for the show's producers, Fosse wanted her to audition for him. He knew that she was good but he did not know whether she would be good *for him*. Fosse was intimidated by her reputation. He had heard that Verdon could be difficult, that she was a high-class snob with an iron-clad pedigree and a hatred of the kind of Broadway dancing she considered to be animated wallpaper.

The producers arranged for them to meet in a dance studio on Broadway at 64th Street. He showed her some ideas he had for the choreography for her number "Whatever Lola Wants." Watching Fosse slithering and stalking his way through the oldest stripping tricks in the book, observing his winks and blinks and finger curls that she could tell came from weeks of careful preparation, she was impressed. As he worked out when she should breathe and laugh and smile and how much, her incredulity became enthusiasm. Her enthusiasm gave him confidence and his confidence increased her enthusiasm. She asked him to do it again and made suggestions, which he appreciated. For Lola's advance on the baseball player Joe Hardy, Fosse had her stop and scratch an itch on the back of her leg with one toe. Verdon found the move hard to do in high heels because they affected her balance. Since Fosse wanted to keep the moment in, he brought to rehearsal a pair of oversized high heels to show her that it could be done. He would tell her that he did this because he never asked people to do what he was not willing to do himself.

The couple was more than compatible. She admired his technique and he admired her body, her enthusiasm, her desire for perfection, and endless energy. Verdon would say that when Fosse got a-hold of her, she was a great dancer but he developed and "created" her. She got the job and they agreed to work together. Abbott was to direct the singers in the show and Fosse to do the dances, even when they appeared in the middle of a song.

Damn Yankees rehearsals began on March 7, 1955, over separate spaces on different floors at the Waltons Warehouse, and the first run-through was held on March 20, 1955. Abbott supposedly had less faith in Verdon's acting abilities so he is said to have minimized her dialogue, until he saw that she had a disarming and comic vulnerability. She credited Fosse as being more helpful to her as an actress than Abbott, who had reportedly told her, "Say the words and get off." Verdon also found that he was equally difficult because he gave line readings. This would make her tear her hair out.

Verdon had done her own research for Lola by spending time on English Avenue observing the attitude of Cuban–Puerto Rican people, and she also learned a pseudo–Spanish accent for the part. She imagined the character as a child, more funny than sexy, in the way she copied Lola Montez and the movie ladies of the '30s and '40s who flared their nostrils and used eye attitude to be sexy. However ,Verdon acted it straight rather than funny, meaning every word. Fosse helped her get the character from the dialogue in the Lola song, and he worked to the classical music of Aaron Copland and Morton Gould which helped him with the oddball phrasing of the dance steps. The Lola number was designed to showcase her combination of sexiness and humor. Fosse and Verdon worked together to present a dance that was a parody of the bump and grind routines that they were both familiar with from their mutual experience in burlesque. It was also a continuation of the comic vamping that Carol Haney and he had employed for "Hernando's Hideaway." Verdon would give sole credit to Fosse for choreographing the number, which was a sign of her lack of vanity and generosity. But an examination of the dance reveals that while his touches are the small movements, the strides and turns are typically hers.

There were two scenes in the play where Verdon was called upon to act and here she was also coached by Fosse. In the scene where Lola tells Joe that she was the ugliest woman in Providence, Rhode Island, Fosse wanted Verdon to reveal a secret about herself to provide the meaning required. He suggested she think about something she did that she now felt guilty about, so Verdon recalled the times when she was a kid and she used to steal things. However she did not like using such personal things in her work to fill in for something in a scene because she worried that she wouldn't be able to remember that thing every night. Verdon felt it was better to have some sort of technique you can call on, just as a dancer does, to prepare to perform. This need would be met with her further studies with Sanford Meisner in her next show, *New Girl in Town*.

Tryouts were held in New Haven with three previews from April 2, 1955, and then Boston for three weeks. One problem that was encountered: Audiences were more interested in the baseball and the character of Lola than the love story between Joe and Meg. She had a late entrance into the story and only had one solo number, "Whatever Lola Wants." Verdon didn't complain because that was not her nature, but she was still aware of the situation. The authors didn't want her to detract from the love story, but it was clear that Verdon had the potential to be a show stopper. They decided to build up her part, giving her two new songs and a new dance, and her character was made more sympathetic. In New Haven, the song "A Little Brains, a Little Talent" was added before "What Lola Wants" in the first act.

Richard Adler was unhappy with Fosse's choreography for the new number. Verdon was doing tiny bumps where she moved nothing but her hips, as if she was adjusting herself inside her panties. Adler felt this was not enough because he said his friends didn't know what she was doing. She apparently became angered at what she interpreted as being spoken to in a derogatory manner. Verdon supposedly replied with expletives, telling Adler that her friends thought what she was doing was terrific. Fosse agreed with Verdon and the number wasn't changed.

Among the other alterations: Abbott had Adler and Ross change the rock music that accompanied "Two Lost Souls" to make it sound like "There Was Once a Man" from *The Pajama Game*. (When Verdon did the show ten years later in Chicago and Westbury, the orchestration was restored to the rock sound.) The number which appeared at the end of

4. Damn Yankees, Bob Fosse and New Girl in Town 49

the first act troubled producer Harold Prince. It featured the baseball players at a party where one of them stood on a chair wearing a gorilla suit under a Yankee uniform, terrorizing them as they danced around him in a game of musical chairs. Verdon was also part of the number, doing *a pas de deux* with George Marcy. At the first preview, Fosse decided to play the part of the gorilla. Prince wanted the number scrapped but Fosse refused to take it out of the show. Abbott convinced Fosse to come up with another number. Verdon would say that she was sorry to see the gorilla ballet go because she thought it was fabulous. Fosse's alternative number was created for the scene where the baseball hero's fan club does an entertainment for him. Thinking of the grunting South American dance that was the current rage, he came up with a duet based on the mambo, and Adler and Ross provided the song "Who's Got the Pain." He worked on the number with Verdon, which was to be danced by her and Eddie Phillips. The performers wore tight black pants, bright Caribbean tops, and the little hats that would become a Fosse trademark. Prince was pleased with this number, which was original in Fosse's use of athleticism.

The show came to the 46th Street Theatre and had a preview on May 2, 1955, which was a benefit for pre-adoptive nursery care by the Spence-Chapin Adoptive Service. It opened on May 5, 1955, and would run to May 4, 1957, there and then from May 6 to October 12, 1957, at the Adelphi Theatre. For the opening night performance, tickets were printed to resemble ballpark tickets, listing rain check provisions, gate numbers and the game being played. "Heart" and Verdon both stopped the show; there was praise for Stephen Douglass and Ray Walston, but the greatest excitement was over her. In the *New York Times*, Lewis Funke wrote that she "gives brilliance and sparkle to the evening with her exuberant dancing, her wicked, glistening eyes and her sheer delight in the foolery." He described Fosse with Verdon as one of the evening's heroes and wrote that the dance numbers "are full of fun and vitality."

Despite the good reviews, the producers continued to tinker with it. They felt it was too long, and also the audiences didn't like how Lola climatically turned back into the ugly old crone she had originally been. The number "Not Meg" was cut and a second act number was moved into the first, which saved twenty minutes. The ending was also altered. Now the Devil changed Lola back in to a beautiful seductress again. Baseball-associated gimmicks used were actual bright stadium lights on the stage and in the orchestra, and hot dogs were sold at intermission. However the box office take was not what was hoped for. Perhaps those who predicted that baseball musicals were jinxed were right. The producers looked at

Stephen Douglass and Verdon in a posed shot from the stage show *Damn Yankees* (1955–1956).

their advertising which had Verdon in a baggy baseball uniform. She looked adorable and funny but not sexy. They replaced it with an image of Verdon in her underwear in her Lola number. This also referenced the number in the show which was funny, and the song, which had become popular after having been recorded by Sarah Vaughan. The "Playbill" cover and the cover of the original cast recording which was recorded on May 8,

1955, were also changed to this effect. Ironically Verdon is dressed in a baseball uniform in some of the photographs taken at the recording session. As a result of the strategy, business rose dramatically. Another reason to change Verdon's costume was that it was felt that the advertising should remove references to baseball because people originally were confused as to whether the show was about the South or baseball. The producers wanted to downplay the sports angle and highlight the popular themes of regained youth as symbolized by Faust and sex.

The show received industry acclaim when it won Tony Awards as Best Musical, Verdon as Best Actress in a Musical, Ray Walston as Best Actor in a Musical, Russ Brown as Best Featured Actor in a Musical, and Fosse for Best Choreography. The original cast recording was released by RCA Victor on June 1, 1955. During the run Verdon would be replaced for individual performances by Sheila Bond, Gretchen Wyler and Devra Korwin.

The *New York Times* of May 15, 1955, reported that Mary Loos and Richard Sale would next film *Gentlemen Chase Redheads* and that Verdon would leave *Damn Yankees* in May 1956 to appear in it. The husband-and-wife producing team said that they had begun to write the story and that they planned to start filming in the summer of 1956. Jeanne Crain was also said to be slated to play a starring role. The plot involved a group of *Time* magazine researchers who dig into a story that redheads, like Cleopatra and Queen Elizabeth 1, still rule the world nowadays. This film was never made.

Damn Yankees was the subject of a photographic essay by Peter Stackpole in *Life* magazine (May 16, 1955). There was also an accompanying article that described the nine months that it took to bring the show to Broadway. Verdon was shown in baseball costume among "The Big Pool of Talent"—the eighty-three participants which includes producers, authors, actors, designers, production staff, singers, dancers, and orchestra. She was one of the fourteen principal actors and referred to as "the Devil's accomplice." In a photo Verdon wore what appeared to be jeans and a sweater as she tried out steps in the rehearsal hall as the other dancers watched. She was also photographed flying with Eddie Phillips on stage in the "Who's Got the Pain" number; with Walston as an irate Satan; and with Douglass performing "Whatever Lola Wants."

Her success was also signified by her getting the cover of *Time* magazine on June 13, 1955. In the accompanying article by Roger S. Hewlett were photographs of Verdon with Stephen Douglass in *Damn Yankees*, director Abbott, Verdon in *Can-Can*, her son Jimmy and his grandparents, and Verdon as a hula dancer at age nine. The article ended with Verdon's idea that she only gave herself five more years as a dancer. It was said that she received many long-term contract offers which she was in no hurry to sign because "I don't want to get lost."

Verdon made the first of two appearances on the television comedy-musical variety show *The Colgate Comedy Hour*. The series was filmed live in New York with segments telecast from Los Angeles. The episode broadcast on July 10, 1955, had George Abbott as special host and was devoted to the songs of Richard Adler and Jerry Ross, specifically those they had written for *The Pajama Game* and *Damn Yankees*. Verdon performed "A Little Brains, a Little Talent" but strangely, Abbe Lane did "Whatever Lola Wants."

In the July 12, 1955, *Look* magazine there was an article about Verdon entitled "Beauty and Baseball." Publicizing *Damn Yankees*, she was seen in photographs from the show as well as backstage in a strapless long black dress, and in the theater alley racing to a matinee. In the last shot Verdon wore a long fur coat and carried two parcels that appeared to contain clothes and a hat. She commented about it, saying that among other things, she had found out that stardom meant you were always in a rush.

On July 21, 1955, Verdon was presented with the Most Outstanding Actress in the Musical Comedy Field Award for her *Damn Yankees* performance by the Dance Educators of America at the Park-Sheraton Hotel. On December 11 she was one of the participants in "Cocktail Revue," the Equity Library Theatre entertainment presented at the Belmont Plaza Hotel. Broadcast on the same night was the *Colgate Comedy Hour* salute to George Abbott. Verdon and Fosse were credited as dancers in the show. She was not part of the national touring company of *Damn Yankees*, which began in New Haven on January 21, 1956, having been replaced by Tybee Afra and then Sherry O'Neil.

Verdon released an album of her singing with Joe Reisman and His Orchestra entitled "The Girl I Left Home For." She appeared on the album cover dressed in black sweater and slacks, red waist sash to match her red hair, and lying on a wooden bench. The album reveals that perhaps Verdon's vocals are better suited to the theater than to records and the concert stage, with a voice that is reminiscent of Helen Kane but with more range. The song choices are an interesting mix of ballads and up-tempo numbers. She does three songs that Betty Grable had performed in the film *Meet Me After the Show* (in which Verdon had also appeared): "It's a Hot Night in Alaska," "Bettin on a Man" and "No-Talent Joe." Another notable choice is a slowed-down version of "I've Got the World on a String" which Frank

Sinatra had made famous with a 1953 recording. The album was reviewed in the *New York Times* by John S. Wilson on February 19, 1956. He wrote that the allure that is such an important part of her stage presence did not transfer readily to disks, so that she was heard on the album in "diminished and diluted form as a comedienne with a minor and little sense of comic projection." Wilson praised her choice of interesting offbeat songs but wrote that she was "unable to overcome a lackluster blandness in her delivery."

Verdon, Ray Walston and Stephen Douglass did a special performance of *Damn Yankees* at New York's Treasurers Club on March 18, 1956. The next day the *New York Times* reported that Verdon and Walston were among the actors who had been nominated for awards by the Lambs for their noteworthy overall contribution to the theater. Silver mugs, emblematic of the traditional pewter mug of the Lambs, would be presented at the group's annual gambol at the Waldorf Astoria on April 21. Verdon was chosen as one of the winners of the awards but Walston was not. It was reported in the *New York Times* on April 22, 1956, that she attended the ceremony to receive it.

In *Life* magazine (March 19, 1956), Verdon was featured in the fashion section modelling new spring clothes. She was seen in one color and eight black-and-white photographs wearing attention-getting outfits from top collections under the headline of "A Star's Fling at Spring. Verdon Teaches Upstaging." The text proclaimed her a seasoned show-stealer and the star of Broadway's *Damn Yankees*, "like any girl who has a little zest, a lot of nerve and enough cash to be able to upstage anyone in a crowd."

For the April 1956 *Theatre Arts* magazine, Verdon authored the article "Musical Comedy. The Theatre's Awkward Adolescent" which was accompanied by a *Damn Yankees* photograph of her with Stephen Douglass. She expressed how she felt about the fact that the dramatic side of musicals was behind the musical side in terms of sophistication and how the idea that the musical comedy had come of age was a false one. Verdon claimed that part of the reason for this was how musicals were created, where lines for the book were often ad libbed in rehearsal by the director and actors. One downside to this practice was that lines often regurgitated the plot which a musical number had just advanced so that an actor mouthed program notes rather than real dialogue. She was also critical of the forms of comedy in musical comedies (frequently gags and pratfalls) did not arise from the dramatic situation itself. Verdon claimed that this kind of material was provided because of a feeling that musical comedy performers were not dramatic actors capable of giving characterizations of any depth. She offered some solutions to the problem, suggesting that the show's book be prepared in advance as much as the musical numbers were, and that directors be employed from the legitimate theater rather than those with only experience in musical comedies. She also suggested that the choreographer's role in the show might be extended to give them complete control of the musical, dance and dramatic direction. Here she admitted that this was an ability not all choreographers had, giving Michael Kidd, Jerome Robbins and Fosse as the only examples she was aware of. This argument prefigured Verdon's insistence on Fosse directing her later show *Redhead*. Other ideas she had were having a librettist-director (like Garson Kanin) work in combination with said choreographers; and that stage directors and writers should study acting so that they could analyze a play and help an actor achieve a truthful performance rather than just mimic line readings given to them. Verdon ended the article on a note of hope: She was confident that eventually a show's book work would catch up with the music and lyrics and they would merge so thoroughly that works of genuine integrity would be the rule rather than the exception.

It appears that Verdon but not Fosse attended the Tony Awards on April 1, 1956, to accept her Best Actress in a Musical statue. The ceremony, held at the Plaza Hotel in New York, was the first broadcast live on television.

An added benefit for Verdon from doing *Damn Yankees* was that she had fallen in love with Fosse. Their working relationship became entangled with their personal one, since it captured the essentials of their attraction. It reflected their needs and was the physical representation of their characters. One of Fosse's dancers said that the dancers talked about wanting to watch the couple make love because they were so exciting sexually together, especially when they worked. Their affair reportedly ended Verdon's relationship with actor Scott Brady, whom she had presumably met on the set of *Gentlemen Marry Brunettes*.

Dancer Svetlana McLee was in the chorus of *Damn Yankees* and had also appeared with Fosse's wife, Joan McCracken, in the Broadway musical *Me and Juliet*. McLee told McCracken of the affair between Verdon and Fosse that had been obvious in rehearsals. When McCracken learned about it, she supposedly told him, "Sometimes the artificial can be very attractive." Fosse filed for divorce to be with Verdon, though sources differ as to when. Some say it was in 1956, others '57.

During her run in *Damn Yankees* Verdon also took dance classes. In July 1956 she acquired a studio several floors above her East Side apartment for her thirteen-year-old son Jimmy, who planned on coming to New York to go to prep school. She also contributed to the reconstruction of the studio, painting, sanding, staining the floors and dividing a room to make a pantry. Verdon rigged a split bamboo blind for the roof of the garden to create a screened-in sleeping area, and replastered a whole wall. This job made her right arm so tired that she had to wear a sling off-stage.

On September 9, 1956, she and the company of *Damn Yankees* gave an Actors Fund performance. Verdon's mother Gertrude died on October 16, 1956; Gwen was unable to attend her funeral because of her commitment to the show. The *New York Times* on October 22 reported that Verdon was set to leave *Damn Yankees* on December 3 and that she would be replaced by Gretchen Wyler. Then on November 19 it was reported that she would leave on November 24. The *New York Times* also announced that Verdon was set to star with Thelma Ritter in *New Girl in Town*, a new musical adaptation of Eugene O'Neill's play *Anna Christie* by George Abbott and Bob Merrill. The show was to be produced by Fred Brisson, Robert Griffith and Harold Prince, the producers of *Damn Yankees*, with Abbott directing and Bob Fosse as choreographer. It was scheduled to open on Broadway in May at the 46th Street Theatre.

New Girl in Town had eventuated after the ending of the working relationship between composer Jerry Ross and Richard Adler, when Ross died on November 11, 1955. This meant that a proposed follow-up to *Damn Yankees* could not happen. Doris Day had told George Abbott about songs that Bob Merrill had written for a planned MGM musical remake of *Anna Christie* which was to have starred her and Thelma Ritter. The film was to have been set in the present among the fishing fleets on the Monterey, California, coast. MGM had four screenplays written for it but none of them worked, so the project was shelved. Liking the songs, Abbott bought the rights and planned a new stage show that he would write the book for and direct, changing the title from *Pay the Piper* to *New Girl in Town*.

Merrill's adaptation had updated the source material but Abbott rejected the idea of modernizing the story. Later Abbott would say that he felt that prostitution was not the problem it had been in earlier times when a girl could be driven into it by economic necessity. Now he thought that a girl could earn a living much more easily. He threw out the eighteen songs Merrill had written and had him substitute nineteen new ones. The original play had been set in 1912 but Abbott changed the year to the turn of the century because he felt that clothes were prettier then. This also allowed the adaptation to exploit the idea of women who were less socially emancipated. The O'Neill source play had run on Broadway at the Vanderbilt Theatre from November 2, 1921, to April 1922. It starred Pauline Lord as Anna and won the playwright the 1922 Pulitzer Prize for Drama. A silent film version was made by the Thomas H. Ince Company for Associated First National Pictures and released in 1923 with Blanche Sweet playing Anna. The MGM version starred Greta Garbo as Anna in her talkie debut and was released in 1930. The new girl of the title was a Swedish-American former prostitute who had come to Manhattan to start a new life and was reunited with her sea captain father.

The producers were unsure as to whether it was best to get an actress and teach her to sing or to get a singer and teach her to act. As the star of their current hit show, Verdon was considered by the producers as a dancer who had developed her singing and acting talents only in the last few seasons, and she was given the script to consider in September 1956. Fosse wasn't sure it was the right choice for himself and Verdon. He felt that the show was more a vehicle for singing than dancing, and that the leading role was designed for a singer with a strong Rodgers and Hammerstein voice. But Verdon wanted the part because she thought that it was an extraordinary opportunity to show that musical theater performance was acting and no different from doing the material as a drama.

Other actresses were auditioned including Ida Lupino and Shelley Winters who couldn't sing well enough, and Marilyn Monroe. She could sing, just not very loud and, since this was before the days of body mikes, the producers decided that she would not be able to be heard in the theater. Abbott also made Verdon audition, an affront to her established stardom. He actually read with her and afterward told her, "Well, that's in miniature, but that's right." For her musical audition, she tried to sing "Good to Be Alive" but she broke in the middle of it. She knew she had given a bad impression but she later said that something about defeat "does something to her" so she asked to audition again in three weeks. Some sources claim that she used the time to take daily singing lessons, while others say that she rehearsed with acting teacher Sanford Meisner, whom Fosse had brought in. Verdon said that she took the singing lessons and only studied with Meisner after she got the part. At her second audition, Harold Prince was sold but Abbott supposedly still had reservations. He wanted a show without dancing and was concerned about casting a non-dancing Verdon. However he agreed to have Verdon play the role, since although his initial choice was not to have a choreographer, she was given dance moments in rehearsal which led to Fosse's involvement.

Her casting would stop her from making her London theater debut in *Damn Yankees*, but it insured a strong box office pre-sale for the new show after the success of the former. Fosse's credit was expanded to musical staging as well as choreography so that now he was also responsible for the direction of the show's songs as well as the dances. He gave a party for the chorus in his one-bedroom apartment on Manhattan's West Side. Verdon entertained the crowd with tales about Jack Cole. Once rehearsals began, she worked with Meisner. Fosse brought in Pat Ferrier to help him create the dances, to do what Verdon would have otherwise done for him.

To show her dedication to the show, Verdon dyed her red hair because she thought that Anna should be blonde since O'Neill said she was in his play. Another factor was that, whenever she was in a show, they talked about the "flame-haired green-orbed Gwen Verdon." She felt that the first thing was always her red hair. When the producer saw the sketches for her costumes, he felt that they were too plain but he was assured by others that Verdon's red hair would make them stand out. That decided it for her. She thought since everybody was depending on her hair, it would be tragic if they said of her in an O'Neill play "the flame-haired Miss Verdon" and they reviewed it like any other show she had been in. She thought "Never mind the color of my hair" because some day it'll turn gray and she wanted to be remembered as good, not just flame-haired. This comment is ironic given that Verdon's hair color later in life was still red, presumably because she did not want to be seen with gray hair.

She decided that she didn't want to play the part as a deep person. Verdon saw that Anna was tragic and pathetic but she also found her funny-pathetic, like Chaplin. "She's confused and not very bright, like a hurt animal," she said. "She tries to be a lady, and it doesn't quite come off, and it's funny and sad, a sort of laughing and crying at the same time." Her studies with Meisner also had Verdon examine her past to relate to the character. Anna had the shame of a former life as a prostitute which she wanted to conceal but feared that something she did would give her away. Verdon had the shame of being a childhood cripple, and always feared that something would stick out or something she did would give her secret away. However after she studied the original O'Neill scenes with Meisner, she was dismayed when they were almost completely cut from the new show. They had been envisaged as dialogue in a spotlight that would lead to a big number. One lost scene that Verdon particularly missed was when Anna tells her father about her former life. As a way to compensate, she transferred the emotions from the cut scenes into the dancing. However, after six months, Verdon found that she hated this way of working, of using her inner resources. She decided to change her approach from working on a character from the inside to working from the outside. To develop the character, Verdon would create a specific walk or a funny little tic or a certain posture. She then added to this with costume and props and found that this affected behavior and the definition of a character.

When Verdon read Laurence Olivier's 1982 autobiography *Confessions of an Actor*, she saw that he adopted the same approach. She would say that she found that Anna's first scene, where she comes into the saloon and meets the father she hasn't seen in years, took more out of her than anything else she had ever done. It left her so exhausted that her back ached. This is because the character was such an emotional mess as well as being physically weak after having been sick and just gotten out a hospital. Trying to show the strain that Anna was under became a terrible strain on any actress playing the role. Verdon demonstrated this with small touches like making her lips tremble when she drank a glass of port.

Fosse developed a whorehouse ballet for the sequence where Anna dreams of her past life. Abbott wasn't sure about the idea but he decided to see what reaction it received. The number was controversial since it involved Verdon in flesh-colored tights, garter belt and a brief corset. In rehearsals one of her breasts would occasionally pop out when she was being carried up a great staircase to an upstairs bedroom. Another part of the ballet had Anna flirting with a young man (played by Harvey Evans, who was then known as Harry Hohnecker) brought into the whorehouse. Evans first met Verdon when he was fifteen and had waited at the stage door for her after a performance of *Can-Can*. In the number his leg shook and rose like an erection in reaction to Anna's flirting. Producer Harold Prince found the ballet revolting and described it as "crotch dancing" and a "Vegas, Crazy Horse in Paris number."

The show had a preview in New Haven on April 8, 1957. Reportedly members of the audience averted their eyes and some even shrieked in horror. The number was deemed too dirty and had to be cut. The police came and padlocked the stage doors and posted a Do Not Enter sign which was discovered by the dancers when they arrived the next day. Sources differ as to how this came about. Some say that the police had acted after having read reviews of the show. One claims that "the police" was actually one crossing guard, summoned by the mother of a teenage girl. Harvey Evans says the producers were responsible for the lockout. He says they went to the city officials, claiming that the ballet material was pornographic, which led to the police action.

When the company moved to Boston in May, the controversy continued.

Abbott and Prince wanted the number out but Fosse and Verdon refused. Three arguments were proffered against the dance. Dream ballets in general were overused. It glamorized the bordello by making Anna's former life as a prostitute appear far more appealing than her present circumstances. And it didn't belong in the show because Anna was not a dancer. Perhaps the most important and persuasive argument was that audiences hated the ballet. They reportedly felt nervous about how it was done without music except for a drum beat, and they expressed their displeasure by not applauding at the end of the number. Fosse and Verdon considered the ballet high art and said that they didn't care what the audience thought, citing how an audience had thrown fruit at Stravinsky. Abbott commented that the act of throwing fruit at a project was not proof of its being high art. Ironically the number drew attention away from the fact that the show was otherwise thought to be mediocre with a weak book and undistinguished songs. The show also suffered by comparison with *West Side Story* which had tryouts in February and which would open on Broadway on September 26, 1957. Another factor that provided an imbalance to the show was the casting of Thelma Ritter in the supporting role of Martha. Since her part was a comic one and Verdon's was more serious, Ritter was getting more attention from the press.

Jack Cole is said to have visited. He had once warned Verdon against working with Fosse, but now he approved. Fosse's whorehouse ballet presumably got Cole's approval because he too liked whorehouse ballets, akin to the "Harlequin Odyssey" he had done with Verdon in 1953. Fosse devised an alternate ballet but Abbott felt it was similar to the original and vetoed it. Some sources claim that the producers went so far as to burn the $40,000 staircase used in the number in the alley behind the theater to prevent the sequence from being restored. Verdon said that she did not know who actually burned the set although she knew it wasn't the producers, Abbott or Fosse. He would eventually restore the ballet, without the staircase but using a few chairs and an orchestration to replace the drum beat.

The opposition to the ballet highlighted an irony that the producers must have been aware of. The best option to save the show was to give Verdon more of what she did best—dancing. However, perhaps perversely, the only time she could attend dance rehearsals was after the show at night, since she was used in the daytime for revisions of her dramatic scenes. Verdon was working until three or four in the morning. Abbott suggested that a waltz number might replace the forbidden whorehouse ballet, but when he appeared at Fosse's rehearsal, he saw the ballet being worked on. Verdon tried to speak to Abbott but was told by Harold Prince that he was too busy. In response she thought, "Then I'm too busy to go on."

Verdon reported sick for three days (one source says that she was out for a week). Did she really have the flu or was she faking it as a strategic maneuver? Reportedly her part was so complicated that it had to be split into four different sections and played by four different understudies. One read Anna's dialogue and sang, and the three others performed the dances. When Verdon returned, Abbott supposedly punished her by refusing to hire a stand-in for her. Fosse finally relented and reworked the ballet but the situation made him vow to never again work with Abbott and Harold Prince. The Boston tryouts also saw Verdon drop out of the last four performances because she reportedly knocked herself out from losing weight. She said that she got worn out because she was required to rehearse new material on her own as well as give performances.

The show was originally set to open on Broadway on May 8, 1957. The preview performance of May 13 was a party benefit for the Children's Village at Dobbs Ferry. On February 16, the *New York Times* announced that the show would now open on May 9. On March 21, they reported that the May 7 preview was to be a benefit for the Rehearsal Club which aided young women seeking theatrical careers. This benefit was later postponed to June 24. The show finally opened on Broadway on May 14 and it ran till May 24, 1958, at the 46th Street Theatre.

It received a mixed review from Brooks Atkinson in the *New York Times*, who wrote that Verdon played with "great style and insight," giving a complete characterization that was "sobering and admirable." He wrote more about the show in May 26 *Times* article on George Abbott. Atkinson said that the finest thing about it was Verdon's reticent, moving performance. "There is nothing hackneyed or superficial about Miss Verdon's acting. It is an illuminating portrait of a wretched inarticulate creature." In *The Times* of June 16, John Martin wrote that Verdon is a "marvelous, instinctive dancer, and once she starts, Pauline Lord and Eugene O'Neill, plot and drama, lines and gags, fade into a kind of gray unimportance. This is not just skill, it is magic."

Fosse got to restore the whorehouse ballet, known as the "Red Light" or "Cathouse" ballet. He prepared for this by rehearsing the dancers and presented the ballet a month after the show opened. The date was June 23, his birthday. This was done without the permission of Abbott or Prince. The songs were also captured in an original cast recording done on May 26, 1957. At the Tony Awards ceremony held on April 13, 1958, at the Waldorf

4. Damn Yankees, *Bob Fosse and* New Girl in Town

Astoria, there was a tie for Best Actress in a Musical for Verdon and Ritter. It lost for Best Musical, Best Featured Actor for Cameron Prud-homme, and Best Choreography for Fosse.

Verdon would say that she was very disappointed in the show because she thought that they were really going to do O'Neill but it changed so much out of town. She says that in the end it was not one of her favorites but it really did more for her than any of the others. People discovered that Verdon could act and wasn't just the "last of the red hot mamas." She only stayed with the show for eleven months, and although this was partly to do with the opportunity to do the film *Damn Yankees*, she said that she was very glad to leave.

In a *New York Times* interview by Lewis Nichols (May 26, 1957), Verdon said she would like to do one more dancing job before she stopped. Verdon said that age does step in and in her case that would be pretty soon, and she didn't want to do a musical show with a lot of dancing and have people on the way out say "But you should have seen her ten years ago." She felt that she could get through one more but she didn't want to grow shaky. Verdon supposed that she could do concerts indefinitely, but not ballet. Dancing required a lot of muscular energy and at some point the legs go. She didn't think that she'd ever been any good at choreography since she did not think she was at all creative, but sometimes she could do something a little different to the steps than what a choreographer like Fosse proposed. Nichols disagreed with Verdon's idea that she was not creative or a choreographer, particularly since the *Damn Yankees* program had a note that one dance was a collaboration between her and Fosse.

Nichols also wrote that she had practically no social life. He said Verdon seldom went to parties, and if she was at one, she froze at any suggestion that she dance or sing. Her main vice was reading. "Lately, it's naturally been O'Neill, but for years I've read Odets, Saroyan, Strindberg." She said she went through periods of reading biographies and historical novels: "I guess you could say that I get literary crushes, but it's not planned reading." Nichols commented that he thought her son Jimmy, 14, seemed a sad, woebegone little figure because she said that he had not inherited his mother's ability to dance. Verdon disagreed, saying that her son was as happy as they come. She added that Jimmy played the saxophone, planned to go to Cornell and then wanted to travel west to be a cattleman. The theater was just not in his bones. That was for others in the family.

During the season, Verdon missed performances. The *New York Times* of May 29, 1957, reported that she was out on May 27 and May 28 for four performances due to a throat ailment. Her stint was divided among Ann Williams, who did the acting, and dancers Claiborne Cary, Pat Ferrier and Marie Kolin. Williams usually played Mrs. Dowling and Ferrier was Moll, and Cary and Kolin were in the dancing chorus. It is not known who filled in for these ladies in their roles for the performances. It was reported in the *Times* that Verdon returned to the show on June 3 after having had an acute sinus condition and bronchitis. However her absences apparently had the producers now seeking an alternate to lessen her arduous task of acting, singing and dancing. The *Times* reported on June 7 that Valerie Bettis had made a bid to act as Verdon's stand-by. However on June 10 it was advised that Joan Holloway, who had followed Verdon in *Can-Can*, had been appointed as her *New Girl in Town* stand-by. Verdon left the show in March 1958 when she was replaced by Evelyn Ward, who appeared to be new to it.

New Girl in Town was one of many shows featured in an article in the Theater section of the *Life* Magazine edition of June 24. The article was titled "Big Run for O'Neill Plays. The late dramatist has his busiest season on Broadway and off–even with music." *New Girl in Town* had joined three O'Neill plays already on the New York stage; *Moon for the Misbegotten*, *The Iceman Cometh*, and *A Touch of the Poet*. The article also featured photographs of Verdon dancing in the whorehouse ballet, and one of her in glad rags arriving at the waterfront bar.

The conflict with Abbott had drawn Verdon and Fosse even closer together. Hal Prince said that they were so in love that it was almost dangerous. She is quoted as

Portrait of Verdon in *New Girl in Town* (1957–1958).

4. Damn Yankees, *Bob Fosse and* New Girl in Town

saying that she would have set her hair on fire if Fosse had asked her to. However it was wondered whether Fosse's commitment to Verdon was as strong, since he was known to also have dalliances with the show's chorus girls. In April 1957, Fosse went to Winston County, Alabama, to get a quickie divorce from McCracken. He and Verdon kept separate residences. He lived on the West Side of midtown and her apartment was on Lexington and 68th. After the show, they and Jimmy would meet to have dinner at Dinty Moore's where they had their own table. Jimmy said that Fosse never tried to behave like a father towards him or even force a friendship. Fosse was funny and frank but still tentative, and Jimmy felt this distance was because of Fosse's own demons.

On June 28, 1957, Verdon was interviewed backstage for the WRCA radio show *Monitor*, and selections from *New Girl in Town* were played. On August 2 she was a guest on the WCBS radio show *This Is New York*. On September 2, the *New York Times* reported that Verdon had been signed to recreate her role of Lola in the film of *Damn Yankees* which was to start production (with George Abbott and Stanley Donen co-directing) after the first of the year. When Verdon had no matinee performance of *New Girl in Town*, she went to Philadelphia in September to join Fosse for the tryouts of a new musical, *Copper and Brass*. Devised as a vehicle for comedienne Nancy Walker, the show had had tryouts in New Haven from September 13 to 21, 1957. It moved to Broadway's Martin Beck Theatre on October 17 and closed on November 16.

On January 7, 1958, it was announced in the *Times* that Verdon would essay the role of Nell Gwynn in a midnight pageant entitled "Imperial Favorites" to be presented at the Imperial Ball of the Waldorf Astoria Hotel on January 10. The event was for the benefit of the Hospitalized Veterans Service of the Musicians Emergency Fund. On January 9, the *Times* announced that she was one of the guest on Dinah Shore's January 19 NBC *Chevy Show*. However Verdon did *not* appear in this particular episode.

On March 11, 1958, the *Times* reported that, although the rumor could not be substantiated, there was talk that Robert Fryer and Lawrence Carr had acquired the musical *Redhead*, which was formerly designated as "The Works." The offering was credited to Herbert and Dorothy Fields, Sidney Sheldon and Albert Hague and the producers planned to start rehearsals in January. Verdon is said to have expressed interest in portraying the feminine lead, and Fosse was reported to be likely to be the director and choreographer. The *New York Times* on March 21, 1958, said she was to leave *New Girl in Town* on March 22 since she was headed to

Hollywood to make *Damn Yankees*. On March 25, the *Times* reported the death of Herbert Fields and said that he just put the finishing touches on the lyrics for *Redhead* which was bound for Broadway in 1959. The show, now set to star Verdon, would take place in London in 1906. On April 7, 1958, it was announced in the *Times* that she had been appointed to the board of directors of the Karen Horney Clinic, which had been open for three years as a low-cost psychoanalytical center for persons of limited income.

In the April 14, 1958, issue of *Life*, Verdon appeared on the cover in white-face as her beloved Harlequin, the broken-hearted 16th century clown *in commedia dell-arte*, photographed by Eliot Elisofon. She was one of eleven actors featured in a photographic essay entitled "Eleven Fine Actors Get Their Dream Roles. Stars Create For *Life* Scenes They Would Like to Do." Verdon is quoted as saying that when she got a new part she always stopped and asked herself how Harlequin would do it, which had helped her a lot.

5

Damn Yankees on Film and *Redhead*

It was the film version of *Damn Yankees* that brought Fosse and Verdon back to Hollywood. While there she visited her parents and saw her son, Jimmy. The couple rented a house in Malibu and used a red convertible he had named "Baby." Being with Jimmy made Verdon want to have another child, though she knew that the time was not yet right.

Co-directed by George Abbott and Stanley Donen, *Damn Yankees* was in production in April and May 1958. It was shot on location in Washington, D.C., Wrigley Field in Los Angeles, and at Warner Bros. Donen is said to have wanted Abbott's input to keep the film consistent with the Broadway production. Warner Bros. were originally interested in casting Cary Grant who wanted to play the part of Applegate, and Cyd Charisse as Lola. It is not known why Grant lost interest; Charisse became unavailable because she was filming the film noir *Party Girl* (1958) at MGM. Two performers were not retained from the Broadway cast. Stephen Douglass was replaced by Tab Hunter as the young Joe, and Eddie Phillips was replaced by Allen Case as Sohovik and by Fosse as the mambo partner for Lola in "Who's Got the Pain." Apparently Phillips had asked for $1,000 to do the film and the studio refused. In contrast Fosse's fee was a hairpiece made by the "Wigmaster to the Stars." The project meant a lot to Verdon because it was the only time they danced together in a film.

She also wanted Fosse with her because she had a hard time with George Abbott previously. Verdon was nervous about doing the film because of him, even though it was Donen who really directed. She felt that Abbott was against her because he didn't like her on camera. Fosse would stand by on set and watch to try and protect her. Fellow cast member Shannon Bolin was told by Verdon that Donen refused to shoot her in close-up, and there *are* no close-ups of her in the film. Verdon said that this became an issue during the filming of the first number, "A Little Brains, a Little Talent." She liked the song and thought that she was very cute and adorable in it. Fosse told Donen that when Verdon got to the point in the number when she talks baby talk, there should be an extreme close-up of her. Donen replied that he couldn't do it. When Fosse asked if it was because he didn't think that Verdon was good, Donen said that was not the reason. He said it was because he thought she was so "disagreeable looking." Verdon claimed that Donen said this in front of her, and this was how she started the movie. Perhaps matters were not helped because Fosse is said to have argued with Abbott and Donen about the way some of the numbers were filmed. An example is how he had wanted "Who's Got the Pain" in as much blackness as possible and only using a single spotlight to follow the dancers. Donen protested and a compromise was reached.

Verdon doesn't make an appearance until halfway into the film. Lola is first seen objectified by her stockinged legs in a negligee with her head under a sheet in a pink bed, when Mr. Applegate (Ray Walston) telephones her to come to Washington. For her first number, "A Little Brains, a Little Talent" she wears a white suit with blue and white striped blouse, and also uses a handkerchief. Her movement is limited to walking around the room, lying on a bed and leaning against a wall as she sings, although she gestures with her arms. For her "Whatever Lola Wants" number, Verdon enters using a Spanish accent as Senorita Lolita Hernando. She is dressed like a vamp, in black flamenco skirt with black gloves, and a black ribbon fascinator and big red flower in her hair. Verdon's act as Lolita is funny because we are aware of the pretense, and also since she is both overt and coy. She drops her act momentarily when she says "home" in her normal voice, but goes into overdrive when she sings the song. She removes her gloves, skirt, throws away her fascinator, and removes her lace capris to reveal a black lace-trimmed body suit. In the number Lola dances around Joe (Tab Hunter) and also touches him repeatedly, ending with her lying across his waist. Verdon provides a subtle silent reaction to Applegate's insulting her for her failure to ensnare Joe, and this is despite her not being given a closeup. It is said that the choreography for both "A Little Brains, a Little Talent" and "Whatever Lola Wants" was toned down from their stage versions to appease film censors. In particular the former number's bumps that were cut are said to explain why Verdon is seen to stand so much in the scene.

For "Who's Got the Pain" Verdon and Fosse are dressed in black pants with yellow shirts and white hats. Unlike the shirt of Fosse, which has black horizontal stripes, her shirt has black and red cherry-shaped baubles and a black fringe, is low-cut and exposes her midriff. The number is filmed mostly in one long shot, and since both dancers are so good, one's eye alternates between them so a second viewing is required to focus on their individual performance. Verdon said that it was very difficult to keep up with Fosse because he was a terrific jumper. He could fly but she couldn't. They would be right in the middle of a take and he'd yell at her to jump. Despite that, she felt it was wonderful. Verdon described the experience as like a jetstream where you just coasted and didn't feel the energy. She said that she didn't even know that she was tired until she stopped.

In "Two Lost Souls" the initial conceit is used for Joe to stop Lola from dancing because he says he can't dance. However it is he who dances before her, and although he will occasionally join her, he mostly leaves her alone to dance. The crowd in the club that surrounds the couple adds to the notion of preventing her from dancing, so that she has to move away in her first attempt with another man who is deliberately bad. As the number progresses it allows Verdon to release her energy and show her dancing ability. When the music changes tempo, she joins other women in a line to dance. Verdon is distinguished from them by her wearing the black dress to their colored ones, and she also has different moves. Joe returns with a chair that she sits on and he slides across the floor with her on it. After the other dancers attach themselves to her, then detach themselves, Verdon dances solo. Then she joins the others in a group dance where they clap and jump and kick and touch the floor and reach for the sky, in a frenzy matched by the music. The number concludes with Verdon standing on Joe's chair and then joining him to sing the end of the song.

Verdon's acting performance is less theatrical than that of Ray Walston and the others; she doesn't yell and tempers her volume for the screen. Lola is vulnerable and touching when she speaks to Joe in her normal voice before the benefit performance. Our fear that it is her new tactic to trick him is allayed by her sincerity. Her later reluctance to help Applegate any further is confirmed when she admits that she loves Joe. Verdon looks beautiful wearing a pink sleeveless sheath with matching pink and blue sparkly wrap in Applegate's apartment, and a black full-skirted dress for "Two Lost Souls" which enhances her dancing. She also wears a striking dark pink dress and coat at the climactic game.

The character of Lola is positioned in the narrative in contrast to the other women, who are mostly middle-aged and plain. The most extreme comparison can be made with Sister Miller (Jean Stapleton) who is loud and gauche and wears an unflattering hairstyle. It's telling that the only young women of any note shown in the film are fan club members at the

Joe Hardy benefit and they look more like schoolgirls than women. There are young women shown as chorus girls at the benefit and female patrons and dancers at the club for the "Two Lost Souls" number, but they get inconsequential screen time. This is presumably done so as not to counter Lola's appeal, but also perhaps because a lot of the ballplayers look more middle-aged than young like Joe. The plot point that Joe is in love with his wife is given a spin in light of his having been transformed into a younger man, who is never tempted by the younger Lola. He kisses her but it is not presented as an act of desire. Lola being a former ugly woman also has a disturbing subtext, since it could be used to judge her present more supposedly beautiful self as less so. When Applegate turns her back into a crone with long gray hair, gray eyebrows, a hooked nose, warts and a hunched back, it is hard to recognize this as also Verdon. Finally, there is something sad about Lola's fate. Although we see that Applegate has turned her back into the beauty Lola, it seems that she will always be in danger of being turned back into a crone and always at his mercy. She sold her soul for beauty and the cost was disempowerment.

Still of Verdon in the 1958 film version of her stage hit *Damn Yankees*. Photograph by Bert Six.

The film premiered in Denver (the location of the Yankees fan club) on September 19, 1958; released in Los Angeles on September 24, and in New York on September 26. The tagline was "It's a picture in a million! Starring that girl in a million, the red-headed darling of the Broadway show, Gwen Verdon!" The original theatrical trailer carried the name of the movie as *Whatever Lola Wants* although the actual name was added parenthetically in smaller letters at the bottom of the screen.

It was praised by *Variety*, Bosley Crowther in the *New York Times*, Clive Hirshhorn in *The Warner Bros. Story*, and Gordon Gow in *Hollywood in the Fifties*. Crowther wrote that Verdon's performance was "one of the hottest and heartiest we've seen in a musical movie in years" and that she "has the sort of fine, fresh talent that the screen badly needs these days." He commented that while she lacks the movie star beauty of Brigitte Bardot and Elizabeth Taylor, she "manufactures her own strong brand of sex" and, while brilliant as a dancer, "her exceptional achievements in this picture are as a comedienne." Crowther wrote further about the film and Verdon in a *Times* article on October 5, 1958. He said that her appearance in the film was the major screen event of the year and that she was an absolute natural for films. Crowther noted that Verdon "may not be too good-looking, by the measuring tape of Hollywood" but that she had a wondrously witty style of acting and was as saucy and fresh as a summer breeze. He also commented that if somebody didn't sign her quickly for another film, then all producers are mad.

The film was nominated for the Best Music Score Academy Award, which is ironic given that a film musicians' union strike had prevented pre-recording an orchestra musical soundtrack score for the rehearsal and filming of the production numbers. The original show recordings were employed for rehearsing and filming and afterwards the vocal tracks were recorded a cappella, without a studio union orchestra on a Warner Sound Department stage. They were then sent to Italy where a symphony orchestra recorded secondary underscore tracks. The film's soundtrack recording was released by RCA Victor in 1958.

It was reported in the *New York Times* on April 14, 1959, that the film was not a box office success. An effort to make it more profitable for its European release was made by changing the title to *What Lola Wants* but it was still unsuccessful. It was known that movies about baseball generally only had appeal in the United States and in Japan, so the European market was relied upon to pick up half of the film's gross. There was future hope that areas in the Caribbean and South America might be more successful, given their becoming increasingly conscious of the sport, but one movie executive said that the hope was "as bright as a spitball in a smog." This lack of confidence was shown by the fact that at the time there were no baseball-themed movies slated for production. A Warner Bros representative said that the film had failed in the United States despite receiving critical raves. The reason given was that it was thought that people who like baseball like to root for or against a team, and this was something that they couldn't do in the movie. Another reason was that baseball was more expensive to film than other sports since you needed two teams and needed to shoot outdoors. Other movie executives had other suggested reasons. One was that women didn't respond because they wanted a great personal story with family appeal. Two successful movies that had baseball themes had such stories, *The Pride of the Yankees* (1942) and *The Babe Ruth Story* (1948), although producer Sam Goldywn felt that the former's casting of Gary Cooper also helped.

A *Damn Yankees* remake was made for television and broadcast in April 8, 1967, by NBC. Directed by Kirk Browning, it starred Phil Silvers as Applegate, Lee Remick as Lola, Jerry Lanning (who would later become Verdon's real-life partner) as Joe, and Jim Backus as Van Buren. In 2009 the film was going to be remade with Jim Carrey as the Devil and Jake Gyllenhaal as Joe Hardy, but production never got underway.

In his autobiography *Tab Hunter Confidential: The Making of a Movie Star*, Hunter says that he had heard that Verdon was considered too old and not pretty enough to play Lola and that she was going to be replaced by Marilyn Monroe or Mitzi Gaynor. Richard Adler said that, according to the Hollywood tradition of that era, Verdon's face was not pretty enough to make her a film star, like Tab Hunter who was almost perfect looking. Hollywood had a narrow definition of pretty, but it was her figure rather than her face that people were attracted to. Hunter's sympathy for her became tempered by an item he had seen in Walter Winchell's column that said that she was disappointed that Hunter had been cast in the film. Hunter also writes that Verdon called him "Tabunter" in a thick New York accent and the rest of the cast followed.

In the summer of 1958, Verdon took her first vacation in ten years. With Jimmy she went to Long Island and spent time cooking and lying on the beach. Of the former, she said that she liked spaghetti with clam sauce. Of the latter, she said that she freckled until they all ran together to form a tan. She also began working privately on her next Broadway role which was not to start rehearsals until November.

In the meantime Verdon did more television. On September 21, 1958, she made the first of three appearances on NBC-TV's music variety series *The Dinah Shore Chevy Show*. It was filmed live in New York's Ziegfeld Theatre with special hosts Janet Blair and John Raitt.

On September 24, 1958, the *New York Times* reported that *Redhead* was slated to open at the 46th Street Theatre on February 5, 1959. This was to be Verdon's next Broadway show, which would play in Washington for a fortnight beginning on December 29 and then have an additional three weeks at the Shubert Theatre in Philadelphia. In the meantime Verdon returned to the *Dinah Shore* show on October 5. The *New York Times'* John P. Shanley described Verdon in it as a one-woman forest fire whose dancing was, as usual, inspired. On October 8, the *Times* reported that *Redhead* was being eyed by NBC who were considering putting up $150,000 for the show. This was half the capital required by producers Robert Fryer and Lawrence Carr. *Times* reporter Sam Zolotow had also added David Shaw to the names of the show's creators, along with Herbert and Dorothy Fields, Sidney Sheldon, and Albert Hague.

Redhead was a musical murder mystery set in turn-of-the-century London against a background of music halls and wax museums. The starring role was the Cockney Essie Whimple, a woman who created wax figures for a museum operated by her two aunts and who learned the identity of Jack the Ripper. It had been written for Bea Lillie; sources say that Lillie had to decline because she was unavailable. Other stars had been approached in the hope that they would either finance it themselves or take it to a producer. Ethel Merman, Mary Martin, Celeste Holm and Gisele MacKenzie had all passed on it. At one point Irving Berlin was commissioned to write the score, but then he changed his mind and backed out.

Verdon was invited by the producers to hear the songs and Fosse went with her. If she liked what she heard, getting financing for the show would be easy. It is said that Verdon, aware of her new power, agreed to do it on one condition: that Fosse direct. Other sources say that the idea of his directing came from the producers, as an alternative to his suggestion that he play a small part. Verdon would later say that a demand that Fosse should direct was not made by her because she was not big enough to do so. However she felt that she couldn't afford *not* to have him as the director. Fosse was approved to direct, with another provision being that Verdon would perform at the backers auditions.

Aware that a Gwen Verdon show was not the same as a Bea Lillie show, the producers hired David Shaw and Sidney Sheldon as librettists. According to one source, Shaw was brought in by Verdon, since he had written "Native Dancer" for her, and that he was hired because Sidney Sheldon refused to rewrite with Fosse. Another source claims that Sheldon and Shaw were brought in to assist Dorothy Fields after her librettist brother, Herbert, died. Yet another says that Sheldon was lured away by Hollywood and that's why Shaw was brought in. In the *New York Times* (June 23, 1958) Lewis Gelb reported that Shaw had been assigned to the show to revise and polish. The rewriting amounted to cutting subplots to make room for dances. Verdon joined Fosse for the casting auditions for five hundred singers, dancers and actors. Richard Kiley was so nervous auditioning that Verdon and Fosse sang with him to give him more confidence, and he was chosen to play opposite her.

Rehearsals began in October 1958 at the Variety Arts Studios. At one rehearsal Kiley reportedly erupted at Verdon when she appeared after an argument began between Fosse and the actor on an acting point. She knew that Fosse was unused to a performer expressing an opposing opinion. Kiley ordered Verdon out of the room, telling her, "You may be the star of the show, but this isn't any of your business." He knew who she was but Kiley still considered her the director's girlfriend. Verdon retreated because she and Fosse found him very imposing and neither would dare abuse him. However this didn't stop Fosse from suggesting that Kiley should cover his receding hairline with a wig, because he felt it was right for the character. Kiley saw the humor in the situation when he tried on toupees. Verdon also had trouble with Sidney Sheldon, whose name she supposedly omitted as the co-author when interviewed. It is not known what the specific problem between the two was.

For "Erbie Hitch's Twitch" where Essie imitates her father, Verdon said she imitated Laurence Olivier's Archie Rice from *The Entertainer*. This was a role he had originated on the London stage in 1957 and had played on Broadway from February 12 to May 10, 1958 (he received a nomination for the Best Actor Tony Award). She found the tongue-twisting words of the song tricky because there were so many of them. Verdon had been asked to perform them as fast as Danny Kaye had done his patter song "Tchaikovsky" in the musical *Lady in the Dark*, where he named fifty Russian composers in thirty-nine seconds. She began by saying the words slowly and precisely, then faster and faster still until her mouth just did it without her having to think about it.

Ten nights of tryouts were held in December in New Haven. Fosse devised a thirty-minute ballet for Verdon in an attempt to compensate for what he felt the book lacked. "Essie's Dream" consisted of five parts: jazz, cancan, gypsy, military march, and music hall with fast costume changes. It was the most challenging dance that she had attempted to date, and Verdon appeared in every section. She entered one on the wings of a table, jumped onto a trampoline, and dove out on the stage horizontally. Verdon claimed that the exertion of the performance made her lose several pounds each night. To keep up her weight she is said to have guzzled root beer floats, hot chocolate, milk shakes and honey. She told a *New York Times* reporter that by the time she hit Broadway, she was also consuming a double orange juice, gobs of whipped cream with her hot chocolate, several pieces of candy, and a chicken and a roast beef sandwich. Verdon claimed that she was having the time of her life and it was the first time that she wasn't scared on stage.

Later she would say that the show may have been her favorite, and that it was a treat working with Kiley. The musical contained what Verdon would say was her favorite onstage moment, when Essie walked into the cloud of smoke that the departing Kiley had produced from his cigar. It also contained her personal favorite of all her musical numbers, "Erbie Fitch's Twitch." Verdon loved the character because once Essie became part of the travelling show, she was a flop. "Erbie Fitch's Twitch" was meant to be the act of an amateur where she would tell a joke that wasn't funny and the other characters on stage would look at her with derision. Verdon found using the Cockney accent easy because her whole family was Cockney. She found that she was so adept at it that she was told to pull it back a bit because Americans could never understand the way a real Cockney speaks.

Verdon felt the most memorable part of the show was the beginning at the wax museum, where she wore a severe wig and had a Jane Eyre look. She had fun being the ugly duckling swooning over Kiley's American because he would look at her as if Essie was the last woman he would ever consider. Verdon loved the innocence of Essie, a quality that she knew that she could project, though she never did it in a calculated way. This innocence came through in a lot of future characters, like Charity and Roxie Hart. In acting class, Verdon did scenes from *The Madwoman of Chaillot*; that character also had an innocence about her along with her madness. In addition Verdon studied singing with Keith Davis, who gave her images to think of when she sang. The most important lesson he gave her was to sing on a speaking level: not to think about notes but to consider yourself as speaking lyrics, which made it seem more natural. Davis described Verdon's voice as a "character voice" which worked for musical theater because a show is about a character so the voice needs to be real. She was playing Essie so she couldn't sound like an opera singer.

In Philadelphia the show got good reviews and did good business. But in the "Pick-Pocket Tango," a row of metal bars from the jail set landed hard on Verdon's feet after a stagehand missed his cue, and she cried out and fell backward. The audience gasped and Fosse yelled for the curtain to come down. He ran to her but she claimed not to be injured. Verdon wanted to keep going but Fosse refused to let her. The trope cry of "Is there a doctor in the house?" came from the public address system, which produced three or five, according to different sources. Verdon was bruised but had no broken bones. Sources differ as to whether the show resumed that night. One says it did and that she wore a pair of slippers under her costume. As the next scene required her to stamp her foot three times at the request of the American, the audience supposedly groaned, dreading what might happen. However, to protect herself, Verdon softly and gingerly tapped her foot instead, which made the audience stand up and cheer. The source claims that the show closed for the next night because Verdon's understudy had left the show after a burst appendix. Another says that the star and the show did not carry on the night of the accident, because Fosse didn't want her to and there was no understudy to replace her. He supposedly went after the stagehand at fault, who was supposedly drunk. Sources also suggest that Verdon's good spirits in the show were only temporary, and perhaps things changed after the accident. She became strained, and criticized the chorus behind her and started missing performances, where she was presumably replaced by her new cast understudies Patti Karr and Allyn Ann McLerie.

The company moved to Washington for a season from December 31, 1958, to the first two weeks of January 1959. Verdon occasionally asked to skip a song because she was tired. This became more frequent so that dialogue had to be altered and song cues dropped to accommodate the change. At one performance, when Verdon asked to drop seven songs, composer Albert Hague objected strenuously. The producer asked him whether he wanted to complain to the Dramatists Guild and close the show and he backed down. Verdon also had the orchestrations for her songs transposed so that, depending on how she felt, she could sing numbers either in a higher or lower key. By the time the show came to Broadway she would be performing in the lower key because it was easier for her to sing. She made an exception when she appeared at an Actors Fund benefit since it was attended by theater professionals.

For the *New York Times* of February 1, 1959, Al Hirschfeld provided four caricatures of Verdon in the show. On the same night she was given a party at the Herwyn Club, where she wore a black sleeveless cocktail dress with a flower in the cleavage. *Redhead* opened on Broadway at the 46th Street Theatre as scheduled on February 5, 1959, and ran till March 19, 1960. The *New York Times*' Brooks Atkinson gave the show a mixed review.

He wrote that when Verdon is dancing it was a delight but when she was not, which was most of the time, it was a "hurrah's-nest of old show paraphernalia."

The original cast recording was made on February 8, 1959, and released by RCA Victor on February 13. On May 10, 1959, John S. Wilson of the *New York Times* wrote that Verdon gave a disarming and virtuoso performance, and seemed thoroughly at home vocally in the English music hall world of the early 1900s. She sparkled through Hague's lively and lusty music and Fields' witty lyrics, giving an added personal filip of bright vitality to a score that Wilson found fresh and engaging. At the 1960 Grammy Awards held on November 29, 1959, *Redhead* tied for Best Broadway Show album with *Gypsy*. On April 12, 1959, at the Waldorf Astoria it won Tony Awards for Best Musical, Kiley for Best Actor in a Musical, Verdon for Best Actress in a Musical, Fosse for Best Choreography, and Rouben Ter-Arutunian for Best Costume Design. Interestingly, Fosse was not even nominated as Best Director.

During the run she was out at times. On April 6, 1959, Verdon was suffering from a respiratory ailment. From August 1 and 2, it was after spraining her left ankle while limbering up. On August 11, it was because Verdon had injured her right ankle on the 10th while dancing in the show. On October 28 and 29, she had a throat ailment. Verdon's stand-in was Allyn Ann

Portrait of Verdon in her stage show *Redhead* (1959–1960).

McLerie. Verdon later summed up the show by saying that it played in New York and then toured but only six performances came together. "Six! Performances when I sang well and danced well. When I did it right."

Verdon scored the cover of *Life* magazine's February 23, 1959, edition. She was shown in a photograph dressed in black sweater and tights with a black tied choker and brown boots. She held a multi-colored and ribboned tambourine, and was backed up by two male dancers. On the cover it said about her, "Gwen Verdon: Her Joyous Strutting Knocks Broadway Cold." The magazine's table of contents referenced the article about her in *Redhead* with "Dancing in dizzy zest in Broadway's newest musical [she] scores season's greatest personal triumph and enjoys herself doing it." The Tom Prideaux article, entitled "Gwen Knocks 'Em in the Aisles," featured photographs of her alone, with Richard Kiley and dancer Kasimir Kokich in the show, and of her doing dance exercises to warm up for the RCA Victor cast recording as two unidentified men watch. Fosse is quoted as saying that in the past Verdon had always seemed to be proving something to herself. Prideaux wrote that the show brought a new Verdon who enjoyed herself and let her audiences know it. George Abbott said that her hard work stemmed from an unfriendliness to her own body. He claimed that Verdon was not at all vain and never dressed to attract attention to herself. She dressed like a gypsy, wearing old slacks that drooled around her ankles. Abbott also said that Verdon did not think of herself as sexy. She was an intellectual actress and you approached her through reason. Prideaux wrote that Verdon was formerly known as a big worrier, but she was now said to be only a part-time one. Fosse advised that when he went backstage to see her after opening night, he expected her to ask how he thought they liked it. Instead Verdon broke into a grin and told him, "I can't believe it. I wasn't nervous at all."

She and Fosse now lived together in a penthouse apartment at 91 Central Park West with a view of the park. Their terrace was big enough for a vegetable garden (where Verdon grew eggplant and zucchini), a ping pong table, and a dog run for her pets. It also allowed the couple to entertain their small group of friends. Most of the apartment's furnishings belonged to Verdon since Fosse was more suited to the gypsy life of living out of a suitcase. They both loved crafts, and on the weekends they would go to junkyards, beaches and second-hand shops to find them. Their prized possessions were old lamps which they refurbished, and not Tony Awards which they kept hidden. The couple also spent their nights off from the theater at home, or visiting friends like the Jule Stynes, the Sydney Chaplins, the Neil Simons, and Buddy Hackett when he was in New York.

For Hackett they would venture out for dinner at Rao's. While Verdon did not have the same love of sports as Fosse, she would join him to watch them on television. She provided beer and pretzels, although her diet was more health-conscious.

Verdon also donated time and resources to New York's Postgraduate Center for Mental Health, a low-cost psychiatric clinic. This was because she was a proponent of psychoanalysis, and also because she wanted to teach children with physical disabilities the benefits of exercise and movement in group therapy. She and Fosse used their terrace to give benefits and fundraising parties to raise awareness for the cause. At one affair with a luau theme, the weather caused a tent they'd set up to blow off and spin down to the park. At a dinner party for David Shaw, the couple met Paddy Chayefsky and he became a close friend to Fosse.

However, the relationship had its problems since Verdon preferred to go home straight after the show, but Fosse stayed out, rehearsing and having drinks with the cast members. He saw other women but tried to be discrete about it out of respect for her. When asked by hairdresser Vidal Sassoon how he kept it from Verdon, Fosse reportedly told him, "Hot showers." He often did not go home at all, preferring to take a room at the Edison Hotel so that he could move from rehearsal room to bedroom.

Verdon attended the 1958 Tony Awards on April 12, 1959, at the Waldorf Astoria Hotel. She was presented her Best Actress in a Musical award for *Redhead* by Ingrid Bergman. Verdon was photographed wearing a short black sleeveless dress with fur trim and cape and white gloves. Fosse's contribution as choreographer and director of the show was also noted in a *New York Times* article by Emily Coleman (April 19, 1959) entitled "The Dance Man Leaps to the Top." Verdon was quoted as saying that he could give you movement to do to suggest a feeling, since a choreographer is never afraid to move you around in the scene. Coleman said that Fosse credited Verdon for the success of their shows together, saying that when you have someone like her you like to have her show off. He said that people like to see people do things because dancing is in great part sheer exhibitionism. Verdon agreed with this idea, though she felt that sometimes a person could make dance an art form. For her it represented just an abundance of energy. It was about feeling good and getting to play all the games that she never got to play as a kid. Verdon said that to dance in a group was the most exciting thing and she had never had that before.

In May 1959 the *New York Times* reported that Verdon had won a Theatre Award for her performance in *Redhead* by the Newspaper Guild of

New York. It was presented to her at the union's Page One Ball on June 26 at the Astor Hotel. The *New York Times* on August 8 reported that Verdon had extended her contract for the show till June 30, 1960.

New projects were offered to her. There was a proposed film version of *Redhead*, and a plan to take Verdon and Fosse to London for a production of the stage show; he would have played the murderer and Verdon would have made her London debut. But it did not happen. Robert Fryer again tried to get the rights to *Chicago* for her but failed. It was said that there were press reports that he had an option on the material with his partner Lawrence Carr, although this proved not to be true.

Verdon made her third appearance on *Dinah Shore*, broadcast on October 4, 1959. She is first seen warming up in her dressing room, wearing a black leotard and waist-sash. Verdon moves in fast motion as per the opening skit that has Shore moving like this. Shore stands in front of a wall of posters from Verdon's stage shows (*Can-Can*, *Damn Yankees*, *New Girl in Town*, and *Redhead*) to introduce her doing "Erbie Fitch's Twitch" from the latter show. (Shore pronounces her name emphasizing the second syllable, as Ver*DON*.) For the number, Verdon is like Charlie Chaplin's Tramp, in a suit, bowler hat and moustache and holding a cane in front of a crowd of on-stage observers. At one point it appears that the cane hits an overhead light since a crash is heard. There are frequent cuts from long shots to closer shots, which diminishes the effect of her performance.

She returns later in the show with Dinah and boxer Ingmar Johannson and both women wear ridiculously oversized coats over their dresses. Verdon is funny in the way she flirts with Johannson. She tickles him and bites his leg, leans back against him as he shows her how to shadow box, and leans forward on him. When he comments that it takes a long time to learn how to shadow box, Verdon replies, "I've got nothing to do for the next twenty years." As she leans facing him, she asks, "How do you hold on in the clinches?"

After Johannson exits, Verdon and Shore remove their coats to sing "I Want to Be Happy" together wearing evening gowns that have side-splits. For the number Shore asks that Verdon not dance and just stand and sing, but she finds this impossible to do. At one point, Verdon puts a scarf over Shore's head and Shore in turn uses it to tie Verdon's hands to her body. This does not hold Verdon down. Verdon is then joined by chorus boys wearing black suits that dance with her and push Shore out of the way. Shore draws a box on the floor to show the area where the women must stay in order to be in camera range, but Verdon will not be limited to being in the box's parameter. Then the chorus boys return and crowd into the box and lift Verdon and Shore. The box is then abandoned as Verdon and Shore both do a Latin dance to end the song. Verdon's rebellious behavior in the number is more playful than vengeful and it appears that some of it is improvised since at times Shore looks genuinely surprised. Clearly the execution of the number had been rehearsed but Shore's reaction also shows that she is a good sport when it appears that a younger performer is trying to cheekily upstage her.

On October 25, 1959, Verdon was to appear as one of the guests on an NBC one-hour tribute to Mrs. Franklin D. Roosevelt. David Susskind was the show's producer. With Verdon still in *Redhead*, it was reported on January 1, 1960, in the *New York Times* that it would leave Broadway on April 16 for the coast, and that in Los Angeles and San Francisco it would be performed at the Edwin Lester music festivals. On January 26, 1960, it was reported that the show would close in New York on March 19 and open in Chicago on March 23. It would then travel to Los Angeles on April 25 and San Francisco on June 6. It was also reported that Verdon said on January 25, 1960, that after the show had run its course she would take a leave of nine months to continue her studies in dancing, singing and acting. She also said that during that period she would appear on television and also in the film of the show with Richard Kiley. This was expected to be produced by the show's producers Fryer and Carr and released through United Artists.

On January 29, 1960, Verdon was interviewed by Charles Collingwood on the CBS news documentary television series *Person to Person*. Two days later she was one of a group of stars to join the cast of the Broadway musical *La Plume de Ma Tante* at the Royale Theatre in a special performance given in aid of the survivors of the Frejus Dam disaster in France. The musical had opened on November 11, 1958, and would close on December 17, 1960. On February 9, 1960, the *New York Times* reported that there was to be a two-hour stage show arranged for the benefit of the new Children's Clinic of the Postgraduate Center for Psychotherapy at the 46th Street Theatre. Verdon was the chairman of the variety show, which was to be followed that evening by the Apres Bal at the Waldorf Astoria.

Around February 1960, Marjorie Beddow is said to have played Lola in *Damn Yankees* in stock after being recommended by Verdon, who coached her to play the part. Verdon travelled with *Redhead* when it went on tour (Beddow became her understudy). The tour allowed Verdon to meet Fosse's family and also visit with her own. While the company was on the road, the couple decided to have a baby and in Chicago they married.

Verdon later said that she felt that she didn't have to be married to have a child but Fosse thought that they should. On April 2 they took out a license and the next day drove to Oak Park, Illinois. Verdon said that on the way she kept asking Fosse if he was sure about getting married and he kept saying yes. She also remembered that he was very nervous and if he had changed his mind it still would have been okay with her. Verdon found a justice of the peace from the telephone book.

On April 3, 1960, in the living room of Gilbert Volk were the minister's wife and their nine-year-old son as witnesses. Verdon said that Volk asked Fosse if he wanted music and he agreed. Money was put into a juke box and Mario Lanza started singing "Be My Love" at the top of his lungs. Then Gwyneth Heneghan and Robert Louis Fosse were wed. It was a secret ceremony. Fosse's family were only a 45- minute drive away in Evanston, but they were not in attendance because they had not been told of the event. Fosse's divided feelings between Joan McCracken and Verdon supposedly had him ask McCracken the day before if she would consider getting back together with him. Presumably her answer was no. Apparently after he had left her for Verdon, Fosse remained interested in his former wife enough to frequently telephone her and also follow her. But once he married Verdon, the attention to McCracken stopped. The marriage was not made public until October 1960 when Fosse's mother Sadie was dying (she passed away on December 19, 1960). Verdon had told fellow *Redhead* actor Pat Ferrier backstage about the marriage after it had happened but asked her not to tell anyone else. However it is said that the press got wind of it a few days after the ceremony. Verdon and Fosse were photographed dining in New York's Harwyn Club and the next day rumors of their wedding were in most of the dailies.

After the end of the Los Angeles run of *Redhead*, Verdon announced her retirement. She thought that by now she was professionally established and the time was right to have another child. Since Verdon was now nearly 36, perhaps she worried that if she continued to dance, she might lessen her chances to conceive. She had decided that she wasn't going to work again until she had a baby and the baby was to be at least two-and-a-half years old before she'd go back. However, given her continuing appearances on television, specifically where she danced, the retirement is said to have been only from the stage. And again, this would be temporary.

6

Semi-Retirement and Motherhood

Verdon's second retirement from performing did not stop her from working in other capacities. She is said to have acted as Fosse's assistant on the musical version of the Preston Sturges' 1944 war comedy film *Hail the Conquering Hero*, renamed *The Conquering Hero*. However Margery Beddow in her book on Fosse claims that his assistants were she and Robert Tucker. Beddow is credited in the Broadway cast as a dancer but Tucker is not.

The star was in attendance at rehearsals at the New Amsterdam Theatre in October 1960 when Fosse had a seizure. He fell to the floor from the table where he had been sitting and struck his head. His arm and leg thrashing, eyeballs rolling and mouth frothing indicated an epileptic seizure. Verdon was in a side chair and went to Fosse, turning him on his side so that he would not choke on his froth and covered him with her sweater. Her calmness suggested that this was not the first time that she had been witness to such an attack. Fosse had for many years taken the seizure medication Dilantin which generally worked, although a lack of sleep and emotional stress could make it ineffective. He had attributed the epilepsy to a head injury from falling from a horse when his foot got caught in the stirrup and he was dragged a distance. (There was no witness to the horse incident so it was believed that the real reason was that the condition was genetic.) A source says that when Verdon came to his aid, she cried out, "Call BUtterfield 8–1234" which was the telephone number for Fosse's psychiatrist. She placed her knee under his head to stop Fosse banging it on the stage, and shooed the crowd away. Fosse's doctor injected him with a sedative. Verdon instructed the show's stage manager, Philburn Friedman, what to do if there was another seizure and she was not around.

The next day she was at Fosse's apartment on Central Park West when the show's book writer Larry Gelbart came for a script conference. Fosse blamed Gelbart for setting off the seizure. Later Fosse would say that he felt the seizure came from his Seconal withdrawal, particularly since he stopped taking it cold turkey. This was something he couldn't admit at the time, since his epilepsy and his drug addiction were secrets held by him and Verdon. They believed that if they were made public, it would cost Fosse work.

When the show had tryouts in New Haven in November, Verdon ran many of the dance rehearsals as Fosse directed. She was particularly annoyed by dancers who "marked" (i.e., walked) through a number that had been choreographed and not perform full out. Verdon asked why they marked for her when they wouldn't have for Fosse, and she was told it was because she was not the show's choreographer. The company moved to the National Theatre in Washington in November 1960, and another argument between the producer, Gelbart and Fosse over cut lines had Verdon drag the director offstage because she was scared that he would have another seizure. Fosse was so unhappy that he told her that he didn't want to go to rehearsal and he clutched a Mexican statue of Jesus screaming, "Why don't you help me?" Verdon led him to rehearsals, sometimes forcibly.

At a production meeting, Fosse made the suggestion that *he* replace the leading actor, Tom Poston. He was even prepared to do an audition after the show. That night as Verdon sat in the theater's back row, Fosse began. She supposedly roared in approval at his performance, although it seemed to be done to sell the casting since what he was doing was unfunny. Producer Robert Whitehead knew that they couldn't cast Fosse and that he could not continue as Poston's director since he had no faith in him. Whitehead spoke to Fosse and he agreed to leave, with two conditions: He wanted to finish his choreographic duties and he also wanted to have the company alone to say goodbye. At the last rehearsal Beddow said that Fosse acted more intense than usual. She commented on it to Verdon, who told her to just do whatever he said and that she would understand the reasons later. After the rehearsal Verdon sat on a stool looking somber, dressed in a mink coat that came down to her ankles over her usual black pants and sweater. Fosse told the company that he had been fired and then he took Verdon's arm and walked off the stage, pausing to turn to say goodbye.

The show opened on Broadway at the ANTA Playhouse on January 16, 1961, and was a flop, only running for eight performances until January 21, 1961. Fosse and Verdon attended the last performance, curious to see what had become of the work. They apparently stood behind the last row. After

6. Semi-Retirement and Motherhood 83

the show Fosse is said to have grabbed the show's composer Moose Charlap and held him against the back wall, swearing at him and demanding to know how he could have done this. Verdon is said to have pulled her husband away and taken him into the lobby. The man accosted turned out to be Robert Griffith, the co-producer of *Damn Yankees*. Another version of this story has Fosse grabbing Griffith from his seat in the audience after the show, asking him if he had come to gloat. Griffith did not answer and Fosse walked away. The first version had Griffith going after Fosse, and Harold Prince, who was seated next to Griffith, followed. Prince found the men in the foyer smiling and embracing with Verdon's arm around both of them. In the second version it was Prince who went after Fosse with Griffith close behind. They supposedly found Fosse on the floor of the lobby in a curled-up position, almost catatonic. Verdon was beside him, stroking his head and telling him that the man he had attacked was Griffith. This comment of hers suggested that Fosse mistook him for someone else.

Verdon's supposed performance retirement ended when she was a guest star on NBC's *Perry Como's Kraft Music Hall*, broadcast on January 18, 1961. In the show she makes several appearances. To the song "Flamboyenco" she does a flamenco dance with two guitarists and a dance chorus. She wears a black polka-dotted layered dress with train and black hat tied under her neck. The guitarists are revealed to be Como and George Gobel, also wearing the same black hats. This isn't a great surprise given that they are placed closest to the camera, sitting in front of the dancers and blocking our view of Verdon. The number stops when she points out that Como has made a mistake in his playing, but she states she will go on and "dance louder." The number stops a second time when the guitarists play another bad note and Verdon and the dancers walk off the stage, after she states that she has never been so humiliated in all her life.

She returns to dance again, wearing an oversized coat over a black sweater and pants. Before the number, Como asks her how she remembers all the steps for a dance number, and she replies that it is the same as remembering all the lyrics of a song he sings. When Como says that he has cue cards, she says that she has the same and Como displays a cue card with dance labanotation. Verdon demonstrates some of the movements when Como points to spots on the card. After she removes her coat, Verdon appears on a white set that has the optical effect of giving her body a white outline and she dances a solo of "Doodle Town Fifers." Then there is a sudden cut to her wearing a topcoat, white blouse and tie and hat. She is joined by the Peter Gennaro Dancers and they dance the

"Mambo Jubilo." Another cut has Verdon and Gennaro dressed in formal clothes. She wears a sparkly corset with a long-backed skirt over tights; she has long black gloves and a feather in her hair. The couple dance to "The Wistful Waltz." Another cut has Verdon seen back in black sweater and pants with a hat with a flower attached to it, joining the dancers for the finale of "Mambo Jubilo." After the number, Como tells her that Gennaro has described her to him as a "dancer's dancer" and Como adds that he thinks she is also a "singer's dancer." She replies that that is very sweet and she thanks him. Gobel joins them and the three sing and dance to a Miracle Margarine song. Verdon kicks and bumps Gobel at the end.

Verdon is back to join Como, Gobel and Paul Anka, and she wears a white evening gown with white gloves. She sings a few lines of "Heart" from *Damn Yankees*, with Anka on piano, and the four laugh in reaction to the unseen audience screaming at Anka as he is about to sing. Verdon faux screams in reaction to Gobel's singing "When the Red Red Robin" and he shakes her hand, and she joins all of the others singing "My Home Town." Como asks Anka to compose a new song and Verdon suggests the line "When the moonlight is bright," before Anka gets taken away by a group of screaming girls from the audience. When Como sits at the piano to compose a song, Verdon suggests a line about a Kraft's noodle chicken dinner which makes the screaming girls return and leads to an advertisement for Kraft. Verdon comes back for the finale of the show, dressed in an elbow-cuffed and belted gray dress. She contributes to the joke that the show is running overtime by saying that they cut five minutes from her dance number, and she, Como and Anka and Gobel all agree to do the cut pieces. She does a few seconds of a dance, then Verdon joins the others to sing Anka's "When the Moonlight Is Bright Tonight." She takes a bow as Como and the chorus sing "I Feel a Song Coming On" and joins Como and his guests dancing under the show's end credits.

The star is said to have toyed with the idea of co-starring with Fosse in a revival of *Pal Joey* at the New York City Center of Music and Drama, but decided against it. However Fosse and Verdon did work with Eileen Heckart on her "Zip" number. The show opened on May 31, 1961, and the planned engagement of ten days was extended by two weeks so that the show closed on June 25. *Can-Can* producer Cy Feuer contacted Verdon to ask Fosse about a new choreography job for the show *How to Succeed in Business Without Really Trying*, then in tryouts in Philadelphia and scheduled to open on Broadway in three weeks. The original choreographer Hugh Lambert was found to be unsuitable. Fosse agreed to supervise him and leave the Fosse name off the show, restaging the musical numbers.

6. Semi-Retirement and Motherhood 85

Verdon said that Fosse didn't want Lambert fired, particularly not after *he* had been fired from *The Conquering Hero*. Verdon accompanied Fosse to Philadelphia and again acted as his dance assistant as well as his gofer, shopping for costumes and props. The company stayed at the Warwick Hotel and Donna McKechnie, one of the dancers, was told by Verdon how she and Fosse would jump all over their bed rehearsing steps in preparation for the next day. The show was the Broadway debut for McKechnie, who said that Verdon was one of her heroes and that she used to wear black velvet ribbons tied around her neck just like Verdon did. The dancer also said that when she first came to New York she found out where Verdon had her dance boots made because she had to have the same boots. Verdon and Fosse prepared and presented a reworked version of the song "A Secretary Is Not a Toy," both wearing identical tight black pants and sweat socks and sneakers. She also wore a heavy white ribbed wool sweater and he a loose white shirt.

The show opened on Broadway at the 46th Street Theatre on October 14, 1961, and was an enormous hit, running until March 6, 1965. Verdon next assisted Fosse on an hour-long ABC-TV musical Timex special, "The Seasons of Youth." Dancer Barrie Chase rehearsed with Verdon and said that it was obvious that she was madly in love with Fosse. Verdon helped him work out an audition number for Chase and also gave him notes as the program was being filmed. She was not being paid to assist him, but Verdon would come in every day to line up chairs and clean up the space at New York's Variety Arts studio. When a costume ripped, she produced a needle and thread to sew it together. "The Seasons of Youth" aired on October 25, 1961.

Verdon made the first of eleven appearances on the comedy-variety hour *The Garry Moore Show* in the episode that was broadcast on October 31, 1961. It was filmed at CBS studios in New York and in it she is said to have done a song-and-dance version of "Daddy." On November 1, 1961, Joan McCracken died of a heart attack in her sleep. She was only 43 years old. A friend of McCracken, Patton Campbell, telephoned Verdon when he heard the news and asked to come to Verdon's apartment. When he arrived he told her what had happened and then she told Fosse. Verdon said that the sorrow of McCracken's death affected him so deeply since he felt, of all the women in his life and despite all of his success, that only she enhanced his life.

Fosse and Verdon did not attend the funeral service held on November 3 at the Walter B. Cooke Funeral Parlor. He supposedly watched from across the street, repeating the alleged behavior he had of watching his former wife from afar after they had divorced. Unlike the later friendship that eventuated between Verdon and Fosse's girlfriend Ann Reinking, she had never managed to form one with McCracken, which makes her absence at the funeral more understandable. At one time Fosse had supposedly offered McCracken the chance to substitute for Verdon in one of their shows. McCracken came to see the show but declined. It was said that the reasons were a resentment of Verdon, whom she felt had taken Fosse away from her, and the sight of Verdon dancing at a level that McCracken could no longer achieve. McCracken was also said to have gone to great lengths to avoid encounters with Verdon. Apparently, once when she was in the city with a friend, she thought she spotted the red-haired Verdon on the street wearing heavy makeup and a blond mink coat. She had her friend hide in a storefront with her until the woman passed. It turned out that the woman was actually Dolores Gray.

In November 1961, Verdon appeared on the *Perry Como's Kraft Musical Hall* Thanksgiving show. Sources differ as to the date of the show—some say it was November 22; others November 26. She is first seen arriving in a truck with the other guest stars, and joins Como to be introduced, wearing a white dress with white hand gloves and a white scarf. She sings "Howdy Neighbor" with the cast who move to a barn set with a haystack. She and Dorothy Collins go to Como and talk about Thanksgiving as a segue into a Kraft commercial. Verdon then pop ups to camera and is joined by Collins to perform "Make Mine Country Style" as a duet. The number has both women wearing overalls over short-sleeved plaid shirts and white hats and white shoes. Verdon has a handkerchief hanging from a back pocket which she proceeds to tie around her neck. The couple dance around a barn set. At one point, Verdon strums a pitchfork as if it is a guitar, and she is shown to be less afraid to pet a horse than Collins. Verdon returns later in her white dress to dance with four male dancers of the chorus to "Skip to My Lou" on a raised platform on the barn set. Regrettably director Dwight Hemion has some of the chorus blocking our view of Verdon by having two of them standing on either side of the camera, although their presence is rationalized as she jumps into their arms to camera at the end of the number.

She returns for a skit with Paul Lynde with him as the Thanksgiving chef. Taking orders for the meal, he asks Verdon if she is anybody and she replies, "I'm beginning to wonder." In her white dress and scarf she is next alone on the haystack, where she places a flower in her hair, finds a boot which she throws away and then a white balloon on a string. She dances on the floor holding the balloon, and runs behind a truck and out of camera range. The number then changes to Verdon in a dark field running in slow motion with the balloon seen as bigger than it was before. The images are distorted with soft focus and extended vertical lines, and Verdon sits in a tree. There is a closeup of her smiling to the camera before she jumps out of the tree and runs again, stopping to dance among trees in a forest. After she jumps again we see her return to the barn set: she is lowered from the ceiling by a string onto the haystack, still holding the balloon. Verdon removes the glove from her hand that holds the balloon and it floats away. She waves goodbye to it with the same hand and the number ends. Verdon is then part of a "Sing a Song" medley. She sings "Buffalo Gals" as she walks among the male members of the chorus on the raised level of the barn set. She dances with two of the men arm in arm on either side of her, moving up and down stairs and comes down to the floor. Verdon joins Como and Collins sitting on the haystack for "We Were Looking Through This Barn" to the tune of "Old MacDonald Had a Farm." After the number, Verdon asks about the promised dinner and comments that Thanksgiving only comes once a year "but it doesn't seem to be coming here at all." The cast sit at a table for the meal.

Verdon returned for her second *Garry Moore Show* (December 19, 1961), which had a Christmas theme. The choreographer may have been Kevin Carlisle. She appeared in four of the episode's musical numbers. In the entrance number, Verdon wears a mink coat and walks through a department store's swivel door carrying presents. Dressed in a sparkling white dress and feathered cap, she then dances to "Greensleeves," with the song's lyrics changed to "The Beautiful Trees of Christmas" and sung by an unseen chorus. The set features three Christmas trees which transform into three female dancers, and they and Verdon are joined by four male dancers. She returns for a second musical number with Carol Burnett and Julie Andrews. The three ladies are dressed in sweats and together they sing "Everybody's Doin' It" on gymnasium equipment, and Verdon scores a laugh from her use of a rowing machine. The skit climaxes with the three dressed as Santa Claus, ringing bells, and getting money donated into a box by the passing Garry Moore. Verdon's final appearance comes within a montage of carol singing. She sings the French version of "The First Noel" as she stands against a window frame, dressed in black and with a glittering necklace

The star was back for her third *Garry Moore Show* appearance on January 30, 1962. She sang and danced to the song "Forty-Nine Percent," and with Carol Burnett sang the finale "Let's Be Buddies." A still exists of the women together for the number, wearing identical white topcoats with boutonnieres, white hats, striped pants and holding canes. Verdon's hat has feathers in it which Burnett's does not.

The *New York Times* reported on February 25, 1962, that Verdon was one of the people to receive the annual *Dance Magazine* award at a cocktail ceremony to be held in March. The award, an abstract statuette in silver, cited her for bringing a disarming warmth, a sure technique, and star quality to musical comedy dancing in ideal synthesis with acting and singing. The organization said that Verdon epitomized the best of all-round performer in today's musical theater of Broadway, Hollywood and television. The *New York Times* of March 21 1962, confirmed that the ceremony was held on March 20 at the Carriage Club. Her award was presented by Paddy Chayefsky.

In Verdon's fourth appearance on *The Garry Moore Show* (February 27, 1962), she sang and danced to the song "Pretty to Walk With" and joined the cast for a sketch called "Palace Intrigue" where Verdon was a charm school teacher. She also teamed with Carol Burnett in the show's finale of "Be a Clown." A still exists of Verdon with Burnett on the show, both of them wearing identical white high-collared smocks and black tights, presumably for the "Be a Clown" number. She returned to *The Garry Moore Show* for her fifth appearance on March 20, 1962. In it Verdon sang and danced in a production number based on the song "Shoo Fly Pie."

On April 1, 1962, WCBS-TV Public Affairs Department broadcast an episode of *American Musical Theatre* which had guests Verdon and Fosse. The show, produced in association with the Board of Education of the City of New York, was "an informal workshop in a series of television biographies of people whose personal contribution to the musical theater had made it a native American art." It was hosted by Earl Wrightson, had students from New York City high schools in the audience, and featured Jay Brockton and the CBS Orchestra. Brockton had been the musical director for *Redhead*. In the show both Verdon and Fosse are dressed in black, she in a sweater and pants with her hair in a ponytail. Sitting on stools close to the audience, they are asked by Wrightson about their pasts, and they also take questions from the audience. Verdon then sang "Whatever Lola Wants" from *Damn Yankees* two ways as a demonstration of staging a musical number. The opening five lines of the song is sung a capella with her sitting on her stool. Then Fosse leads Verdon to a stage where there is a bench so that she can sing the song in full, with movement and musical accompaniment, to him playing Joe Hardy sitting on a chair. Wrightson gives Verdon a towel for her neck after her performance.

She comments on the influence of the baggy-pants Picasso clowns on her work. Verdon then performs "The Pony Dance" from *New Girl in Town*. Fosse joins her in the dance, but unlike the first number, director Anthony Farrar violates the performance at one point by obscuring the dancers with a shot from the audience's point of view. Fosse talks about Verdon, describing her as an extraordinary talent and says that the things that impress him most about her are her enthusiasm, her desire for perfection and endless energy. He also says that she has intuition of what he wants when he has an idea. Verdon next performs the pantomime dance "Merely Marvelous" from *Redhead* in a white-petticoated polka dot skirt over her clothes, putting on a white glove that has been left on a table. Verdon and Fosse do "Who's Got the Pain" from *Damn Yankees*, and wear hats for the number. She confesses that when she is good she takes a singing and dancing lesson every day, and when she is bad she misses them and always regrets it. Verdon claims it requires a great deal of work and discipline which is compensated by having the fun she does on stage which makes you forget the pain of learning it.

Fosse then leads Verdon in a "then-I-choreographed" singing and dance medley which features brief excerpts from "Hernando's Hideaway" from *The Pajama Game*, "Steam Heat" from *The Pajama Game* with hats, "Shoeless Joe" from *Damn Yankees*, "Mu Cha Cha" from *Bells Are Ringing*, "Sunshine Girl" from *New Girl in Town* with Verdon holding a hat, "Herbie Fitch's Lament" from *Redhead* with Verdon wearing a hat and holding a cane; and "Brotherhood of Man" from *How to Succeed in Business Without Really Trying*.

It is reported that Verdon attended the April 29, 1962 Tony Awards which were held at the Waldorf Astoria Hotel. On May 21, 1962, Verdon and Fosse were part of the program for the third City Center of Music and Drama "Showcase of Stars" for the benefit of the Children's Asthma Research Institute. They were assisted by a chorus performing in the "Don't Kick It Around" dance from *Pal Joey*. The *New York Times* of May 9 reported that show's producer was Jean Dalrymple and its director John Fearnley. But in its report on May 22, it says that Dalrymple was the director.

Verdon returned to *The Garry Moore Show* for her sixth appearance on June 5, 1962. Fosse was also a guest and together the couple sing and dance "I Wanna Be a Dancin' Man," a song originally performed by Fred Astaire in the MGM musical *The Belle of New York* (1952). In the number Verdon corrects Fosse's singing "man" with "girl" to refer to the fact that she wants to be a dancing girl. The couple wear identical white blouses, black pants, white socks, black shoes and cane hats, with a set that has a giant cane hat on the curtain behind them. A photograph in the *New York Times* on June 3, 1962, shows that Carol Burnett, Fosse and Verdon also appeared in a dance number where they appear to wear white chef outfits.

The star had been counselled by her doctors not to get pregnant because of her age, although there was nothing specifically physically wrong with her. When she failed to conceive, the couple consulted pregnancy specialists, kept charts of Verdon's temperature and monitored her menstrual cycle, and scheduled lovemaking sessions. However she still was not pregnant. Fosse's sperm was then tested and it was determined to be "slow," which meant that the couple would not be able to conceive in the natural way. They considered adoption as a better option, and then they proved their advisors wrong: Verdon became pregnant. (Fosse jokingly observed that the best way to get pregnant seemed to be to start adoption proceedings.) It might have seemed wise for Verdon not to keep working. But according to Neil Simon's memoir *Rewrites*, she worked again with Fosse on his next musical.

He was asked by Cy Feuer and Ernie Martin to choreograph *Little Me*, a new show to star Sid Caesar. It was written by Simon and based on the Patrick Dennis novel *Little Me: The Intimate Memoirs of That Great Star of Stage, Screen and Television/Belle Poitrine*. Since Feuer wanted to direct and since Fosse now would only work as a choreographer-director, they agreed to be credited as co-directors. It was during the auditions that, one source claims, Verdon learned she was pregnant. Apparently she was at home because she had not been feeling well. When her doctor told her the news, she telephoned Fosse backstage. When he found out, Fosse apparently let out a yell, dropped the receiver, and ran out into the street. Verdon feared that her husband had fainted upon hearing the news, but he was actually just happy and had to shout it out to the world.

Rehearsals for the show took place at the Variety Arts studio. Cy Coleman recalled when he first met Verdon: She came waddling down the aisle with the also pregnant Joan Simon. The women were both laughing and comparing the size of their bellies. Neil Simon writes that, weeks before rehearsals began, Fosse had worked out the dances with Verdon and a pianist. She would help him flesh out the numbers with both of them playing everyone's part. Verdon went with Fosse when the show moved to the Erlanger Theatre in Philadelphia in October 1962. Then after seven weeks it moved to Broadway and opened on November 17 at the Lunt-Fontanne Theatre. Despite a newspaper strike, the show was a success and ran till June 29, 1963.

6. Semi-Retirement and Motherhood

Fosse took Verdon to Chicago for Christmas to show off her pregnancy to his family. The family put on a Christmas revue for her, drawing a curtain across the middle of the living room and doing numbers from *The Pajama Game, Damn Yankees* and *How to Succeed in Business Without Really Trying*. They had costumes copied from the *Damn Yankees* movie and played the soundtrack recording for "Who's Got the Pain." Fosse's seventeen-year-old niece Cindy was to do the number in a variety show at Amundsen High and he and Verdon coached her in every detail of the number. Verdon was back on *The Garry Moore Show* for her seventh appearance on January 1, 1963. She did a dance entitled "Ecstasy" and joined Carol Burnett and Roy Castle in the finale "My Mother Was a Lady."

On March 4, 1963, Verdon gave birth to Nicole, a variation on the name Nicholas that Fosse had wanted if they had a boy. He had chosen it as a tribute to his uncle but later when he wanted to appear more literary he said he got Nicole from F. Scott Fitzgerald's character Nicole Diver in his novel *Tender Is the Night*. Dorothy Fields, the lyricist of *Redhead*, is said to have come up with the middle name Providence, based on the fact that the Fosses had wanted a child for so long, had tried so hard and had almost given up all hope.

In a *New York Times* article (April 26, 1963) it was reported that Fosse was working on a new stage show of his own conception to star Verdon. The article did not state what the show would be about other than it was an offbeat idea, dominated by movement and dance, and something that he had been thinking about for five years. Fosse was to begin discussions with producers Robert Fryer and Lawrence Carr who had previously worked with the couple on *Redhead*. On May 6, 1963, Verdon attended a party celebrating the 40th anniversary of *Time* magazine, held at the Waldorf Astoria. In her eighth *Garry Moore Show* appearance (May 21, 1963) she sang and danced to a song called "Love" and joined the cast for the finale of "Haven't Got a Nickel." Verdon was again by Fosse's side at rehearsals and backstage from May 29, 1963, when he performed in a revival of *Pal Joey* directed by Gustav Schirmer, Jr. The show was at the New York City Center for their Light Opera Company; it would only run for fifteen performances until June 9, 1963.

In the May 1963 edition of *Horizon* magazine, Verdon was photographed by Hans Namuth sitting on the sand in front of a modest beach house on Long Island that she and Fosse were said to occupy. She wore a pink short blouse with white long sleeves and pink pants and was barefoot as she sat in front of a tangle of brush and broken-down wooden fencing that was positioned between her and the two-storey brownstone house behind her. The fencing was meant to anchor the dune against the Atlantic storms though its dilapidated state suggested that it now had little protective benefit. Fosse was not in the photograph and the house looked small, with pink frames and silver shutters on the windows and doors. The raised back veranda had beach towels slung over a railing and a beach mattress on the porch, and sun hats hung on what appeared to be a clothes line. The accompanying prose was written by William K. Zinsser. He reported that the house was originally part of an Army quarantine camp built at Montauk Point during the Spanish-American war and later moved to its present location near Amagansett. The Fosses bought it four years ago and used it all year as a weekend retreat from their city schedules. Zinsser also mentioned that Verdon liked to make collages for her living room from driftwood, bits of broken glass, and other beachcombing discoveries. It is noteworthy that she did not include her baby in the photograph.

Despite her previously announced retirement from the stage and the birth of Nicole, Verdon was now keen for another comeback. Verdon felt that when her daughter was three, that would be the right time when she could safely leave her to free herself for one last triumph. This was planned as a show with Fosse that would top what they had done with *Redhead*, but this time, something that they had created for themselves. Verdon would spend the meantime searching for the right material, something that was new and challenging and personal to both her and Fosse, with dance potential for him and a leading role for her.

7

Sweet Charity

Verdon was still interested in *Chicago* but Fosse was more taken with the idea of musical versions of either one of two foreign films. They were Mario Monicelli's crime comedy *Big Deal on Madonna Street* (1958) and Federico Fellini's drama *Nights of Cabiria* (1957), winner of the Best Foreign Language Film Academy Award. He had seen the latter film in the spring of 1962. Fosse felt that it had the better role for Verdon of the waifish prostitute Cabiria (played by Giulietta Masina) who looks for love but only finds heartbreak. She could be likened to a modern-day Harlequin which was Verdon's personal archetype. Though a male figure, she would explain that the Harlequin was a well-rounded, sensitive person who is transformed by suffering when his heart is broken and which makes him a man. He has the twirl of blue paper in his eye to represent tears and a flower on his nose as a symbol of unattainable beauty. He hunts for love, not realizing that it is right in front of him. Verdon could relate the Harlequin's object of desire of Columbine to Fosse. However she hated the film and found it depressing.

Another possibility was suggested by *Redhead*'s producer, Robert Fryer: a musical of Truman Capote's novella "Breakfast at Tiffany's" which had been made into a romantic comedy film by Blake Edwards and released in 1961. Fosse imagined doing all three properties as a three-act musical or just two of them as a double bill of one-act musicals. Maurine Dallas Watkins was opposed and again refused the rights to *Chicago*. Verdon talked to the playwright who supposedly lived in a Florida nunnery. She felt it was ridiculous to discuss the idea of a musical of her play just after the 1962 Cuban missile crisis. Watkins was considered eccentric but also wise about a possible nuclear event only ninety miles from where she lived. She also considered that a murderess was hardly the appropriate subject for entertainment, though one might think that she had overcome this idea when she wrote the original play. Verdon suggested that Watkins' royalties could be paid to the nunnery instead of Watkins, but she still wouldn't agree. Other sources claim that Watkins lived with her mother in Florida, though still as a recluse. She only let a few close friends know of her whereabouts, and even her agent had to write to her via a post office box in Jacksonville. When Sheldon Abend took over as her new agent, he hired a private detective to find Watkins, particularly since he knew that *Chicago* was a property of potential value. After she was found, telephone calls were made and a date was set for a meeting, and then broken. Watkins would listen with interest and then give the same answer: no.

Verdon felt that Watkins warmed to the idea of giving the rights to her because her take on the material was that it was a huge comment on the press as much as it was about the murder. However the author remained firm. She had turned to religion, and specifically to astrology, to inform her life decisions. This included not allowing any new productions of her work, although Watkins also took into account what she read in *Variety* about the risks and costs of stage productions. The other sources also claim that Verdon's approach came through writing to her. Watkins had told Verdon that Ann-Margret was also interested in the rights though perhaps this was untrue and just a test. In reply Verdon said that she should go with her if that was the better way to get the property done. This generosity was something Watkins may not have expected of a performer. While she continued to deny Verdon the rights, she still felt that she was the best choice. The writer held onto the play's rights until her death in 1969.

The focus shifted back to *Nights of Cabiria*. Fosse screened the film for Robert Fryer and Lawrence Carr in their office with Verdon in attendance. The producers supposedly loved the movie but Fosse knew it was still a hard sell. It was not a happy romance and it ended on a sad note. Fryer said that he wasn't sure it was right for a Broadway show and, to Fosse's surprise, Verdon agreed with him. She found Cabiria to be pathetic, a poor creature who gets pushed aside and knocked down, and is so desperate for love that she picks up a chicken and hugs it. Carr was the only one who agreed with Fosse and encouraged him to stay with it because he liked the story's big little heart.

The rights were obtained and Fosse flew to Italy to discuss the project with Fellini, who wished him well but expressed no interest in becoming involved with the musical. Setting the show in a dance hall changed the minds of Cryer, Carr and Verdon, since it made the piece more theatrical and blurred the prostitution line. The girls at the Tango were paid to dance. They were hostesses but not hookers, though what they did after they turned in their dance tickets for a commission was up to them. Verdon liked the idea of Cabiria as a hostess because in New York prostitutes were either elegant with posh lives (whom nobody would have any sympathy for) or bums (that nobody would care about). Fosse rationalized the change since he said there was something ugly about a prostitute in America, although it was all right in Italy. He wanted to get to the nearest thing to a prostitute which he thought was a promiscuous girl who sold something for money—a dance, her understanding, conversation, something. Verdon was concerned that playing the role would make people compare her to Masina or be disappointed because of the material's unhappy ending. She felt that American audiences preferred happy endings where the girl gets the fella and eight kids in Scarsdale, although she knew that not many people ended up that way.

Fosse decided to write the book himself to avoid having to deal with the problems of collaboration. He had done uncredited work on the script of *Redhead* and believed this gave him the experience to go solo. In nine pages he outlined a one-act musical and showed it to Verdon, but she remained unconvinced. She found the character and milieu stridently unglamorous. She also reminded Fosse of the unpopularity of his whorehouse ballet in *New Girl in Town* where audiences didn't want to see seedy goings-on. He consented to engaging Martin Charnin as a co-writer and planned to use *Nights of Cabiria* as the basis for the first act of a two-act musical to be called *Hearts and Flowers*. Their priority was to fit the material to Verdon's strengths, and Charnin learned that Fosse was to be the controlling force in all aspects of the production. For three weeks they worked together and by June 1963 there was a first draft of sixty pages. It was submitted to Fryer and Carr, and then Fosse cut off all contact with Charnin, and tried to find a composer. Cy Coleman expressed some interest but only if he could have Dorothy Fields to write the lyrics. She was interested but would not commit because the second-act musical had not been decided upon. Fosse then looked for another writer for the second act, his experience with Charnin somehow not inspiring him to want to work with him again. He found Elaine May but discovered that she was slow to work.

In the meantime Fosse signed on to direct and choreograph a new musical about Fanny Brice called *Funny Girl*. Brice was to be played by Barbra Streisand. Fosse later claimed that he was responsible for casting Streisand, but other sources claim that he thought Verdon could have played her. He supposedly asked the producers to replace Streisand with Verdon, but they turned him down. Fosse said that he worked on *Funny Girl* for seven months although another source claims that it was only one. He quit in September 1963, unhappy about producer Ray Stark. The show opened on March 26, 1964, at the Wintergarden Theatre and was a huge hit, running until July 1, 1967.

Verdon saw a change in Fosse thanks to their daughter and proclaimed that he was a fabulous father, and that being one gave him a new happiness. It was this new happiness that also made him want to give Verdon the best show she ever had. When Robert Fryer bought the rights to "Breakfast at Tiffany's," this financial commitment made Fosse shelve *Nights of Cabiria*.

She returned to *The Garry Moore Show* for her ninth appearance on November 5, 1963. Verdon presented a modern version of "Two Little Maids from School," sang and danced to "St. Louis Blues," and joined the cast in a sketch about a harried husband who plans to do away with his wife. She made the first of six appearances on the CBS musical comedy show *The Danny Kaye Show* in an episode broadcast on November 20, 1963. It was filmed in Los Angeles and in it Verdon performed three dances set to nursery rhymes:"Pop Goes the Weasel," a jazz version of "Three Blind Mice," and a lullaby ballet, all with the Tony Charmoli Dancers. She did two duets with Kaye, "Two of a Kind" and "What Is a Woman." The latter is said to have been spoken by Kaye as she danced. Verdon also performed two sketches. One had Verdon, Kaye and Harvey Korman playing a band of strolling players who try to help a medieval prince remember how to laugh, by jestering and square, flamenco, ballet and vaudeville dance. A photograph of Kaye and Verdon in costume for this number appeared in the *New York Times* on November 17, 1963. The second had Verdon and Kaye as a married couple, which one source describes as newlyweds and another as a couple celebrating their anniversary. They stop at a drive-in-restaurant and suffered from pratfalls caused by the staff.

A source claims that Verdon appeared on *The Jimmy Dean Show* in December 1963 but this is not confirmed. The television series, filmed in New York, was a "down home" musical comedy program that catered to country and western performance, but also featured popular music artists.

She also made her tenth *Garry Moore Show* appearance on January 7, 1964. Verdon did a special dance to the song "I've Got the World on a String." The number was choreographed by Kevin Carlyle who used sign language to teach dance to deaf mutes. Before the number Verdon explained how she understood and could speak fluently in sign language because of the deaf mute girl she befriended at school. In it, she wears a long-sleeved black dress with a white ruffled collar and white gloves. For the song we hear Verdon singing as we see her sign. She is backed up by five female dancers who also sign the words to the song, and Verdon and the dancers have their own spotlights. As the song progresses, two more backup dancers are revealed sitting in front of Verdon, and they also sign. Then the other dancers disappear and Verdon dances alone on the bare stage (which is now more brightly lit) until she is joined by male and female dancers. The number climaxes with Verdon and the backup dancers all signing and back in spotlights, and ends with a closeup of her gloved hand. The number also includes some unusual titled camera coverage of the dance.

On January 27, 1964, Verdon was one of a number of people making speeches at Madison Square Garden. This was in dual tribute to President Kennedy, who had died on November 22, 1963, and to Sol Hurok on his fiftieth anniversary in show business. The program was presented by the women's division of the Federation of Jewish Philanthropies of New York. Verdon made her eleventh and last *Garry Moore Show* appearance on April 14, 1964. On it she did a song and dance to "I'm Old Fashioned." On April 17, the 16th anniversary ball of the Bedside Network of the Veterans Hospital Radio and Television Guild was held at the Grand Ballroom of the New York Hilton. Verdon was one of the committee members for the event and the proceeds were used to support the guild's volunteer services in more than one hundred hospitals for veterans. On April 22, Verdon was one of the reported 1200 guests at a party at the Texas Pavilion of the World's Fair for Governor John Connally who was still recovering from a wound received at the time of the Kennedy assassination.

In April 1964 Robert Fryer heard from Truman Capote's literary agent, Audrey Wood, about the "Breakfast at Tiffany's" project. Capote had a problem with the idea of Verdon playing the story's heroine, Holly Golightly. She was written in the novella as a girl of nineteen, and Capote had already been stung by the casting of Audrey Hepburn in the movie version, since she was 32 by the time the film was released. Verdon at 38 was also deemed too old for the part by the author, and it didn't help her case that she was about to become a grandmother by her son. Capote agreed to meet with her. It was hoped that when he saw how young-looking she was, he would change his mind. Fosse initially wouldn't allow it, despite the fact that Verdon had no problem with the idea. Or perhaps she did but she knew that a small humiliation was worth the price of securing the rights. Audrey Wood brought Capote to the Fosse apartment for breakfast. Fosse may have felt that she looked great and that musicals aren't realistic anyway, but Capote decided that Verdon did indeed look too old. The option money was returned and that was the end of that.

Capote would later approve 30-year-old Mary Tyler Moore to play the part in a musical adaptation, although the show closed in Broadway previews in December 1966.

Quotes from Verdon about Carol Haney were published in the *New York Times* on May 12, 1964, two days after Haney's death. Verdon said that Haney was like a great, big husky puppy dog that never knows when it's tired. She was so enthusiastic about everything that she never noticed the strain. When people asked Haney to slow down, she'd just babble on about some new project. On May 24, 1964, Verdon was a presenter at the 1964 Tony Awards held at the New York Hilton Hotel, which was broadcast live for television.

She was then back for her second guest appearance on *The Danny Kaye Show*, broadcast on September 23, 1964. On the show Verdon sang and danced to "Downtown." She also appeared in a skit entitled "Jerome the Bachelor," a spoof involving a group of bashful bachelors. In the fifteen-minute skit Verdon is dental technician Renee Miller, the blind date of Kaye's shoe salesman Jerome. It initially scores laughs from the awkwardness of the blind date and then climaxes in slapstick comedy when Jerome's tie gets caught in Renee's dress and, when removing it, he rips off her dress. But it ends with touching pathos where the couple decides to go out together, and they are saved from being presented as pathetic fools. Verdon is vulnerable and funny when presenting her character's shyness with a man. Renee is first seen meekly entering the room where Jerome is. The medium shot has Verdon with a bow in her hair and wearing a sleeveless dress and pearl necklace. She gets laughs from her repeated furtive glances, shoulder shrug and a comic smile at Jerome, and a long shot reveals that she wears a flower-patterned dress with a frilled trim and also shows her holding her hands together. Verdon supplies a desperate laugh of affirmation when it is revealed that it is Renee's first trip to New York. She also gets more laughs from her "Yes?" after Jerome nervously clears his throat, her panicked reaction to Jerome touching her neck after the clasp of her necklace opens, and when she asks if he can fix it.

A still exists of Verdon and Kaye standing together, with her in a white high-necked layered blouse and black skirt. In her third *Danny Kaye* guest appearance (November 25, 1964), Verdon sang "I've Got Rhythm" and she joined Kaye in two skits. One was about a husband and wife squabbling at breakfast; in the second, she, Kaye and Harvey Korman did a parody in the movie musical style titled "The Elopement."

On December 19, 1964, the *New York Times* reported that producers

7. Sweet Charity 99

Robert Fryer, Lawrence Carr, and Joseph and Sylvia Harris planned to bring Verdon back to Broadway after an absence of five years in a two-in-one show. One segment was to be a musical adaptation of *Nights of Cabiria* and the other an original work by Elaine May entitled "The Larger World of Faith." May was also said to be adapting the Fellini film with Fosse directing and choreographing. The music would be by Cy Coleman and the lyrics by Dorothy Fields. It was announced that the show would go into rehearsals on July 19, 1965, and open in New York on October 28 after tryouts in Detroit and Philadelphia.

Verdon was back for her fourth *Danny Kaye Show* guest appearance on December 23, 1964. She sang "There's a Lull in My Life" and "The Song Is Ended." She danced with Kaye in the show's opening Christmas Waltz and in a fantasy dance where they played rejected dolls in in a child's room. Verdon also joined Kaye and Harvey Korman in an espionage comedy sketch titled "The Spy Who Got a Cold." She was photographed with Kaye for an article on the show in the December 20, 1964, edition of the *Washington Evening Star* television magazine "The Sunday Star." The article was entitled "Gwen Verdon: A Dancer with Elfish Humor" and the color photograph had Verdon in a blue and green patterned dress.

Around this time there was a rumor that Verdon had been considered for the leading role in a new musical adaptation of the Arthur Laurents play *The Time of the Cuckoo* entitled *Do I Hear a Waltz?* However this is a rumor that Laurents denied. The musical had a book by Laurents, music by Richard Rodgers (who also produced), and lyrics by Stephen Sondheim. The director was John Dexter. Ultimately cast in the role of Leona Samish was Elizabeth Allen. The show would open on Broadway on May 18, 1965, at the 46th Street Theatre and had a reasonable run until September 25.

Verdon assisted Fosse on his next show, a musical entitled *Pleasures and Palaces*. Rehearsals began in early 1965 in New York and she left Nicole at home with their Brazilian nanny, Hermocinda. The show moved to Detroit from March for six weeks of tryouts. Another source claims that Verdon brought her daughter on the road with her and that her first word was spoken while she was in a hotelroom: The word was supposedly "bellhop." The tryouts were not well received and Fosse rehearsed script revisions as Verdon worked on the dances and at night she watched the performances with composer Frank Loesser. The producers eventually decided to close the show on April 10, 1965, and not take it into New York.

On Verdon's fifth *Danny Kaye Show* (February 10, 1965) she appeared in two skits. The first, "Top Hat, White Tie and Green Socks," also features Kaye and Harvey Korman. In this three-act comedy she plays a tempera-

Danny Kaye and Verdon in a still for her guest appearance on the February 10, 1965, *Danny Kaye Show*.

mental musical comedy star who looks for a leading man to star in her next stage show and decides on an accident-prone delivery boy (Kaye). In the second, Verdon is the wife of Kaye and demands that he ask for a raise from his boss in the office. A still exists of Kaye and Verdon singing. She is dressed in a Little Bo Peep–type dress with white puffy sleeves and a white lace apron over a dark full silk skirt. The *New York Times* published a still from the show in an article by Paul Gardner called "Warming Up with Gwen" on February 7, 1965. The still showed Kaye and Verdon in the "Top Hat, White Tie and Green Socks" number where she wears a dark top and short skirt and white socks and heels. In the photograph the pair stand back to back, both of them holding their arms outstretched with hands touching. Jack Gould, reviewing the number for the *Times*, lambasted it.

Paul Gardner interviewed Verdon for the article at the Oak Bar of the Plaza Hotel, where she wore a puffy badger cap, mink coat and mink jumper. She explained her fondness for mink by telling him that when she first came to New York it was so cold that a policeman had to help her off the street so she was determined never to be cold again. Verdon also smoked during the interview. She told Gardner that she knew that she couldn't keep dancing forever but she kept her legs in shape with daily ballet lessons and let Sanford Meisner worry about her dramatic motivations. Verdon admitted that being a happy-go-lucky person made her want to avoid tragic acting parts that other actresses seem to want. The Actors Studio had refused her admission and also refused to let her audition, possibly because they felt that she hadn't suffered enough on the musical stage.

Verdon revealed that she planned to return to Broadway in the fall in the two one-act musicals, which may be called "Two Choruses of Melancholy Baby." The following year she would probably have her own television series, which she described as a situation comedy where she would play a married woman. Verdon said that it was necessary to make the character married because that was the only way she could play a seduction scene, since she felt that you could do anything as long as you were married on television. She bemoaned the fact that television seldom allowed time for perfection and that even the dancing on television was a lot better than it looked but so much of it looked alike. This was because you always had to wear black to get a clean line, and you were photographed from the same angle and never in profile. Verdon commented that dancing before a camera only becomes interesting when the camera is part of the number. Dancing was action and she thought it should be photographed like a fight or a Western. Verdon felt that some of the best television dancing was done on the new ABC musical variety series *Shindig!* (She never appeared on the show, which ran from September 16, 1964, to January 8, 1966.) The star said that after she finished *Redhead* she had a minor knee operation. She also had taken a vacation from work after marrying Fosse and having Nicole because she felt that she couldn't do two things at once.

Fosse held a backers' audition at Delmonico's with a reading of the material for the unnamed two-act musical. This revealed that Elaine May had barely completed her half of the show, which had an alternate title of "Robbers and Cops." Apparently in May's musical, Verdon was to have played a cat burglar and would wear suction cups on her hands and feet which would have allowed her to crawl straight up a wall. Naturally such a stunt would have been extremely dangerous, which probably insured that it would be abandoned. Another reason given for the loss of the piece was that it too strongly resembled another Broadway-bound musical, *Drat the Cat!*, which had a society jewel thief as its heroine. That show had book and lyrics by Ira-Levin and music by Milton Schafer, and would open at Broadway's Martin Beck Theatre on October 10, 1965. It lasted eight performances.

Fosse's *Nights of Cabiria* was further along though the presentation still gave the impression that it had been rushed. It was apparent that Fosse's draft needed more stage time than a one-act piece allowed to explore the relationship between Cabiria and her beau, Oscar. In May 1965 Fosse turned for help to David Shaw, one of the book writers on *Redhead*; Shaw's ex-wife had suggested *Nights of Cabiria* to Fosse in the first place. However this didn't work out. Neither did approaching Abe Burrows, the director and book writer of *Can-Can*. Fosse next tried Hugh Wheeler with whom he had worked on the abandoned *Breakfast at Tiffany's*. Wheeler rewrote the first seven scenes and then told the director that he didn't think that he was a good match for the material.

In the summer the Fosses rented an East Hampton cottage which was only a few steps away from the beach. He had decided that he now did not want a collaborator and he wrote alone for five days. Then he got a call from Robert Fryer who had approached another writer—Paddy Chayefsky. Fosse went back to Manhattan for a meeting. Chayefsky had a surprising interest in musical comedy and he had written the book and lyrics of the musical *No T.O. for Love* which had been produced in London in 1945. But then Fosse gave up on the idea of working with Chayefsky on the project and he returned to Long Island to finish the show's book on his own. He even came up with a pseudonym for himself, "Bill Lewis." But neither "Bill Lewis" nor Fosse would end up as the credited author on the project.

The *New York Times* of July 8, 1965, reported that Elaine May said that her half of the two-act musical had been withdrawn. Robert Fryer is quoted as saying that the adaptation of *Nights of Cabiria* had developed into a full evening's presentation, which is why May's contribution was dropped. She also reported that she was planning to do a screen version of her piece, which never eventuated. It was reported that Fosse was the adaptor of the Fellini movie and that the name of a collaborator would soon be announced. The title of the show was for the first time given as *Sweet Charity* and the Broadway opening date was now December 28, 1965. On July 22, 1965, the *New York Times* reported that the Palace had been booked to host the show and it would be the first legitimate attraction at the former vaudeville house since it was built in 1913. It had been recently been purchased from RKO Theatres by David Nederlander of Detroit and his sons and they planned an extensive reconstruction job.

In July 1965 Fosse telephoned his friend Neil Simon who was in Rome for the shooting of his screenplay *After the Fox*. Fosse had by now completed a first draft for the two-act musical and asked Simon to read it and for help in making it better and funnier. One source claims that Simon agreed to help because he had no other writing assignments to complete at the time, but others, including Simon, say that he was too busy to take on anything else. Therefore Simon agreeing to look at Fosse's draft was done as a favor out of their friendship. The draft was reportedly posted to Simon by Fosse the day after their telephone call and marked for urgent delivery since rehearsals for the show were scheduled to begin in August 1965. The script arrived eight days later, despite the urging packaging, and Simon read it. He felt that Fosse was wrong. It didn't need humor—it *desperately* needed humor. And given the start date for rehearsals, it needed it fast. Simon made a few suggestions, like removing the lines he felt didn't work and inserting what he hoped were funnier ones. The script was sent back to Fosse. Three days later Fosse called again and told him that he loved the new lines and wanted more.

To press his point, a week later the director arrived in Rome accompanied by a tape of the score. In Simon's hotel room Fosse moved the furniture against the wall to free up dance space. He then played the score and performed the proposed dances to the audience of Simon and his wife Joan. When the writer saw what Fosse had done he was hooked. Fosse left the next morning and Simon structured a schedule so he could work on *Sweet Charity*. He had difficulty with it because it was not the kind of book he would have done, and therefore to work further on it required him to start from scratch—a total rewrite. Verdon would say that one of Simon's greatest additions to the book was the idea for "If My Friends Could See Me Now," to give the first act something pleasurable and uplifting for Charity. Presumably it was Fosse who added the scene's hat and cane.

Other sources, like the *New York Times*, give a different timeline to Simon's working on the show. They say that the original rehearsal book was credited to Fosse's Bill Lewis aka Robert Lewis Fosse, and that Simon was brought in on October 1, 1966. Simon's commitment led to his logically asking for full credit for his work. Having become the most popular playwright on Broadway, he did not want to be a co-author and he had the clout to make such a demand. What had begun as a friendly favor was now a business relationship where theatrical billing and credit was essential to justice and ego. Fosse agreed to the demand although he believed that he had done the major effort on the script. He also knew the commercial sense in having a show advertised as having a book by Simon.

To research *Sweet Charity*, Verdon accompanied Fosse to Times Square dance halls to observe the girls. The palaces were open from noon to four a.m. and the girls ranged in age from 18 to 50. At one place the women were in their forties and dressed in the past. Verdon sensed that some seemed trapped back in the '30s. Others must have thought it was still 1942, with Lana Turner hairdos and wedgie shoes, or Veronica Lake with that hairdo. Another thought she was Joan Crawford with those plastic shoes. They were tough and Verdon was a little scared when one caught her eyeing her and asked what she was staring at. She approached one who was knitting, who explained that she took the job to pay for the baby that was due in five months. Her husband was in Korea and she became a hostess because she didn't know to do anything else. If the women made dates after work as prostitutes, Verdon never found out about it, though Fosse said that he saw more groping than dancing. He paid for their time and found them interested in him and attentive; he told the women how he was doing research for a show and listened to their stories. Fosse found that he was more successful when he went without his wife since she was more conspicuous in a room full of dancers. Fosse also observed the 1960s dances that were performed in the clubs and after his tour he would go to his studio to work, lacing all of the dancing threads together.

Verdon supposedly also went undercover and worked as one of the girls. Despite being in her forties and a grandmother, her firm and supple body made her fair competition to the ones half her age. Verdon worked in a tiny, dark upstairs hideaway dance hall on Broadway as a dance hostess; she and the others were protected by wooden dividers from the men until one of them paid for a dance. She felt that the younger women found something romantic in the faded grandeur of the dance hall, an attitude that was presumably lacking in the older women.

Fosse had taken an apartment on the eleventh floor of 850 Seventh

Avenue to get away from Verdon's ménage and the toddler Nicole at 91 Central Park West. He worked at the Variety Arts rehearsal studios on the dances for *Sweet Charity* though sometimes he would drag Verdon to the studio in the middle of the night to help him realize steps he had dreamed up in bed. She would say that he tried to get her up, but when she was out, she was out, and the next morning Verdon had usually forgotten everything. After that, Fosse would just let her sleep.

In the summer the couple holidayed in their Amagansett beach house which was their first substantial financial investment. Verdon also used their considerable earnings in more real estate in one of the most expensive resort communities in the country. Fosse would joke that he paid the bills and she bought houses but he was wise enough to recognize that she had the greater head for business. Verdon also liked to socialize in the area, to go to and to give parties. The latter had her supply beer, corn on the cob and filet mignon cooked on the charcoal grill, while Fosse would instigate a ping-pong tournament. Among the guests were the Simons with their daughter Nancy, who lived just up the street.

Fosse had gotten past any hard feelings over the *Sweet Charity* book which Simon had pared down to a series of scenes that resembled comic sketches, which after all was his specialty and which served to link the songs. The only two long scenes had Cabiria renamed as Charity hiding in the closet of the Italian movie star where she spends the night as he entertains his girlfriend, and the elevator scene with Oscar. Verdon would say that the movie star scene including the closet scene came from Fosse. The movie star scene is in Fellini's original, although Cabiria hides in his bathroom and not his closet. Simon also retained Fosse's original opening image of Charity being shoved into the orchestra pit (representing a Central Park pond) by her purse-snatching date.

The decision to change the prostitute Cabiria into the dance hostess Charity was made as a concession to modern morality although the implication that she is also a prostitute remained. This plot point allowed for Oscar's eventual rejection of her because he cannot accept her sexual history. Making Charity a hostess also permitted Fosse to show the sleazy Broadway dance hall where she worked and the seamier side of show business that he knew so well. The expected lighthearted entertainment for a musical comedy had an underbelly of sadness since its heroine was a victimized innocent loved by what Fosse called an emotional pacificist, i.e., someone afraid to feel.

The book cut some of the even darker material from the screenplay, like Cabiria being pushed into the river at the beginning which nearly causes her to drown and how in the climax she asks Alberto to kill her. Fellini's Cabiria was a tough, abrasive and rather unlikable Roman streetwalker who behaved more aggressively than Charity, evident by her general attitude and her attacking a prostitute who makes fun of her. This was changed since Charity had to be likable for us to empathize with her as a girl who wanted to be loved. The film's plot point of Cabiria as an aging prostitute was an issue that was not carried over into the book, and the ambiguity about whether Oscar marries Cabiria was also not repeated. In the film he revealed that he only wanted the money she obtained from selling her house as a dowry, and he did not express a disapproval of her life as a prostitute. Another lost plot point is the idea that she was short of stature which was highlighted when she and Alberto Lazzaril—the Vittorio Vidal character—danced together. This loss is a surprise given the difference in heights between the 5-foot 3 Verdon and the 6-foot John McMartin who was cast as Oscar.

All the other parts were cast with dancers and this included Verdon, who at age forty got herself into shape for the part. Dancer Lee Roy Reams told the story of how he knew at the audition that Fosse didn't like him, he thought because he wore ballet tights and not dance pants. However Reams felt that Verdon did like him because she kept looking at him as they worked through the male dancers' auditions. It got down to two dancers left for the part of Young Spanish Man. Reams wasn't worried by the fact that the other dancer was Puerto Rican, since he had taken Spanish at university, and he got the part because his trills were better. Reams said that Verdon and he began a friendship and that she was always very kind to him. He also saw the moment when Fosse commented that a move of his that Verdon had executed was no good. She defended it by saying that it was wonderful and Fosse responded with "Everything I do looks good on you." Fosse said that he could never tell if it was really good or not.

One of the show's stage managers Paul Phillips got the job thanks to Verdon. He had known her son Jimmy when he, Jimmy, was in the national company of the comedy *Take Her, She's Mine* which Phillips was also the stage manager for. In March 1963, when Verdon was in hospital to give birth to Nicole, Jimmy was taken to hospital by Phillips for an appendix operation. His parents needed to be called for permission for the procedure so Jimmy told Phillips that his mother was Verdon—something that he had kept secret from the company. Permission was given and Jimmy had the operation. This meant that he could not do the show, so Phillips filed in for him, and also gave the additional paychecks he earned to Jimmy. A year or so later, Phillips received a phone call from Verdon who told him that she wanted him as one of the stage managers for *Sweet Charity*. Phillips was thrilled because he needed a job and he joined the company on the first day of rehearsal.

Rehearsals began in August 1965. Verdon joined Fosse at Variety Arts and he discovered anew the excitement of seeing his steps on her body. He said that working on the show together rekindled their love and that he couldn't believe how talented she was. In turn Verdon saw that he was grinning, not at the results, but at her. Believing he was being pleased by her was more stimulating than rousing an entire audience. They would pop in for a midnight sandwich at Dinty Moore's. Then, as waiters cleared the tables and scrubbed up, if something ignited them the couple would go the Dinty's kitchen and rehearse more.

Fosse had trouble with the "Big Spender" number, telling Verdon that it stank and that he couldn't finish it because he didn't know what to do. She said that he started getting in a panic about what he could do because all the women dancers were waiting for him. Verdon kept telling him to finish it by doing it badly and then he could fix it. So he went out and she stood right next to him and she would finish his sentences when he tried to say what he wanted. Verdon said that he wanted them to come down and entice men. Some sources claim that Fosse's block came from his ambivalence towards the underside of life that the material confronted him with, but he managed to finish the number. Verdon also had input into the stage design for the show since it came from the way she thought and the way her brain and Fosse's brain worked. The proscenium was fractured into jagged pieces, the way a child would make it. To this Fosse added filmic touches of silent-movie titles, fast scene changes, and iris-in techniques for closeup effects.

Verdon made her sixth and final *Danny Kaye* guest appearance which was broadcast on December 1, 1965 before *Sweet Charity* rehearsals had begun. She performed a western dance to the song "Mexico" sung by fellow guest star D'Aldo Romano, and appeared in a skit as a liberated woman. A still from the show shows Kaye and Verdon singing with their arms outstretched as they stand in front of a staircase.

Since Charity did not appear in the numbers "Big Spender" and "Rich Man's Frug," she acted as Fosse's assistant for them. Lee Roy Reams felt that Verdon did not present herself as the show's star. She was part of the company as much as she was part of Fosse. There was no set delineation of responsibility, although natural tendencies emerged. Fosse as the director kept watch over the bigger picture while Verdon the dancer honed in on the details. One dancer said that Verdon could break the steps down in a way that he could not. Having done his shows for so long, Verdon had an eye on how to do them technically—she knew how to get where he wanted to go.

The dancers laughed at costumer Irene Sharaff's pleas to be careful with her expensive and delicate glittering dresses (made from French silk) with silk stockings and hand-sewn beads. The effort of both of the chorus numbers exhausted them and, as expected, the clothes did not survive the first dress rehearsal performance. They were scrapped and Verdon came up with the solution. But first she had to deal with her own costume. Sharaff had designed a range of costumes for Charity to wear in the show. These included a lime green dress with a purple slip underneath, designed in a fishhook style with a very tight bodice that flared out at the bottom. She had started rehearsing in a Norman Norel evening gown with a slip in it, but finding that she didn't need the slip, she cut it off. She then reverted to the slip, with a handbag with a rope on it. The handbag was useful because it allowed Verdon to change between scenes. Sharaff had designed a costume for her that was similar to the slip that was covered with crocheted black balls. But the balls kept falling off and getting in the way. They didn't allow for a clean line and she couldn't sit down with them. Also, Verdon thought the dress should be like a uniform, very much like Edith Piaf. It was felt by Fosse and presumably Verdon that the impact would be stronger if she stayed in the same little black dress. However a costume was used for the number "There's Gotta Be Something Better Than This." It was hot pink and had a big swishy skit and Fosse had her do the costume change onstage. This sometimes caused an audible gasp from the audience when Verdon's nearly nude body was revealed. Although she looked sensational, it was still thought to be shocking to see a middle-aged woman like that. A further costume crisis occurred when Verdon's first scene in the dance hall was upstaged by a handmade robe sewn with big and colorful patches and sequins and beads worn by a chorus girl. Fosse ordered it out.

Verdon's solution for the other dancers occurred when they went for lunch and she had the seamstresses make up similar shifts with individual variations. When the dancers returned an hour later, they had new and more practical costumes. Dancer Gene Foote says that Verdon bought eight identical black sheaths from Lerners. She slit them up the side, took a piece off the original costume and stuck them somewhere, and the helmets finished the new costumes. Another source claims that the costume problem came from Fosse because he felt they overpowered his numbers, specifically "Big Spender." He said that he hated them and that they were too bright and shiny, not seedy enough. Fosse also commented that the seven little circles to indicate seven sequins in her sketches became blinding sequins on stage. In response Sharaff supposedly stormed down the aisle with a collection of sketches and threw them in his lap. She reminded Fosse that he had previously approved them and it was Fosse who had them spray-painted to tone them down. Dresses that had cost thousands of dollars were painted over the sequins and the frilly trims were ripped off. One source even claims that Fosse personally did the spray-painting. Kathryn Doby, one of the company dancers, reported that she had a paisley print dress and every single pattern on it was sequined and beaded. She thought it was so beautiful that it belonged in a museum, but it was not suitable for that kind of chorus girl. Doby also agreed that the costumes were upstaging and impractical, like the gloves that slowed down fast costume changes. She said that Fosse had Sharaff take her costume and put it on a mannequin, and it was the designer who sprayed it until there was practically nothing left of the original. This was naturally not a pleasant experience for her and Doby said that she could see the agony on Sharaff's face.

This was not to be a show about costumes but rather a vehicle for Verdon to showcase her unique combination of sexuality and humor. To highlight this fact, the poster art used her opening pose from the show, peering over her shoulder with a come-hither look of impure innocence. One hand casually rested on her jaunty bottom, one knee was locked and the other playfully bent, the foot rested back on her high heel with the toe up in the air. The look represented the distillation of Fosse's interest: minimalism with precise movement and detail for effect. Even Verdon's curled pinkie on the hand that she had on her thigh was meant to show dance in stopped action. The broken look of Charity, being pigeon-toed and knock-kneed like the young Verdon in her orthopedic braces, also said resilience. She said that she had taken the posture from the perfume salesladies at Bloomingdale's, whose feet burned from standing in heels and who shifted the weight from one foot to another. Verdon also took the kind of movement she observed from teenagers and the way they would sit with their legs wrapped around each other. This movement was used for the show's opening number which demonstrated Charity's goofy and nutsy nature.

Verdon built the character of Charity from the dance hall women, and the image of Cabiria hugging the chicken. The actress felt that the woman just wanted something to love. Although the sign for the show would read that it was the story of a girl who wanted to be loved, Verdon believed that it was really the story of a girl who wanted to love someone.

She again took what she had learned from Olivier to help create her character, beginning with the dress, her discovery of a need for a handbag, and then the discovery that she had to get off her feet because they were killing her most of the time. These details piled up and when you added the song lyrics, it was quite a combination. The handbag had a rope for a handle since Fosse wanted Charity to have a swayback look.

Another aspect was Charity's use of foul language. Verdon had seen many young girls who used it though they weren't even aware that it was foul because it was the only language they knew. This was equally true of Charity because she didn't know that she was saying things that were offensive. She told Vittorio Vidal that if someone insulted her, she would answer with "Up yours." Verdon decided that the line should be performed just like you might say, "Oh, eat a banana" or "Take a flying leap to the moon." The vulgarity was lessened because of the character's kind of innocence.

She also worked on how to integrate the songs into the character. Before rehearsals began, Verdon started to learn the song lyrics and the music for the show, as always. She sometimes worked with a pianist, and sometimes the composer would make her a piano dub of just the music. As Verdon learned her dances, she realized that she had to breathe and that she wouldn't be able to sing that long when she was required to do both simultaneously. She had to figure out when was the best time to breathe on these occasions. She found one place in "If My Friends

Portrait of Verdon from the stage show *Sweet Charity* **(1966–1967).**

7. Sweet Charity 111

Could See Me Now" where lyricist Dorothy Fields did not want her to breathe. Fields asked her to breather after "pow" but Verdon found that she couldn't sing that far into the line without breathing. A solution was to breathe on "landed," and then take a big breath. Then her dress exploded, popping open in response to the deep breathing. So the next time Verdon had to breathe not quite so vigorously, and Fields had no more comment on the line's delivery.

Before the company began tryouts, Fosse and Verdon had lunch with 20th Century-Fox executive Robert Linden in New York about an offer from Hollywood. George Cukor was making a new musical called *Bloomer Girl* to star Shirley MacLaine. It had been originally produced on Broadway in 1944 and was a smash hit, but Fosse had concerns about the timing. He decided to wait before making the final decision but the project was cancelled by Fox in March 1966.

Sweet Charity had tryouts in Philadelphia at the Shubert Theatre from December 6, 1965, and in Detroit at the Fisher Theatre from December 22. Cy Coleman said that after the first preview there were lines around the block. It was also reported that in Philadelphia police were called in at ten a.m. after reviews came out. This was to supervise a line of prospective ticket buyers who pushed their way to the box office. The stampede became a riot and the box office was closed until the pandemonium subsided. The show sold out its run and scalpers were said to have got two hundred dollars for a ticket that would only cost ten dollars on Broadway.

Fosse had fun rehearsing his wife and John McMartin in their hotel's bathtub with the shower curtain drawn to capture the claustrophobia that Oscar felt in the elevator scene. However the team was concerned that the show made such a demand on Verdon and feared that it would end prematurely, the way *Redhead* had. This first became apparent when she refused to sing the two slow songs in the show, "Where Am I Going" and "Poor Everybody Else." It was thought that perhaps Fosse agreed with her but he allowed Verdon to be the one to take the flack, since the director's limited enthusiasm for slow songs was well known. She argued to Coleman that she had a small voice and that she would do one of the songs but not both. Fosse told Coleman that he could pick the one to be dropped. When the composer hesitated, he was told that if he did not choose, then the choice would be made for him. "Poor Everybody Else" was cut. (Coleman would later use it his 1973 Broadway musical *Seesaw*.) Then Verdon refused to sing "Where Am I Going." She had decided that she hated it and she begged Coleman to cut it. One source claims that her ego was dented by the fact that the song had been recorded by Barbra Streisand

and released prior to the show's opening. However Streisand's version was not released until after her television special *Color Me Barbra* (broadcast on March 30, 1966) in which she performed the song, after the Broadway opening.

The director found he had to differentiate between the show's needs and his star-wife's. He had to recognize whether she was incapable of performing the number convincingly or just afraid to try. Fosse decided that the song was to stay and in reaction, Verdon made herself unavailable for some performances. Another approach she had was to skip the song altogether; the *New York Times* (April 17, 1966) reported that she had done this at matinees. It said she also dropped the opening number, "You Should See Yourself," although both songs were said to be restored for the evening performances. Robert Fryer would explain that Verdon did so out of illness. When he was asked why audiences were not warned of the planned omissions, he replied that it was something that he would talk to his star about. When one audience member wrote to her complaining, Verdon supposedly divided the ticket cost by the length of the show and sent him a refund for the amount of minutes he missed. If it is true that she was bothered by the Streisand comparison over "Where Am I Going," she was presumably less concerned over the fact that Peggy Lee had performed "Big Spender" before the show opened. This was done by Lee in her act in New York's Copacabana nightclub and perhaps less of a concern since Verdon did not sing the song.

The Fosses were joined by Nicole, her nanny, and Paddy Chayefsky for the tryouts. The show was considered a hit. The director was particularly pleased with a bit of vaudeville business he had added in the scene where Charity hides in the closet, which always got a laugh. He had her light a cigarette and blow the smoke into a clear plastic garment bag and zip it shut, fearing discovery. However something else happened in the same scene that was not as funny: Also in the closet with Verdon was a feather boa and she inhaled one of its feathers. Afterwards she complained of respiratory trouble and in a few days she was wheezing. Still Verdon made every performance and continued to coach the dancers for hours after each show. Then she found it difficult to breathe and said that she could feel something in her throat. Apparently the duck feather from the boa had wrapped around her vocal chords. Verdon kept playing in the show until her voice grew so raspy and her discomfort so intense that it was decided to take her to a hospital. The next performance was cancelled to allow her understudy, Helen Gallagher, to run through the part. (She had been also cast as Nickie so *her* understudy, Elaine Cancilla, filled in

7. Sweet Charity   113

for that part.) Gallagher would play Charity for a week but Verdon came back fully recovered for the Broadway run, and Gallagher and Cancilla assumed their original roles. During the Broadway run, Gallagher would again get the opportunity to play the title role during Verdon's absences. She would say that when she was initially asked by the producers to play a secondary role in the show and be Verdon's stand-by, she agreed without qualms. Gallagher claimed she might have had trouble doing so for a star she did not respect but she found Verdon unsurpassed. She said she would wait in the wings and watch her dance and wonder what muscles she was using for a particular move. Verdon moved like spun spit and no effort showed. Gallagher never thought that she ought to be in her place because Verdon belonged there. She also felt proud that she was there to make an actress feel secure when she was needed.

It was reportedly in the tryouts that Simon added the idea of Oscar being a claustrophobe who gets stuck in an elevator with Charity. However some sources claim that it was one of the first ideas that he had suggested to Fosse after reading the draft. Fosse had supposedly had the couple first meet in a group therapy scene which Simon disliked. What gave the writer the new idea was a real-life experience that supposedly occurred one day when he was attempting to leave the Jefferson Hotel to go to the theater with his wife Joan. Their elevator stalled and, Simon being a claustrophobe, he panicked as they waited to be rescued. Joan tried to keep Simon calm by playing trivia games with him but he kept getting more and more agitated. Sweating profusely, he removed his jacket then his tie, fanning himself with his hat. When they were finally rescued and the elevator opened into the hotel's lobby, the couple disembarked but then he suddenly told Joan that he had to get back in. Simon told her that he needed to go back to their room to write down the scene they had just lived through, which he did.

The tryouts also highlighted what was seen as a weak ending. Fosse had asked Stanley Donen to see the show and this was something he agreed with. Simon had ended with Charity being left at the altar by Oscar and again being pushed into the lake as she had in the play's beginning. McMartin playing Oscar said that people in the audience, specifically women, already booed at him after the show so he dreaded a proposed *darker* ending. Simon resisted Fosse's request and kept his ending. Charity emerged from the lake with hope, even after a cheap gag with a good fairy who turns out to be a television advertising shill. Verdon told Margery Beddow she had proposed a different ending. In hers, a hot dog and souvenir vendor appeared next to Charity after she emerged from the lake and he gave her a balloon. She wrote a note and said the words aloud: "Whoever you are and wherever you are, I love you" and then tied the note to the balloon and released it to the sky. However, this ending was never used.

When the show came to New York, Verdon reportedly decorated her Palace Theatre dressing room in shades of Army khaki green. After ten previews from January 18, 1966, it opened on January 29. Accompanying the *New York Times* article on January 23 about the Palace was an Al Hirschfeld caricature of Verdon in the show. The theater renovations included a reduction in the seating capacity, with the second balcony closed. Some say this was Fosse's idea because he wanted to establish intimacy with the audience and felt that the crows' nest seats worked against that. Verdon would say that it was her idea since she felt that the sightlines would not give ticket buyers a good view of the performance.

The opening date had been postponed from December 28, 1965, and then from January 25, 1966, because the renovations were taking longer than expected, according to a spokesman for the show. The day before the opening, Fellini gave Verdon a cornetta—a curved horn that was the traditional symbol of good luck. The opening night crowd included Verdon's father who flew in from California. Also attending was Martin Charnin, Fosse's abandoned collaborator, who would eventually succeed in a suit against the show's producers for payment for his contribution. The opening night party was originally planned to be held at the Rainbow Room in Rockefeller Center but changed to the Skylight Roof of the Waldorf Astoria Hotel. Ed Sullivan was one of the attendees which no doubt helped Verdon mend the rift between them.

The show received a mixed review from the *Times'* Stanley Kauffmann on January 31, 1966. He partly blamed Fosse for Verdon's "playing so unremittingly in the brave-pathetic vein that she frequently repeats effects," though he acknowledges that she was a first-class performer. On February 25, 1966, in the *Times* was another mixed review by Clive Barnes, though he wrote that Fosse's choreography for Verdon gave her gamine charm its full chance. The show was a hit and would run till July 15, 1967. The image of Verdon's black slip and rope-handled bag was also marketed on program souvenir books and shopping bags in Times Square. The show was nominated for nine Tony Awards including Verdon for Best Actress in a Musical but only Fosse won for Best Choreography. Verdon was beaten by Angela Lansbury in *Mame*.

The original Broadway cast recording was made on February 6, 1966, and released the next day. The album featured opening night party interviews including one with Verdon. She said that she wasn't nervous before the show because she usually got very calm (but she didn't know if that was good). She said she liked the show and wasn't tired after it, because she liked Charity since she was so hopeful.

The cast recording was reviewed by John S. Wilson in the *New York Times*. He wrote that Verdon worked wonders with her oddly charming voice, and though the score was not one that added magnificence or soaring lyricism to a song, it was not one that has much to be magnificent or lyrical *about*. Wilson said that Verdon's primary contributions were touches of color (illuminating what might otherwise be ordinary lines) and perceptive shadings of expression that helped to bring out ideas that the composer and lyricist have not made explicit in their songs. Verdon helped to make a generally adequate score seem better than it was.

Some of the theater's renovations proved to be problematic during the run. The old dressing rooms had been removed to expand the backstage area and a high-speed elevator rose ten flights above the stage to new ones. Verdon was critical of this alteration since she felt that the basement should have been restored so that players could change there during the show. Air conditioning had not been included in the renovations, and to cope with the record summer heat, a fan blew over a block of ice. Verdon apparently placed a thermometer backstage and when it recorded the temperature as 107 degrees one day the matinee performance was cancelled. She also reported that dancers fainted onstage from the heat. Another unfortunate event occurred when a workman accidently broke into a sewer line which resulted in waste floating all over the basement. The cast complained to Actors Equity and the union suggested the producers buy the performers galoshes. Verdon said that there were rats backstage as big as cats, and roaches that she photographed with a shoe next to them to show their size. Between the heat and the fumes, people began to get sick. The producers did nothing to solve the problem until Verdon got an attorney and sued Equity for non-representation, which finally led to things getting fixed. She told Equity that she would not do the show until the problems were solved and she refused to go on, although her standby did. They then closed down the show the next day and cancelled the next matinee but that night there was air conditioning. It was said only the dancers' loyalty to Fosse made them stay and endure such unacceptable conditions.

Verdon was off for six shows in the week prior to May 16, 1966, because of a virus ailment. She was replaced by her understudy, Helen Gallagher, although it was reported that the absence of Verdon meant a drop in earnings for the show. Gallagher also filled in when Verdon went on a two-week vacation from July 11 to 25 and then from June 30, 1967, when she left the show after emergency surgery. Gallagher was replaced in her role of Nickie by Charlene Ryan, who stepped out of the chorus. Lee Roy Reams says that he gave his notice on opening night because he had been offered three times the money to work with Juliet Prowse. He reported that on his last night on the show, when his Young Spanish Man was meant to pull Verdon out of the orchestra pit, she refused to give him her hands. Rather she placed her feet in his face, so he had to pull her up by them. Reams interpreted that as a sign that she didn't want him to leave.

Verdon was interviewed by the *Times*' Rex Reed in an article entitled "I Never Wanted to Be Special" (February 6, 1966). The interview took place in her Palace dressing room where she sprawled on her chaise lounge. He described his subject as tall, freckled, with big bones and long muscles and a head of hair that looked like a tomato surprise that just exploded. Verdon actually asked Reed not to write about her flame-colored tresses, and she defended wearing a mink coat over her rehearsal pants by saying that she didn't want to catch cold because she was sick so much of the time. Verdon commented that everybody wanted to know what she had been doing since *Redhead* and she told Reed that it included getting married, some television, taking dance lessons from Cyd Charisse's sister-in-law and having Nicole. The star said that she also had stomach trouble and two of the top specialists in New York treated her for ulcers and hepatitis when she was actually pregnant. Verdon reported that after sixteen working hours a day, she and Fosse now planned to do nothing for a while except stay home with the baby. To sustain her energy in the show she drank beef bouillon with soda crackers and two tablespoons of cottage cheese for the potassium. Verdon also took a special formula vitamin pill that Cornell University made up for pilots on bombing missions during the war to keep the fat built up on the nerve ends. She felt that she would never make another Hollywood movie because their idea of a movie star is a girl with a big bosom who can do a couple of chorus kicks. Verdon believed that she was not box office so asked rhetorically, who would pay to see her in a movie? Another problem was that she did not think she was sexy and that she only kids sex, like in the Lola number in *Damn Yankees*.

Verdon also talked about what she saw as a character flaw: It took her a long time but once she decided to do something, she tried so hard to make it perfect that she was never satisfied. Verdon doesn't classify it as ambition, since she also did carpentry and approached it the same way.

7. Sweet Charity

She and Fosse were photographed in their New York apartment on March 24, 1966, by Martha Holmes for *Life* magazine. Verdon wore a dark checked dress with light jacket and scarf and sat in a chair smiling up at Fosse, who sat on the chair's left arm. In an article by Thomas Thompson on *Sweet Charity* that appeared in the March 25, 1966, *Life*, he reported that Verdon was forty-one years old and a grandmother but you would never guess it from the way she "prances with legs, arms and tangerine hair flying." The article also featured photographs of Verdon in the show, as well a shot of Fosse with her in her dressing room after a matinee performance with her seated wearing a robe. The main photograph for the article is Verdon in Charity's little black dress and handbag, with her right leg raised and her figure backed by pink lights.

During one *Sweet Charity* matinee, Verdon heard that Fosse had chest pains and she was unable to be with him because she was required to stay for the evening performance. Later Fosse denied having the pains but implied that he faked them to make his wife give an even greater performance that night. However the director became bitter about the show, feeling that Verdon undeservingly got more credit for it than he. Cary Grant saw the show and told Verdon that she was the strangest actor he had ever watched. When she played a happy scene he cried and when she played a sad scene he laughed. This particularly irked Fosse since he had directed Verdon to do this. Perhaps his frustration also came out of how her performing in the show left him alone at night, and his amphetamine use which made it difficult for him to sleep. These things would supposedly lead Fosse to seek the company of other women. Ironically he would never go to see Verdon in her dressing room before or after the show once it had opened, and never took her out afterwards. Others in the *Sweet Charity* cast saw that she appeared lonely, and brief visits to cheer her up extended to hour-long ones where they gossiped and sewed stuffed animals for Nicole. Ruth Buzzi said that she was in there most nights of the week. Care was taken by Verdon's visitors not to mention her absent husband, a subject the leading lady also never brought up.

She herself felt that the high point of doing the show was going home at night because it was so exhausting. She didn't know it when she was on stage but by the end of the evening she was just dead. *Redhead* may have been the most difficult show to perform in terms of acting, singing and dancing, but she was thirty-five when that opened. Verdon found that there was a big difference between what her body could do at thirty-five and what it could do at forty-one. It must not have escaped her notice that many of the chorus dancers were teenage girls, which made her feel even older. Perhaps by comparing herself to these girls, she felt obsolescent. Verdon was also afraid that the show would be her last, and once commented to a reporter backstage that she hoped that all the fuses would blow so that she wouldn't have to perform.

She made her first of six guest appearances on NBC's *The Merv Griffin Show* on an episode broadcast on March 29, 1966. On April 3, 1966, in New York, Verdon appeared as the mystery guest on the episode of *What's My Line?* which was broadcast on May 15. On April 4, the *New York Times* reported that Verdon had asked the owners of the Palace that the 301 seats in the unused gallery be made available at no charge to servicemen and drama and dance students. Joe Nederlander reported that he was all for it and that the seat covers would be removed and that section of the house would be spruced up so that arrangements could be made by the next week. On April 5, Verdon rode an elephant called Sweet Charity. It was part of the benefit held at the Ringling Brothers and Barnum & Bailey Circus in Madison Square Garden to help the French Hospital.

On April 17, 1966, the *New York Times* reported that it would be Chita Rivera and not Verdon who would be taking the show to London. A date was not given for the opening though rehearsals were set to take place in December 1966 or January 1967 depending on the availability of Fosse. On April 29, 1966, Verdon was to attend the Bedside Network of the Veterans Hospital Radio and Television Guild's 18th anniversary ball at the Waldorf Astoria Grand Ballroom. (She was one of the vice chairman of the ball.) The proceeds were to help the network continue to bring leading professional entertainers to Veterans Administration hospitals. Verdon also helped to arrange a benefit gala on June 8, 1966, at the Society of Illustrators with proceeds going to the Postgraduate Center for Mental Health. Sponsored by the women's division of the Center, it would include a discotheque, buffet and an exhibition of contemporary illustrations. On July 31, 1966, Verdon was honored by the dance teachers' organization, the Dance Masters of America, at the teachers' annual ball at the Statler Hilton Hotel. She received a plaque in recognition of her contribution to the art of the dance.

Verdon was a guest on the NBC *Late Show* hosted by Sammy Davis, Jr., which was broadcast on August 5, 1966. On August 17 she was a guest of host Bob Newhart on the show. The *New York Times* reported on August 29 that Verdon made her second guest appearance on *The Merv Griffin Show*. However, according to other sources, the same guest stars actually appeared on the show on July 20, 1967. There is a clip on YouTube of Verdon on the show with Adam West and Burt Ward being interviewed about

Batman, and it is dated September 1, 1966. Verdon says that the *Batman* television series is educational for children and cites the examples of how they look before crossing the road and clean their teeth. She is wearing a white lace dress with spaghetti straps and a white ribbon in her hair.

On September 25, 1966, Verdon modelled a white crepe Geoffrey Beene dress with big ruffles around the neck for a fashion show ballet produced by the American Ballet Theatre Company and the Fashion Designers of America. The event was held at the St. James Theatre. The proceeds were applied to the matching fund grant made to the Ballet Theatre in 1965 by the National Council of the Arts and were to be used for increased salaries for the company and a new four-act production of *Swan Lake.*

Verdon returned to *The Ed Sullivan Show* for her second appearance, which was broadcast on October 2, 1966. Sullivan says in his introduction that down through the years he has aged considerably trying to lasso her for his show. In the show she performs "I'm a Brass Band" and with the Company dancers. The number begins in a filmic way with an extreme closeup of Verdon's face so that we can see her powder-blue eyes. It then cuts to a long shot of her in spotlight. She wears the Charity signature black dress covered with a blue coat with pink interior lining, black high boots, and a black ribbon in her hair. Lights come up on a set which has a blue backlight and an archway with a banner which reads "Charity Is in Love" with the wording surrounded by colored heart shapes. Verdon removes the coat which she throws around as she sings before tossing it off-stage. She is joined by the male dancers and the backlighting changes to orange. Verdon claps her hands and the sound of a cymbal is heard and the music changes to a faster tempo. She is joined at different times by two dancers, or four, or all the dancers, as they appear behind her and follow her around as she dances. The dancers also sing the song to Verdon, and the number ends with her being handed back her blue coat and a suitcase by hands off-stage. The orange lighting changes back to the blue and she holds the coat over her shoulder. Verdon then presents the suitcase which has "Almost Married" written on it on the edge of the stage, which she hides behind as she finishes singing the song.

Verdon was back on *The Merv Griffin Show* on October 13, 1966. On November 13 she was one of the entertainers at the annual dinner dance of the National Tay-Sachs and Allied Diseases Association at the Grand Ballroom of the Waldorf Astoria. Besides research into Tay-Sachs and other diseases, the agency supported a 17-bed children's ward at the Brooklyn Jewish Chronic Disease Hospital. On December 2 she was on the dance committee for the Champagne Supper at the Rainbow Room arranged in aid of hemophiliacs. She returned to *The Merv Griffin Show* on November 22.

Fosse said that it was when he went to California to work on the film version of *Sweet Charity* that the marriage to Verdon became strained. His alleged philandering was one thing, presumably something she could tolerate while he remained based in New York, even when he was required to go out of town for show tryouts. But Fosse said that when he wanted to work away, that things changed. No doubt the strain increased when it was decided that Verdon was not be cast in the film.

8

Sweet Charity on Film

Joseph E. Levine had purchased the film rights to *Sweet Charity* following its stage premiere. It was to be produced by Universal Studios, where the head man Lew Wasserman wanted Shirley MacLaine to play the title role. Fosse wanted Verdon for the film and rallied for her. It was reported in Bernard F. Dick's book, *City of Dreams: The Making and Remaking of Universal Pictures* that Verdon was originally considered for the film with Jack Lemmon playing Oscar to ensure a box office name. However, this idea was vetoed by Universal who wanted MacLaine because of her box office value. She had just made the successful comic crime thriller *Gambit* (1966) for Universal. She was also known as a musical-comedy star because of the film version of *Can-Can* though that film had been a box office flop. The issue of age also presumably came into play. Although Charity's age in the stage show was not made specific, MacLaine was nine years younger than Verdon. And perhaps George Abbott's refusal to give Verdon closeups in the film of *Damn Yankees* was weighed against the idea that MacLaine was considered more camera-friendly. Wasserman set Ross Hunter to oversee the new film and MacLaine was signed. It was she who asked for Fosse to direct (the actress claimed that Wasserman didn't know who he was). MacLaine also claimed that Verdon didn't wish to play the part. Fosse did not get along with Hunter, who wanted to change the look of the show and sanitize the character of Charity. An example was that he didn't want her to say "Up yours." MacLaine supported Fosse and convinced Wasserman to let Hunter go. He was replaced by Robert Arthur.

Fosse wanted Verdon to work on the film. He asked her how she felt about MacLaine's casting, and his wife told him that it was fine. This was perhaps Verdon's greatest test of generosity, and she supported Fosse because she felt that the property was one that he had instigated. The film could only be made with a successful movie star, which Verdon knew she wasn't. She also knew that if Fosse passed on the film because of Verdon, that someone else would do it. She agreed to join her husband in Hollywood after the show closed on Broadway on July 15, 1967.

Verdon was on the dance committee for a champagne supper dance and midnight auction held at the Rainbow Room on December 2, 1966, to benefit the National Hemophilia Foundation. She returned for her third *Ed Sullivan Show* appearance (March 5 1967). Verdon performed "If My Friends Could See Me Now" with James Luisi from *Sweet Charity*. She plays the scene with Vittorio Vidal that leads to the song, wearing the Charity black dress, stockings and black shoes. The set is Vittorio's bedroom. Verdon's singing is interrupted by the two exits and entrances of Vittorio as he brings her his popping top hat and cane. She scores a laugh by straightening up the bed when he returns and catches her jumping on it. At the end of the song, Vittorio (Luisi) returns and kisses Verdon's hand.

On April 14, 1967, she attended the 19th Anniversary Ball for Bedside Network at the New York Hilton Hotel. She was co-chairman of the dinner dance. On June 22 she underwent emergency surgery for a cyst at the New York Hospital, which ended her run in *Sweet Charity* on stage. It was reported in the *New York Times* on October 13, 1968, that Verdon had turned down the title role in the Broadway production of Tennessee Williams' play *The Seven Descents of Myrtle* to be with Fosse in California. Myrtle was a sometime prostitute and former showgirl, who has recently married a tubercular neurotic youth who is an impotent transvestite overly attached to the memory of his late mother. She dwells in a fantasy world of romantic illusions and takes up with her husband's multi-racial half-brother. Williams had suggested Verdon for the part; it would have been her straight play debut. But producer David Merrick could not wait for her to become free, and Estelle Parsons was cast instead. The play, directed by Jose Quintero, opened at the Ethel Barrymore Theatre on March 27, 1968, and ran for only twenty-nine performances.

Rehearsals had begun with MacLaine in the fall of 1967 in advance of Verdon's arrival. Fosse worked with Sonja Haney as his assistant. Verdon brought Nicole with her to California and joined Fosse in a rented house in Westwood, close to the ocean that they loved. Although the couple was sharing a home, Fosse was seen at the Universal Studios commissary with a girlfriend. Verdon was said to have been a distant presence when she attended rehearsals, hovering without meddling, like a mother at a school dance. Occasionally she would do barre work in an empty studio by herself. Verdon could also be seen whispering in Fosse's ear.

Some were surprised at how she could keep up such a congenial attitude under the circumstances. John McMartin, who was retained for the part of Oscar for the film, said that he felt Verdon's heart must have been broken over MacLaine's casting. The moves were her moves, but he found her stoic. Chita Rivera, who was cast as Nickie, commented that the fact that Verdon was there at all blew her away, but dancers do what they have to do. Verdon did it for Jack Cole and for Fosse, and Rivera sensed no resentment coming from her. Verdon just did the job. That was her point of view in work and in love. Lee Roy Reams, another member of the stage show cast in the film, commented that it was horrid to watch Verdon showing MacLaine the choreography. He felt that MacLaine was wonderful but after seeing Verdon do it, anything else was an imitation. Others may have thought that being Fosse's dramaturge and ubiquitous assistant was a sad and selfless position for her to take but she thought it was a good deal for her, considering the alternative.

One evening Richard Kiley and his wife Pat Ferrier came to dinner. Ferrier had danced with Verdon in *Damn Yankees* and *Redhead*, and Verdon confessed to her friend her fears of growing older. She admitted that it wasn't age or death that worried her as much as the idea of her dancing coming to an end. Verdon had sacrificed her career somewhat by going into semi-retirement to have Nicole, and now the biological clock was running out on her. She felt that she had passed her peak now just as Fosse was reaching his. Naturally the situation was complicated by the fact of Verdon being his wife, but she also saw herself as the guardian of his style, its oldest representative and its most expert practitioner. She knew more about Fosse's work than anyone else and was an unbeatable back catalogue for him, which made her essential even after her body gave out. He used Verdon with Haney to watch the dancers so that he was freed up to focus on the camera.

Verdon taught all Charity's routines to MacLaine. They became very good friends. According to MacLaine, it wasn't in Verdon's nature to be competitive; she attributed this to the idea that dancers were a special breed. MacLaine said that among the things that Verdon taught her were secrets of how to balance steps with breaths, and tricks with hats. However Fosse said that it was MacLaine's idea to add a hat trick from "Steam Heat" to "If My Friends Could See Me Now" that wasn't in the original choreography. This was evidence that MacLaine was not just to be a carbon copy of Verdon's performance. MacLaine said that Verdon also brought her several photos of people she thought the screen character should look like. Verdon's contribution to the film also included dubbing the dances of Sammy Davis, Jr. With his gold jewelry hung on her, she shook to get the sound of all those chains. She said this was done to save money.

The *New York Times* of October 13, 1968, reported that Verdon was considering a part in the play *Her Bed, His Couch* by Lawrence Roman which was to be produced by Frederick Brisson. What made her hesitate was the choice of director. She claimed if she was going to fail she wanted to fail with the best. Verdon wanted Fosse but he was still working on the film *Sweet Charity*. The role she had been offered was a prostitute (again) who has a relationship with a psychiatrist. The play was not produced. Verdon said she was interested in doing something worthwhile off–Broadway and that she would work for a lot less than money than thought. While in California, Verdon made the first of two guest appearances on the CBS family comedy series *The Carol Burnett Show* that was broadcast on October 16, 1967. In the show Verdon sang "The 59th Street Bridge Song."

The Ed Sullivan Show's twentieth anniversary episode was broadcast on December 10, 1967. This was Verdon's fourth appearance on the show and on it she performed "Nothing Can Stop Me Now!," a Leslie Bricusse-Anthony Newley song from the musical *The Roar of the Greasepaint—The Smell of the Crowd*, with a chorus of six dancers in white uniforms. Verdon is heard before she is seen in the number, singing as two dancers holding white drums pass Sullivan. She emerges from the largest drum which is brought on stage by two other dancers; on it is written "Congratulations Ed." Pushing through the drum's cover, she wears a white majorette outfit with a black angled slash, slit-skirt and high white boots, and she holds a baton. Sullivan remains on stage next to the drum, and she hits a smaller drum and a cymbal on a drum as they pass her. The large drum is moved and Verdon gets out of it to dance with the chorus. The dance includes the chorus beating drums as she dances around them, and all the dancers marching together after the drums are raised off the floor. The choreography suggests it was done by Fosse, with its use of the group in synchronized movement, recalling the "I'm a Brass Band" number from *Sweet Charity*.

The staging has an interesting change when a curtain behind the dancers is opened to reveal an orange-colored backdrop, with the raised drums hanging in the air. The original six chorus dancers are replaced by twelve soldiers dressed in white, holding rifles, which Verdon dances around. She runs over to Sullivan, gets on her knees and holds his legs until she is pulled back onstage by the chorus dancers where a red material backdrop is raised. They are joined again by the soldiers and, together with the dancers, all the men lie on the floor, then salute for the number's end, as Verdon salutes standing in front of them. We then see the chorus dancers and Verdon leave the stage and exit the theater through the audience.

However she returns to Sullivan for him to hug her and introduce her to the audience. Verdon thanks him and also says thanks to her boys.

Production got underway on *Sweet Charity* in 1968. On the first day of filming, the studio's publicity department held their customary invitation to the press to visit the set. There was a heavy turnout of reporters and photographers. Fosse posed with MacLaine and when Verdon was recognized among the onlookers she was asked to pose with the star. She agreed and it was then revealed to the press how Verdon was coaching MacLaine in how to play the role that she had created. The press harped on this angle, and while it generated added publicity for the film, it surely did not make Verdon happy. During filming Verdon was photographed with MacLaine in costume in rehearsals for "I'm a Brass Band," and with Sammy Davis Jr. in costume in rehearsals for the "Rhythm of Life" number. She was also photographed on the set for "If My Friends Could See Me Now" with MacLaine, on the set of "Big Spender" with Fosse, and with Fosse and MacLaine on the set on MacLaine's birthday on April 24. Filming ended in June 1968.

The film was released on April 2, 1969. Fosse was said to have been so agitated at the New York premiere on April 1 that he abandoned Verdon, who had accompanied him, seeking solace in the Maiden Lane Dance Hall in Times Square. He didn't leave her alone since she had Richard and Pat Kiley.

It received a mixed review by Vincent Canby in the *New York Times*, who wrote that it was haunted by the presence of Verdon. Canby noted that although MacLaine often looks like her, "she never succeeds in recreating the eccentric line that gave cohesion to the original." Canby wrote further about the film in the *Times* article "Is the Cost of *Charity* Too High?" There he said that it tried to ignore the fact that the show was largely successful because of the unique quality of Verdon. Pauline Kael called the film a disaster. It received a mixed review by Clive Hirshhorn in his book *The Universal Story*, but John Baxter in *Hollywood in the Sixties* gave praise. It was a box office flop and not even Universal's attempt to salvage it with a more upbeat ending, where Oscar returns to Charity, saved it.

It's impossible to compare MacLaine's acting performance in the film with Verdon's in the stage version of the show since there is no equitable material available. However a viewing of the film, and the television appearances of Verdon doing "If My Friends Could See Me Now" and "I'm a Brass Band," can provide a comparison in terms of singing and dancing. While Verdon does not have a great singing voice, it is serviceable.

MacLaine's likability and sensitivity compensate somewhat for her weaker singing voice which underwhelms some of the songs Charity sings. An example of this is the "Where Am I Going?" number in which MacLaine's vocal is bad. One can accept MacLaine's voice as it is since Charity is not a professional singer, only a professional dancer. Additionally it adds to the vulnerability of the character. However when Chita Rivera and Paula Kelly sing "There's Gotta Be Something Better Than This," we can hear what a difference a good voice makes.

MacLaine's dancing is better than her singing but it is not as good as Verdon's. This is apparent despite the fact that Verdon's coverage is limited by the mechanic of television filming, where the performance is mostly photographed straight onto the dancer in one long take. MacLaine's performances are viewed with the techniques of cinema. Fosse utilizes editing, different camera angles, and closer coverage which breaks up the flow of a live performance. The effect is influenced by the more realistic sets and locations and costume, since "I'm a Brass Band" provides Charity with a new marching band outfit with striking red long rubber boots and a white hat which sometimes obscures MacLaine's face. One could argue that Fosse is so eager to impress that the focus moves from MacLaine's performance to his directing.

The perception of the superiority of Verdon is colored by the fact that she introduced the moves she performs in the two mentioned numbers, which inevitably makes MacLaine's copying of them disappointing. Another swaying factor is the idea that Verdon was denied the film opportunity so that there is an inherent resentment of MacLaine appropriating the numbers. There is a rumor that MacLaine had an uncredited dance double named Michelle Graham for the film. However it is not as obvious as, say, the dance doubles used for Jennifer Beals in *Flashdance* (1983). Rivera and Kelly may be better dancers but one's eye is drawn to MacLaine when the three are together in the "There's Gotta Be Something Better Than This" number. This explains why MacLaine is a movie star and the two others are not. And also perhaps why Verdon was not.

Verdon was on the committee for the 20th anniversary ball of the Bedside Network which took place on May 3, 1968, at the New York Hilton Hotel. Verdon made her only appearance on the ABC talk show *The Joey Bishop Show* on August 30, 1968. She was next a guest on the CBS comedy *The Jonathan Winters Show* on September 25. Verdon danced to "Sweet Talk" and she and fellow guest Peter Graves joined Winters in a movie spoof of *Planet of the Apes* called "Planet of the Chickens."

She then appeared on the NBC special *The Bob Hope Show* (October

14, 1968), participating in a comedy sketch that ran for over ten minutes. The first part had her seen as Miss Violet C. Drab in a parody of *The Dating Game* called *Celebrity Blind Date*. Introduced as being from Cedar Rapids, Iowa, she is dressed in a black sweater with white collar and yellow corsage, white gloves, a black striped skirt and yellow belt, and black feathered hat which moults. She is called "a reject from *Let's Make a Deal*" by the host and she shakes fearfully. Verdon gets laughs from her nervous behavior and makes this shrinking violet pathetic but touching. The three celebrity blind dates are Los Angeles Rams player Crazy-Head Craniac, movie star Warren Beagle (played by Hope), and the author-playwright Tennessee Gofar. Clearly all are unsuitable dates, being respectively, dumb, vain and presumably gay. To play the game, Violet asks them questions. When she asks Beagle how he would describe himself, he tells her to picture someone between Rock Hudson and Cary Grant. This makes Violet shriek in pleasure. When she asks him if he only had one night to live, who he would want to spend it with, he replies Dr. Christian Bernard. This makes her swoons and she says she loves the way he sounds. Violet chooses Beagle as her date and Verdon cries comically when he is revealed to her. She clutches him, repeating, "Oh I could die," and falls to the floor, holding him by a leg as he moves away from her. Beagle walking off-camera, still being held onto by Violet, is the end of the first part of the sketch.

The second part of the sketch shows Beagle in his apartment, waiting for the date. Violet arrives wearing an orange and brown sleeveless dress with a frilled trim, orange shoes, a fur stole, white large earrings and an orange ribbon in her hair. The scene is a reverse of the one Verdon played in *Sweet Charity*: This time, her character is *not* found charming by a famous man. Regrettably, Beagle's attempt to be nice to her is begrudging, and Violet only captures his interest by knocking him unconscious and kidnapping him. However the narrative undercuts the premise of Violet being desperate for attention and Beagle being full of himself when she finds his kisses disappointing. Verdon makes Violet sweet in the way she says hello to Beagle when he enters the room. Her throwing a glove away when she drinks champagne recalls her glove-throwing from the *Damn Yankees* performance of "Whatever Lola Wants." Violet turns on a radio and dances frantically to the music, moving too fast for the tempo, and she slow-dances with Beagle. The scene also features what appear to be improvised moments. Verdon has a stumbled line reading over "Boy, I've seen a sick mackerel with better pucker power than that" which makes Hope laugh in a surprised reaction. When Violet hits Beagle on the head with the champagne bottle which doesn't break, this leads to him ask, "Is that the right bottle?"

Verdon returns for two dance numbers with Lee Roy Reams and Bud Vest which were choreographed by Fosse. For "Cool Hand Luke" the dancers first appear in shadow for the first minute of the two-minute number. A partial light eventually comes on the dancers, who wear brown Spanish pants outfits with ruffled shirts and black sombreros. For the two-and-a-half-minute "The Tijuana (Mexican) Shuffle" number they are in light. Verdon smokes a cigar and the men have mustaches. The men wore brown shirts, Verdon a brown sweater. The dances incorporate some of Fosse's patented moves. Verdon remains positioned between Reams and Vest during the entire two numbers. The second dance includes slapping the floor and ends with the dancers in shadow as they had begun. A snippet of "The Tijuana Shuffle" appears on the *Highlights of a Quarter of a Century of Bob Hope on Television* special, seen on NBC on October 24, 1975. "Cool Hand Luke" was later featured as part of the Broadway show *Fosse* for which Verdon was the artistic advisor.

She next made her only guest appearance on the CBS musical comedy hour *The Jackie Gleason Show* (November 16, 1968), filmed in Miami Beach, Florida. Also in 1968, Verdon, Kathryn Doby and Louise Quick did "Big Spender" at Madison Square Garden for a benefit for the Chicago Seven. On July 25, 1971, an article in the *New York Times* reported that in 1968 Verdon had flirted with the idea of playing Bananas in John Guare's play *The House of Blue Leaves* but would not make a commitment. The part was eventually played by Katherine Helmond in an off–Broadway production at the Truck and Warehouse Theatre and ran from February 10 to December 3, 1971.

From January 13 to 17, 1969, Verdon made the first of three independent appearances on the CBS daytime talk show *The Mike Douglas Show*. She was the co-host for the week for the show, which was taped in Philadelphia. On the January 17 episode Verdon first appears in a white split-skirt with jacket with a silver angled stripe and white knee-high boots. Introduced with the song "Hey, Look Me Over" from the Broadway musical *Wildcat*, she does some high kicks, and she brings out the show's guests Jack Lord, Lionel Hampton, Paddy Chayefsky, and Cy Coleman. Douglas shows a framed black sketch on white background that the three-and-a-half-year-old Nicole did of Verdon three years earlier, and one of her four Tony Awards. When asked if she is neat at home, Verdon admits that she has one rotten miserable drawer that she allows herself. She says that she thinks you've got to have one thing like that in the house to indulge yourself but otherwise her house is very neat. Douglas knows that Verdon is neat because he has secretly taken snapshots of her dressing room which he shows the audience. She laughs and comments, "How dare you call it a dressing room? I've been in a phone booth all week."

When asking about her early career as a dancer, Douglas shows several photograph of her. These include one from *The Mississippi Gambler*, of her dressed for a Watusi dance in black body and face makeup and white costume with white feathers, and one of her as Eve in *Can-Can*. When Douglas comments on her scanty costume, she says that she had more clothes on then than she has on for the show with him. Verdon reported that the picture shown was going to be the cover of *Look* magazine, and they printed it and all the magazines were sent out but the post office refused to let them to go through the mail. So all the magazines were recalled and the picture was put on the inside and they put Eisenhower on the cover, which the post office accepted. This presumably refers to the March 8, 1955, edition.

Douglas asks Verdon how she got the part in *Sweet Charity* and she jokingly replies, "I'm a friend of the director." Verdon tells of one show that *she* wanted very badly that she was not wanted *for*: *New Girl in Town*. Douglas says that he found out that one of Verdon's secret desires was to perform on Broadway holding a mike. He asks her why she is so thrilled by it, and Verdon tells him because when she sees people on television and in nightclubs holding the mike, she thinks they look at ease and casual. He hands her a mike and sings "I've Got a Crush on You" for Nicole with piano accompaniment, as photographs of Nicole are shown as a baby and as a little girl.

After the commercial break, Verdon is dressed in an off-white shirt with a red tie and gray slacks. Jack Lord places a pink lei on Verdon when he appears and she and Douglas kneel at a table of luau food. The head chef of Trader Vic's, Louis Low, who provided the food, makes an appearance. Verdon eats the smoked raw fish that Low cuts and offers, and says that it is good, and wipes her hands on the blue tablecloth. Back in the chairs, Douglas speaks of his distaste for eating raw fish and Verdon says that she has eaten raw octopus where all the little tentacles touch your face. Following Lionel Hampton's appearance Verdon introduces Paddy Chayefsky. He talks about his play *The Latent Homosexual* which he refuses to do on Broadway, and which she considers brilliant. Verdon describes his protest as very important and Chayefsky claims that it is against the future as a "technocratic society" in which people's only function is to produce and consume.

She removes her lei and joins Cy Coleman at the piano. He accompanies Verdon as she sings "You Should See Yourself" from the stage version of *Sweet Charity*. The coverage of this performance is disappointing since the camera partially views Verdon behind Coleman and she is blocked by his piano microphone. He reports that Verdon worked on the film though he doesn't say that she wasn't cast as the title character, and that he admires her precision. She jokes that she's like the IBM machine Chayefsky was talking about, though he did not specifically mention IBM machines; rather cogs in the wheel of machinery. Douglas brings out a chorus of little girls in colored leotards and white stockings to perform "Big Spender" using a metallic rail. They don't do the original Fosse choreography, but this is not a surprise given their age. After the number Verdon speaks to some individually, and she comments that she knows Mrs. Yvonne Hall as the person who worked with the girls because Nicole has been on one of her shows. Verdon says that the girls did a beautiful job. When the show's guests are back sitting in chairs, Coleman talks about how Andre Previn tried having computers compose music independently. Verdon says it did not work because he had to go back and fix it. Coleman says the World's Fair Expo had computers approximating the sound of instruments to which Verdon comments, "Be careful. We'll have another musicians strike." Under the show's closing music, Douglas thanks her for a delightful week.

On January 22, 1969, she was one of the 500 stage friends attending a 35-minute tribute before the matinee of *Mame* at the Wintergarden Theatre to Lawrence Carr, who had died on January 17. Verdon reminisced about Carr, and in response to her request the audience gave a standing ovation to him because she said he always wanted to know what it felt like to get one.

She returned to *The Ed Sullivan Show* for her fifth appearance on March 2, 1969. She plays a girl put in a crate and shipped to a desert location for a sheik's entertainment. When the box is opened, Verdon is reading a book, and says, "My agent said he booked the Sahara. But the Sahara Sahara?!" She gets out of the box and is dressed in a pink body stocking with pink tail and gold vest, gold waistband, gold necklace, and a gold headband with pink flowers. After being chased by the sheik, Verdon entraps him in her crate and dances for his four male guards, whistling "Big Wind Blew In from Winnetka." She also sings lines from "Jeepers Creepers," "Is You Is Or Is You Ain't My Baby," and "Stout Hearted Men." Verdon takes the swords from the men saying, "C'mon fellas. Hand over the hardware," and adds, "Talk to them nice, they'll do anything." She then leads a group dance with the guards and the three belly dancers, as we see that the sheik uses a sword to progressively cut his way out of the box. When the sheik has cut a hole in the top of the box, the guards direct Verdon to a carpet on the ground. She poses on it and the carpet is lifted into the air. An optical effect is used for the flying of the carpet for her escape, as she waves goodbye to the guards. The sheik jumps up and down in frustration.

Verdon was a Tony Awards presenter on April 20, 1969, broadcast live by NBC. The show took place at the Mark Hellinger Theatre and she presented the award for Best Choreography to Joe Layton for his work on the musical *George M*. Verdon appears to the sound of "If My Friends Could See Me Now." She is dressed in a long high-collared black dress with a tie and striped patterned sleeves, and her hair is teased up at the back and swept off her forehead. Verdon states that, of all the creative people involved in making a musical successful, the choreographer is by far the most underrated, overlooked and underpaid. She laughs and then reveals, "I don't really believe that but my husband's a choreographer and he told me to say it." On May 2, 1969, Verdon was co-chairman of the ball that honored the 21st year of the Bedside Network at the New York Hilton Hotel.

On *The Ed Sullivan Show* (June 1, 1969), Verdon, Marie Lake and Dee Erickson performed the dance "Mexican Breakfast." She wears a yellow pants suit, a yellow blouse and neck-scarf, and has sunglasses in her hair. The dance was choreographed for Verdon by Fosse. The photographic coverage sometimes uses closer angles rather than long shots which is passable because the angles don't get too close so as to lose the effectiveness of the performance. It is also cyclic as it opens and closes in an extreme long shot of the three ladies posed in a spotlight. This 1969 number received a modern review when Beyoncé used it as inspiration for her 2008 music video "Single Ladies (Put a Ring on It)." Directed by Jake Nava, it was shot in black and white, unlike "Mexican Breakfast" which was in color. It has choreography by Frank Gatson and JaQuel Knight and incorporates J-Setting choreography. Beyoncé said she saw a video of "Mexican Breakfast" on YouTube "and I said, 'This is genius.'" She advised that they kept a lot of the Fosse choreography and added the down-south J-Setting, where one person does something and the next person follows. The song has a faster tempo than the original and the costuming is also different. The video caused a sensation and won the MTV Best Video, Best Choreography and Best Editing Awards.

Verdon made her only guest appearance on the NBC talk show *The*

Joan Rivers Show which was taped in New York and seen on June 22, 1969. In Hollywood she made the first of two appearances on the ABC variety and talk show *The Dick Cavett Show*, broadcast on July 7. She made her only guest appearances on the ABC family musical comedy show *The Hollywood Palace* in an episode broadcast on October 11, 1969. In the show Verdon sang and danced "The Psychedelic Stomp" which was set in a Western bar with male dancers, and she participated in a Beatles medley. In the latter she sang "Can't Buy Me Love" with Bing Crosby and Engelbert Humperdinck, "With a Little Help from My Friends" with Dick Shawn and Bobby Gentry, and joined the cast in "Ob-La-Di, Ob-La-Da." She begins singing "Can't Buy Me Love" standing at the back of the stage wearing a black glittery sleeveless dress with a large white feather boa around her neck. After dancing among four dancing boys, she pushes them away separately and joins Crosby and Humperdinck on a raised step to continue "Can't Buy Me Love." Verdon then leaves the men, singing an "uh-uh" to follow the song's lyrics of "no." For "With a Little Help from My Friends" she joins Dick Shawn and Bobby Gentry on the steps and they lock arms until Shawn leads her offstage. For "Ob-La-Di, Ob-La-Da" Verdon is back on the steps with the men and the chorus dancers behind them. All the lead performers step down onto the floor to stand in line and sing the song. The coverage of this last number oddly includes the audience in the bottom of the frame, necessitating that the performers remain in a long shot.

On October 12, 1969, Verdon was a co-chairperson for supper parties held at the homes of Mr. and Mrs. Herbert Steinmann and Mr. and Mrs. Alexander Farkas after the world premiere of the film *The Madwoman of Chaillot* at the Plaza Theatre. The evening proceeds went to aid the Postgraduate Center for Mental Health in its cooperative research with the Maferr Foundation. Verdon's second and last guest appearance on *The Carol Burnett Show* was broadcast on November 3, 1969.

The Fosses retreated to Amangansett for the summer of 1969. The marriage was strained by the fact that neither had an income, and the couple were living off their savings. He accepted an invitation to dinner with the Hal Princes and the Neil Simons. Fosse claimed that Verdon's absence was due to illness, but the feeling was that they didn't want to be together. The Princes and the Simons planned on spending the rest of the summer in Majorca and invited the Fosses to join them, but he did not answer. But it was at this dinner that Fosse learned that Prince would not be directing the film version of *Cabaret*, that he had directed on Broadway. It had been a monster hit running from November 20, 1966, to September 6,

1969. The film was going to be made at the Bavaria Studio in Munich and would be Fosse's next directing job.

Verdon returned to *The Merv Griffin Show* which was broadcast on January 6, 1970. Also in January, Fosse rehearsed with Verdon and six male dancers the number "It's a Fine Fine Day" that he had choreographed for her next appearance on *The Ed Sullivan Show*. This would be her seventh and final appearance and was broadcast on February 1, 1970. For the number Verdon was dressed in a sparkly gold striped jacket with black tights and a gold-trimmed black hat. The number is another that seems to have been inspired by "I'm a Brass Band" from *Sweet Charity*. After she did the number, Sullivan calls her over for a chat. After asking if she can say hi to her father, she says "So long, pop. I'll see you Tuesday." She made her second guest appearance on *The Dick Cavett Show* on February 9, 1970. Verdon was back on *The Merv Griffin Show* for her final guest appearance on April 27, 1970. She also returned to *The Mike Douglas Show* for her second week of co-hosting duties from May 4 to 8, 1970. With Cyril Ritchard, Verdon appeared on the PBS biographical drama series *NET Playhouse*. The episode, broadcast on July 14, 1970 (some sources give it as November 26, 1971), was divided into two parts and the one featuring her was entitled "Actors Choice." In it she and Cyril Ritchard read pieces written by Lewis Carroll, including a portion of *Alice in Wonderland*. Verdon made her only guest appearance on the ABC television talk show *Girl Talk* on August 24, 1970.

An article in the *New York Times* by Jean Hewitt on September 7, 1970, on the demand for organic food reported that a few months prior Verdon had bought a supply of ladybugs and praying mantises to wipe out the insects in her organic Central Park West rooftop garden. The article included a photograph of a praying mantis in her garden. It was reported that Verdon grew organic tomatoes and shipped them to her summer home in Southampton, Long Island, for her family to eat there, and there was an accompanying photograph of tomato plants in her garden. Additionally there was a photo of Mrs. Ben Sackheim who was said to have shared Verdon's garden. Verdon was quoted as saying she estimated that 75 percent of the food she served Fosse and Nicole was organic. When they ate out, Verdon preferred dockside seafood restaurants where the catch was as fresh as possible. Her motto was "Keep it simple, keep it pure." Verdon decried convenience foods, saying that anything organic could be prepared in an hour.

On November 1, 1970, she was among those singing hits from the Dorothy Fields songbook for a tribute paid to the lyricist at the Museum of the City of New York. Verdon also made her only guest appearance on the NBC variety program *The Don Knotts Show*, broadcast on January 26, 1971. In the show she performed "I Won't Dance" and "It's a Fine Fine Day." She also dueted with Knotts on "Do You Love Me?" and joined him and his other guests, the King Cousins and Tommy Smothers, to sing "Mame." Additionally, she appeared in a skit with Knotts playing his cleaning lady who doesn't understand English.

She was a performer at *The 1971 Tony Awards* which were held on March 28 at the Palace Theatre. Verdon appeared four times in the evening as part of a salute to 25 previous Best Musical Tony winners to celebrate the twenty-fifth anniversary of the awards. She first appears for *Can-Can* briefly doing the title dance, including high kicks and cartwheels and a split. She wears black tights with a black draw-string blouse, blue-striped white billowy skirt, white pantaloons, a black choker, and a blue ribbon in her hair. After doing the final split, Verdon is helped up by a man and handed the envelope to present the award for Best Choreography to Donald Sandler for *No, No, Nanette*.

The tribute to *Damn Yankees* has her singing "Whatever Lola Wants" with Ray Walston. Verdon appears through a silver curtain, dressed in the same black tights but with a black senorita skirt with red petticoat and a red flower in her hair. There's an insert shot of the audience when she slips down her skirt, under which she wears a tiny black skirt and a corset over her body stocking. (On Dick Cavett's show in 1977 she explained that television censorship could never allow her to show the act of taking off her clothes even though she never totally stripped for the number.) The number is abbreviated from the original, as many of the numbers in the evening are, but she retains some of the Fosse choreography including the removal of gloves and the shaking of her bottom.

Verdon returns with Richard Kiley for *Redhead* and they perform "Look Who's in Love." He is seated on the set with the 1959 year display on it and she sits on a lower level in between his legs and holding onto his left leg. The pair stays in the same positions for the whole performance. Verdon wears a black dress with white blouse and black triangular pattern on the front, white gloves, and a black ribbon in her hair. She is also seen under the closing credits of the show singing "There's No Business Like Show Business" with the cast.

9

Children! Children!

According to Verdon, Sally Bowles in *I Am a Camera* was the dream role that she never got to play. It was written by John Van Druten as an adaptation of Christopher Isherwood's book *The Berlin Stories* and been staged successfully on Broadway from November 28, 1951, to July 12, 1952. Verdon had seen Dorothy Tutin do it in London in 1954. Fosse had been offered the chance to direct the stage musical version earlier but had declined.

The film of *Cabaret* was in production in Germany from February to July 1971. Verdon agreed to join Fosse when he said he had a crisis over costumes, and she brought Nicole with her. The time that Verdon was in Berlin included Nicole's eighth birthday on March 4. The Fosses stayed at the Hotel Residenz in the town of Schwabing on the outskirts of Munich. Verdon joined the company of actors and dancers in late-night card games.

She enjoyed Liza Minnelli and was not envious of the way that Fosse was transforming her into a spectacular dancer. Verdon also worked on the star's personal style, creating the Louise Brooks–style helmet look of her hair with a widow's peak. It was supposedly her idea that Sally Bowles had emerald-green fingernail polish, although this feature of the character came from Christopher Isherwood's source novella.

It was not a surprise that Verdon would have an affinity with Bowles since she was not far removed from her own Charity persona, another hopeful and eccentric but luckless waif. Fosse could not see Minnelli playing Bowles in damask which was the costume designer's choice of material, and he was so distressed about her look that Verdon "butted in." She went to junk shops and antique stores in Paris to find authentic period clothes. Verdon found the purple dress with the beaded centerpiece that Minnelli wore for the title song. She gave Minnelli a vest that belonged to Fosse that the star wore without a shirt for the "Mein Heir" number. Verdon also contributed some of her own clothes like a shawl that she had brought with her, her green blouse used for "Maybe This Time," and her kimono.

Her emergency rescue also brought the fighting factions of the production together since the crew loved her. Verdon's faith in people was contagious and it reflected back upon people having faith in her. Fosse had begun a relationship with another woman whom he had met months before. She was Ilse Schwarzwald, the interpreter he had been given in the film's pre-production period to help him communicate. Their romance extended into production and Fosse promoted her to production secretary. People noticed that Ilse resembled Verdon, something which became more apparent when Verdon arrived in town. She innocently chatted with the German girl on set, unaware of the affair that was common knowledge to everyone else. Fosse had initially tried to keep it a secret but soon he was publicly declaring his love for Ilse. While she was not the first woman he had had an affair with, the situation was different now because the Fosses were in Europe, where he no longer made an effort to hide his philandering from his wife. Another difference was that Fosse told Ilse that he was now only staying married to Verdon for Nicole.

Matters might have come to a head when Verdon learned about Ilse from the man she was living with—some sources say he was Ilse's husband. He apparently sent her a note telling all, including a warning about Ilse's expensive tastes. But Verdon's reaction was more sarcastic than angry, and to the crew's amazement, she decided to stay on in Munich to work on costumes and makeup and with the dancers. One makeup tip that she contributed was to put melted crayon on eyelashes for a startling effect. Verdon said that she did all the girls using melted Crayola so that they could have different colors. Again her generosity over her husband's work took precedent over her personal feelings, particularly as she was not paid for her services. Cynics might have believed that Verdon's attitude was based on a refusal to show her suffering. If she did, people might think that Fosse did not love her and then she would lose her title as his queen. It was better for her to stay strong, because there was dignity in transcendence. But this attitude would only work for Verdon for a time. Others observed a serious weight loss that they attributed to her grief.

Verdon solved another costume crisis that occurred with the number "If You Could See Her (The Gorilla Song)." She flew back to New York to Brooks Costume to handpick a gorilla costume to replace the blue velour one provided by designer Charlotte Flemming. Other sources claim that Fosse's complaint was just about the head of the costume. Verdon flew back to Munich with the costume's head on her lap. This head was enormous and rather unusual because it had a ring through its nose. This was presumably the same ring that Joel Grey in the film places in the female gorilla's nose as an engagement ring. Grey commented that the head looked like Verdon's head if she were a gorilla, that it was very much her kind of stage persona. In the film the sparkling eyes and big smile of the gorilla do perversely recall her. Looking past the idea of the bestial love of a gorilla as an example of the perversity demonstrated in the club's array of sexual proclivities, one can read a parallel between Verdon's relationship with Fosse. He is represented by Grey's M.C. and she is the gorilla, who wears a feather in her hat which is a look that Verdon often used. She is the pathetic female, with unconventional looks, who is led by the nose by a man who claims to appreciate her individual qualities, but only feigns sentiment. Yes he will marry her, but he will also hold her gullibility up for ridicule.

Upon her return to Munich, Verdon walked in on Fosse with a couple of German girls and that was the last straw for her. She went back to New York and sent a letter to her husband in Berlin, where he had gone for the end of location photography. In it Verdon stated that she loved Fosse, but that they had to separate because he had been cheating on her from virtually the moment they had met. The separation also meant that she no longer wanted him living in their apartment, and he moved to a two-bedroom apartment at 58 West 58th Street. Fosse told a friend that he cheated because he was constantly thrown into a situation with beautiful women but he had always made it clear that he was married and that the affair would lead to nothing big. But after the letter, Fosse dove into the relationship with Ilse, making it sound as if it was practically his wife's fault.

In Madrid after the end filming, he called Verdon and asked her to meet him at the Simons' rented villa in Majorca. She agreed and met him at the house. Hal and Judy Prince were staying at the mountaintop near the Simons. The Princes and the Fosses had drinks in Palma and then Fosse and Verdon went back to the Prince house for dinner. The couple spent a week together but their fighting resumed and they learned that a reconciliation was not possible. They endured a dance performance by the Simons' fourteen-year old daughter Ellen which she had created as a farewell gesture to them. Then supposedly Neil Simon asked them both to leave when neither Fosse not Verdon could muster the enthusiasm to pay the girl a compliment. They spent their last night together in a hotel in Palma and then Verdon went back to New York and Nicole.

She would later say that she was living like a wife and a mother, which was really what she wanted to be, but she was the wrong kind of wife for him. Verdon thought that Fosse outgrew her. He started writing and he was involved in all kinds of things, and she was so involved with Nicole she didn't really care if she worked or not. She said that the hardest thing was that she was honest with Fosse but Fosse would say that it was his fault that the marriage failed and that it had to do with his work. When he worked, he shut everything out. Fosse said that he tried harder with Verdon than with his other two wives, but marriage was a disaster for him. He likened it to one big closing in New Haven. Verdon thought that the marriage failed because she didn't know what he wanted, but they remained friends after they separated. Verdon's sustained friendship with Fosse allowed him to regularly visit his daughter in her apartment, and also to Verdon working with him again.

On June 21, 1971, Verdon was one of 100 women handing out leaflets in front of Bloomingdale's and Alexander's department stores that claimed that the spiralling cost of living was linked to the war in Vietnam. The women wore sandwich boards reading "Don't Buy War" and they asked shoppers to postpone doing anything for one day, as a protest against the war. They also handed out "shopping lists" of 1971 "war prices" for such items as eggs and coffee as being sharply higher than "peace prices" for the same goods in March 1961. On October 7, Verdon was one of the many celebrities participating in a benefit reception to raise money for the New York Public Library's theater collection. She was photographed with auctioneer Timothy Tetlow displaying a poster of Sarah Bernhardt's 1900 Farewell American Tour during an auction, wearing a white long-sleeved high-necked jacket with a row of buttons on the left side.

On November 15, 1971, Verdon was chairperson of a conference meeting to raise funds to prevent the Research Library of the Performing Arts of the New York Public Library from closing as planned on January 1, 1972. Under the auspices of the Actors Equity Association, artists for these programs would donate their time for a series of "Nine O'Clock Crisis Concerts." These were planned to be held in the Library and Museum of the Performing Arts Auditorium on December 6, 13, 18 and 20, 1971, and January 14, 1972. On December 18, Verdon led dance shock troops to give a couple of the fund-raising concerts. In 1971 Verdon had also modeled the furs of Ben Kahn at a show at the Park Lane Theatre in aid of the Actor's Guild.

On January 13, 1972, it was announced in the *New York Times* that Verdon had been cast in the theatrical thriller *Children! Children!* by Jack Horrigan. She asked Louis Calta to please not write that she was making her debut in a straight play, preferring to say that it was the first show in which she didn't sing or dance. But Calta did not do as she asked. Verdon explained the difference was that using "straight play" implied that she had not done any acting in such plot-ridden shows as *Sweet Charity, New Girl in Town, Damn Yankees,* and *Redhead*. She asked: If she wasn't acting in any of those shows, what was she doing?

Verdon was to play Helen Giles, a woman recovering from a nervous breakdown who took the job as babysitter to three malevolent children. The story was set in a Gramercy Park duplex on New Year's Eve. Unbeknownst to Helen, the children had caused the demise of their last sitter and they planned a similar fate for her. It was to open on March 7, 1972. Director Joseph Hardy described it as a suspense play with social and psychological implications. It was produced by Arthur Whitelaw, Seth Harrison, Ben Gerard and Hardy. There were no out-of-town tryouts scheduled. Verdon said the extraordinary thing about it was that it was very funny yet terrifying.

On February 16, 1972, she was one of many speakers who gave a brief speech of greetings and good wishes to welcome back the Ritz Theatre to Broadway as a legitimate playhouse. The space had begun life as such fifty years earlier, but had then served as a radio and television studio and most recently as a porno theater. Verdon was to appear in the theater in her new Broadway play and the producers of the show had refurbished it. This included mounting on the theater walls and displayed in the playhouse old programs, pictures, records and memorabilia they had found in the Theatre Collection of the Museum of the City of New York.

After thirteen previews from February 24, 1972, *Children! Children!* opened on Broadway on March 8 and closed the same night. It was lambasted by Clive Barnes in the *New York Times* who wrote that the acting of the entire cast, including Verdon, was indescribably bad and that it seemed ill-advised in its effrontery. She talked about the experience on *The Mike Douglas Show* on June 14, 1976. Verdon said that during the previews, material was taken out and nothing was put in its place so that the opening night performance was 65 minutes without an intermission. She was reminded of the show business adage to never work with children or animals and this show had her working with three children and two cats. After Verdon was advised that the show would be closing the next day, she went back and got the cats. She later commented that Jack Horrigan had refused to do any rewriting and a lot of cutting was done by the director, whose name recalled the character in *Damn Yankees*.

Verdon was back as a Tony Award presenter on April 23, 1972. The ceremony was held at the Broadway Theatre and broadcast by ABC. She appeared with Alfred Drake to present the Best Actor in a Musical Award

Unidentified child with Verdon in a portrait for her stage show *Children! Children!* (1972).

to Phil Silvers for *A Funny Thing Happened on the Way to the Forum*. She wore a lime green and yellow-lined bare-shouldered dress with a tie to the neck and her hair in a longer style to her shoulders. The couple were introduced by Peter Ustinov as having six Tonys between them. Drake corrected Ustinov by saying that actually they had eight Tonys and Verdon explained that the eight were their own and the two they had come to present. She then laughed and said to Ustinov, "I worried you, didn't I?" Verdon was also among the show's cast under the end credits holding a ukulele as they all sang "I Want to Be Happy."

On May 15, 1972, she danced and sang "If My Friends Could See Me Now" from *Sweet Charity* as part of the entertainment for the Songwriters Hall of Fame induction evening at the Grand Ballroom of the Americana Hotel. On May 16 Virginia Lee Warren (the *New York Times*) confirmed Verdon's continued support for organic food. She reported that Verdon had taken a turn behind the counter of the food store devoted to organically grown foods, Greenhouse Association. The work schedule was said to entail a commitment for each of four months of the year, of two periods of three and a half hours making a total of 21 hours annually. On May 22, Verdon pushed a motorized vacuum cleaner along 73rd Street as part of the five-day community clean-up of the West Side between 60th and 73rd Street by the Neighborhood Environmental Action Team. The team was a coalition of residents, merchants and property owners formed in January to improve the neighborhood. On May 26, Laurie Johnston of the *New York Times* reported that Verdon et al. were to make an appeal on behalf of the research libraries of the New York Public Library. More funds were needed for the Library to qualify for a Federal grant from the National Endowment for the Humanities.

On May 31, Verdon was part of the invited audience at Liza Minnelli's NBC television concert directed by Fosse, *Liza with a Z*, performed at the Lyceum Theatre in New York. It was broadcast on September 10. Verdon can be seen eight times in long shots in it. Seated between Chita Rivera and Fred Werner, she wore a green dress with a green scarf, and is shown applauding each time we see her. She next appeared in the ABC variety special *The Perpetual People Puzzle* which was broadcast on June 19. In it she sang and danced her way through "Chicago" in a Kennedy airport terminal. The show was executive produced by Al Perlmutter and was lambasted by John J. O'Connor in the *New York Times*.

At this time it is said that Verdon involved herself in the activities of the social psychologist Karen Horney. Verdon's frustration over the lack of substantial work also had her talking about starting an employment office for out-of-work dancers since she could sympathize with them. At Verdon's urging, Fosse joined her and Nicole for the summer in the Hamptons. After a year of unhappiness over the separation she had decided to become a marital pioneer. Always generous, Verdon now acknowledged what could be considered as a form of second marriage. One source says that Fosse only attended on weekends since he was too busy working during the week. The gathering together as a family for croquet, ping-pong and dinner may have been a lie but he did it for his daughter because he wanted to be a good father. Fosse considered it a date with Nicole since she lived with Verdon, and the difference between the two he considered was vast because the women had a day-to-day interdependence. Observers noted Verdon's behavior when Fosse was with her, as if she was in denial about where he was for the rest of the week. She lined up social events like lunches and barbeques for him, perhaps so that they would not have to be alone. The sad truth seemed to be that the couple didn't have much else to talk about except their daughter. Verdon would present as the hostess at the charcoal grill, the Broadway star with a cookout apron over her jeans, a figure from a magazine story about stars at home. Fosse humored her by acting the role of weekend husband and father but the difference was that he made no secret of his girlfriends in the city. Verdon said that Nicole repeatedly asked her why she (Verdon) didn't mind these women and Fosse being in other relationships. She told her daughter that it was better for him than being lonely, and since he had so many dark clouds over his head, they should let him have a few days of sunshine. Fosse's growing circle of writer friends, like E.L. Doctorow and Peter Mass, who also lived in the Hamptons, joined the couple. Observers wondered if the charade was intended to fill the need to sentimentalize the couple as glamorous and celebrated show business legends.

Despite appearances, Fosse still supposedly retained a resentment of his wife, and perversely used it in his next stage show, *Pippin*. It opened in Washington on September 20, 1972; the character of Fastrada was the title character's evil stepmother, and modelled on Verdon. She was played by Verdon lookalike Leland Palmer, who would later play the Verdon character in the film *All That Jazz*, and here she wore a red wig. Cast members felt that Fosse did this to give his wife a kick in the pants and there were rumors that Verdon would go to Washington to see the show.

On August 15, 1972, the *New York Times* reported that Verdon had recently played softball at East Hampton, Long Island, as part of a benefit game for Democratic presidential campaigner Senator George McGovern. On August 20 she was one of 75 guests at the Amagansett House of Plimpton which held a fund-raising party organized by Mrs. Victor Rabinowitz for the Attica Defense Committee. The inmates faced indictment for a 1971 uprising in the prison.

Verdon made her only guest appearance on the ABC anthology comedy series *Love, American Style* in the episode vignette "Love and the

9. Children! Children! 143

New Act" (September 29, 1972). She played Estelle Mayberry in the vignette written by Peggy Elliott and directed by James Sheldon. On October 12 Verdon was among the entertainment line-up at the supper party held after the premiere of the film *Lady Sings the Blues*. The event was also a benefit for the National Association for the Advancement of Colored People's Project Rebound. On October 27 she sang a medley with Chita Rivera and Cass Elliot at a Madison Square Garden benefit for George McGovern called "Star-Spangled Women for McGovern-Shriver." The three sang "Heart" but with words changed to reflect the evening's agenda. The musical director was Bobby Rosengarten. On December 4 Verdon helped at an auction at the Dalton School to raise money for a scholarship fund.

On December 6, 1972, the *New York Times* reported that she was to finally star in a musical revival of *Chicago*. The show was to be produced in the next year's Broadway season by Robert Fryer and James Cresson in association with Martin Richards. Fosse was to direct and choreograph. Songs would be by John Kander and Fred Ebb. Verdon was to play Roxie Hart, the heroine of the Maurine Watkins play, and Fosse, Kander and Ebb were said to be currently at work on an original treatment of the three-act comedy. Rehearsals were scheduled for the next fall for an opening in the winter. On January 28, 1973, the *Times* wrote more about the show. It said the rights were obtained after the death of Watkins, when her estate was controlled by her mother; the deal was brokered with the help of Watkins' agent, Sheldon Abend. Another source claims that the deal could only be made after both Watkins *and* her mother died and the rights were transferred to Abend. Yet another source said that Verdon herself bought the rights to the play.

Verdon was part of the cast of the CBS special *Ed Sullivan's Broadway* which was held at the Ed Sullivan Theatre and broadcast on March 16, 1973. Verdon was first seen under the opening credits coming out of Sardi's wearing a high-collared mink jacket. She mugged for the camera, waving for a taxi, getting into one and waving goodbye to the camera as the car drives away. Verdon was then introduced with the other cast members, wearing a black blouse with tie, floor-length black skirt and blue feathered vest. Sullivan read from a column he had written (dated May 8, 1954) about the opening night of *Can-Can*, although the show opened on that day in 1953. The column said that along with the new Cole Porter score, the new smash brought a new powerhouse talent to town packaged inside a red-haired blue-eyed dancing lady named Gwen Verdon. He promised the next time she came to Broadway in a show, her name would ride high above the title, which is exactly what happened a year later when the 46th Street Theatre marquee proclaimed **Gwen Verdon in *Damn Yankees*.**

The number she performs is "Who's Got the Pain" and she does it with Harvey Evans. The number's staging varies from that seen in the film version of *Damn Yankees* since it begins with the dancers sitting slouched in chairs. They wear black outfits with brown leather vests and black hats. Regrettably, the set is a pattern of upstaging chairs and arched frames with a mirrored-wall. Verdon and Evans score a laugh in the way they end the number after leaving the set and returning to poke their heads out from the wings, smiling and waving their hats. She also joined the cast in a medley tribute to the Broadway shows produced by Hal Prince. Dressed in a dark green dress with tie and sparkly dark green jacket, Verdon sang "Whatever Lola Wants" and danced with Evans. She also joined Julie Harris and Evans to sing "Side by Side" and later stood with Ethel Merman and Jack Cassidy as the cast and chorus sang "To Life" from *Fiddler on the Roof* for the closing of the medley. The show was reviewed by Howard Thompson in the *New York Times*, who wrote that Verdon "does nicely" by her *Damn Yankees* number.

Verdon was a performer and presenter at the 1973 Tony Awards which were held on March 25 at the Imperial Theatre and broadcast live by ABC. The show had the theme "The Wide World of Broadway" and included broadcasts from other venues in London, Vienna, Zagreb, Milan, Paris, Tokyo, and a high school in Wichita Falls, Texas. Verdon appeared in the opening number, first seen in a silver pants suit sitting on steps. She is joined by Paula Kelly, Helen Gallagher and Donna McKechnie wearing the same outfit and the four women move to the stage and sing and dance to a song about the show's theme. The women put bottle hats on their heads to do "The Bottle Dance" from *Fiddler on the Roof*, then discard them to dance to "America" from *West Side Story*, and "The Rain in Spain" from *My Fair Lady*, "The Flesh Failures (Let the Sunshine In)" from *Hair*, and an unidentified song from *Gypsy*. The latter gives Verdon a brief solo moment to dance where she also does a cartwheel.

She returns in her opening number costume with Alan King to present the award for Best Actor in a Play to Alan Bates for *Butley*. Verdon accepts the award on Bates' behalf (he was unable to attend because he was performing the play in Los Angeles). She errs in calling Bates "Mr. Butley" and is corrected by King. Verdon appears to be sitting next to Fosse in the audience when Ben Vereen passes to thank them after he is announced as the Best Actor in a Musical for *Pippin*. However, she is not seen sitting next to Fosse when he is announced as the Best Director of a

9. Children! Children! 145

Harvey Evans and Verdon perform "Who's Got the Pain" on the television special *Ed Sullivan's Broadway.*

Musical for *Pippin*. This may be because she returns for the finale of the show, a reprise of the opening number. Verdon is seen in the back row of the cast as they sing the song. Under the show's end credits she is also seen kissing and talking to Stephen Sondheim, and hugging and talking to Ben Vereen.

The *Times* reviewer John J. O'Connor criticized the fact the opening number used a pre-recorded soundtrack. He said it was well performed by the four ladies but it violated the idea of the "aliveness" of theater and the immediacy of a stage production that television can capture.

On March 27, 1973, Fosse won the Best Director Academy Award at the ceremony held at the Dorothy Chandler Pavilion in Los Angeles. One of the people he thanked in his acceptance speech was Verdon. He described her as a dear friend. She was not at the ceremony but at her East Hampton house. Fosse called Nicole to ask her what she thought of the show. Verdon told him that when he won the award, Nicole screamed so loud that she thought she had broken something in her throat.

In the *New York Times* on April 1, 1973, it was reported that Verdon was to teach a modern dance course for 100 physical education teachers for one night a week in New Jersey schools. The course was jointly sponsored by the New Jersey Association of Health, Physical Education and Recreation and the state's Department of Education. With her associate Siegfried Gerstung, Verdon guided the teachers through a strenuous two and a half hours of rhythmics geared to show the interaction between all types of physical education and the dance. She commented that she always wanted to teach but lacked the necessary educational credits to instruct public school children. Verdon's recourse, to teach the teachers of children, left her somewhat pessimistic about the knowledge that the average physical education teacher had about their body. It saddened her that so many of the teachers had not been schooled in body movement because in Europe teachers were better prepared. Verdon found that her pupils were both unskilled and unusually inhibited, and hence taught to their own limitations. The article had her photographed giving direction to Bethany Chapple, Bayonne High School's 280-pound, six-foot-four football coach, one of the ten men taking the course.

On May 1, 1973, rehearsals began for the 20th annual Deering-Milliken Breakfast Show, a yearly garment industry revue held at the Waldorf Astoria. Verdon was one of the headliners for the event, which took place on May 30. An audience of approximately 2500 buyers, store shoppers, managers, and soft-good merchandisers were invited to 73-minute live morning and afternoon shows. The fast-paced music and comedy events were designed to show how Milliken fabrics would look on customers. They had a dozen performances. It was directed by Robert Moore and had book by Arnold Horwitt and choreography by Alan Johnson. Ann Reinking was among the chorus dancers; this is where Verdon said that she first met her. However this seems inaccurate as Reinking was in the cast of *Pippin* which had opened on Broadway in 1972 and she was also a chorus dancer in *Liza with a Z*.

The *New York Times* (May 31, 1973) praised the show in an article that also had photographs. Verdon was in one of them with Robert Morse, where she appears to be wearing a short nurse's uniform and cap. An article on the show in the *Spartanburg Herald-Tribune* (July 1, 1973) also had photographs, with Verdon in three of them. In one she kneeled on a couch where Billy De Wolfe sat, he playing the Devil and she his ace seductress. Verdon is dressed in Milliken with black pants and a black and white sweater with white collar. The show is said to have incorporated an updated version of the Faust story with Morse playing Dexter Bailey, a newly dead department store head who arrives in Hell. De Wolfe was Diablo and Verdon was Nina who, learning of Bailey's lack of interest in sex, says, "He must be from the Harvard School of Business." The second photograph was of the Agilon special and had Verdon kneeling on the floor, holding the legs of Robert Morse, wearing a black and white short dress and backed up by a girlie chorus. The third had her as part of the cast production photograph standing on the stage.

For the summer of 1973 Fosse decided to rent his own home in Quogue, a village not too far from East Hampton where Verdon and Nicole were. His decision was made because he wanted to be with his girlfriend Ann Reinking, and knew that she could not stay with his wife. Verdon was seen to suffer with Fosse's relationship with Reinking because she could tell that it was serious. It also didn't help that Fosse began expressing anger toward her, after a stay in the Payne Whitney psychiatric hospital. His anger toward Verdon was described as violent, based on his envy of her and how it had been perceived that in their working relationships, she was the star.

She starred in the ABC made-for-TV horror movie *Deadly Visitor* which was broadcast on July 3, 1973. It was directed by Lela Swift. Verdon played the proprietor of a haunted boarding house at the turn of the 20th century. She took in a writer as a boarder who found himself haunted by the ghost of a previous female tenant.

Verdon, interviewed by Barbara Delatiner for the *New York Times* (July 22, 1973), she said that she enjoyed spending her summers living in East Hampton which she had been doing since 1958. Verdon liked being considered "just plain folks" and not a celebrity, and that being one was not something she would sacrifice home and family for. She enjoyed riding buses, and started after her bike was stolen from in front of the St. Regis Hotel in Manhattan. Verdon found them faster than cabs, certainly

Portrait of Verdon in her made-for-TV movie *The Deadly Visitor* (1973).

cheaper than limousines, and preferable to subways which she hated. The only downside to her bus travel is that she found that people were scornful when they recognized her, treating her as if she were invading their territory. Otherwise she found the area a pleasure, being able to walk around without makeup which was accepted. In the city if Verdon went without makeup she felt that people wouldn't like it. They would say that she had gone to pot since they expected instant glamour all the time. At her house Verdon also had six cats and a German shepherd.

Nicole, ten years old, wanted to have a yard sale to sell the massive furniture that Verdon had collected over the years that she found would not fit into the dream house. Verdon was currently renovating and trying to talk Nicole out of the yard sale because she would just as soon call in an antique dealer to get rid of it all. She was concerned over the fuss a Gwen Verdon yard sale would make and also about what people would think. The house meant a lot to her because she bought it because she didn't want to live in California, which she didn't like despite the fact her father and son were there. Despite a need for privacy Verdon did not consider herself a recluse, being very much a part of the social scene with a wide circle of friends in many fields besides show business. The summer would see her working for the local Democratic party campaign and raising funds for Guild Hall, the town's cultural center.

On July 29, 1973, Verdon appeared at the John Drew Theatre in East Hampton in an evening entitled "Gwen Verdon and Friends," also called "Divertissement of Dancers." It was produced, written and narrated by James Lipton and had music by Cy Coleman. The event was held as a benefit for Guild Hall. On November 10 and 11, 1973, Verdon was among the artists who participated in the bazaar and auction at Lincoln Center to benefit the New York Public Library's Performing Arts Research Center.

On November 11, she attended the gala benefit performance of the National Ballet of Washington at the City Center in New York. She performed in Act Three of *The Sleeping Beauty* as Little Red Riding Hood, wearing a costume of white dress and red cape. Verdon said that all her life she wanted to be in a real ballet and now she had the chance. The *New York Times*' Clive Barnes wrote that Verdon was darling and proved what some people had always suspected: that she should have been a ballerina all along.

On November 18 she presided over a celebrity auction at the New York Public Library to benefit the Performing Arts Research Center. On December 9 Verdon attended an art show and auction at the Postgraduate Center for Mental Health, in support of her past work for disturbed children. In 1973 she also advertised for Colgate Toothpaste for Colgate with MFB. The copy read, "If Colgate is just a kid's cavity fighter, how come Gwen Verdon won't brush with anything else?" The print advertising showed a photograph of her in black leotards and holding a tambourine in front of a class of girl dancers. What made the photo interesting is that Verdon's body was horizontally dissected by the out-of-focus outstretched arms of two of her pupils.

In early 1974 Jack Cole, very ill from cancer, was admitted into the UCLA Hospital. However it was too expensive for him so according to Paul Phillips, Verdon was called by his friend David. He wanted Cole to be in the Motion Picture and Television Memorial Hospital, the Actors Home in Woodlands, California. The problem was that they didn't know who he was. Verdon supposedly called Lana Turner and Jane Russell and told them both to call the home to get Cole admitted. This was achieved within two hours of the stars making the phone calls. (Gene Kelly was also said to have helped.) Cole was there until February 17, 1974, when he died. In his *New York Times* obituary (February 20, 1974), Verdon was quoted about his influence. She said that when you see dancing on television, that's Jack Cole. In Paris, what they call "Le Jazz Hot" is all Jack Cole.

It was Verdon's doing "Who's Got the Pain" on *Ed Sullivan's Broadway* that had her agree to do a summer revival of *Damn Yankees.* She rejoined Ray Walston in a production directed by him which ran at the Arie Crown Music Theatre at McCormack Place in Chicago from March 26 to April 14, 1974. Playing the part of Joe was Jerry Lanning, and Harvey Evans joined Verdon in the show's rendition of "Who's Got the Pain." After rehearsals Verdon invited Evans and Lanning to dinner. Evans became unavailable, and the meal between Verdon and Lanning began the first and only extended love affair of her life after Fosse. They would live together on and off for several years. Twenty years her junior, he was the son of restaurateur Al Lanning and retired torch singer Roberta Sherwood. Verdon commented on love around this time in her life by saying that "as one gets older and wiser you realize you're not going to fall into that deep ditch of despair. You may get hurt. But you've had a good time." The affair may have helped Verdon's apparent unhappiness over the show, since she was said to be have been overweight and unable to dance Lola the way she had when she was younger. The season was planned to last for three months which would give her time to get in shape, and then arrive in New York in the midsummer. This would then allow Verdon to follow with rehearsals for *Chicago* in the fall. The *Damn Yankees* tour ended at the Westbury Music Tent; it did not go into New York.

10

Chicago

Fosse worked with John Kander and Fred Ebb on *Chicago* from the spring of 1974. Although he had said that he was more interested in doing films, Fosse agreed to do the show as a thank you to Verdon. After all that she had given him and all that he had taken, it was his way of giving back. Fosse was also aware of the box office interest that their reteaming meant, and this would help to assure Nicole's security which he felt was his responsibility. He had told Lionel Chetwynd in a 1974 *Penthouse* interview that Verdon was one of the greatest performers that he had seen in his life. He likened doing the show to doing something for Jolson, since he thought she was *that* great.

Despite these feelings, the couple working together again would be problematic. One new factor was that the contract for the show granted Verdon a good piece of the profits and also provided for a limited pre–Broadway run. It also specified star billing with her name as large and prominent as the show's title on posters and promotional materials which were all subject to her approval. Additionally, Verdon had approval of all creative elements including casting, scenic design, lighting, costumes, compositions, orchestrations, libretto, dance music and orchestrations, and understudies. All these advantage were presumably because she had the rights to the source play. Fred Ebb heard that the show was Fosse's divorce gift to Verdon, although the couple never divorced. Hoping that it would be a hit, he gave her an enormous percentage of it, the royalties from the show being his form of a divorce settlement in terms of cash. Fosse also left the royalties for it to Verdon in his will.

The relationship between Fosse and Verdon had improved, perhaps because both of them had new romantic partners, and also because of her growing respect for Reinking. Verdon said that Reinking was good for Fosse because his use of her as a dancer extended his own talent. Reinking said that Verdon had always been exceptionally good to her. She as Fosse's girlfriend became an ally to Nicole, which also helped the Fosse-Verdon relationship to become more amicable. Reinking knew Fosse's pain of frustration over the time he missed with his daughter, and also was aware that Verdon never stopped loving him. Reinking said that his wife continued to love him in a way that he never did her and that was why Verdon was so good to her. She knew what Reinking was up against and knew that if you loved Fosse there were good and bad sides. Reinking respected Verdon as Fosse's legal wife and Nicole as his only child, and Verdon was smart enough to know that she had to retreat if she wanted to stay close to her husband.

On May 6, 1974, Verdon received the Mother of the Year Award from the Talbot Perkins Children' Services at their 24th annual Mother's Day Luncheon at the Waldorf Astoria Hotel. She was honored for her outstanding services to underprivileged and physically handicapped children. On June 9 Verdon attended a street fair at the Central Park West block at 69th Street to raise funds to provide five lunches a week for senior citizens of Project Find.

She also sold her house in Amagansett for a bigger place in East Hampton with more land. This new land wasn't near the ocean as the former house had been: Set back from Spring Close Road, it was more private and more a country house with trees and lawns instead of sand and brush. The sign out front read "Verdon-Fosse." She added a swimming pool. Fosse was no longer welcome since Jerry Lanning was now living there with Verdon in the summer. One evening she took her new lover to a party held by the Aurthurs, and came across Fosse and Reinking. However the expected scene of jealousy did not occur. It helped that Fosse preferred his home in Quogue on Long Island to East Hampton. While Fosse may have enjoyed the distance from her, he still didn't appreciate her affair with Lanning and told her so. Fosse knew that this was the height of hypocrisy since it was inconsistent with his own demands for freedom, but that is how he felt. He might accept the double standard of his girlfriends seeing other men, but Verdon doing so was another matter.

In the summer of 1974 Verdon joined Fosse at the Broadway Arts rehearsal space and began to step through *Chicago*. After a month he brought in Kathryn Brody and Tony Stevens to assist. Stevens says that he got the job because of Verdon's urging. They had worked together in several Ed Sullivan shows and some specials. He remembers how she told Fosse that he was a snazzy dresser, which Stevens thought was kind of weird. Some evenings Nicole and her parents would go to a Chinese restaurant for dinner like a regular family. The difference was that Fosse would go home to his own place afterwards. Verdon also attended a rough cut screening of *Lenny,* the director's new film; he had arranged for a few close friends to see it. This was before it was officially released on November 10, 1974. She joined the others in telling Fosse that it is was wonderful.

Fred Ebb would call Verdon and Fosse geniuses but also both difficult to work with and abrasive, Fosse especially. He told himself that what you had to remember was that kind of attitude is only offensive when there is no talent behind it, and Ebb said that ultimately it did not bother him a lot. He said that you got your money's worth for what you put up with. The relationship between Fosse and Verdon was a complicated one, as they were complicated people. Despite the problems, Ebb still loved them both. Fosse had co-written the book with Ebb and their working relationship was good until they came to a couple of difficult scenes in it. Ebb said the director on a couple of occasions would take out his frustrations on him when he was the handiest. John Kander was spared this treatment because he always knew when to leave the room. Later Fosse told Ebb that he picked on him because he was vulnerable. Kander said that their friendship with co-star Chita Rivera helped them cope, since she made them laugh and the three of them held each other up a lot.

The July 28, 1974, *Times* reported that *Chicago* was scheduled to open on Broadway on December 10 at a theater soon to be announced after a four-week tryout in Philadelphia. Joining Verdon in the cast were Rivera and Jerry Orbach and rehearsals were now scheduled for September. Rivera had been a replacement dancer in *Can-Can*; she said that she watched and idolized Verdon in it. She said that when she auditioned, Verdon advised her to find her own role, which is something that Rivera did not forget. Apparently the advice was meant to be good-natured and not as resentful as it sounds. Verdon is said to have asked for Rivera's part to be enlarged in *Chicago* so that the show would be a two-hander and take some of the pressure off her. She also felt it better, given her age, that Rivera be given the more athletic dance moves. On September 18, 1974, the *Times* reported that the venue for the show would be the 46th Street Theatre and the opening date would now be January 7, 1975.

Dance rehearsals for *Chicago* began at Broadway Arts on October 26. In November the cast had their first table read, Tony Walton presented his model of the set, and Kander and Ebb played their songs. Verdon was shocked when she saw Fosse: He was puffed up and he had a funny voice. Fosse had recently had another seizure and pain in his upper arm. He asked Phil Friedman to make him an appointment with physician Harold Leder. After the reading Fosse clutched his chest and he was taken to New

York Hospital. One source says that the doctor's appointment was made for 2 p.m. that day and after the reading Fosse attended a dancers rehearsal. Halfway through it he told the show's general manager Joseph Harris that he was unable to continue because of chest pains. Another source claims that Fosse had also been experiencing numbness in his left hand and shortness of breath for weeks. He went to the hospital's emergency room with Harris and producer Robert Fryer. It was supposedly Harris' idea that they go to the hospital rather to Fosse's doctor's office, after Friedman had been told by Leder to do so. The doctor was waiting in the emergency room when the three men arrived. After examining Fosse, Leder paged staff cardiologist Edwin Ettinger. He in turn made an examination. An electrocardiogram test showed that Fosse was going to have a heart attack.

In the meantime the show's rehearsals continued. Verdon reportedly asked where Fosse was a dozen times and was told that he had yet to return from an appointment. She and Rivera worked on the "All That Jazz" number, although other sources claim that they worked on the trial scene, and Verdon was practicing knitting. At 4.30 p.m. Harris supposedly called from the hospital and asked that Verdon go there. Friedman found her and told her. Calmly she changed her shoes in the rehearsal room and her clothes in the ladies room and left the building, careful to keep the news private and contained. Friedman said that she went through the experience like an actress. She supposedly considered that a heart attack was, in a way, what Fosse wanted. Not to die, but to come to the cliff's edge of death, kiss it, then turn back. Verdon thought that it put him in touch with his talent, like fighting producers, who in a sense were like heart attacks and terminal illnesses, with their cruel and insistent reminders of time running out.

Fosse was put into the Intensive Care Unit. When Verdon arrived, he asked her to not keep him in the hospital. He hadn't officially suffered a heart attack yet, but his doctors felt that it was inevitable. The chest pain was a sign of clogged arteries and a reduced blood flow to the heart. He was angry at being kept against his will and he was desperate to go back to work: Verdon told the doctors that he was staying and asked for the medical papers to sign. As his legal wife she had authority over certain medical matters and presided over the paperwork, later worrying that the hospital would not release Fosse after his surgeries if the bill wasn't paid.

Rehearsals for the show were cancelled and the company was told about Fosse. Some sources say that they were told he had had a heart attack, but others claim that they were told he was suffering from exhaustion. Whatever the case, he would need four months to recover. Verdon said that the company would be looked after in the interim. Fosse is said to have given some of the dancers personal loans. Verdon was described as being like their mother, holding them close, and she threw parties to keep up their spirits. She was presumably afraid that if one dancer left, it might inspire more to go. Although Verdon wanted them to get pickup gigs, she knew that if the company disintegrated, schedules would disappear. She also presumably feared that the show would be delayed further and she would be too old to do it. However, putting aside these fears, Verdon threw the cast a party. Fred Ebb said he also threw them a party which Verdon and Rivera co-hosted.

After being given an angiogram, Fosse was told that Ettinger recommended immediate surgery. He was to have a single cardiac bypass performed by Dr. William Gay. Ettinger wanted to take a vein from Fosse's leg to put into the heart muscle to bypass around the area of artery narrowing. The patient protested. As a dancer, he didn't want his legs tampered with. So an artery underneath the chest cage was used instead. At the time Ann Reinking was herself in Roosevelt Hospital for a back injury, and she kept in touch with Fosse by phone. Verdon also kept her informed, which the younger woman found extraordinary and generous.

Fosse's open heart surgery took place on November 15, 1974. He was visited by Verdon in the recovery ward where he was put on an ice mattress to reduce his temperature. She said that he had shakes and tremors in convulsion. On the other side of Fosse, a nurse bathed a 22-year-old man and splashed water all over Verdon and the patient. She took in the sight of Fosse with a tube in his nose and wires and a heart monitor with a white dot blipping across the screen. Two young women appeared and asked for his autograph and Verdon shouted at them to get the hell out and ran into the hall to get help. When she returned, they were gone. Nicole tested her father's love, telling him that if he really loved her, he wouldn't die.

Verdon stayed with him and slept on a sofa in the lounge at the end of the hall. She saw herself as Fosse' wife again after five years and, despite the circumstances, felt that this wish had come true. She even reportedly told Ethel Martin, her old friend from her Jack Cole days, that she thought that she and Fosse would get back together. Verdon assumed this came from how happy Fosse was that she was with him in this crisis. Despite what may have been wishful thinking on her part, Ettinger was amazed by Verdon's sensitivity to the situation since the ward was visited by Fosse's many girlfriends. Ettinger didn't know which one was more important and to whom he should relate information about the patient's condition, but he saw how Verdon treated them all with warmth. It seemed to him that she considered them all family, and she was the brood hen.

After Fosse was moved into a private room, the staff had a strict "immediate family" only rule for visitors. Verdon broke the rule by bringing in the girlfriends, like Kim St. Leon, who she fibbed was her daughter. Some sources claim that children were not allowed into the room, which necessitated Verdon sneaking Nicole in. This provided for the anecdote that she painted her daughter's eleven-year-old face with makeup, strapped chunky platform shoes on her feet with heavy-duty rubber bands, supplied bust pads, and had her wear a wide-brimmed floppy hat. However some sources say that Nicole as one of the immediate family *was* allowed in, even after Verdon had passed off St. Leon as her daughter, explaining that Nicole was her other one. Naturally she accompanied her daughter when she was at Fosse's bedside so that the child would not be too upset by the sight of him connected to machines by wires. Soon the immediate family rule was relaxed and Fosse received many more visitors.

After Reinking was released from her hospital stay, she came to see Fosse. She was nervous about his wife being there but Verdon supposedly put her at ease. Reinking said that Verdon knew how things should be and did the right thing. Ettinger observed the two women together and considered that their confidence was like that of two sisters. However, unlike Verdon who had natural dignity and formidable powers of self-control, Reinking erupted at the sight of her rival, St. Leon. Reinking reportedly yelled at her to leave because she felt that she didn't belong. Verdon insisted that she stay, because she cared for him and he cared for her. Reinking was unconvinced. Verdon took them into the corridor while Fosse slept. St. Leon was no match for the older Reinking, but Verdon said that she felt like a lady gangster, laying down the law to the two girls. They were pacified enough to return to the room and although the two remained unfriendly, Verdon managed to keep the peace. The situation made both St. Leon and Reinking evaluate the kind of person Verdon was. Reinking was afraid that there would be competition between them but instead she found a reserved graciousness. "Friendly-careful" is the phrase Reinking used. St. Leon was more deferential, saying that Verdon transcended being Fosse's lover and that she was always the one for him, being his alter ego. St. Leon thought that it was his need for physicality with other women that broke the marriage though it would break any marriage.

Fosse had a second heart attack. Some sources claim that this was due to his not taking his recovery seriously, like his continuing to smoke.

Another claims that it was a reaction to seeing a bad television review of the film *The Little Prince* (1974) for which Fosse had done a dance sequence as the Snake for director Stanley Donen. Reinking told Tom Buckley in the *New York Times* (January 4, 1980) that she was sitting with Fosse when he had the second attack.

The dolling-up that Verdon was said to have done to sneak in Nicole to see her father is described in another source as having being done for the Thanksgiving dinner that Verdon held in Fosse's hospital room. This source describes Nicole as wearing eyeliner, false eyelashes, mascara, and green eye shadow. She is said to have worn her mother's jazz pants, her mother's shoes (secured with rubber bands), and a hat. Reinking would also be invited to the dinner, to show that Verdon acknowledged her relationship with Fosse. For the meal, Verdon set out a tablecloth on his bed with silver and dishes. She also provided a kind of wine which was crushed fruit punch with 7 Up in a carafe, and the accompanying food was (to no one's surprise) completely organic. The only wrinkle in the proceedings occurred when the chief nurse refused to admit the violinist that Verdon had engaged. Fosse recovered and was discharged from the hospital on December 10, 1974. A Christmas party was thrown by Verdon for Fosse with the company of *Chicago* at her Central Park West apartment. However he had not moved back in with her since he had decided to go back to his own home on West 58th Street.

In January, Verdon, Fosse and Nicole attended the nightclub act that Chita Rivera had put together at a small West Side cabaret room called the Grande Finale. Rivera had been unable to hold out for the *Chicago* postponement. She had to pay for her daughter's enrollment in a private school, and devised an act with dancer-choreographer Tony Stevens (Fosse's assistant choreographer on *Chicago*). This act was also written by John Kander and Fred Ebb. Rivera would perform her act for two months, which included taking it to Los Angeles, and by the time she returned to New York, Fosse was ready to start up again.

Verdon made the first of two guest appearances on the CBS children's program *Captain Kangaroo* on March 5, 1975. It was filmed in New York. *Chicago* resumed rehearsals in March 1975 after a postponement of three months. It was thought that the normal anger and depression that anyone would experience after heart surgery flavored Fosse's new take on the show: make it more edgy and bitter. His relationship with his wife had also changed. Although he had begun the show for Verdon, Fosse now behaved resentful for having to go through with the obligation. However this resentment was also linked to his reverence for her. Their relationship had always been strongest when they worked together and it was said that their love was rekindled in the rehearsal room. It wasn't easy because there were arguments, pushing and pulling, passive aggression and misunderstandings but also total trust. He was trying to get Verdon to dance her best but he wasn't yet completely fluent in her older body. He could be impatient with her and once she responded by saying, "They can pack his heart in a sawdust box for all I care."

Others observed the tension between them. At first they behaved like old friends and then she would say something bitter to him. Fosse may have been Verdon's number one fan as an artist and a performer but Tony Stevens saw that there were personal issues going on underneath. The hurt and pain that they had seemingly inflicted upon each other was apparent. Stevens was surprised that some of the things Fosse asked Verdon to do were so unattractive and nasty. But she did them. An example was the staging of the number "Funny Honey." He felt that the number was tawdry and that Fosse made Verdon look unattractive in Roxie's drunkenness. It may have been appropriate for the number but some felt that it appeared that he was trying to destroy her. This ignored the fact that Verdon was no doubt aware of his intention, knowing him so well, and she could salvage herself no matter what he asked. Perhaps that was the reason he was doing it, so that she would do something to outshine him and showcase her talent further. Verdon later told Bob Aurthur that Fosse's apparent cruelty and inflicting of pain had a purpose. He did it to get a response that would advance the creative process. She also felt that there was a connection between this behavior and his self-destructive habits since they put him in touch with his talent and it was the way he was creative. Stevens saw the struggle between the two of them over the number. Verdon would try to raise the style and Fosse would lower it. Stevens found that she had a dark side too and she thought some of it was funny, but not all. Chita Rivera was particularly upset by how she felt that Fosse was presenting his wife among dancers groaning and humping in the "Razzle Dazzle" number. She commented to Fred Ebb, "That's the great Gwen Verdon up there and look what they're doing."

The ending for the show was another source of disagreement. Verdon felt that Roxie needed to have a triumphant moment to take back power and win the day after everyone runs out on her, like "Rose's Turn" in *Gypsy*. But Fosse wouldn't have it because he wanted Roxie to end up wounded. Some thought this was because Fosse wanted Verdon to be wounded to keep her from walking away with the show, as he had feared she had done in the past. Others considered it a Fosse strategy to keep her fighting as

Roxie fought for her own moment. Ironically he would not cater to Rivera's demand for more dancing for her in the show because he felt this might show up Verdon.

The company moved to Philadelphia for tryouts. The first preview was a disaster. Some members of the audience were terrific but there were also walkouts. The reviews were savage. Fosse would seek solace after each performance at the Variety Club in the Bellevue-Stratford Hotel, although Verdon's absence was notable. Perhaps she felt humiliated by Fosse's blatant references at rehearsals to sleeping with the girls in the show. Perhaps she didn't want to be witness to his old habits of smoking and drinking that she knew would inevitably kill him. Gene Foote played Aaron in the show and said that cast members were getting notes one day and Verdon and Rivera were on the stage. Fosse said he had individual notes to give to them but they said it was okay to do so in front of the others. Fosse told them that he realized that they were both very big stars but in one number it would be very nice if they could dance together like chorus girls. And in particular, he told Verdon that she needed to shake her

Verdon (left) and Chita Rivera in their stage show *Chicago* **(1975–1977).**

shoulders. She told him that he knew that she couldn't shake her shoulders.

The new ending consisted of two numbers, "It" and "Loopin' the Loop." It began with Verdon playing the saxophone and Rivera the drums and ended with the both of them dancing triumphantly and thanking the audience. The documentary *The Music of Kander & Ebb: Razzle Dazzle* includes home movies of this number. Verdon said that she made up a tune on the sax and it was orchestrated, which she found very funny because she thought both she and Rivera were terrible on the instruments. Verdon also commented in the documentary, "[Fosse] was never interested in just entertaining the audience—he could go for the jugular vein." However this ending wasn't thought to work. Tony Stevens said that Verdon screamed and cried and hollered in the theater's lobby because she had had it with Fosse. She felt that the cynical ending wouldn't satisfy the audience. He went to Kander and Ebb and they wrote "Nowadays" as a replacement.

Ann Reinking says that the song came from Fosse, asking for a list of all the things that life had to offer for the two characters. The next day it was played for Fosse, Verdon and Rivera. Ebb said that Verdon wanted to sing it by herself although it had been devised to be sung by both women. Rivera said that her co-star demanded it, and that this was the first time she had seen Verdon stand up to Fosse. The emotion of the confrontation supposedly brought Verdon to tears and her body started to convulse. Fosse had the song played again with Verdon singing it. Rivera claimed that she couldn't get through it because she was so upset. Fosse still disagreed and thought that she ought to sing it with Rivera. Apparently this turned into a terrible ruckus which made John Kander eventually leave so he wouldn't have to witness it. Kander said that Rivera began crying and handed notes to Ebb saying "Give it to her!" Another source claims that Rivera joined Verdon singing the song when Verdon couldn't get through it and Rivera told him this was how the number was going to be done. She supposedly told Fosse that she didn't care what he thought of her or how he felt about Verdon. Verdon claimed that she knew Fosse's decision to have the women split the number was designed to provoke backstage tension that they could transfer onstage to their characters. But despite this, she still wanted to sing it alone. His choice prevailed and the song was done as a duet. Ebb and Kander went backstage after the first night that it was performed as such. They congratulated Verdon who supposedly told them, "You see, if you only stand up to him, you'll get exactly what you want." This comment seemed cryptic since neither of them had stood up to Fosse, and when she had, she didn't get what she wanted.

Anther out-of-town problem was the number "My Own Best Friend," a take-off of the over-dramatic Edith Piaf ballad. In the middle of it Verdon and Rivera sat back to back and had long monologues about their lives. After watching the show one day in the first week of previews, the two women were seen sliding across the stage. Apparently they had written their monologues in the glow-tape on the floor and they were both moving to read them. The next day, the monologues were cut. Verdon would comment that the show was Fosse's mix of theater and politics, and his reaction to Watergate. The corruption in his home town in the 1920s was reflected in the show's series of vaudeville acts. Verdon also said that Fosse brought sensuality to the stage—not just being sexy, but real eroticism.

On April 27, 1975, the *New York Times* reported that *Chicago*'s preview period had been extended by two weeks and opening night was now to be June 3. After 24 previews from May 12 the show opened on Broadway on the third and ran until August 27, 1977. Verdon appeared at the opening party at the Rainbow Room wearing a low-cut sequined spaghetti-strap dress and feather boa, with Nicole.

The show received a mixed review by Clive Barnes in the *New York Times*. But he praised Verdon's superlative knock-'em-in-the-aisles performance that glittered like gold dust, saying that she danced her heart out and that her voice was all candy innocence—but also naughtily suggestive of untold viciousness. A Walter Kerr article in the *New York Times* on June 8, 1975, featured an Al Hirschfeld caricature of Verdon. Harris Green's *New York Times* article of July 20, 1975, "Is the Broadway Musical Changing Its Tune?" included the comment that Verdon was not what she once was but she was still something at half-speed.

The original cast recording was made between June 17 and 22, 1975. It was reviewed in the *New York Times* by John S. Wilson (August 31, 1975). As he had done with *Pippin* to bolster box office, Fosse again made a one-minute television commercial for *Chicago*, although oddly it did not feature Verdon or Rivera. Rather it showed chorus girls in flimsy costumes dancing slowly and writhing on the floor singing "All That Jazz."

During the run, Verdon missed performances. She was replaced by her understudy Lenora Nemetz on July 28 and from July 30 to August 7; by Liza Minnelli from August 8 to September 13; and by Ann Reinking on February 7, 1977. Minnelli stepped in while Verdon recovered from a minor throat ailment, said to have occurred after she sucked down confetti thrown at her in the "My Own Best Friend" number. She was expected to return on September 15, 1975. Minnelli had seen the show in Philadelphia, when she had gone with Goldie Hawn as they were interested in doing the movie version together. She supposedly suggested herself to replace Verdon when she was told by Fred Ebb of the crisis. Verdon may have felt a twinge of resentment, despite the fact that she liked Minnelli, but that would have been overridden by the profit the star's presence in the show would mean for Verdon's investment. Her appearance was kept low-key with the producers posting a chaste billboard outside the theater and a *sotto voce* announcement before the show. No mention of her was made in the Playbill. But Minnelli's dates were quickly sold out. The losses that had been made with Nemetz were now more than made up for. Minnelli was said to be doing the show as a favor to her friends Fosse, Kander and Ebb, and presumably she also saw it as a grand rehearsal for the movie. Fosse was said to be concerned over Verdon's reaction to the reception Minnelli got in the show (audiences were on their feet as if they were at a rock concert). Security guards were stationed on the street at the lip of the stage to keep them back. A press embargo was imposed so that no new reviews would be written but it was lifted after Clive Barnes threatened a *New York Times* boycott of the future shows of Fryer and Cresson.

Barnes wrote in the *Times* (August 15, 1975) that any comparison between the stars was silly. He likened it to comparing a white wine with a red wine, since Verdon was a dancer who sang and Minnelli a singer who danced. Barnes said that both were separately and distinctively adorable. The article increased box office sales and Minnelli was presented with the key to the city by New York Mayor Abe Beame on the stage. The increased sales continued after Minnelli left and Verdon returned, so the former's appearance had worked well for the show. The latter also proved that Verdon still had popular appeal, even if it was not as fervent as that of Minnelli.

During the run there had been talk of Verdon and Rivera role-switching, in true repertory tradition, but that never materialized. After returning to the show and playing it for two years, Verdon wanted to do other things. She was replaced by Reinking after Verdon trained her in the part. This act was typical of her generosity, but perhaps more so, because she knew that Reinking was also her replacement as Fosse's love interest. Verdon would later say that the replacement had extraordinary symmetry because pieces simply fell into place. She also said that she had no desire to go down in the Guinness Book of Records as the oldest dancing star, and laughed with mischievous glee when she added, "Chita's going to do that!" The critical belief was that Reinking at 26 was too young for the part which had been vacated by the 51-year-old. However her greater physical ability did allow Fosse to make adjustments in the show to tailor it for his new leading lady.

As with *Sweet Charity*, the movie version of *Chicago* also eluded Verdon. Fosse was interested in doing it but never came up with a hook for transferring it from stage to screen. Then he said he wasn't interested because he didn't want to make another movie musical. Also, Fosse had resolved after *Sweet Charity* never to do onscreen what he had already done on stage. He likened it to trying to go back to an old girlfriend. Producer Marty Richards continued to urge him to make the film; Fosse finally relented and planned to attend the first production meeting on September 24, 1987. He died on September 23 and Richards shelved the idea. Over the years various actors and directors were rumored to be interested or attached to the project, and in 2002 it was finally made by director Rob Marshall with Renee Zellweger as Roxie. Chita Rivera was given a token cameo in the film, but not Verdon, who died in 2000.

The June 5, 1975, performance of *Chicago* was a binary benefit for the American Music and Dramatic Academy which taught dancers to act and actors to dance. The second part of the benefit had a scholarship inaugurated in Verdon's name at a supper party at Sardi's.

She was interviewed by Clarke Taylor for *People* magazine article published on June 23, 1975. Verdon commented on her prostitute roles coloring her world view of love, and her championing of causes which had seen her support candidates Adlai Stevenson, Gene McCarthy and George McGovern. Her other life included teaching dance to instructors and therapists who worked with brain-damaged kids. She also served on the board of directors of New York's Postgraduate Center for Mental Health.

Verdon continued her practical passion for organic gardening, food-buying cooperatives and domestic crafts. She had decided that Nicole would learn that you didn't have to get mayonnaise off the supermarket shelf—you could make it! And Verdon wanted her to know that there was a time when people did things like make soap, lace and so forth. Her personal life now consisted of her son Jimmy, who was an actor and trucking operator, her daughter Nicole, and Jerry Lanning. The article had photographs of Verdon in *Chicago*, at the first night party with Fosse, Nicole and Lanning, and on the terrace of her Central Park West penthouse. It was reported that it was once owned by press lord William Randolph Hearst and set up for his starlet mistress, Marion Davies. Verdon now lived in it with an aviary of twenty birds, six cats, and her organic garden. In this latter photograph she stood in front of an iron gate, leaning against a brick wall and wearing a white sweater and pants with a dark belt and a dark scarf.

On July 22, 1975, Verdon, Rivera and Orbach were guests on NBC's news and talk series *The Today Show*. After being out because of illness, Verdon return to *Chicago* on September 15 but after working three nights, the show was halted because of a musicians' strike. She was on call in case the strike was settled in time for the performance. Verdon said that it was like being adrift because she got so psyched up to do the show that she didn't dare let down. She always thought backstage was like a prison yard with everyone pacing around. Verdon had received a telephone call from a stranger calling from Rome asking if the show would play the next Saturday matinee and she had to advise the caller that she didn't know. When the caller said that they would come the following Saturday, Verdon told them to come on backstage and say hello. If the strike was to continue, Verdon suggested that the show go back to Philadelphia. They could run a bus service or make a deal with Amtrak to have dinner on the train and then bus people to the theater for a nine o'clock curtain. She was concerned about the effects of an extended strike. Verdon wished that New York City could accept the fact that it was an attraction, like topless dancers and gambling were in Las Vegas. She felt that tourists came to the city to see the Empire State Building, crime in the streets, and the Broadway Theater.

On September 27, 1975, Verdon was one of the Actors Equity members who spoke at a musical rally in Shubert Alley. They stressed the threat the continuing strike posed to the theater and allied industries, like charity organizations dependent on benefit parties to raise funds for the sick and aged and needy, and pressed demands for a speedy settlement. Musicians union Local 182 was seeking to raise their present salaries in a new three-year contract with the League of New York Theatres. The rally saw cast members of affected shows sing selections from their programs, without musicians. The crowd of almost 400 held placards that read "We Want to Work" and "Don't Let Broadway Die" and circulated petitions urging the governor and mayor to intervene without delay in the contract negotiations. On October 11, Verdon undertook work to organize an ad-hoc committee of Actors Equity to enact a twilight street rally to again protest the continuing musicians' strike which had left theaters closed for 24 days to date. The rally included a live a cappella performance by five Broadway stars on a stage in front of the Brothers and Sisters restaurant at 355 West 46th Street. The strike was settled on October 12th and the show performances resumed.

Verdon was back for her second guest appearance on *Captain Kangaroo* for the episode that was broadcast on October 22, 1975. On

November 2 she was the hostess for a celebrity auction at the New York Public Library to benefit the library's Performing Arts Research Center. One of the items for sale was the kimono worn by Liza Minnelli in *Cabaret*, which was originally Verdon's. She and Chita Rivera appeared on the CBS comedy variety series *Saturday Night Live with Howard Cosell* in the episode on November 8, 1975. The two stars performed "Nowadays" and "Honey Hot Rag" from *Chicago*. Verdon made her one guest appearance on Dinah Shore's talk show *Dinah!* which was broadcast on November 11. It included a salute to *Chicago* from New York where she was joined by Rivera.

On November 13 Verdon was named one of the three 1975 Women of Achievement by the New York's Women's Division of the Anti-Defamation League Appeal of B'nai B'rith at the division's luncheon at the Hotel Pierre. The benefit included a fashion show and a tribute to the charter members of the A.D.L.'s newly organized Women of Commitment. She went with Nicole and Paul Phillips to see Margot Fonteyn and Rudolph Nureyev on Broadway during their farewell performance at the Uris Theatre (November 18 to 29, 1975). Verdon's name had been imprinted on a flyer as one of the celebrities scheduled to appear at a rally at Times Square on November 24. The rally was organized to demonstrate against budget cutbacks in the city that had resulted from the presidency of Gerald Ford. Verdon did not appear for the event.

On January 7, 1976, she attended the opening of a new show at the Grand Finale in New York with Rivera. On April 12 it was reported in the *Times* advertising section that Verdon had become a spokesperson for the Shaeffer Pen with Doyle Dane Bernhach. Her hands and signature was used for a campaign entitled "Sign It with Shaeffer" where they were seen signing a program for *Chicago*.

Verdon was simply a present nominee for Best Actress in a Musical for *Chicago* at the 1976 Tony Awards held on April 18 at the Shubert Theatre and broadcast on ABC. She does the usual pleased reaction on camera where all the nominees are shown, and when the winner is announced: Donna McKechnie for *A Chorus Line*. Verdon would say that McKechnie could not act and that she was just playing her own story. A June 5, 1977, *Times* article by Patricia Bosworth told about the drama behind the Tony Awards. McKechnie's position in *A Chorus Line* was viewed as being that of a featured player. When she was announced as being nominated for the Best Actress category with Verdon and Rivera, the two supposedly reacted with anger and refused to attend the Tony nominating party. McKechnie said that it was director Michael Bennett who demanded that the nominating committee put her in the Best Actress category, which she heard had enraged Fosse. She realized how political the awards were, with Fosse viewed as the older director-choreographer and the belief that his show should therefore be recognized more than Bennett's. Any bad feeling that McKechnie's winning may have caused seemed to be overlooked later when she was cast in the national tour of *Sweet Charity*.

In Shirley MacLaine's book, *Sage-ing While Age-ing*, she reported that she brought Verdon into her rehearsals for her first one-woman show to teach her the new kind of dances. The show would run on Broadway from April 19 to May 1, 1976, and then July 9 to 24, 1976, at the Palace Theatre. The director was Tony Charmoli and the credited choreographer Alan Johnson. MacLaine says that Johnson had been hired on Verdon's recommendation. On May 9, 1976, Verdon performed at the Star-Spangled Gala, a benefit revue at the Metropolitan Opera House. It was held to raise money for operating expenses for the Performing Arts Research Center which was part of the New York Public Library. The center had suffered from the evaporation of city government funds and had recently been forced to cut staff and hours of operation, and now appealed directly to the public for financial assistance. The event was produced and directed by James Lipton. Clive Barnes in the *Times* reported that Verdon and Chita Rivera "played it cool" in numbers from *Chicago*.

According to the May 23, 1976, *Times*, Verdon had agreed to be the ballet mistress for a project to revive and reconstruct the theater dances by Jack Cole by the American Dance Machine. It was to done under the auspices of the Eugene O'Neill Memorial Theatre in Waterford, Connecticut. For the next eight weeks she was to lead special daily classes in the style of Cole's choreography. Then there would be another eight weeks of reconstruction and rehearsal of the works which would be filmed and recorded in Labanotation. The 25- minute film *Recollections* would go on file in the Library of Congress and also clips from Cole's films and TV shows as well as reminiscences by his dancers. On the August 25 *Times*, Clive Barnes reviewed the American Dance Machine show held at the Newport Festival. The program Cole was said to be divided into three parts: "Vocabulary," *Recollections*, and a reconstruction of dances from Kismet. Barnes wrote that in the film, Verdon talked beautifully about Cole.

In September the company would perform the dances in public in Connecticut and in New York, where lecture demonstrations would also be held on the whole range of Cole's style. Verdon was one of the many dancers to bring their own memories to bear on the reconstruction of the very numbers that she herself had helped to create, like ones from *Magdalena* and *Alive and Kicking*. She said that it was time that ballet in Broadway shows received real recognition. Verdon felt that some of the production numbers were out-and-out masterpieces and most were far superior to what had been seen on the ballet stage. She said that she had had some of the greatest choreographers create dances on her body, and it was scandalous that she should be the only one who really remembered them. Verdon was grateful for the work of the American Dance Machine because she felt that if the dances and dance styles weren't handed down to future generations, they would be lost forever.

In the summer of 1976 Fosse began working on a screenplay about his life and his own imagined death that would become the film *All That Jazz* (1979). He and writer Bob Aurthur interviewed everyone who had been around at the time of Fosse's heart attacks and surgery. This covered almost a hundred people and included Verdon. She told Aurthur that she felt that Fosse hated her when they first met because he was jealous of her. Verdon felt that he was jealous of all his girls and that Death was the only real affair of his life. This was the reason she was never really jealous of the other women in his life. Verdon also told Aurthur that she was a magnificent tool for Fosse because she absolutely trusted him, and that he had confided to her about his demons which would make him angry and deranged. On the subject of marital fidelity, Verdon said that he didn't take advantage of a double standard that saw her remaining faithful. Fosse was more the victim of the double standard. Interviewee Nicole expressed her dealing with her mother's boyfriend Jerry Lanning when he sometimes acted like a father.

Fosse would deny that the film's scenario was autobiographical, and the pseudonym Joe Gideon was used. Interviewed later in the *Times* by Moira Hodgson he would rationalize this by saying that he kept declaiming that the material was autobiographical to avoid people calling the film self-indulgent. However, he admitted that there was a lot of himself in Gideon, and that an artist should draw more from himself and less than others. The narrative included a character obviously based on Verdon, the estranged dancer-actress wife who the director-choreographer owes a show to. The production went ahead when Columbia Pictures agreed to finance it, with Fosse directing.

On June 11, 1976, Verdon appeared live on the WOR-TV charity benefit telecast "One on One" to aid the mentally retarded. She made her last guest appearance on *The Mike Douglas Show* in the June 14, 1976, episode. With Chita Rivera, Verdon performed "Nowadays" and "Honey Rag" from

Chicago. For "Nowadays" they wore white top hats with silver trim, white tail jackets with a white flower in the lapel, white body suits, black semi-stockings and silver shoes, and used canes. The outfits lacked the heart shapes on the crotch that were part of the stage costumes, presumably because they were considered too racy for television. After "Nowadays," the week's co-host Hal Linden appears on stage for some patter and the women exit. They then return wearing white split skirts with a silver belt over their body suits to dance "Honey Rag." Again the stage costume heart crotches were absent.

They were brought out again to be interviewed by Douglas and Linden. Verdon wore a black suit with white polka-dot blouse, a black polka-dot bowtie, a sparkly headband, and black earrings. Douglas told about his admiration for dancers because of the physical injuries they could sustain, and Verdon commented that often an injury resulted from the fact that you couldn't walk but you could still dance. When he mentioned Fosse having an individual style, she said that the really good choreographers demanded that you act the dancing. Verdon added that a shoeshine and smile would get you nowhere in the dance field. She also talked about her experience of doing *Children! Children!* Verdon said that at a Saturday matinee of Chicage the youngest women in the audience were 45 and they would scream all the Women's Lib expressions like "Right on!" She felt that ladies were a much better audience for the show because it was very naughty and risqué, to put it mildly. However Verdon had seen men and women in the evening (whom she assumed were married) who enjoyed the show, with one man in particular who seemed to enjoy Rivera too much and was punched in the face by his wife. Verdon also told how audiences sang "All That Jazz" along with Rivera but in a very syncopated way, so that when she paused, they would sing the "jazz."

On June 21, 1976, the *Times*' Bernadine Morris reported that Verdon had recently been one of the models at a showing of Israeli fashions, organized by the National Women's Division of State of Israel Bonds. The luncheon was held at the Waldorf Astoria in New York. On November 24, 1976, Verdon was the guest on the WNYC-AM radio show "Conversations from Circle in the Square."

11

All That Jazz

After she left *Chicago* in 1977, Verdon sometimes joined Fosse and Reinking for dinner after the show. The dance assistant Tony Stevens commented on her friendliness towards her professional and personal replacement, saying that the peculiar extended family was very sophisticated and very New York. He also felt that Verdon lived with the situation, whether she was happy about it or not. By now Nicole was attending the Dalton School in Manhattan. As the girl became a teenager, she apparently began to resent what she saw as her mother's overprotectiveness. An example was when she put her daughter into a taxi, she would take down the name and hack number of the driver. When someone else sent Nicole home in a taxi, Verdon would insist that they do the same. She also became aware of her daughter's physical development. Although she had trained in ballet for years, Nicole had the biology of a Fosse dancer with burlesquey curves and a knowing smile. This attracted boys, which added to her mother's concern.

Verdon made her second appearance on *The Dick Cavett Show* which was broadcast in two parts on December 5 and 6, 1977. It focused on the American Dance Machine and she appeared with dancers Debbi Bier Prouty, Morgan Richardson, and Amy Levine. Verdon wore a black long-sleeve leotard with black tights and a silver belt throughout the entire show, and had her hair in a ponytail. She looked uncharacteristically thin, perhaps even underweight. The performances took place on a bare stage with back lighting with an unseen band. The lighting was dimmed when Verdon sat with Cavett on canvas chairs to talk.

Cavett asked her about her past as a dancer, which segued into her talking about Jack Cole as the first choreographer to bring jazz to a Broadway show and his influence on ethnic dancing. Verdon and the dancers demonstrated an African ritual dance and then Cole's 1942 number "Wedding of a Solid Sender" which was based on a real Watusi ritual dance. She next talked about Agnes de Mille as the first to bring ballet to musical theater to have the dancers perform as characters in the show as in *Oklahoma*! Before Cole and de Mille, dancers would just do maid-dusting numbers or Tiller dancing with high kicks in a chorus line. In *Carousel*, de Mille had dancers combine ballet and soft-shoe. Verdon does dancing walks from Michael Kidd's *Guys and Dolls* and Fosse's *Damn Yankees*, and Chaplin's dancing walk. She also does a Jack Cole Cuban walk. Verdon and the dancers do "The Telephone Song" from the stage show *Cabaret*, which was choreographed by Ron Field who worked with Cole, and then Cole's East Indian dance. She continued her history of dance influences on musical theater with modern dance which was used by Cole, de Mille, Kidd and Jerome Robbins, talking through the moves that the dancers make when they perform de Mille's funeral dance from *Brigadoon* and Kidd's mute dance from *Finian's Rainbow*. Verdon next demonstrates stripper movement that was used by Cole and Kidd for Eve in the "Garden of Eden Ballet" from *Can-Can*.

Verdon teaches Cavett the first tap-dance she ever learned, "The Shim-Sham." He also shows her a tap time step that he said Fosse is envious of because he could not master it. The first half of the show ends with Cavett and Verdon wearing straw hats to do hat tricks and shtick. In the second half, they talk about the period when the choreographer became the show's director, and Verdon mentions *New Girl in Town* and the controversial ballet that was censored. She also talks about the Pony dance from that show and does it with the dancers, as well as Fosse's audition dance that was influenced by de Mille. The new choreographer-directors demanded that dancers be able to sing and act, and Verdon explains how to breathe when called upon to sing and dance. She gets a laugh when she tells Cavett, "It ain't easy, pal." She does different funky dances of Fosse and Pete Gennaro, to demonstrate the next influence of dance music into musical theater. Verdon calls the first "Bubbles" but it resembles "I'm a Brass Band" from *Sweet Charity*. She explains that the difference between the two numbers is that Fosse had the bump beat going to the back, whereas Gennaro had it going forward. Another influence was elegant Spanish dance which is demonstrated with "America" from *West Side Story* and "There's Gotta Be Something Better Than This" from *Sweet Charity*. The latter number has an added poignancy because once again it reminds us that Verdon did not get to do the film version.

Verdon points out that Cole's estate did not get royalties after his death, since he was not credited for the choreography for the revival of *Man of La Mancha* which had opened on Broadway on September 15, 1977. She said that the American Dance Machine had referred the matter to volunteer attorneys for the Council of the Arts and arbitration was in progress. The list of influences finishes with that of the American cowboy. Verdon joins the dancers for Bob Fosse's cowboy dance, which appears to be the same as "Cool Hand Luke," with all wearing black cowboy hats.

She next resumed her film career in what amounts to a cameo appearance. On December 16, 1977, Verdon was one of the Guests at Heartland in the finale of the jukebox musical *Sgt. Pepper's Lonely Hearts Club Band* (1978) directed by Michael Schultz. The film was shot from October 1977 to March 1978 on location at Tower Records in San Francisco, the MGM backlot, Century City in Los Angeles, and at Universal Studios. Verdon appeared in a standing group shot and wore a long-sleeved black dress with choker and uncharacteristic long hair as she sang and moved to a reprise of the title song. It is apparent that more than one take of the group was filmed since the people on either side of her differ in different shots. She was one of an enormous roster of celebrities invited to sing in the finale, a group that had been originally envisaged to imitate the famous cover of the Beatles album which depicted the band posing in front of a collage of some of their favorite historic figures and celebrities. It is reported that to attract the group, formal invitations were engraved and sent to virtually everyone in the entertainment industry. Those who accepted were treated to first-class transportation to Los Angeles, limos, luxurious hotels, champagne, a lavishly catered dinner and private tents for each of the stars in the studio's garden room.

The surreal screen musical was based on the stage show *Sgt Pepper's Lonely Hearts Club Band on the Road* by Robin Wagner and Tom O'Horgan which had a brief run off–Broadway at the Beacon Theatre from November 17, 1974, to January 1975. It was released on July 24, 1978, with the taglines "Only their music could conquer the forces of evil," "A splendid time is guaranteed for all," and "A fantastical, musical adventure!"

Variety described the finale as a celebrity olio. The film was lambasted by Janet Maslin in the *New York Times* and Clive Hirschhorn in *The Universal Story*. It was not a box office hit, and the soundtrack sales were equally disappointing.

On March 2, 1978, Verdon appeared as a guest artist in the Houston Ballet at Jones Hall as the debutante in Sir Frederick Ashton's "Façade," a 1931 musing on dance style. The piece was staged by Richard Ellis with costumes borrowed from the Joffrey Ballet. The *Times*' Anna Kisselgoff wrote that Verdon caught the silly ecstatic state of a giddy woman swept away by a slinky Latin Lover, danced by Ben Stephenson. The writer noted that it had long been the dancer's ambition to dance with a ballet company and, while this was not a classical role, it was still a difficult one to make convincing. Kisselgoff also reported that after her performance, Verdon was showered by flowers from the wings and, in return, she gave Stephenson her orange garter and threw a rose to the conductor, Charles Rosenkrans. On March 27, 1978, she attended the Broadhurst Theatre for the opening night of Fosse's new show *Dancin'* that he had choreographed and directed. Verdon was also photographed at the after-show party at Tavern on the Green, wearing a choker with her outfit which would become a staple of her wardrobe in her later years.

Chicago's national tour began on September 12, 1977, in Boston. After playing Miami Beach and Detroit, it came to the Blackstone Theatre in Chicago. The run began there in February 1978 but Verdon joined the company in April, replacing Penny Worth as Roxie. Verdon continued when the show moved to the Dorothy Chandler Pavilion in Los Angeles from May to June 1978 and then to the Orpheum Theatre in San Francisco from June 27 to August 5. In Los Angeles at the Civic Light Opera production, some of the language of the show was modified by Cy Feuer and Ernest Martin who had helped produce the original Broadway show. They also asked that the number "Class" be cut entirely. Fosse and Verdon both objected to the requested changes and the company petitioned against them. She had otherwise campaigned against censorship, being on the New York Board for Commisssioners of Libraries and having had seen libraries take "unacceptable" works off the shelves. Ultimately minimal changes were made.

Verdon commented in the *Biography* episode on Fosse that around this time, she was worried about her husband and his use of Dexedrine. Verdon reasoned that Fosse acted this way, even though he knew better, because he felt he was running out of time.

Fosse had originally planned to start filming *All That Jazz* in early 1978 but the casting of Richard Dreyfuss as Joe did not pan out. Production would go on hold for six months until the replacement, Roy Scheider, was available. This was after Fosse had been persuaded by the producers not to play the part himself. When Scheider was ready, filming began in October 1978 in New York. Fosse cast Leland Palmer as Audrey Paris, the character he had based on Verdon. In her book *Sage-ing While Age-ing*, Shirley MacLaine reported that he had wanted her to play the part of Audrey, but she declined because she felt she couldn't dance well enough any more. MacLaine was interviewed in the Mark McLaughlin documentary *Hollywood Singing and Dancing: The 1970s* and spoke about Fosse's desire for authenticity for his film. When she told him that her playing Audrey was as unauthentic as his Gideon character dying in the film, Fosse replied that if she would play Audrey then he promised that he would be dead by the first preview. She still passed.

Scheider said that Verdon was at rehearsals and at the shooting of some scenes, like the Air-otica number. After Fosse would film a certain part of it, he would go to her and ask what she thought. Verdon would offer her opinion, in the same way that Joe does with Audrey. When the film went over budget, Columbia Pictures closed it down before it was finished. Luckily 20th Century-Fox agreed to finance the shooting of the final scenes after they were shown a rough cut. This explains why the film has two studio credits. When shooting was over, Verdon was allowed by Fosse to see a rough cut. She supposedly evaded him after the screening, then walked home in silence with Nicole. Verdon called Fosse the next day to tell him what their daughter had said about the film—that she thought that the daughter was the only one who cared whether Joe Gideon lived or died.

The film was released on December 20, 1979, with the tagline "All that work. All that glitter. All that pain. All that love. All that crazy rhythm. All that jazz." It was praised by Vincent Canby in the *New York Times* but received mixed reviews in *Variety* and in Clive Hirschhorn's book *The Columbia Story*. However, it was a box office hit and also earned Academy Award nominations for Best Picture, Best Director and Best Actor.

Palmer in the film resembles Verdon, except that she wears her hair in a fuller, longer style and does not have the same fire-red hair color. Audrey as Verdon is shown to be a consultant to Gideon as he asks her opinion on casting. This is not surprising given that she is playing the lead in the show they are doing and the dance numbers that he choreographs. At the auditions Audrey's kindness is shown when she stops the Nicole character, Michelle (Erzsebet Foldi), from pointing and laughing at an inept dancer, and her humor is shown when she laughs at Gideon's pleasure at watching dancing twins.

The film has some interesting moments for her. Audrey laughs to herself and to Joe when the Fred Ebb character, Paul Dann (Anthony Holland), sings the number "Take Off with Us." When she is rehearsing a solo dance number and Joe enters the room, she does not let him see her falter, presumably fearful that he will replace her. He tells her that he is only doing the show because Audrey wants to play a part she is too old for. She replies that he is only doing the show because of guilt over her, for never going one day when he was faithful to her. Earlier Joe had told Angelique (Jessica Lange) that he screwed up his marriage to Audrey because he cheated every chance he could get. After viewing the "Take Off with Us" number that Joe has revamped into Air-otica, Audrey tells him it's the best work he has ever done, but she is angry and calls him a son of a bitch. At the cast table-read of the script, she gives him a look when Joe admits that he is not too familiar with it, and more when she reads lines that everyone else thinks are funny. Audrey has another good moment when she explodes at Nurse Blake (C.C.H. Pounder) after getting a bill from her for Joe's treatment, since the nurse had initially refused to do anything when he had had his second heart attack.

We see Audrey dance at the solo rehearsal and for the "Hospital Hop" after the show's company is told about Joe's hospitalization and they have a party. She also sings and dances in the climactic hospital hallucinations medley. Audrey is the main vocalist for "After You've Gone." The number shows that Palmer's singing voice is not like that of Verdon and it is photographed more for Palmer's vocal than for her dancing. Fosse does not showcase her in the same spectacular way he does for Ann Reinking for "You Better Change Your Ways," which suggests that perhaps Palmer does not have Verdon's individual dancing style.

Audrey Paris (Leland Palmer) and Joe Gideon (Roy Scheider) as alter egos for Verdon and Bob Fosse in *All That Jazz* (1979).

Verdon also appeared in the documentary *Hollywood Singing and Dancing: The 1970s*. She talked about how the narrative of *All That Jazz* was not that accurate in terms of her life with Fosse and was made more theatrical than real. She gave Gideon's drug-taking as an example since she claimed that if Fosse was as drugged-up as the character, he would have never been able to work. Verdon acknowledged that the character's womanizing was closer to the truth and reported how she would tell auditioning women to wear revealing clothes and full makeup because she knew that Fosse was turned on by it. Later she said that the character of Audrey was not like her at all, though she thought the film was magnificent. Verdon cited the scene when Gideon is rushed to the hospital after having a heart attack as an example of Fosse's theatrical fiction. In the film, Audrey is sad but in real life Verdon was not. She was more mad because Fosse wanted to get out of the hospital, and she had to use the fact that they were not legally divorced to keep him in hospital. She said he hated her for it but he was obviously very ill and it was clearly the best thing to do.

Roy Scheider commented on Verdon and Fosse in the *Biography* episode on Fosse. He said that he found Verdon to be a sincere and principled person but Fosse was not. To Fosse, she was like a model of decency and yet there was something rueful and bad-boy about him that Verdon found attractive too. Verdon later also spoke about the film to Charlie Rose in an interview broadcast on March 9, 1999. She said that the closest thing to the truth in it was the relationship between the Nicole character and the Reinking character.

On December 3, 1978, Verdon joined Peter Gennaro to dance at the Shubert Theatre to celebrate the 50 year anniversary of the Neighborhood Playhouse's School of the Theatre. The evening was also a fund-raiser for the playhouse's new repertory company.

In February 1979 Verdon was asked by Fosse to supervise the touring company of *Dancin'* since he was busy filming *All That Jazz*. This was to perform simultaneously with the Broadway show which would run until June 27, 1982. Fosse was co-producing the tour and he apologized to her for offering what he considered such a lousy job. Verdon said she was grateful for it. She commented that when you get older and can't cut it any more, the greatest thrill was to work with dancers who could. Verdon later said that she didn't like the job, because she didn't like being the boss. Kathryn Doby had overseen the Broadway production until she left to be in *All That Jazz*, and Verdon took over with what Doby considered less than perfect results. Doby wanted the dances done the way Fosse had envisaged but she thought that Verdon tried to make them a little easier. The short cuts she suggested she said were more practical, and Verdon also insisted on derivations that were unknown to Doby. An example was one number which she thought had come from "Who's Got the Pain." Since Fosse was absent, Verdon was the deciding voice despite Doby's objections.

Verdon went out to the Coast and auditioned 260 girls, from which she only chose two. Back in New York she logged five- and six-day work weeks to prepare the company, which made its debut in Los Angeles. Even after the show had opened, Verdon continued to work with the dancers, particularly since some of the cast members only had six-month contracts, so she had to line up replacements.

In a *Times* article by Tony Chiu (July 24, 1979), Verdon commented that she regarded herself as one of the best choreographic assistants around, but she had no desire to create her own show. This feeling had come after her unhappy experience at the Lido in Paris in 1949. Verdon was also watching for a Broadway comedy to perform in after she had finished her duties on *Dancin'.* She said that good scripts were rare and that another problem was people's perception of her that might stop her from being cast in such a role. To many she was still a dancer and they didn't consider her an actress. The article featured a photograph of Verdon with fellow dancer and dance master Christopher Chadman demonstrating a step at the King Studio. In it she wore her hair tied up and had a long black-sleeved sweater and pants.

Interviewed in the November 1979 issue of *Life*, Fosse spoke about how Nicole had lived with him when she attended Manhattan's Dalton School after things had gotten uptight between her and Verdon. He saw that the problem was having two women in the same household, and also that his wife was more strict with their daughter than he was. Then in 1978 Nicole went away to the North Carolina School of the Arts.

On December 2, 1979, Verdon attended the Kennedy Center Honors gala at the White House in Washington, presumably to support Martha Graham, one of the five artists honored for lifetime achievement in the performing arts. She was reportedly greeted at the reception by Rosalynn Carter and Joan Mondale since President Carter and Vice-President Walter Mondale were unavailable. The event was filmed to be televised by CBS on December 29, 1979; Verdon cannot be seen in the viewed footage. On December 23 she coordinated a gala with James Lipton for the American Ballet Theatre at a theater as a benefit for their unemployment-support fund. The gala was followed by a dinner at Tavern on the Green.

11. All That Jazz

On May 18, 1980, Verdon participated in a gala performance at the Shubert Theatre to mark the 10th anniversary of the Puerto Rican Dance Theatre. On July 12 she and Nicole attended the Grand Opening of Laundry in East Hampton. On August 28, Verdon presented the film of *Damn Yankees* with composer Richard Adler at the Film Makers of the Hamptons Festival devoted to "Music and the Movies" at Guild Hall's John Drew Theatre. On October 19, she was hostess of the Celebrity Auction at the Bruno Walter Auditorium of the New York Public Library's Lincoln Center branch to benefit same. Reporting on the event in the October 20 *New York Times*, Laurie Johnston said that Verdon commented on the celebrities who had been collected to join her in the running of the auction. She told the audience, "I hope you're impressed with this stageful of people—I was about to faint when I saw them all." Verdon also told the audience that she expected a lot from them since they were outnumbered by the celebrities.

She mounted an abbreviated version of *The Nutcracker* at the John Drew Theatre in East Hampton to be performed on December 22 and 23, 1980. The corps de ballet was made up of students from the American School of Ballet, the American Ballet School and the Joffrey Ballet School. The show, choreographed by Kirk Peterson, marked Verdon's debut as a producer, sharing the honor with Peter S. Diggins, Peterson and Gary Chryst. She also appeared in it, waltzing in the first act as Clara's Mother Ginger, and in the second act wore the pink sequined ball gown that Gertrude Lawrence wore in *The King and I*. Verdon's interest in the production came from the fact that Nicole was currently studying at the American School of Ballet and she made her professional debut in the Arabian dance in the show. Verdon said that she had done everything for the show, from casting, to begging costumes, to buying point shoes, and even raising the money for their mini-budget. She also acted as a housemother by putting up all the dancers at her place, and in the city when they rehearsed there.

The project began in October when Verdon attended a ballet performance at the John Drew. It was sold out and the audience went crazy so she asked Anthony Stimac, the managing director of the theater, if they had ever done a *Nutcracker* there. When he told her no, she said that she could do it. Verdon decided to go ahead because she thought it would be great fun. She thought that raising the money would be the biggest problem but it worked out well. The budget was obtained partly from the John Drew Children's Workshop and friends, including Fosse whom she asked to pay for new leotards and skirts. Other help was provided by the local high school whose band lent their uniform tunics. The children's mothers made costumes that couldn't be borrowed.

Verdon commented about her daughter's debut, saying that she had left her career choice up to her. Despite being around dancers and knowing the demands it made and the discipline it took, it is what Nicole wanted. Verdon said that when it came to dance, motherhood went out the window. When all of the kids auditioned, she watched her daughter and forgot who she was, and realized that she was really good. Verdon was already planning to do the show again the next year in East Hampton. Next time she wanted to do it with a larger company and at the high school where there was a bigger stage and more seats. Verdon had compromised for this production by only having seven of the sixty snowflakes that choreographer George Balanchine had in the New York City Ballet's production. Next year she wanted at least ten.

On March 18, 1981, Verdon attended the opening of "Paul Revere's Ride," a one-hour musical version of the Boston epic poem which told of the silversmith and his involvement with a British spy. The show was a benefit done by the Performing Arts Repertory Theatre at the Martin Theatre in the Dalton School, with a book by Allen Cruikshank and John Allen, lyrics by Jill Gorham and music by Malcolm Dodds. There was a reception that Verdon attended after the show. On April 5 she was elected by a group of drama critics and editors as a new member into the Theatre Hall of Fame in "A Tribute to Broadway" at the Uris Theatre. Membership required that a person had a career spanning at least 25 years on Broadway and more than five major credits. The event was sponsored by Revlon and featured performances by Ann Reinking and the American Dance Machine.

On April 14 Verdon attended a fund-raising gala for the Paul Taylor Dance Company at the City Center. She was also part of the entertainment, being in the chorus of the song "From Sea to Shining Sea," (Rudolph Nureyev placed a glass on her backside) and as Betsy Ross (who got her thread stuck). On May 17, the *New York Times* reported that Verdon had given her support to the novel *Mirrors* by James Lipton which was published by St. Martin's Press. The novel was described by the author as a tribute to dancers—not to the glory of a Fonteyn or a Nureyev but to all the Broadway "gypsies" who share the spotlight and never possess the limelight. She was quoted as saying that "at last dancers (usually mute) have a spokesman."

She was interviewed by Suzanne Daley at her Central Park West penthouse for the *New York Times* of May 17, 1981. Daley said Verdon's hair was now the color of peach ice cream and that her dining room was sparsely furnished with oak antiques and little trees in big pots. On one wall were pen and ink drawings that Nicole did several years earlier; there were no signs of her Broadway past. By this time Verdon and Fosse had been separated for ten years. She told Daley that she could still dance but would no longer consider doing a Broadway musical because she couldn't dance for as long as she used to be able to. Verdon said there was no point working on technique because that boat left the dock a long time ago. Dancers died twice: the first time when they realized they were no longer the kind of athletes they were. It was a hard realization and you could either mope around or just go on. She chose the latter, trying her hand at producing, and putting together an abbreviated version of *The Nutcracker* at the John Drew Theatre.

In the summer Verdon planned to go to China on a teaching and performing tour of six cities, accompanying Ben Stevenson, the artistic director of the Houston Ballet. She was to assist in teaching dancers at the Peking Dance Academy some of Stevenson's ballets. She found that the Chinese were rigid dancers because they use a very old Russian technique so Verdon planned to teach theater dance to help them use emotion to act the dances. All in all she was happy. Life had been terrific to her which made her truly appreciate even a blade of grass, and an ant crawling up it. For the future Verdon most of all wanted to make the transition from musicals to comedies. She wanted to play a woman her own age—a wacky 50-year-old woman.

In June 1981 Verdon was presented with the National Film Society's Artistry in Cinema Award for lifetime achievement in musical comedy at New York's Sheraton-Center. One of the speakers at the ceremony was Francis Ford Coppola who would later cast Verdon in his film *The Cotton Club* (1984). He also read her a congratulatory telegram from her friend Gene Nelson.

Also in June, Verdon hosted the Showtime television special *The American Dance Machine: A Celebration of Broadway Dance*. Directed by Philip Gay, the show was a stage performance recorded at the Brooklyn Academy of Music. It was performed by the American Dance Machine company and guest artists as part of their initiative to put rescued Broadway dance numbers in front of an audience. Wearing red silk pajamas and briefly a white shawl and black hat and clogs, Verdon introduced the dances and songs presented. She also did some brief dance moves as part of her introductions. These included a ballroom dance with Lee Roy Reams, who said that he never got to dance with her in *Sweet Charity* on stage. Reams said she choreographed this dance for them in the style of the Fred Astaire-Ginger Rogers number "The Continental." Verdon also led the marching dances for their bows at the end of the show. While her eye-line sometimes made it apparent that she was reading the introductions, Verdon also inserted some humor into her duties.

On August 7, 1981, Verdon and Christopher Chadman produced an all-star evening of cabaret dance entitled "The Great White Way Cabaret." On August 8 the team also produced, directed and choreographed "An Affectionate Look at 50 Years of American Musical Theatre." Both events were part of the weeklong festival celebration of the 50th anniversary of East Hampton's Guild Hall acknowledging "50 Years of American Dance."

Verdon made a guest appearance in the two-part episode of the CBS comedy and war drama *M*A*S*H*, "That's Show Biz" (October 26, 1981). It was written by David Pollock and Elias Davis and directed by Charles S. Dubin. The series was a follow-up to the film *MASH* (1970) directed by Robert Altman, about the staff of the 4077th Mobile Army Surgical Hospital in the Korean War. In the episode, Verdon played Brandy Doyle, an ex-stripper who was part of an U.S.O. tour troupe that visited the unit when one of their singers, Marina (Gail Edwards) needed an appendectomy. Because of road restrictions, they are forced to stay for a few days in the camp, and the troupe gets to do a show in the hospital's post-operative ward. Brandy sings and dances to "Cuddle Up a Little Closer, Lovey Mine" and also appears as a nurse in the comedy sketch of Freddie (Danny Dayton).

Brandy has two subplots: She has to make Margaret (Loretta Swit) less nervous about sharing her tent with her, and she has a romantic interest in Colonel Potter (Harry Morgan). The first subplot is resolved after Brandy confesses that she is just as lonely as Margaret, being a divorced woman—although Brandy has had five husbands. This plot point also has her show that she wears a hairpiece to demonstrate that her appearance is constructed. The second subplot has her accept Potter's invitation to share a bottle of Scotch in his tent, since he knows her from her days as a stripper. This pays off the point that Brandy feels that the soldiers she entertains only see her as an aging burlesque performer who parodies her sex appeal. The idea that she wants to seduce Potter or that he might violate his marriage vows to sleep with her is resolved when he falls unconscious from drinking, whereas Brandy holds her liquor.

Verdon amusingly sashays and vamps as Brandy, and the subplots allow her to demonstrate Brandy's bravado and vulnerability. One's disappointment in not seeing her dance is rationalized by her playing a stripper and not a dancer. Dubin's direction of the troupe's musical numbers presents them in the reality of the improvised performance space. Our view of the entertainers is hindered by the framing of those observing them. Dubin also employs cutaway reaction shots. Verdon gets a funny line after Brandy gives patients dirty cookies. When a soldier starts to read one, she says, "Please, fellas. There are women present. Speak up so we can hear ya!" For the "Cuddle Up" number, Verdon wears a silver shimmery long dress with a leg split and garter, feather boa, and long pink gloves with jewelry. To visit Potter, Brandy wears red silk lounging pajamas which recall Verdon's costume from the *American Dance Machine* television special, and at one point she does a stretch-kick as she lies on his bunk. The morning after Brandy has stayed in Margaret's tent, as she approaches the truck to leave the camp, she shows her a hip thrust dance move which Margaret copies. Brandy also kisses Potter goodbye on the mouth twice; he doesn't object, which suggests that there is a mutual attraction. The star said that she loved doing the episode. She played a lady "who was over the hill who had a crush on a man who was also over the hill but love is love so it doesn't matter how old you are." Verdon didn't have to play old as a character part with lots of added wrinkles because she admitted that her age was obvious and she already had the wrinkles.

In January 1982 she made a guest appearance on the ABC television soap opera *All My Children* playing Judith Kingsley Sawyer, a prim, mean-spirited mother. Verdon was a fill-in for Carol Burnett, whose husband suddenly became ill. When asked why she had recently joined the cast, she replied, "I wasn't asked before."

From February 4 to 13, 1982, a new revue was presented as a work in progress at the Hudson Guild that had musical staging by Verdon. "Vamps and Rideouts," based on the music of Jule Styne, starred the show's conceiver Phyllis Newman, Pauletta Pearson and George Lee Andrews. The director was James Pentecost and the choreographer was Dennis Dennehy.

12

The Mature Actress

Verdon made her only guest appearance in the NBC musical television series *Fame* in the episode "Come One, Come All." It was broadcast on March 11, 1982, written by Hindi Brooks. The show told the stories of the students and faculty of the New York City High School for the Performing Arts. Verdon's appearance reunited her with Albert Hague, who was in the regular cast and who had composed the score for her Broadway show *Redhead*. She played Melinda MacNeill, the mother of student Montgomery MacNeill (P.R. Paul); Melinda has been asked to appear as the celebrity guest in the school's Parent's Nights event. She is also asked to take over the show as director, when the original director falls ill. Melinda is said to be a movie star who has appeared in the musical comedy *Good News* (1947) dancing "The Varsity Drag," and Verdon gets to dance in a scene with the school's dance teacher Lydia (Debbie Allen) when they improvise a dancing number.

The conflict of the narrative occurs when it is believed that Melinda has her own agenda. The school gets upset when she asks that the theme of the night be a 1920s motif and when she asks that agents be invited, presumably to see her and not the students. Lydia reminds her that the night is meant to showcase what the students have learned to do, rather than what Melinda is asking, and that Melinda has chosen the 1920s motif because that is *her* strength. We see Melinda rehearsing the dancers with the "Black Bottom" number and that two students are unable to do a comic burlesque routine she has also suggested. After Melinda withdraws from the night, we see two of the preferred numbers by the students: an unmemorable clown routine by Montgomery and an awfully choreographed dance to "Sing, Sing, Sing." The teleplay presents Melinda as a phony who walks out on the show when she gets a film offer. She is presented as selfish for not watching Montgomery's rehearsal performance, and her shame is expressed with the cliché of smearing her makeup mirror to cover her reflection. Melinda also gets points scored off her with Lydia's imitation of her speaking voice, and when she admits that being at the school has made her realize that she is no longer young. We never get to see the number that Melinda had planned to do in the show, which works against the idea that she was only doing it as self-promotion. We also tend to side with Melinda's stance on the students in the show. Their attitude of refusing to do what they don't like seems to mark them as amateurs; professional performers have the discipline to make whatever they have to do work. Melinda's accusation of amateurism also stings Lydia, who otherwise claims that the students have to "pay" for their desire for fame in sweat.

Verdon has a good dramatic moment when Melinda confronts Bruno (Lee Curreri) and threatens to take him out of the show. She smiles when she sees that Angelo Martelli (Carmine Caridi) recognizes her before he speaks, as if this a moment she has lived before, and she is warm and funny otherwise. Regrettably Verdon outclasses everyone she faces in the show, and this includes Debbie Allen in their dance number. Although we are grateful that Lydia's "Evolution of the Dance" includes Jack Cole, her "modern" dancing lacks Melinda's precision and control, something that the fringes on Lydia's pants help to show. It also doesn't help that director Robert Scheerer cuts from long to medium shots of the women dancing, as he will also use cutaways in the climactic finale rehearsal. The evolution number also suffers from the contrivance of it being obviously choreographed but presented as supposedly improvised by the two dancers. However, it does let us see Verdon strike some very Fosse-style poses and we are grateful for the chance to watch her dance again, even when her performance is compromised as it is here. Allen reported that when she was trying to explain to Verdon the concept for the dance in the scene, Verdon replied, "Honey, just tell me what you want me to do."

Verdon assisted on a May 24, 1982, benefit for Ballet Today, Brett Raphael's new dance company, which included a performance of "The Magic Bird of Fire." This was a rock-disco reimagining of Stravinsky's Firebird Suite that Fosse choreographed for Nicole. It was held at New York's Fashion Institute of Technology Haft Auditorium. Verdon worked on her daughter's costume (a feathery unitard) and acted as intermediary between Fosse, Nicole and Raphael. She and Ann Reinking came for the show, but Fosse only attended the dress rehearsal as he needed to leave for Vancouver to work on his new film *Star 80* (1983).

On January 11, 1983, Verdon introduced the alumni guests at the first program of a gala benefit for American Ballet Theatre II at the Joyce Theatre. On March 23, HBO screened a documentary entitled *Strippers* which Verdon narrated. Directed by Robert Deubel, it explored the art of the

Debbie Allen dances with Verdon in the *Fame* episode entitled "Come One, Come All."

striptease via the lives of six of the world's most famous strippers: Lydia Thompson, Josephine Baker, Gypsy Rose Lee, Little Egypt, Carrie Farrell, and Sally Rand. The special incorporated rare film clips, still photographs, and recreations to tell the story of how the striptease began and how it prospered.

Verdon was mistress of ceremonies at a revue at the Music Hall in Tarrytown for the Theatre League of Westchester for performances from

12. The Mature Actress

April 21 to 24, 1983. The revue, entitled "The Broadway Songbook" presented memorable moments from the Broadway musical theater in its prime. Verdon also joined in the revue's finale dancing having been persuaded to participate by the chairman and creative consultant of the Theatre League, Stanley Greene. He said that he simply wrote her a letter about the league's purpose, to bring Broadway musical entertainment to Westchester County, and it contained the proviso, "I'm going to pester you until you say 'Yes!'"

She appeared in support in the ABC made-for-TV movie *Legs*, broadcast May 2, 1983. This story of life backstage with the famous chorus line was the first film to be shot in Radio City Music Hall. The film was written by Jerrold Freedman from a story by Brian Garfield, and directed by Freedman. In it she played the Rockettes' choreographer Maureen. Verdon has a sizable part, appearing in thirteen scenes. She is repeatedly shown in the rehearsal room, wearing black pants and sweater, sometimes with colored blouses, and can be seen teaching a few simple dance steps.

Times reviewer John J. O'Connor wrote that she projected her own very special brand of vulnerability. He wrote that Verdon was lovely, no more so than when she suddenly begins gliding gracefully about the floor of the rehearsal stage. Interviewed about the film, she said that the Rockettes were an institution and the current 36 were a different breed of woman. Most women in chorus lines wanted to get out and dreamed of going to modern dance or ballet. For the Rockettes, however, the goal was just being a Rockette, with one dancer in the current line having been there for 26 years. Verdon felt that the group were singularly dedicated and saw their work as more than a dance job. They were not interested in being an individual on the stage; they had made that adjustment.

Also on May 2, 1983, the ABC television special *Parade of Stars* was filmed. It would be broadcast on May 22, 1983. It was produced by Alexander H. Cohen, directed by Clark Jones and performed at New York's Palace Theatre as a celebration of the stars who had entertained at the legendary theater during vaudeville and after. Verdon is first seen as a silhouette behind a white screen labelled "Sweet Charity." Rather than burst through it, she moves around it for a dialogue scene with a man playing Vittorio Vidal. Verdon wears a black dress with a sheer blouse that has odd puffy sleeves and catches at the elbows, with a black sparkling bow in her hair. Jones films Verdon in medium shot for the dialogue scene and as she sings the beginning of "If My Friends Could See Me Now," and alternates between medium and long shots. At one point he has Verdon sitting on set steps but still in a long shot, and stays with long shots for Verdon's dance with Vittorio's pop-up hat and cane. The number is abbreviated from the original show but, given Verdon's absence from the film version, it is still wonderful to see her do the number on a stage. The performance also has added poignancy since, at 58, she is obviously not in the same physical or vocal shape as 23 years prior. However Verdon does not embarrass herself in her attempt. She returns for the end of the show's "Give My Regards to Broadway" number and takes a bow, and then is seen with the full cast for the finale singing "Playing the Palace" as they walk in a circle. Verdon wears the same outfit she had before, and can be seen doing kicks in time with the music under the closing credits.

Stephen Holden wrote in the *Times* (May 4, 1983) that the show was produced to aid the Actors' Fund, and the $200,000 that it was expected to raise would go toward the building of a nursing home adjacent to the Actors' Retirement Residence in Englewood, New Jersey. The *Times'* John J. O'Connor wrote on May 23 that Verdon's number was one of the show's first-rate moments.

She next played a small supporting role in Francis Ford Coppola's musical crime drama *The Cotton Club*. The film was in production from August 22 to December 1983 with reshoots done up to March 1984. It was shot at the Kaufman Astoria Studios in New York, with location shooting taking place in Grand Central Station, where Verdon appeared in a scene. The screenplay by Coppola and William Kennedy was based on a story by Kennedy, Coppola and Mario Puzo, which was suggested by James Haskins' pictorial history of the Cotton Club. Verdon played Tish Dwyer and there is the suggestion that she is a former star who is now a dancing teacher. When she meets Gloria Swanson (Diane Venora) at the Club, Tish reverts the expected when she tells her, "You're my biggest fan." Verdon appears in three scenes and is heard in a fourth, although she has little of consequence to do. She is given a close-up for the moment when Tish speaks to the Club's owner Owney Madden (Bob Hoskins), and in the last scene of the film she briefly dances in long shot, showing a dancing woman at Grand Central Station a better tap dancing move.

The film opened on December 14, 1984, with the taglines "It was the jazz age. It was an era of elegance and violence. The action was gambling. The stakes were life and death," "Where crime lords rub elbows with the rich and famous!" and "Welcome to the Cotton Club. Where Crime Lords rub elbows with the rich and famous. Where deals are made, lives are traded. And the legends of jazz light up the night." It was praised by Roger Ebert in the *Chicago Sun-Times* but lambasted by Richard Corliss in *Time*, Vincent Canby in the *New York Times*, and Pauline Kael in *The New Yorker*.

Canby called Verdon one of the supporting actors who is "on and off so fast that their use seems to be profligate." It was not a box office success though it received Academy Award nominations for Best Editing and Best Art Direction and Set Decoration.

A pre-opening screening for *Star 80* was held on November 9, 1983, and Fosse made it a benefit for one of Verdon's favorite causes: the Postgraduate Center for Mental Health, the oldest low-cost psychiatric clinic in New York. The benefit was to specifically aid a newly opened division devoted to counselling patients in the performing arts. Dr. Harry Sands commented that it was necessary because of the constant rejection that was experienced by those in the profession which could be psychologically devastating. This fact had considerable irony given the subject of the film was actress Dorothy Stratten, who was murdered by her husband Paul Snider. A cocktail party at Le Train Blue in Bloomingdale's preceded the screening and there was an after-party at Tavern on the Green with dinner and dancing.

Verdon appeared in a small role in the made-for-TV comedy *The Jerk, Too* (1984), a sequel to the film comedy *The Jerk* (1979). The sequel was directed by Michael Schultz with a screenplay by Ziggy Steinberg and Rocco Urbisci and based on characters created by Steve Martin and Carl Gottlieb. She appears in only one scene as a bag lady, singing and dancing with protagonist Navin Johnston (Mark Blankfield) to the duet "You're Just in Love" from the musical *Call Me Madam*. Verdon wears layered clothes including a red-flower purple hat, pink shirt and scarf, brown jacket, purple skirt, pink gloves, and red shoes. The bag lady's movement is less choreographed than that of the dancers supporting the couple. Her bulky skirt hampers her agility and the scene is badly photographed as a dance performance since the dancer's legs are often cut off with medium shots. Verdon scores laughs from the beginning of the scene where she provides silent reactions to Navin's reciting a letter to his mother.

The film was broadcast on January 6, 1984. The DVD has the tagline "He's not stupid. He's a jerk." It is said that the movie was designed as a pilot for a TV series that never materialized.

Verdon made a guest appearance on the NBC comedy *Gimme a Break!* in the episode "The Center" (April 19, 1984). The show focused on Nell Harper (Nell Carter), the nanny for the family of the widowed chief of police in Glenlawn, California, Carl Kanisky (Dolph Sweet). The episode was written by Jeff Franklin and directed by John Bowab. In it Grandpa Stanley Kanisky (John Hoyt) visits a senior citizen's center where the director is Lilly Le Thrill (Verdon). A former stripper, she has a crush on Andy

(Ray Walston), a resident of the center. The climax is the annual spring fling ballroom dance which the kids also attend and play their own music. Lily and Andy are handcuffed together and locked in a closet to work out their situation.

Lily being the center's director and not a resident spares her the narrative jokes about age that are incorporated with the invasion of some youth center kids. However points are scored off her for being a four-time widow, and with Lily's over-eagerness when she pulls down Andy's jacket and tells him, "I want to cook you dinner!" He is said to be wary of her because he still misses his deceased wife, rather than not finding Lily desirable, and the conclusion provides a tentative resolution in the way they hug but don't kiss. The episode also creates an expectation that Lily will have a romance with Grandpa, which is not met.

Verdon appears in three scenes and her wardrobe is uncharacteristically drab in color. She sports a gray suit with an olive green jacket, and at the dance wears a tan blouse with black long split-skirt. Lily adds some embellishment to the drabness by having a purple waist scarf under the suit jacket, and a choker and sparkly belt to her dance outfit. Lily's split dress also allows us to see Verdon's legs when she is carried into the closet. We also briefly see Verdon dancing a slow dance with Grandpa, and comically dancing in reaction to the bad dancing of youth center kid and dance partner Russell (actor unidentified). Her performance ranges from broadly comic with the overuse of hand gestures, to slyly comic as when she bumps when recalling her act as a stripper, and poignant stillness when talking to Andy in the closet. It's nice to see Verdon reunited with Walston. She gets some funny lines and situations. When she talks of being a stripper, she says that she wore a map of America and as she danced she'd toss out the states, and Lily is funny when she objects to Andy's cancelling the dinner with "I'm already defrosting." He rejects her by saying that there's lots of fish in the sea, and Lily responds with, "You couldn't catch a fish at Marineland." When she dances with Russell, she comments, "You're very brave to do this in public."

The star was a performer and presenter at the 1984 Tony Awards held on June 3, 1984, at the Gershwin Theatre and broadcast on CBS. The cast was announced in a series of Al Hirschfeld caricatures on a backdrop curtain, with Verdon's being of her in *Sweet Charity* that was seen in the *New York Times* of January 23, 1966. She first appears to sing "Nowadays" from *Chicago* with Chita Rivera in a medley of songs by John Kander and Fred Ebb. Both ladies wear black top hat and tails, with a white flower in the jacket, body suits and a neck choker, and carried canes to do the number.

12. The Mature Actress

The hats are sparkly and the chokers are bejewelled. The number is covered by alternating long and medium shots, and the latter suggests that perhaps the white jacket flowers could be bejewelled broaches. (The *Times'* John J. O'Connor described the Rivera-Verdon number as delightful.) She was back in a black sequined jagged gown with splits and black choker to present the Best Choreographer award to Danny Daniels for *The Tap Dance Kid*.

On July 2, 1984, Verdon served as one of the emcees at the first New York International Ballet Competition at City Center. She also joined arms with the other masters, Tony Randall and Kitty Carlisle Hart, and they careered exuberantly off the stage together at the evening's end.

From August to December 1984 Verdon filmed the supporting role of Bess McCarthy in the science fiction comic-drama *Cocoon* (1985) on location in Florida and the Bahamas. She had been cast after the first choice of director Ron Howard, Joan Bennett, turned down the role. Verdon would also receive screen credit as "special music and dance coordinator" for the film. In his DVD audio commentary Howard says that this job involved Verdon choreographing Bess' dance number "That's What We Call Dancing." Bess is the dance instructor at the Sunny Shores St. Petersburg Retirement Community in Tampa, Florida. Verdon is heard singing "That's What We Call Dancing" before she is first seen, and her role presents her as one of the more active of the women who populate the home. The screenplay by Tom Benedek, based on a story by David Saperstein, centers on three "geezers" who discover that the swimming pool in the neighboring house has been appropriated by aliens. The Antareans, led by Walter (Brian Dennehy), energize the pool to provide a lifeforce for the alien clamshell-like cocoons that house his ground crew and that have been moved to the pool from their resting place at sea in the sunken city of Atlantis. The geezers find that the pool water has rejuvenating qualities. Bess marries Art Selwyn (Don Ameche) before joining the rest of the geezers and their friends as they accompany the aliens to a spaceship for a new life.

Bess, like the wives of Joe and Ben, are reactive characters. The difference with Bess is that she is a single woman who is romantically pursued by Art. Verdon's best moment is Bess' smile of post-coital happiness after the men have found that the pool has restored their virility and the three have made love to their respective partners. Holding a hand-fan, Bess says, "I feel so nice today I can't tell you." Ron Howard teases us with the suggestion that we will see Verdon dance in a ballroom sequence but then he quickly cuts away from her dancing with

Ameche to "Dancing in the Dark" when the couple is enveloped by the crowd. The screenplay provides an exchange of double entrendre at the ballroom when Bess tells Art that everything is happening so fast, and he asks, "Are you talking about last night?" One scene where Bess watches Fred Astaire and Ginger Rogers dance "The Continental" in *The Gay Divorcee* (1934) on television is also notable for a color picture on the wall of her house of Verdon in a 1956 *Esquire* magazine pin-up. We also see Verdon in a long shot in a bathing suit, when Bess uses the pool.

The film was released on June 21, 1985, with the taglines "It is everything you've dreamed of. It is nothing you expect" and "Beyond the innocence of youth, and the wisdom of age, lies the wonder of ... *Cocoon*." It was a box office hit and received praise from *Variety*, Janet Maslin in the *New York Times*, and John Stanley in his book *Creature Features*. Pauline Kael in *The New Yorker* called Verdon one of the actresses who "bring the film the bearing of major performers." The film earned Academy Awards for Best Visual Effects and Best Supporting Actor for Don Ameche.

In October 1984 Glenn Loney's book *Unsung Genius. The Passion of Dancer-Choreographer Jack Cole* was released by Franklin Watts publishers. It featured photographs of Verdon in rehearsals with Cole for *Alive and Kicking*, and in performance. The rehearsal photograph displays the respective roles the couple played in their relationship, with Cole sitting in a chair and she sitting on the floor beside him.

In the winter of 1984 Verdon was invited to a party held by Fosse at his Quogue home, and she met his new girlfriend Phoebe Ungerer. As she had accepted Ann Reinking, Verdon also seemed to accept this new girl in order to stay friendly with her husband. She even took her by the arm and introduced her to guests as if it was her home and not Fosse's. This relationship would change after Fosse died.

On February 17, 1985, Verdon appeared on ABC-TV's *Night of 100 Stars II* at New York's Radio City Music Hall. Aired on March 10, 1985, it was a celebrity benefit for the Actors Fund of America, featuring music, songs, dances and comedy. The show was to raise money designated as a building fund for an extended-care facility to be built adjacent to the Actor's Fund Home in Englewood, New Jersey. The number of stars varies according to sources: some say it was 308, others 288. However many, they participated in a seven-hour marathon that was edited to three hours for television. While they worked without pay, the luminaries had perks like complimentary limo service and accommodations at the New York Hilton. Rooms were stocked with Taittinger champagne, Perugina chocolates, Haagen-Dazs cream liqueur, caviar and croissants—gifts from some of the corporate sponsors who had underwritten the production costs. The hotel also provided a staff of trouble-shooters. The company was given a pre-performance party at the Rainbow Room, and "21" was converted into a private canteen. After the taping, the stars were transported back to the Hilton for dinner and danced to Woody Herman's band. Verdon was part of an eight-and-a-half-minute song and dance act entitled "A New Pair of Shoes" which was written by John Kander and Fred Ebb. Tap dancers wore white clothes and red shoes, with a set that was an elongated horizontal white stage under a lit metal arch. Verdon appeared in top hat and tail-coat over a white leotard, and had only a few seconds worth of solo dancing.

On February 25, 1985, she attended the New York Telephone's Gala Music Tribute Dinner and Stage Performances for her and Cy Coleman. It was held at the Waldorf Astoria Hotel to benefit the Postgraduate Center for Mental Health. Verdon was photographed wearing a black dress with a rose pattern with lime green waist-sash and lime green hat.

She was sent by Fosse to prepare a revival of *Sweet Charity* for the Los Angeles Civic Light Opera Company's summer season. He supposedly hadn't wanted the show to be revived, but then heard that it going to be produced with or without him. Fosse was busy preparing the stage show *Big Deal* which is why he allowed Verdon to fill in for him. *Fame*'s Debbie Allen was cast in the title role. John Boab replaced Fosse as director, and Verdon coached Allen and supervised the show's choreography. Allen said that Verdon never told her how to play the role of Charity because "she's too great an artist to do it like that." The original show's choreography had not been notated clearly so the dances needed to be reconstructed from memory. There was raw footage taped from a Japanese tour of the show and the film version, but it still was a Herculean endeavor. Fortunately Verdon's recall of the show and her part were flawless, (Ann Reinking claimed that Verdon had a photographic memory). However, she also contacted every dancer she could who was in the original company to help.

While in Los Angeles, Verdon made a guest appearance on the CBS medical drama *Trapper John, M.D.* "All the King's Horses..." broadcast on March 31, 1985, focussed on the Korean War *M*A*S*H* unit veteran Trapper John McIntyre (Pernell Roberts), who operated as chief surgeon at San Francisco Memorial Hospital. The episode was written by Gene O'Neill and Noreen Tobin. In it Trapper and his son, Dr. John "J.T." McIntyre (Timothy Busfield), are on vacation in South Lake Tahoe. J.T. saves five-year-old Megan Hughes (Maia Brewton) from drowning in the frozen lake but her uncle, outspoken TV personality Lawrence Kolleeny (Tony Roberts), is critical of her treatment. Verdon appeared in the secondary plot back in the San Francisco Hospital as Rosemary Taylor, a professional gambler who is wealthy and thrice married; she's in the hospital for knee surgery after exerting herself doing aerobics. She pretends to have a crush on Dr. George Alonzo "Gonzo" Gates (Gregory Harrison) but actually schemes with him to sting his associate Dr. Justin "Jackpot" Jackson (Brian Mitchell).

The Rosemary plot introduces the idea of a woman 30 years older than a man interested in a May-December romance. Its supposed implausibility is what sets up Jackpot to lose his money since he gambles against her getting Gonzo. Jackpot is also conned into the bet because of Gonzo's expressed attitude of using Rosemary for her money, and that he could learn to love her. The idea that the setup is a sting is suggested by the fact that most of Rosemary's scenes take place with Jackpot rather than Gonzo, which makes us question the veracity of her crush. What saves this potentially offensive narrative is the way Verdon as Rosemary is presented, since she is photographed to look very attractive. She wears a series of high-necked colored pajamas and robes, and a white fur piece over a white suit when she is discharged. Verdon gets two notable lines. She tells Jackpot, "[Gonzo is] a big fish but I bet [long pause] I could land him," and is funny when asking Gonzo, "Would you care to play some strip blackjack? I'm a good loser." Director Charles Siebert probably used a hand-double for the shot where Rosemary does card tricks for Jackpot to demonstrate her profession.

Portrait of Verdon in the *Trapper John, M.D.*, episode "All the King's Horses…."

In April 1985, Verdon and Chita Rivera reunited

at the Music Hall in Tarrytown to perform "Nowadays" from *Chicago*. They wore the red silk Halston pajamas designed for them and Liza Minnelli when they appeared in the Lincoln Center tribute to John Kander and Fred Ebb. Rivera described the number for the show with Verdon, saying that they didn't do cartwheels. They did a little bit of walking and a little bit of singing, but there was a lot of style. After the pair agreed to perform the number together, Verdon asked that a message be sent to Rivera: "Tell her my red costume fits." Rivera commented that that she thought that Verdon was the best of the best and she kept telling her that they should put on their rhinestones and go to Vegas, but Verdon wouldn't do it. Rivera added that sharing the stage with her was a memory that would stay with her for the rest of her life. "Any time she wants to do anything, it'll be all right with me. I'll be ready—I'll even get the top hat and the cane." The number was the grand finale of a performance by the American Dance Machine. The evening covered a multiplicity of benefits: for the Theatre League of Westchester, the Westchester Lighthouse and the American Dance Machine itself. It was also the centennial celebration of the Music Hall.

In the *New York Times*, Alvin Klein reported that Verdon now divided her professional time between performing—only in non-musical roles, mostly "cameo" appearances in films and on television—and passing on her pointers about style and showmanship to individual performers and entire companies. Recently she'd trained Mikhail Baryshnikov in jazz dancing and advised the Peking Ballet about American musical comedy technique. Verdon commented that the need was fulfilled: "It's more exciting than doing eight shows a week." She had given up jumping and splits and was on her way to supervising the staging of a new touring company of the musical *Dancin'.*

Fosse joined Verdon in June 1985 to put the finishing touches on the *Sweet Charity* revival. At a technical run-through, dancer Jane Lanier observed how Verdon seemed to experience it as Charity. She was practically dancing the part in her seat and going through everything that Charity was going through. Fosse was unhappy, claiming that director John had missed the material's innermost core. After the first act and a break for lunch, Fosse asked to see the show again from the top and then gave notes. His credit as production supervisor was changed to director as Bowab left. Fosse also revised Verdon's work with Allen. He pronounced that what they had done with "If My Friends Could See Me Now" was awful. Verdon responded defensively that she had not choreographed it, and Fosse blamed himself more than her since she had respectfully restaged his original work. His taste and technique had developed in 20 years and the revival allowed him the opportunity to rework some of the material. Fosse was also aware that Allen lacked Verdon's qualities, and he had to perform the number for her to show her how he wanted it. The show opened on July 16, 1985, at the Dorothy Chandler Pavilion of the Music Center and ran till August 31.

Verdon made the first of four appearances on the CBS crime action adventure series *Magnum, P.I.* which was filmed in Hawaii with Tom Selleck as Hawaii-based private investigator Thomas Magnum. The episode "Going Home" (October 31, 1985) was directed by Harry Harris and had a teleplay by Chris Abbot-Fish from a story by Gene Donalds. In it, Magnum returns home to Tidewater, Virginia, after an absence of fifteen years for the funeral of his grandfather (played by Selleck's real life father, Bob). His return also brings up the resentment he has towards his stepfather Frank Peterson (David Huddleston). Verdon plays the role of Katherine Peterson, Magnum's mother. The character had previously been spoken of in the episode "Try to Remember" and was then named Martha. She was first seen in the episode entitled "Home from the Sea," named Katherine and played by Susan Blanchard. After "Going Home," Verdon would continue to play the character in the series.

In the episode she is in twelve scenes but only has one change of wardrobe. For the funeral Katherine wears a blue suit, and later changes the jacket for a brown one, and then she wears a red and purple skirt with red jacket. Verdon's hair looks more blonde than red here, and though her eyes are watery at the funeral we don't see tears. Her voice is heard before she is seen, as Magnum watches black-and-white home movies of his grandfather with a younger actress playing Katherine and a younger actor playing Magnum. Verdon gives a good performance as Katherine and her best sustained moment is perhaps the monologue she has talking about Frank's flying.

The first of Verdon's three guest appearances on the ABC family comedy *Webster* was "Hello, I Must Be Going," broadcast on January 1, 1986. The show, filmed in Hollywood, was set in Chicago where the title character (Emmanuel Lewis) was a five-year-old black boy adopted by white retired football player George Papadapolis (Alex Karras) and his wife Katherine (Susan Clark). The episode was written by Mike Scott and Daryl G. Nickens and directed by Joel Zwick. In it Verdon plays Charlotte, Katherine's globe-trotting, much-married aunt, who pays a surprise visit and is set up by matchmaking Webster with George's father Papa Papadapolis (Jack Kruschen).

12. The Mature Actress 195

This romance between elder characters includes physical attraction but not the expected happy ending, since Papa as a homebody is ultimately incompatible with the restless traveler Charlotte. Additionally her sudden disappearance from the story via a note she leaves is rationalized by the idea that coming and going without any warning is part of her style. The teleplay's level of wit is demonstrated with Charlotte's comment about the postal service in India: "And after you lick the stamp there's always that lingering taste of curry."

Verdon is given five different outfits which include a full-length black fur coat and fur piece, long skirts and high boots and a sparkly silver blouse. She sings part of the song "Tenderly" with Kruschen and does a slow-dance with him. Her naturalistic performance stands in contrast to the hand-gesturing amateurism of the regulars. Zwick's staging incorporates the cliché of Webster crushed between Charlotte and Papa as they advance to each other.

The star next made a guest appearance on the CBS action-crime drama *The Equalizer* which was filmed in New York. In "Unnatural Causes" (February 12, 1986), Robert McCall (Edward Woodward) is a retired British intelligence agent turned private detective who helps threatened clients to equalize the odds against them. The episode had a teleplay by Susan Woollen, Coleman Luck and Scott Shepherd, based on a story by Woollen, and was directed by Alan Metzger. Verdon was in a subplot as Kelly Sterling, a retired operative and now owner of the K-S Associates Animated Displays Company that makes window displays for department stores. She is called to assist McCall in the case of a serial killer named Mr. Goodheart (Kevin Geer) who targets lonely middle-aged single women responding to a Lonely Hearts newspaper advertisement. McCall is delayed getting to Kelly's warehouse where she has invited the killer to visit her. McCall's attention is taken by the actress and call girl Sally Ann Carter (Kim Delaney) who is being beaten by the pimp Anza Serrato (Bobby DiCicco).

Verdon appears in three scenes, and only gets to wear two different outfits. The first is a fur coat and underneath a brown-and black-patterned high-necked sweater with black skirt and boots and gold waist-band. The second is a red high-necked sweater with scarf and brown skirt and boots. Kelly gets a laugh leaving the phone message for McCall: "Mr. Goodheart is showing up at eight o'clock. I sure as hell hope you are too." It is a shock to see Verdon the victim of violence as Kelly, struck by Mr. Goodheart when McCall arrives. It leaves her with a head wound.

She returned to *Webster* in the episode "There Goes the Bride"

(March 14, 1986). Like her previous episode, this one was written by Mike Scott and Daryl G. Nickens and directed by Joel Zwick. In it Aunt Charlotte visits to get married (for the sixth time) to a 28-year-old Pamplona poet named Ramon Fernandez Garcia Guzman (she calls him Raul). Katherine (Susan Clark) and George (Alex Karras) offer to have the wedding in their home. Charlotte is nervous because she has previously always eloped. The episode's title prefigures the fate of Charlotte, but this is prefigured by her behavior in her previous episode "Hello, I Must Be Going."

The idea that Raul is a younger man for Charlotte prefigures that the wedding will not take place. It also underlines the idea of her as a desperate older wealthy woman chasing an unsuitable love interest and perhaps being exploited by an opportunist, although Raul is a cipher because he never appears in the episode. The fact that Charlotte runs out on the planned wedding to elope in Bora Bora reverses the expectation that she also sees Raul as an opportunist, although her leaving a note rather than telling Katherine about her leaving seems cruel. This cruelty is lessened when Charlotte leaves the wedding gown and encourages her niece to use it for the formal wedding that she never had.

The teleplay also features a sly comment on Verdon as a dancer. Charlotte asks to dance with Webster (Emmanuel Lewis) at the proposed wedding and he fears that she will not be able to keep up with his dancing, which he demonstrates. After she sees his dance, Charlotte acknowledges that he is right, calling him "hot stuff," although the boy's moves are nothing special. Perhaps her admission is meant to not insult Webster, but it still reads as an insult to Verdon as a former dancer. The teleplay has some amusing lines. Katherine tells Charlotte that it isn't every day that she gets married, and Charlotte replies, "It just seems that way." When it is learned that the organist for the wedding is dead, Katherine cries that he signed a contract, and Charlotte replies, "I think he found a loophole." Charlotte tells Webster about Raul when she says, "Katherine wants him to wear a tuxedo. It took me two hours to convince him to wear shoes."

Verdon wears four different outfits and a wedding dress, although unlike the previous episode, the time and days passed for her stay are not indicated. Charlotte's wardrobe (including a fur hat and a fur piece) demonstrates the idea that she is a wealthy woman. The white wedding dress provides for a laugh line when she tells Katherine, "I really feel funny wearing white. My past screams red." In this episode Verdon's performance incorporates the same excessive hand-gesturing as the regulars, which lessens her professionalism. She gets a nice moment when Charlotte tells Webster that she doesn't like everyone making a fuss over her wedding, and smiles when she adds, "I'm the one who likes to make the fuss." Charlotte also gets a laugh over her wedding gown when she tells Webster to wait for her "while I ditch this lace."

It was rumored that Verdon took over the technical direction of *Big Deal* temporarily when Fosse was ill with a virus. The show had previews from April 1, 1986, and opened on April 10. It was said that she was able to do this since she was in New York supervising the rehearsals of the *Sweet Charity* revival at the Minskoff Theatre which was having previews from April 15. On April 20, Verdon attended the Second Annual Mr. Abbott Award for Lifetime Achievement in the Theater which honoured Fosse at the Marriott Marquis Hotel in New York. For the event she wore a black satin dress with sheer overlay top, lace sleeves and black choker.

Sweet Charity opened on April 27, 1986, and ran till March 15, 1987. Frank Rich of the *Times* wrote of Debbie Allen that "if she somewhat lacks the vulnerability of the original Charity, Gwen Verdon, she is almost eerie in her recreation of her predecessor's Chaplinesque gait and sparkling gymnastics." The show won Tony Awards for Best Revival, Michael Rupert for Best Featured Actor, Bebe Neuwirth for Best Featured Actress in a Musical, and Patricia Zipprodt for Best Costume Design. Allen was nominated for the Best Actress in a Musical. Neuwirth, who played Nickie, commented that she thought Verdon was a genius. For "Hey Big Spender" she advised the dances to use the silences in the number to show that they were just not standing. She said "Put it in neutral and rev!"

Interviewed by Thomas Morgan in the *Times* (May 28, 1986), Allen said that she was coached by Verdon in a Los Angeles studio for a West Coast run of the show about a year ago, and that dancing with her was like playing a duet with Miles Davis: "It's an artistic high." Allen admitted that Verdon was real tough, but tough with a soft edge, and she shared stage pointers and offered the advice of someone who had been there before. Since Charity is in every scene but two, Allen was reminded that the show was all night long. Verdon told her where she could rest in numbers, and since there were only a couple of places where she could do that, she had better take advantage of them. Allen also said that Verdon gave her space but never gave her line readings.

The star was also interviewed for the article. Verdon said that when Fosse decided to revive the musical, she had only agreed to help him find former dancers who remembered it. She soon discovered that she remembered the dances better than anyone else. Verdon and her assistants taught the dance routines, and Fosse directed the scenes in Los Angeles. She said that she had memories about the show once she saw Allen doing it but she didn't have to remember it any more because it was there. It was terrific for her to see the show because Verdon never saw it when she was in it and she never knew how she looked doing it. She said Allen was doing everything she ever did. The only thing that might look different is that the movement on her (Verdon) may have looked more balletic, and it looked more athletic on Allen, but that may have been because Allen was younger than Verdon was when she did it. She said of Allen that she learned so fast that she knew it was Allen's role the minute they started working together.

Verdon made a guest appearance on the short-lived NBC television comedy *All Is Forgiven* in the episode "I Can't Say No" (May 29, 1986). It was written by Ian Praiser and Howard Abbott Gewirtz and directed by Jeff Chambers. The show was centered on New Yorker Paula Russell (Bess Armstrong), the newly appointed producer of the soap opera *All Is Forgiven*. In the episode Verdon played Bonita Harrell, an actress and former movie star guest starring on the show, and also the ex-girlfriend of the show's director Wendell (Bill Wiley). She is shown to be manipulative and described as "poison" and an "evil woman" which gives her an edge. The writers also show that Bonita retains her sexual allure to Wendell, despite his awareness of her mistreatment of him, and it's always good to see a mature woman presented as a sexual being.

Verdon appears in three scenes and her performance is theatrical which is appropriate for an actress and a woman who pretends to have desire for a man to get what she wants. Her over-gesticulation also matches the same tendency in some of the other performers who act broadly or just plain bad, like Wiley. Presumably to match the character's self-confidence she wears two form-fitting silk outfits, with a red blouse and green pants with green waist-scarf recalling the red silk outfits Verdon wears in her *M*A*S*H* episode and the *American Dance Machine* special. She also wears a black fur piece which suggests the wealth that Bonita left Wendell for and that she now lacks. Bonita is seen smoking in her last scene, presumably to add to the character's duplicity. This scene also has Chambers use what appears to be a body double when she displays a leg. Verdon is given a long reaction shot at the end. She gets a laugh from a moment when she turns her head away from Wendell's attempt at a kiss, with the excuse of "Fever blister."

Verdon attended the closing night of *Big Deal* on June 8, 1986. The show had received a mixed review by Frank Rich in the *New York Times* and had not been a hit. From September 1986, Verdon appeared in the supporting role of Vera, the manageress of the Alamo Beauty Shop in

Austin, Texas, in the comedy *Nadine* (1987). Set in 1954 and filmed on location in Austin by writer-director Robert Benton, it stars Kim Basinger as Nadine Hightower, a beauty shop manicurist who has had art studies taken by photographer Raymond Escobar (Jerry Stiller). When she goes to retrieve the photos, she finds Escobar dead and in her photo file there is a map of confidential Highway Department plans for a superhighway. The man who has killed Escobar for the plans, Buford Pope (Rip Torn), has Nadine's art studies, and he will kill to get the map back. Verdon only appears in two scenes.

The film was released on August 7, 1987, with the taglines "The cops want HER. The killers want HIM. THEY want a divorce. Ain't love grand!" and "They're a Couple on the Run ... from Each Other." It was praised by the *Times*' Vincent Canby, who also commented that Verdon could have done more if she'd had the material. It received a mixed reaction from Roger Ebert in the *Chicago Sun-Times* but was lambasted by Pauline Kael in *The New Yorker*. The film was a box office failure.

Verdon made her second guest star appearance on *Magnum, P.I.* on

Nadine Hightower (Kim Basinger, left) is not impressed by the offer of money from Vera (Verdon) as witnessed by Vernon Hightower (Jeff Bridges) in this lobby card for *Nadine* (1987).

February 11, 1987, in the episode "Forty." It was directed by Russ Mayberry and had a teleplay by Bruce Cervi. It focused on the fortieth birthday of Magnum (Tom Selleck) and his meeting Chinese television news reporter Linda Lee Ellison (Patrice Martinez). Since she is involved with John Walter Costa (James Luisi), an arms dealer, this helps him investigate Honolulu's Chinatown "wolf" gangs. Verdon's appearance amounts to a cameo, with her shown in only one scene and her voice heard in two voicemail messages. She is seen in bed in a purple nightgown answering Magnum's call, and her three lines are stock.

In the fall of 1986, Verdon coached Ann Reinking to replace Debbie Allen in *Sweet Charity*, with Fosse directing. Reinking took over the role in October 1986. Fosse's alleged harsh treatment of his star was said to be softened by Verdon, as if to protect the increasingly ill director. She knew that Reinking had to be strong to play the part of Charity, one of the most demanding in musical theater. Perhaps in an attempt to differentiate her from Verdon, it was decided to have Reinking wear a bleached-blonde wig as Charity. However, inexplicably, publicists refused to replace the face of Allen with Reinking's on the Playbill program. Although Reinking stayed with it till March 1987 box office receipts were said to be disappointing. This meant that a national touring company of the show would be required to recoup costs, and would not star Reinking.

Verdon attended the rehearsal of the show on October 19, 1986, after it was learned that the musical director, Stanley Lobowski, had died from a heart attack. Knowing this would have upset Fosse, she came with copies of Uta Hagen's book *Respect for Acting* and passed them among the company. Verdon was aware that he had little respect for the book, so when he arrived and saw everyone reading it, he laughed. Her relationship with Fosse had gotten closer with their reunion in the show. She would even come to the rehearsal studio before him to pick up the garbage. They began dressing in the same button-down shirts and slacks, with Verdon in blue and Fosse in black. It was even said that they could feel each other's presence in the room. Once she stopped in the middle of working onstage with the company and told a dancer that he had arrived. When they looked around they saw that Fosse was standing at the back of the house. On May 4, 1987, Verdon presented one of the 36th annual Capezio Dance Awards and $5,000 to Fosse at a ceremony at the Juilliard Theatre. She called her husband's contributions to the dance world "unique," "risky" and "provocative."

Verdon made a guest appearance on the ABC drama *Hotel* in an episode entitled "Second Thoughts" which was broadcast on May 20, 1987.

The show was set at the elegant St. Gregory Hotel in San Francisco, managed by Peter McDermott (James Brolin). It is often visited by famous guest stars who have a romantic encounter. Filmed in Hollywood, the episode was written by Sandra Kay Siegel and directed by Vincent McEveety. Verdon played Iris Lloyd.

She was a presenter at the 1987 Tony Awards which were held at the Mark Hellinger Theatre on June 7, 1987, and broadcast live on CBS. Verdon wore a black sequined dress with net lace long sleeves and net chest trim and a black choker. She was joined by Fosse for the Best Choreography Award. He commented that it has been said that the art of choreography is only about 50 percent conception, and that the real test of your talent is getting a number of people in a room who are just a little crazier than you and who can try and live out that thing in your head; "And sometimes, if you're very lucky, you can find someone who dances it better than you ever dreamed it." Fosse said that Verdon hated for him to say anything nice about her but for him that "someone" was her. She smiled and thanked Fosse as the audience applauded her. He let her read the nominees and read the winner: Gillian Gregory for *Me and My Girl*. Verdon also stayed on stage as Fosse read the nominees and announced the winner for Best Director of a Musical; Trevor Nunn and John Caird for *Les Miserables*. Nunn said in his acceptance speech that just to be on the same stage as his two presenters overwhelmed him. One surprise that evening: Neither Verdon nor Fosse appear to join the show's cast onstage to applaud the award given to George Abbott.

On June 22, 1987, Verdon was one of the many Broadway and Hollywood stars who celebrated the one hundredth birthday of Abbott (his real birthday was June 25). The event held at the Palace Theatre in New York was alternatively titled *Happy Birthday, Mr. Abbott!* and *The Night of 100 Years* and benefited the Actors Fund of America. In the archival record of the evening viewed, Verdon is only fleetingly seen amongst the collection of female stars introduced to the song "The Most Beautiful Girl in the World" sung by Arthur Rubin. She wears a black long dress and speckled black and white jacket and matching scarf, and holds a rose like all the other ladies. She cannot be seen at the end when the cast all sing "Heart" from *Damn Yankees*. An article about the evening in the *New York Times* by Andrew L. Yarrow does not even mention Verdon, which perhaps suggests that her appearance was limited to the opening introduction of Abbott's 18 leading ladies.

13

Fosse Dies

On June 23, 1987, Fosse turned 60 and he threw a party at his Quogue home, which Verdon attended. Then the couple reunited again to start rehearsals at the Minskoff Theatre for the national touring company of *Sweet Charity*, in which Donna McKechnie had been cast. As Fosse worked alone in a neighboring studio, Verdon and Mimi Quillon prepared McKechnie. McKechnie says that when it came time to learn the closet scene, she was asked if she wanted to do Chita's version, Ann's version, Debbie's version, or Verdon's version. McKechnie found this a no-brainer and told Verdon that she wanted to do Verdon's version and that was the version they did. When she expressed her concern about playing the role, Verdon told her that if she could get through the first act, then she would be fine. After McKechnie finished a run of the first act, she looked over to her teacher and saw Verdon's face full of emotion. Verdon made her feel that something important had happened and that's why McKechnie says that Verdon was the most generous person she met in her entire life. She felt that Verdon gave her part of her soul, and although she taught a lot of people, it was that experience being alone with her that she valued. McKechnie says that when Fosse came in to look at what she and Verdon had done, he watched and then asked her, "Are you going to do her version or my version?" McKechnie was torn between Fosse as the director and Verdon whom she considered a goddess. She looked at Verdon who was miming "my version." However she told Fosse she would do his version.

The show's pre-sales were disappointing so Fosse and Verdon decided to take the jobs that would have normally been done by stage managers and dance captains. They travelled with the show, beginning in Toronto in July 1987 where it opened at the Royal Alexandra Theatre, and then on to Philadelphia. On September 23, 1987, Verdon was in Washington with Fosse for the opening night at the National Theatre of *Sweet Charity*. Perhaps aware of his growing dependence on his wife, Fosse's girlfriend Phoebe Ungerer did not come to Washington. The show was still doing badly at the box office which he could not understand since he felt it was in wonderful shape.

During the day the couple attended a production meeting with the various departments. Fosse supposedly coughed throughout. They were told that the morale of the company was low because they were concerned with being underpaid and that the tour was being rushed. After the meeting, the company split into groups to rehearse individual pieces. At five-thirty he dismissed the company for their six-thirty half-hour call. He then spent the next hour with the orchestra, Verdon by his side. She reportedly spoke to the drummer about a couple of things he had to catch in "If My Friends Could See Me Now." After six they left the theater to change for the opening night.

They headed toward the Willard hotel, where they had separate rooms. One source claims that Verdon accompanied Fosse because, when she saw him leaving the theater, she sensed that something was wrong. Another says that when Verdon saw him talking with the stage manager on stage she hadn't recognized the man who looked so ashen and gray. When she did and saw him leaving, she ran after him. At the hotel he changed into a tuxedo and the couple left to return to the National. Fosse reportedly fell to the ground on the far side of the crosswalk, a few steps from the curb, on the intersection between Pennsylvania and Fourteenth Street. Another source claims that he fell even before Fosse and Verdon made it to the hotel. In his DVD audio commentary on *All That Jazz*, Roy Scheider claims that Fosse laid down on a bench. In the 1999 *E! True Hollywood Story* re-enactment, Fosse falls in a park near a bench. In the same special, Ben Vereen says that he understood that the couple were walking across a park. Verdon later told the press how Fosse's attack had occurred in his hotel room and not in the street, presumably in an effort to cover up the truth.

Fosse's eyes were said to be half shut and his complexion was green. A crowd gathered around the scene and traffic clogged the intersection. Verdon thought that he had had another seizure but it was his final heart attack. Some claim that she asked for someone to call an ambulance. Verdon dropped to her knees and held Fosse's head in her lap. Others say that she ran around pushing people out of the way to disperse the crowd, knowing how embarrassed he would be about such a public commotion. Others say that this running around pushing people out of the way occurred to allow paramedics to get to Fosse. One source claims that a doctor appeared from the crowd, listened for a heartbeat, and then began to pound on Fosse's chest. Fosse told him to stop because he was hurting him and said that he was all right. Fire trucks were said to have arrived before the ambulance, which appeared after 20 minutes. With Fosse inside, the ambulance proceeded to George Washington University Hospital, a mile and half from where Fosse had collapsed. It arrived at the emergency room at 6:48 p.m. and at 7:23 p.m. he was pronounced dead. Another source claims that Fosse was worked on for 90 minutes before the pronouncement.

Back at the theater, the absence of the couple was felt to be a sign that the show was going to close. But Peter Kulak, the general manager, had heard the news of Fosse's death and informed the company after the curtain calls. The opening night party was still held at the Old Ebbitt Grill since the producers felt that getting drunk would ease their sorrow. The tour would only last for three months and it reportedly did not recoup the investment.

After Fosse's death it was reported that Verdon went back to the hotel where she was sedated. Fosse's body was held at a Washington funeral home where there was a brief viewing. She refused permission for it to be flown back to New York with her. The couple had had a longstanding agreement that they would never travel together to protect their daughter Nicole, in case something happened to the both of them. Although this now seemed ridiculous given that Fosse was already dead, Verdon insisted. A hearse was arranged to drive him back, and she followed in a limousine. Fosse's body was cremated on September 24, 1987, at the Trinity Church Crematory in New York. That night the lights were dimmed on Broadway for one minute as a tribute to him. Verdon was apparently specifically irked by a quote from Bernard B. Jacobs in the *New York Times* article on Fosse by Jeremy Gerard published on September 25, 1987. While he had said some complimentary things about Fosse, Jacobs also stated that he was not a very nice man and that he could be nasty to other people. She blamed Jacobs for aggravating her late husband's ill health in the way he produced *Big Deal*.

Sources differ as to the size of Fosse's estate. Some give it as $1 million, others $4 million, which included the Quogue house and over a million in cash. The bulk of it was divided between Verdon and Nicole. Verdon wrote a letter to New York Hospital, expressing her appreciation to the surgeon who had performed the bypass on Fosse. She said that he had given her husband a great seven years and that he had lived them fully and never suffered another pain. Verdon wrote that it was true that Fosse had died because he would not change his behaviour; however, his attitude was that these were his bonus years.

She and Nicole took the urn with his ashes to Quogue and scattered the ashes along the beach. Verdon then went to Fosse's house where she found Phoebe Ungerer. Despite the four years of friendliness she had shown the girl, Verdon apparently now gave her notice to vacate. Verdon gave away a few items that she knew Fosse would have wanted specific friends to have. An example was his box of Havana cigars which she gave to Budd Schulberg. He said that when she did so, Verdon reminisced about Fosse, their marriage and the wonderful life they had together. She talked about family fun and barbecues at the house, as if they had a conventional marriage, which it certainly was not. Although Verdon had never lived in the Quogue house, she decided to keep it and sell the places she owned in Bridgehampton and East Hampton because she felt she had too many. It was to be kept exactly as it was, with the same furniture and dance studio which Nicole would use. Verdon was Fosse's widow and acted like it, wiping away the reality of Ungerer's relationship as her husband's last.

On September 29, 1987, she bumped into Donna McKechnie after the memorial service held for Michael Bennet at the Shubert Alley Theatre. The last time the women had seen each other was the day Fosse had died. McKechnie said that Verdon hadn't wanted anyone to call her because she wanted to be alone for a while. They fell into each other's arms and McKechnie wept. Verdon worked to keep herself together and told her friend that she was just barely okay. McKechnie thought it was obvious that she did not want to talk about it in the street and that she seemed very upset. The women then had what McKechnie likened to a Pinter exchange. Verdon said, "He lives inside you" and McKechnie told her, "Yes I know." Another report had Verdon saying that they "keep them alive inside." Then she disappeared.

Verdon's third appearance on *Magnum, P.I.*, "Infinity and Jelly Doughnuts" (October 7, 1987), was directed by John C. Flinn III and had a teleplay by Chris Abbott. It sees Magnum (Tom Selleck) in a coma after being shot and having out-of-body memories of what led to the shooting. After he comes out of the coma he continues to have memories which eventually lead to his discovery that his shooting was done as revenge by Father Timothy (Richard Narita), one of the people by Magnum's bed in the hospital. Verdon is another visitor as Magnum's mother Kathleen Peterson; she has little of consequence to do. It is ironic then that she received an Emmy Award nomination for the show as Outstanding Guest Performer in a Drama Series.

The star wore three different outfits: a pink suit with white blouse, a pink blouse with beige pants and a colored scarf, and a brown and white patterned dress. Verdon gulps nervously upon meeting Higgins (John

Hillerman) at Magnum's bedside and gets teary-eyed when speaking to her son. She gets a funny line when she asks Magnum after he has regained consciousness, "Did you miss me? Well, of course you did. Why did I even ask." A hilltop scenes between her and Selleck reveals their difference in show status. The wind that blows in the scene is behind Verdon, dishevelling her hair, but it blows in front of him in a more flattering way.

On October 30, 1987, a memorial took place for Fosse at the Palace Theatre. Verdon is said to have stood at the entrance and personally greeted the mourners as the bereaved widow, dressed in black. Verdon reportedly did the same at the end of the service, stationed at the rear of the theater and thanking those who came. She wore a smile and behaved convivially to keep the event as "up" as possible. Verdon was not one of the speakers at the event but she is said to have compiled a film retrospective of Fosse's work for the occasion. Another source claims that the film was prepared by Stanley Donen and she asked that it be altered. What Verdon supposedly wanted out was a scene from *Give a Girl a Break*, the 1953 MGM musical that Donen had directed Fosse in. However other sources say that the film *was* featured in the retrospective. She also supposedly used her prerogative to veto the idea that dancers from *Sweet Charity* perform the Fosse Combination. Verdon only wanted men to speak for Fosse, and the only actor to be Roy Scheider.

That night a wake was held at the Crystal Ballroom of New York's Tavern on the Green. Over 200 people attended, including Verdon. Fosse had bequeathed $25,000 to 66 friends in his will so that they could have dinner on him but stipulated that they had to donate the money back to the party budget. The division of funds came out to $378.79 to each friend. He did this so that they would feel more like investors and therefore be more likely to show up. Once again Verdon presided over the evening, asking that the restaurant owner keep the press out, though some made their way in. Again she stood at the doorway greeting the guests, shaking hands and kissing people. Another source said that she was in the restaurant foyer to greet people and, with the help of a few servers, also passed out champagne flutes to the guests. Phoebe Ungerer attended; one wonders what Verdon's greeting to her would have been. Especially after she had just evicted the younger woman from what was formerly her home. Kathryn Doby reported that Verdon would not talk to Ungerer the whole night, which made Ungerer cry. But Verdon continued to be gracious to Kim St. Leon, whom she had greeted at the memorial and then at the restaurant. St. Leon apparently thanked Verdon for interceding in the battle with Ann Reinking at the hospital when Fosse had his heart attacks, something she had not been able to do previously. Reportedly in response to the whispered thanks, she smiled and closed her eyes for a moment, as if she had just heard a touching reminiscence.

During the evening Verdon and Nicole got up on stage and did a dance. They were later joined by Ann Reinking, who performed an Irish jig. After dinner Ben Vereen called for people to dance, and Verdon and Fosse's girlfriends joined him. Another source claims that this occurred at midnight. They all supposedly formed a circle around Verdon, who urged Fosse's writer friends onto the floor to enter the circle of women. She wanted them to demonstrate the steps they had learned from him. After they did so, Verdon, Reinking and Nicole were left in the circle to dance together. Their eyes were closed, their hips rolled, and their arms snaked upward. John Rubenstein said that they hugged each other and were "being hot performers and hot with each other." He described the dynamic being expressed by the wife and a girlfriend and daughter as a "complex, almost demented relationship." In the *E! True Hollywood Story* episode on Fosse, Daniel Melnick stated that the dance was begun by Reinking and Nicole, who were joined by Verdon. Some found the celebration of Fosse's death in this manner to be inappropriate and they left. Other Fosse dancers joined the women on the floor and did a ritual dance to the beat of the disco music. Eventually the rest of the crowd joined in. It was said that such a scene could only have been created by Fosse.

Verdon played the supporting role of Edith Cooper in the CBS-TV movie *Best Friends for Life*, on January 18, 1988. Filmed in Waxhaw, North Carolina, it was directed by Michael Switzer from a teleplay by Cynthia Whitcomb based on the novel by Shelby Hearon. The film centered on the friendship between Harriet Cahill (Gena Rowlands) and Sarah "Coop" Cooper (Linda Lavin) which began when the women were children. Their relationship is tested by their different social circles, the deaths of their husbands, new romance and serious illness. Edith was presumably a relative of Sarah, perhaps her mother. On January 26, 1988, Verdon was one of the guests at the opening night of *The Phantom of the Opera* at the Majestic Theatre.

She made her fourth *Magnum, P.I.* guest appearance in the two-part episode "Resolutions" (May 1988). Written by Stephen A. Miller and Chris Abbott and directed by Burt Brinckerhoff it was the finale of the series where Magnum (Tom Selleck) rejoins the navy. Magnum returns to Virginia for his forty-first birthday, then goes back to Hawaii to reunite with his former girlfriend Linda Lee Ellison (Patrice Martinez), is the best man at the wedding of Rick (Larry Manetti), and finds Lily Catherine (Kristen

Carreira), the daughter he believed to be dead. Katherine Peterson (Verdon) appears in five scenes, and she wears three different outfits. They are a purple suit with white blouse, a striped blue and white jacket with blue skirt, and a white sweater with black blouse and black skirt. Verdon's best moment is when Katherine tells Magnum how after her husband had died she would sit in his dark clothes closet to talk to him. She is not in any new scenes in the second part of the episode.

On June 6, 1988, it was reported in the *Times* that Verdon was working on a PBS documentary on Fosse's career and said she was contractually obligated not to release the rights to his dances for a proposed tribute until that program was broadcast. On September 9 she attended the Center Theatre Group and the Ahmanson Theatre Evening Tribute to Neil Simon and Bobby Fryer at Century Plaza Hotel in Los Angeles. Verdon wore a black dress with horizontal stripes and black choker.

She returned to *Webster* for her third and final guest appearance in the episode "Take My Cousin, Please" (November 4, 1988), written by Simon Muntner and directed by Lee Bernhardi. Verdon's Aunt Charlotte makes another surprise visit, this time accompanied by orphan Bobby (Jonathan Brandis). The regulars Katherine (Susan Clark) and George (Alex Karras) do not appear in the episode since we are told that they have gone to the mountains. However they have left Webster (Emmanuel Lewis) behind with Papa (Jack Kruschen). Charlotte tells how she plans to adopt Bobby when she returns to New York. Webster helps Bobby to admit that he is not the good kid she thinks he is: He is shown to be an opportunist who is using Charlotte for her money, and then a thief when he steals money from her purse. Webster can't bring himself to tell Charlotte after he oversees her telling Papa that Bobby is a good kid and her whole life. She walks in on Webster when he attempts to return the money Bobby has stolen, so it appears that *he* has taken it. A rationalization is provided for Bobby's behavior since he believes that Charlotte will be like the previous parents he has had and also "cut out on him." Webster asks Bobby to test her and she passes the test, after he confesses. She tells him that it must have been hard to admit and she forgives him. Bobby has learned his life lesson and gives Webster a community center raffle ticket prize he has won, before leaving for New York with Charlotte.

Verdon wears three different outfits in the episode to suggest Charlotte staying three days, including boldly colored purple and dark green suits, with furs that again show that she is wealthy. Like the prior episode she employs the same over-gesturing as the other actors, and although she has nothing remarkable to do, she is still a likable presence. Verdon only gets one good laugh line in reference to Charlotte imagining being a mother who wears a bathrobe and great big fuzzy slippers and watches TV all day. This is when she asks Papa, "Can Mr. Ed still dial a telephone with a pencil in his teeth?"

Verdon came back to play Bess Selwyn in the *Cocoon* sequel *Cocoon: The Return* (1988) which was filmed on location in Miami, Florida, and San Rafael, California. Ron Howard had declined to direct the film, and Daniel Petrie took the reins. The film has the geezers from the original returning to Earth five years later as the alien Antareans want to retrieve the cocoons they have left in the sea. A complication arises when the St. Petersburg Oceanographic Institute take one of the cocoons they have found at sea, opens it, keeps the alien that is inside and names him Phil (Wendy Cooke). The Antareans and their human friends retrieve Phil so that they can return him and the other cocoons to their planet. Some of the geezers don't go back, but Bess (Verdon) is one who does. The screenplay by Stephen McPherson was based on a story by McPherson and Elizabeth Bradley. The narrative now has Bess learn she is pregnant, and her decision to go back to the alien planet is made since only there can she live to raise her child. Verdon is shown briefly dancing with Art (Don Ameche) in a nightclub, but her best scene is when Bess tries on cocktail dresses when the women go shopping. She looks fetching in a black dress with colored ruffles, black scarf and black hat. Verdon also has a dialogue scene with Art where Bess explains her rationale for returning to the alien planet, giving her more to say than she had in the original film.

The film was released on November 23, 1988, with the tagline "This holiday season, journey to the most wonderful place in the universe ... home." It was lambasted by Rita Kempley in the *Washington Post*, Richard Schieb on *Moria: Science Fiction, Horror and Fantasy Review*, and John Stanley in *Creature Features*. The film was a box office failure.

In 1988 Verdon received an honorary degree from Hamilton College. She made a guest appearance on the NBC comedy *Dear John* in the episode "The Second Time Around" (March 9, 1989), written by Wayne Terwilliger and directed by Art Wolff. The show was filmed in Hollywood and centered on abandoned Manhattan husband John Lacey (Judd Hirsch) who joins the One Two One Club, a support group for divorced and widowed people convened by Louise Mercer (Jane Carr). It was a remake of a British comedy series of the same title. In the episode Verdon plays John's old flame Yvonne, an older woman who was his first 30 years prior when he was 15. The age disparity between the two is made from her being the grandmother of adult children, although her age is never stated. John's initial reluctance to return what he assumes is a romantic interest soon gives way to his desire for her. Yvonne at first laughs at John making a pass at her when he gropes a breast. She tells him that she had felt guilty for her past behavior which she saw as her taking advantage of him because she was lonely. However now she loses the guilt because she sees that he has turned out to be a terrific guy. The couple's kiss on the mouth seems only out of friendliness but then a second kiss suggests that perhaps they will sleep together again. This is another television episode where a mature woman is shown to be a sexual creature and is found to be desirable by a somewhat younger man.

The star appears in two scenes and wears two different outfits. There is a blue jacket with blue patterned scarf, black skirt and black gloves, and then a black wrap over a blue sparkly patterned blouse with black skirt and red scarf. Verdon gives a competent performance although the teleplay provides her with no witty lines or any great emotional scenes to play. However, her appearance does fit the bill for Yvonne's sustained attractiveness, without an obvious display of sexuality.

Verdon was credited as production consultant when *Damn Yankees* opened at the Darien Dinner Theatre on April 16, 1989. She reportedly supervised the dance numbers that featured Lola (played by Gwen Arment). The show was directed and choreographed by Bick Goss and ran for three months. On April 18 Verdon attended the First Annual Broadway Musical Hall of Fame Induction Cocktail Party at Letizia Restaurant in New York City. She wore a dark green jacket and skirt with black outline, a black waist-bow, and black-green-and red–patterned blouse with matching necktie. On April 23 she was one of the 30 female inductees to the Player's Club at its 100th anniversary benefit at the Shubert Theatre. She was photographed at the cocktail party at Sardi's Restaurant before the event, wearing a black gown with horizontal stripes, green scarf, and choker. This was the same gown Verdon wore on September 9 at the Center Theatre Group and the Ahmanson Theatre Evening Tribute to Neil Simon and Bobby Fryer at the Century Plaza Hotel in Los Angeles.

She was one of the contest judges at the Love Ball, a celebrity fundraiser sponsored by the Design Industry Foundation for AIDS in Manhattan on May 12, 1989. Footage of Verdon being interviewed at the event appears in a documentary by Jennie Livingstone entitled *Paris Is Burning* (1990). She speaks about the black male gay performers who do the vogue dance that had originated in 1987 in the ball circuit and hit the mainstream after Madonna had a hit song about it in 1990. Verdon found the vogue performances exciting because they were so "theatrical." She presented a

$50,000 check to the House of Sweet Charity, a trio of Harlem apartments that was to become home for homeless voguers with AIDS. On May 13 Verdon attended the Friars Club Roast of Alan King at the Waldorf Astoria Hotel. She wore a black gown with netting overlay and sleeves and a large necklace. The star was a presenter at the 1989 Tony Awards, held on June 4, 1989, at the Lunt-Fontanne Theatre and broadcast live on CBS. She wore a brown, pink and white blouse with ruffled neck which was tied to the waist of a brown skirt. Verdon first curtsies to the company of *Jerome Robbins' Broadway* who had just performed. Then she announces the nominees for Best Direction of a Musical, racing through the names (and stating that she is nervous) before declaring the winner to be Jerome Robbins. On June 8 Verdon was presented with the New York State's Governor's Art Award at the Grace Rainey Rogers Auditorium of the Metropolitan Museum of Art. The event was filmed, produced and directed by Patrick Connelly for the New York Network.

Verdon played the small supporting role of Alice's mother in writer-director Woody Allen's comedy *Alice* (1990). The film was shot (starting on November 6, 1989) at the Kaufman Astoria Studios and on location in New York. Verdon said that, like other actors who appeared in the films of Woody Allen, she only received the pages for her character rather than the complete script; she didn't know if the film was to be a comedy or not. The unnamed character is spoken of before we see her. The ex-boyfriend of Alice (Mia Farrow), Eddie (Alec Baldwin) describes her as a "third-rate actress" with "infantile ideas on politics." Dorothy (Blythe Danner), Alice's sister, comments that Alice is just like their mother as a kept woman and she calls the mother a drunk. In an imagined conversation with her, Alice says that her mother drank herself to death with margaritas after her husband died, and the mother comments, "You know I could never resist the taste of salt around the rim of a glass." Alice tells the Muse (Bernadette Peters) that her mother was a movie actress who made two or three films and then was persuaded to retire by her husband. However her mother corrects her when she says that she married her husband after the studio had stopped offering her work. She calls herself "no more than a pretty face" who was lucky that her husband came along to look after her. Alice will tell her mother that she found her charming but misguided, and her mother says that Alice had "stars in her eyes" when it came to how she viewed her parents.

The star appears in two scenes, wearing the same outfit, a beige dress with jacket. In the first, she is silent as Alice and Dorothy observe her open a window and then watch her husband cut a birthday cake with a sword. In the second she speaks and makes the character vulnerable, the quaver in her voice hitting the emphasis on "killed" for the line "I would have *killed* myself." Allen uses the conceit of movie lights on Alice's mother in the scene, and he has her speak the "salt" line off-camera with the camera on Farrow's reaction.

The film was premiered on December 12, 1990, at Alice Tully Hall, Lincoln Center, in New York City. Verdon wore a long black coat, black leather gloves, a purple boa with necktie, and a bejewelled necklace. It was released on December 25, 1990, with the tagline "A younger man and a bolder woman." It was praised by Vincent Canby in the *New York Times* and received mixed reviews from Peter Travers in *Rolling Stone* and Roger Ebert in the *Chicago Sun-Times*. It was a box office failure but Allen received a Best Original Screenplay Academy Award nomination.

Verdon was credited as dance consultant for a revival production of Paddy Chayefsky's play *The 10th Man* which was set in an Orthodox Synagogue in Mineola, Long Island, in 1959. The production opened on Broadway on December 10, 1989, after 35 previews from November 10. It was directed by Ulu Grosbard and only ran until January 14, 1990, after being panned by Frank Rich in the *New York Times*. Rich made no mention of the choreography in the show.

In November 1989 Kevin Boyd Grubb's book *Razzle Dazzle: The Life and Work of Bob Fosse* was published by St. Martin's Press. It featured photographs of Verdon on stage in *Can-Can*, *New Girl in Town*, *Redhead*, *Sweet Charity* and *Chicago*; rehearsing *New Girl in Town* with Fosse; in

Portrait of Verdon in *Alice* (1990).

the film version of *Damn Yankees;* and with Fosse on the 1960 television salute to the American Musical Theatre. There were also candid photographs with Fosse and Ray Walston holding their respective Tony Awards for *Damn Yankees,* with Fosse at New York's Harwyn Club in 1960, with the creative staff (including Fosse and Debbie Allen) of the *Sweet Charity* revival, and with Fosse and Nicole at the *Dancin'* Tavern on the Green party. The book was the first Fosse biography released; Verdon described it as "cut-and-paste." Grubb notes in his foreword that Verdon had declined to participate in the writing of his book, although he said he had interviewed her twice previously for unrelated projects. In his final chapter, Grubb reports that Verdon was now a licensed theatrical electrician who remodelled old barns and stables. He also wrote that Central Park West apartment was devoid of anything about her career.

In the summer of 1990 Verdon visited Russia, to accept an award for Fosse's films, and the White House, where she was one of the former acting students who honored Sanford Meisner. She also co-starred with Patrick O'Neal in a production of *Love Letters* which ran at Beverly Hills' Canon Theatre from June 26 to July 1. Verdon was interviewed by Michael Buckley at her home in the Hamptons for an article that appeared in the August 6, 1990, *TheatreWeek*. Also present were a cat and Nicole's weimaraner which was named Flash (Bob Fosse's nickname). Verdon ended the interview by saying that her future would involve more movies and TV. Going back on the stage, and trying to do eight shows a week for a two-year run, was now beyond her. After more than 60 years on the stage, she didn't really care if she ever went back on it again. Accompanying the article were photographs of Verdon in the film of *Damn Yankees* and as a chorus girl in *The Merry Widow*.

She appeared in the Nick Doob–directed documentary *Sanford Meisner: The American Theatre's Best Kept Secret,* seen on PBS's *American Masters* on August 27, 1990. In her interview, conducted by Stephen Harvey, Verdon said that she didn't really like being in front of an audience, so to know her world—what she was and who she was—was a cocoon and her protection and Meisner supplied that. Later she commented that she liked being on stage with the characters in a show. But as far as performing for an audience, and her loving them and them loving her and all that stuff, she didn't go for that. On September 17, 1990, Verdon attended the UJA–Federation of New York event honoring Cy Coleman at the Pierre Hotel in New York City. She wore a black dress with a frill-necked bodice and dark green necklace.

Martin Gottfried's book *All His Jazz. The Life and Death of Bob Fosse* was published by Bantam Books on November 1, 1990. It featured photographs of Verdon doing "Who's Got the Pain" with Fosse in the film of *Damn Yankees* and with him in rehearsal for *New Girl in Town*, the famous photograph of her seated and looking unhappy as George Abbott rehearses Thelma Ritter in the same show, in *Redhead*, and a 1980 Eva Goldstein photograph with Fosse in East Hampton where she is looking at the camera and he is not. Gottfried admonishes Verdon for having continued as Fosse's first lady while he lived apart but undivorced from her, and for acting like a presidential widow after his death. However he acknowledges that she perhaps understood Fosse better as a dancer who could no longer dance and as the portrait he presented of himself in *All That Jazz*. Verdon would say that she hated the book because she thought that the author was so inaccurate.

In 1990 she appeared in the PBS documentary for *Great Performances: Dance in America* entitled "Bob Fosse: Steam Heat," directed by Judy Kinberg. The special had her sitting by a pool talking about Fosse, wearing a blue and white vertical-striped blouse. Verdon talks about her life and separation from Fosse. The special also included "Who's Got the Pain" from the film of *Damn Yankees*, her with Fosse at the 1978 Tony Awards, singing and dancing to "I Wanna Be a Dancin' Man" with Fosse on a 1962 *Garry Moore Show*, and footage from her 1966 *Ed Sullivan Show* appearance doing "I'm a Brass Band" and "If My Friends Could See Me Now." Verdon is heard singing "Merely Marvelous" from *Redhead*. That same year she was also interviewed by Ed Wilson for his CUNY-TV show *Spotlight on....*

On June 8, 1991, Verdon hosted the New York City debut of Chicago's Hubbard Street Dance Company at Carnegie Hall. This was part of the New York International Festival of the Arts which ran from June 8 to 23 and featured more than 60 performing acts from 23 countries in 28 sites. Lou Conte, the artistic director of the company, said that Verdon had approached him about getting Nicole an audition. She later would sit on the advisory board, and had told him that her daughter wanted to be a ballet dancer but didn't have the ability. However Verdon still wanted Nicole to audition since she believed that she did have the ability to be a dancer in a non-classical mode. Conte arranged the audition but nothing came of it. He said that he thought it was all Verdon's idea that her daughter audition, and doubted that Nicole herself was even interested. Although Nicole would dance in other venues, she would go on to pursue a degree in interior design and study architecture.

On March 24, 1992, Verdon attended the opening night of the stage

Verdon promoting the documentary on Bob Fosse on *Great Performances: Dance in America*.

show *Jake's Women* at the Neil Simon Theatre in New York City, with Nicole. She wore a black dress with black coat and gold necklace. On April 14 she appeared at the sixth annual Easter Bonnet Competition to benefit Broadway Cares/Equity Fights AIDS at the Palace Theatre. This was the first of three times that she would appear at the event. She wore a dark green dress with black coat and a red AIDS ribbon.

Verdon made a guest appearance on the HBO comedy series *Dream On* episode "For Peter's Sake" (June 20, 1992). The show centered on Martin Tupper (Brian Benben), a Manhattan book editor. The gimmick for the series was that it featured clips from old films which were used as metaphors for Martin's reactions, as well as cable television swearing. The episode was written by David Crane and Marta Kauffman and directed by Betty Thomas. It has Martin needing a book about someone dying from AIDS as the publisher's major Christmas release, and choosing dying author Peter Brewer (David Clennon). Verdon plays Peter's mother Kitty and appears in two scenes. Her voice is first heard on Peter's intercom, and Kitty appears in a red suit with black scarf. Verdon plays comedy lines, like telling Peter, "Chicken is not meat, it's chicken," after he tells her that he doesn't eat meat, and responding to his "I don't have room in the fridge" with "You'll just have to eat more." She also supplies poignancy when asking Martin, who pretends to be Peter's lover, to promise to take care of her son. Verdon's second scene occurs after Peter had died and she is in his empty apartment. She wears a black blouse and pants with a gray jacket and supplies stillness in her sadness. Kitty's character provides the counterbalance to the script's tactless jokes about AIDS and gay men, since she is accepting of her son and his situation.

In 1992, Verdon, as the custodian of the Bob Fosse and Gwen Verdon Collection, made a gift to the Library of Congress of 54, 840 items in 328 boxes and 114 containers covering material from 1960 to 1987. It included production, project and performance materials, including scripts and set designs; business and personal papers and correspondence; songbooks, printed music scores and choreographic notes; photographs, posters and scrapbooks; and audio-visual materials. On January 25, 1993, she attended the 21st Annual Theatre Hall of Fame Induction Ceremony at the Gershwin Theatre in New York City.

Verdon made a guest appearance in the NBC crime drama *Homicide: Life on the Street* episode "A Ghost of a Chance" (February 3, 1993). The show, filmed on location in Baltimore, was set in the police homicide department of that city. The episode was written by Noel Behn and based on a story by Tom Fontana, and directed by Martin Campbell. The narrative has three police investigations, one of which is the death of Thomas Doohen (John Habberton) led by John Munch (Richard Belzer) and Stanley Bolander (Ned Beatty). Doohen's wife Jessie (Verdon) calls the police to her home after he collapses from a heart attack and she fears he is dead. He revives but the police are called back again when he suffers a second attack and is now definitely dead. Medical examiner Carol Blythe (Wendy Hughes) determines that the death is murder because Jessie admits to dragging his unconscious body and throwing him down a flight of stairs into the house's cellar. Bolander refuses to charge Jessie because he finds it more a case of death by neglect. Verdon only appears in two scenes as the gray-haired 80-year-old Jessie, with spectacles on a chain and a powder-blue suit. She expresses her resentment of her husband who had refused to take her to Paris for their sixtieth wedding anniversary. The fact that Verdon received an Emmy nomination as Guest Actress in a Drama Series for this performance is a surprise because it is so brief, and the writing doesn't allow the actress to do much with the part.

She next made a guest appearance in the Fox comedy television series *Key West* in the episode "Gimme Shelter" (March 9, 1993). The episode was written by Kathryn Baker and directed by Chuck Bowman. The series, filmed on location in Key West and Miami, centered on Seamus O'Neill (Fisher Stevens), a New Jersey factory worker and wannabe writer who wins the lottery and moves to Key West where his idol, Ernest Hemingway, had lived. Seamus takes a job as a reporter for *The Meteor*, a local newspaper, and meets the various eccentric locals. As Sister Grace, Verdon wears a nun's habit, alternating between an all-black coif and veil over a white wimple and black dress, and an all-white outfit. Grace is from Atlanta and visiting the island's parochial school. She tracks down the island's high end prostitute, Savannah (Jennifer Tilly), a former student, at Gumbo's bar to ask her to help the school's sex education teacher Sister Margaret (Miryam Halvorssen) with her class. Most of Grace's scenes are with Savannah, and Grace has to endure a long one where Savannah berates her for supposedly disapproving of her life, a matter not helped by Tilly's shrill voice. Grace gets a redemptive backstory scene where she tells Savannah that she used to be Irma Molestski from Detroit, a wild child who sought refuge from her life in the church. Bowman violates Verdon's speech by cutting to a shot behind her, rather than staying on her face. When Grace asks about Savannah's life, Savannah tells her that she has a feeling that Grace already knows all about it. Grace replies, "Perhaps, but I'm very willing to listen to your version."

In the spring of 1993 Verdon received the New Dramatists Lifetime Achievement Award at a luncheon ceremony where co-workers Richard Adler, Chita Rivera, Cy Coleman, John Kander, and Fred Ebb gathered to pay tribute.

On February 4, 1994, Verdon attended and spoke at a program at the Walter Reade Theatre by the Film Society of Lincoln Centre entitled "Capturing Choreography: Masters of Dance and Film." The evening was curated by Joanna Ney as a tribute to Jack Cole, and his work was represented in 19 film clips. Associates spoke about him, with Verdon providing the aside that Cole used to call Betty Grable "Thumper." On March 29, 1994, she made her second appearance at the Easter Bonnet Competition which benefited Broadway Cares/Equity Fights AIDS at the Minskoff Theatre in New York. Verdon and Bebe Neuwirth were presenters.

Her next acting job was the supporting role of Etta Bell in the four-hour miniseries *Oldest Living Confederate Widow Tells All* (1994), broadcast on CBS on May 1, 1994. Directed by Ken Cameron with a teleplay by Joyce Eliason based on the novel by Allan Gurganus, it was filmed on location in Madison and Milledgeville, Georgia. Etta is a resident of the rest home where the 99-year-old Lucy Honicut Marsden (Anne Bancroft) resides in Falls, North Carolina, for the year leading to Lucy's one hundredth birthday. Unlike Lucy who has white hair, Verdon retains her red hair for the character, who says that she is 72 though later admits to be older. She is also spared the terrible old age makeup that afflicts Bancroft.

Verdon appears in nine scenes and she uses a Southern accent. Etta's interest in watching television soap operas prefigures that of Verdon's Ruth in *Marvin's Room*, though here it is shown to be an interest shared by most of the home's residents. Etta is funny in her flirting with another resident, Professor Taw (E.G. Marshall); her face falls after he refuses to dance with her at the home's Western Day. He tells her, "I would rather die," and Lucy's responds, "One dance with Etta and you probably would." This is then rationalized as a compliment to Etta when Lucy tells her, "You sure can move." Etta's upbeat spirit is temporarily broken after she has a mini-stroke and she expresses a depressive state to Lucy who visits her in hospital. However she returns to her old self when Etta is seen wearing a big hat at the town ceremony for Lucy's one-hundredth birthday. Cameron also supplies lots of shots of Etta reacting to Lucy's speech, and Verdon also gets to dance twice in the narrative. The first and best opportunity is at the home in reaction to seeing the Dixie Cups, a group of dancing residents. Etta tells Lucy that they wanted her to be one of them but "I'm just plain not old enough," and she joins the dancers after she says, "I could show them a thing or two." Verdon's dancing has her swirling the skirt of her purple dress but, regrettably, Cameron uses cutaways and headless shots of Etta as if to suggest her dancing is done by a double. Verdon's square dancing on the Western Day only has her seen in a group of dancers.

The show was praised by Patricia O'Conne in *Variety*. John J. O'Connor (the *New York Times*) wrote that Verdon was delightful. The show won Emmy Awards for Cicely Tyson as Best Supporting Actress in a Miniseries or Special, and for Art Direction, Costume Design, and Hairstyling.

On May 12, 1994, Verdon attended a Tribute to Bob Fosse at the Film Forum in New York City. She was photographed wearing a black gown with a white collar and black choker, with a sparkling bodice and a jewel at her cleavage, and a red AIDS ribbon. On May 19, she attended the 45th Annual New Dramatists Lifetime Achievement Award Salute to Neil Simon at the Marriott Marquis Hotel in New York. She wore a black short skirt and jacket with white blouse and black tie. Verdon was photographed at the event with Carol Channing, as well as with Simon and Bebe Neuwirth and Lucie Arnaz. The show was broadcast on NBC on the same night.

13. Fosse Dies

On June 12 Verdon was a presenter at the 1994 Tony Awards which were held at the Gershwin Theatre and broadcast live on television on CBS. She appeared with Jean Stapleton and the 106-year-old George Abbott on stage at the end of the salute to musical revivals sequence that opened the show and climaxed with "Heart" from *Damn Yankees*. The three sat in a bleacher box set that was moved to the front of the stage and Verdon helped Stapleton get Abbott on his feet to receive the audience's standing ovation. She was dressed in the same outfit she had worn at the Fosse Tribute, at the Film Forum. Verdon also raised Abbott's right hand to wave back at the crowd and she tried to stop the applause by pointing to her watch to indicate that they had to keep moving with the show. She spoke about how the three of them were together for *Damn Yankees*, praised Abbott's contribution and also said that he was still involved in the theater and announced his forthcoming next birthday. Verdon then spoke into his ear to ask if they should get on with the show, to which Abbott replied that it was a good idea. With this he sat back down and Verdon, Stapleton and the audiences all applauded him. Stapleton read the names of the nominees of the Tony for Best Revival of a Musical and Verdon announced the winner as *Carousel*.

She made the first of two guest appearances on the NBC comedy drama series *The Cosby Mysteries* in the episode "Our Lady of Cement," which was broadcast on September 28, 1994. The series was filmed in New York and centered on Guy Hanks (Bill Cosby), a retired New York City Police Department forensic scientist, who occasionally helped his friend Detective Adam Sully (James Naughton) on cases. The episode was written by Alphonse Ruggiero, Jr., based on a story by Robert Van Scoyk, and directed by Philip J. Sgriccia. The narrative has Guy revisit his first case when the body of Mrs. Olivia Bellini is found entombed in cement in a renovated building. Russell Bonner (actor unknown) was imprisoned for the murder in 1973 and the discovery of the body makes the conviction questionable. Verdon's appearance amounts to a cameo, since her character has no impact on the plot. She plays Yolanda, a restaurant owner, and is in two scenes wearing what appears to be the same outfit, a beige print blouse and skirt with a red scarf. In the first scene Verdon has no lines and simply passed a plate of food to Guy. In the second, she only has a few lines, where as the older woman to Sully's younger man, she flirts. After Sully sees her and says her name, she asks what she can do for him, with raised eyebrows. He replies, "I bet you know," and she adds, "You got me."

Verdon returned for her second *Cosby Mysteries* in "Self Defense," broadcast October 5, 1994. Written by Edward Tivnan and directed by E.W. Swackhammer, its narrative has Hanks (Cosby) investigate the shooting by Sully (James Naughton) of police officer Tom Casey (Larry Attile) during an arrest. Verdon cameo-ed as Yolanda and again her appearance had nothing to do with the plot. This time she only has one scene, where she wears a purple suit and big red-patterned scarf. She gets some mildly amusing dialogue. Guy tells Yolanda that he dreamed that they ran away together, and she replies, "I can't run. I've got a heart condition." When Sully tells her he dreamed that they walked away together, Yolanda says, "Oh, babycakes. Walking is such a bore. "

In his Metropolitan Diary column in the *New York Times* on May 31, 2004, Joe Rodgers reported an entry by Pietro Allar of a sighting of Verdon in 1994. He told of how he came across a group of teenagers break-dancing in the theater district. Allar was in a rush but was unable to push his way through the huddle of observing out-of-towners. He became increasingly irritated until he happened to glance over, and saw Verdon at the front of the crowd watching the dancers. She had a bright-eyed look of delight and pride on her face. No one else seemed to realize that they were all in the presence of the famous theatrical dancer, who was clearly excited by the raw urban routine being performed before her.

14

Charity One Last Time and *Fosse*

Verdon was one of the speakers at a memorial on June 5, 1995, at the Majestic Theatre for George Abbott, who died on January 31, 1995. Her greatest memory of him was how he would tell performers to stop acting and simply to speak the lines.

The star next played the supporting role of Ruth Wakefield in the film drama *Marvin's Room* (1996) directed by Jerry Zaks. This was an adaptation of the stage play by Scott McPherson which had been originally produced by Chicago's Goodman Theatre on February 19, 1990, and then played off–Broadway at Playwrights Horizons, opening on November 15, 1991. The film was shot at the Disney/MGM studios in Orlando, Florida, and at the Kaufman Astoria Studios in New York from August 14 to October 28, 1995. The narrative centered on the Lacker family: Marvin (Hume Cronyn), his sister Ruth, Marvin's daughters, Bessie (Diane Keaton) and Lee (Meryl Streep), and Lee's sons, Hank (Leonardo DiCaprio) and Charlie (Hal Scardino). Lee, Hank and Charlie come from Ohio to Florida to visit when they learn that Bessie has leukemia and needs a bone marrow transplant. The story emphasizes the supposed importance of family, particularly in a crisis.

Ruth lives with Marvin and Bessie, and dresses in Florida bright colors and pastels. Verdon's customary red hair is blonde here and she looks physically heavier, presumably to represent Ruth's sedentary existence. She has an electronic anesthetizer as a cure for back pain; it's wired to give her a jolt that provides for a running gag when Ruth is hugged and screams in pain before the jolt of electricity. The jolt also makes the automatic garage door open. Verdon uses teary eyes to make Ruth vulnerable, and she scores a laugh with her shocked reaction to watching a rape on her television soap opera, *SunRise City*. We also see her crying when watching a wedding on the show. Ruth's childlike nature is paralleled with

Charlie, whom she befriends and who does her makeup for the wedding. Although it is proposed at one point to put Ruth in a retirement home, her mental and physical competency is contrasted with Marvin, who is bed-bound and non-verbal. However, it is noted that Ruth's TV show is heard playing at the home when Bessie and Lee visit to check it out. Verdon's best sustained scene is perhaps the one in the hospital when she visits Bessie, explaining Bessie's absence to Marvin and noting how he has a nurse looking after him, in lieu of his daughter. The actress brings a funny and innocent charm to her deception and the conceit that the nurse is imaginary. This is particularly in regards to how when the nurse carries Marvin to the bathroom and Ruth tells him that he must be flying. It's just a pity that we have to be told about this behavior rather than have it shown to us, since we do wonder whether the nurse would try to correct Ruth's fantasy for Marvin's sake.

Verdon said that she had gotten used to playing mother roles after her appearances in *Alice, The Cotton Club* and the *Magnum, P.I.* television show. But Ruth was different because she was not a mother but was old and crippled. Verdon approached the part as one she would have played on stage. An important thing that she had learned from Fosse was economy, whether in movement or acting. To this Verdon added the need for research and preparation to know who the character is and then to become the character. She found working on the film a joy because she felt that Streep, Keaton and Cronyn were all brilliant in it, and they were all so smart that it made her feel dumb. Verdon used this feeling. She deduced that Ruth, like herself, had been a crippled child and that as a result she never really had a youth. It was when Ruth finally got out of pain that she started living and playing games. She started being a teenager, which made her seem slightly cuckoo though in reality it was that she had her innocence for the first time. Now she could enjoy things in a way that she never had before and she expressed this like a child. Verdon felt that Ruth had earned her innocence.

The film was released on December 18, 1996, with the taglines "A story about the years that keep us apart.... And the moments that bring us together," "Open your heart. There's room," and "Sometimes the people you know the least ... are the ones you need the most!" It was praised by Emmanuel Levy in *Variety* who said Verdon had a "superlative supporting turn." The film was not a box office success. Keaton was nominated for the Best Actress Academy Award.

On October 15, 1995, Verdon was given the Life Achievement Award at the 2nd Annual Los Angeles Dance Awards ceremony held at the Century

City Club. She was presented the award by Mitzi Gaynor and Alan Johnson. Gaynor described her as a very special Jack Cole dancer, "Jack's muse.... She was an extension of Jack.... She did it even better than he did and in heels." Accepting the award, Verdon stated that it was not for her, but for Cole. She also said that Fosse had left a posthumous fund for the training of dancers (over a hundred thousand dollars) which she gave to LA Dance to provide dancers with scholarships.

In the summer of 1996, Verdon appeared in a minor supporting role in the three-hour CBS miniseries *In Cold Blood* (1996). Shot in Alberta, Canada, it was broadcast on November 24, 1996. Based on the Truman Capote book which had been made into a film by Richard Brooks in 1967, the teleplay centered on Dick Hickock (Anthony Edwards) and Perry Smith (Eric Roberts) who rob and kill the family of farmer Herbert W. Clutter (Kevin Tighe) in Holcomb, Kansas, on November 14, 1959. They were executed for the crime on April 14, 1965. Verdon played the part of Sadie Truitt, who collected the mail from passing trains at the Holcomb station. She appears wearing an arm in a sling because it is claimed that she was hit by the mail bag thrown from the train. Verdon is seen in five scenes, some silently. She gets a close-up when she says that she is scared after the killings. Her best moment is her half-smile in reaction to the nervous condition of Connie Clutter (Gillian Barber), making her withdraw from a room.

The film's tagline was, "The horrifying true story that shocked the nation!" It was praised by Jeremy Gerard in *Variety* and Howard Rosenberg in the *Los Angeles Times*, and was nominated for the Outstanding Miniseries and Best Editing Emmy Awards.

Margery Beddow's book *Bob Fosse's Broadway* was published by Heinemann on August 5, 1996. In her prologue she thanks Verdon for her help and encouragement. Verdon attended the opening night performance of the Broadway revival of *Chicago* at the Richard Rodgers Theatre on November 14, 1996. She said about Ann Reinking, who played the role of Roxie Hart, that it was perfect that she was doing it. "'She's been through the mill and that's what that character is about." This was a reference to the fact that Reinking, now 46, was only 26 when she originally replaced Verdon in the part in the first production in 1977.

On January 7, 1997, Verdon was at the Marquis Theatre in New York City when Liza Minnelli opened in the stage musical *Victor/Victoria*. Minnelli filled in for Julie Andrews who had starred in the show since it opened on October 25, 1995, and who had gone on vacation. Verdon wore a black outfit with red-striped scarf. In January she attended the 63rd Annual

Drama League Awards at the Pierre Hotel in New York City. She wore a black dress with gray patterned jacket and gray blouse. She was photographed at the event with Ann Reinking.

Verdon made a guest appearance on the CBS family fantasy television series *Touched By An Angel* in the episode "Missing in Action," broadcast on April 13, 1997. The show, filmed in Salt Lake City, centered on three angels that God has sent to Earth to help troubled people. The episode was written by Rosanne Welch and Christine Pettit and directed by Tim Van Patten. The troubled soul here is 80-year-old George "The Colonel" Zarko (Darren McGavin); Monica (Roma Downey) is assigned to help him find the joy in living and to follow God's plan for him to make a difference in the world. Her fellow angel Tess (Della Reese) changes her into an old woman and she moves into his latest home, Spring Valley, run by Stephanie Hancock (Christina Pickles). Verdon played Monica's new roomie, widow Lorraine McCully, though she retains her trademark red hair as opposed to Monica's gray. Lorraine is revealed to be a pianist. She appears in seven scenes and gets two outfits to wear—both sweatsuits. One has a blue fish-patterned jacket with colored scarf, and the other a fruit-patterned jacket with scarf.

Lorraine has the joy in life that George lacks. Monica asks her to share it with George, and this helps him fulfill God's apparent plan, which seems to be that he become the home's new cook. Lorraine's memory loss is demonstrated when she can't remember the word "platonic," but she is astute enough to see that George has a romantic interest in Monica, winking at her after George holds Monica's hand at the bingo game. Her playing the piano leads to the resolution of the second plot point of the episode, concerning Mrs. Hancock, and Lorraine's learned connection with George also suggests that romance between them is possible. Verdon has three good scenes, with the second allowing her to present teary eyes when George is able to tell the fate of her missing-in-action husband, James. The last has her listening to Mrs. Hancock's confession of why she has locked the piano away, and then has her touch Mrs. Hancock's hands to forgive her.

On April 26, 1997, Verdon attended the opening night of the Broadway musical *The Life* at the Ethel Barrymore Theatre and the opening night party at the Supper Club. She was photographed sitting with Chita Rivera, wearing black slacks and a sparkly brown jacket. On May 20 Verdon attended the New Dramatists' 48th Annual Spring Luncheon Salute to John Kander and Fred Ebb at the Marriott Marquis Hotel in New York City. She wore a white outfit with red jacket and red tie. Verdon was photographed at the event with Chita Rivera, Jerry Orbach, and Liza Minnelli.

Roy Harris' book *Eight Women of the American Stage*, published by Heinemann on September 15, 1997, featured a chapter on Verdon with a photograph of her in *New Girl in Town* and a Hirschfeld drawing of her in *Redhead*. The 17-page chapter was comprised of his memory of seeing her in *Sweet Charity* and a brief biography. It also had an interview that had her discussing her early life, *Can-Can, Damn Yankees, New Girl in Town, Redhead, Sweet Charity, Chicago*, and her later acting career.

Verdon made two guest appearances on CBS' *Walker, Texas Ranger* an action crime drama series filmed in Texas. It centered on a martial artist who battled crime all around the state of Texas. Her first episode was entitled "Forgotten People" and it was broadcast on October 25, 1997. It was written and directed by Tony Mordente. Verdon played Maisie Whitman, a woman who has checked into the Quiet Rest nursing home to investigate the death of her female best friend, who died after being there for three weeks. The Texas Rangers also send C.D. (Noble Willingham) into the home to investigate. He learns that the head of the home, Dr Janet Monroe (Gail Strickland), is using patients as guinea pigs to test a banned experimental Alzheimer's drug, PSL-130, so that they can sell it to pharmaceutical companies.

Maisie appears in ten scenes and her character's love of dancing is suited to Verdon's past. She gets to wear a collection of multi-colored outfits with floral patterns and a hat with a flower in it. Verdon's look is a little different here as Maisie's hair is brushed off her forehead, and she seems physically heavier. We see Verdon dance although it is nothing too challenging for her (Maisie is supposed to be an amateur dancer). The character also allows Verdon to play on two levels. Maisie uses her dancing to pretend to be senile to the home's staff, but she is normal with C.D. whom she realizes is also not who he pretends to be. In Verdon's best scene, Maisie tells C.D. how she ended up in the home, with the suggestion that perhaps her relationship with her best friend had a lesbian element. She uses a pause for emotion when telling her story, and also humor when Maisie tells Janet "I think not" after she is told to get out of the doctor's office. This scene also has Maisie punch Janet unconscious to stop her from shredding incriminating documents. While it is unique to have Verdon punch another actor in her film canon, it regrettably fits the cartoonish quality of the treatment by director Mordente. Maisie gets a comical scene with religious overtones when she challenges God as to why He does not answer her prayers. When moonlight moves over the photograph of her and her friends, she tells God that she interprets that as a sign of being heard. Maisie is also shown to have courage when she dances with the orderlies to act as a decoy for C.D. once we have seen how they are liable to pick anyone who has challenged them as the next drug guinea pig. In the climax she acts as the lookout for C.D. when he searches for evidence, and we hear Verdon scream when Maisie is caught and held by the neck. The shaky voice of Verdon gets an unintentional parallel with that of Gail Strickland, whose voice is apparently the result of suffering from dysphonia.

Verdon appeared on the cover of *In Theatre* magazine (February 6, 1998) with Chita Rivera with the heading "Gwen & Chita and the Broadway Bears." Both women were dressed in black and holding teddy bears, with Verdon's yellow bear dressed like Charity Hope Valentine of *Sweet Charity* in the signature black dress and with a heart tattoo on the left arm. The bear also had red hair and a black hat. She made an appearance on the CBS family drama *Promised Land* in the episode "Undercover Granny" (March 26, 1998). Filmed in various cities in Utah, the show centered on the members of the Greene family, who travel across the country in a trailer in search of adventure and to help people along the way. The episode was directed by Timothy Van Patten and written by Arnold Margolin. In it, Hattie Greene (Celeste Holm) goes undercover in a home for seniors to investigate possible elder abuse.

Verdon was credited for the musical staging of a concert of *Sweet Charity* performed at Avery Hall in Lincoln Center on June 15, 1998. The one-night-only show directed by John Bowab was a benefit for the American Foundation for AIDS Research and Broadway Cares/Equity Fights AIDS. It was put together in three weeks. There was a week of pre-production with Verdon, Kathryn Doby, who had appeared in the original stage production in the ensemble and the film as a dancer, and Mimi Quillin, who had appeared in the 1986–1987 revival as Mimi. There followed two weeks of rehearsal with the performers. Bowab said that he rehearsed Robert Goulet alone in his Las Vegas home, and then Marla Maples in her Los Angeles home, and rehearsed with individual ladies in New York. Bowab then pieced his work together with Verdon's. He said that she did her own adaptation of the show's book to make the one-night event the most accessible, though Verdon retained some of the original dialogue. She was photographed in the first week of rehearsals wearing black and a blue denim jacket. Verdon was also filmed rehearsing "If My Friends Could See Me Now," performing the number side by side with Debbie Allen. Verdon is seen in front of Allen doing the steps so that Allen can watch her; she wears glasses and is in black clothes without the jacket.

Another filmed moment has Verdon singing the song with Allen and Bebe Neuwirth. Cy Coleman said that Verdon worked hard putting the evening together. Everyone wanted her to participate as a performer in at least one of the segments. She finally consented to do the closet scene because, "No one does this scene better than I do!"

The star appears in the show as one of the alternate actresses playing Charity, coming from the closet in the scene in the apartment of Vittorio Vidal (Robert Goulet). She is not dressed exactly in character but still in a similar black dress with a sheer sleeve covering and carrying a shoulder bag. Verdon takes a plate of food from the meal that Charity has been offered, then returns. She acknowledges the audience's applause but is unable to get out her line until finally Charles Nelson Reilly as Manfred roars to her, "What did you want to say? What are you trying to say?" Verdon then says the line, "If you get a chance, I'd love a cold beer" and goes back into the closet. She is also seen hiding behind the closet door when Ursula (Marla Maples) enters. Charity puts on Vittorio's black top hat and hides amongst clothes when Ursula moves to open the closet. She reacts against Ursala hitting the door when she says, "Why do I torture myself?" Verdon accidentally makes the door set slip toward Ursula and falls, which gets a big laugh from the audience. She pulls the closet door, which is on wheels, back into position with the assistance of a crew member and the audience applauds. In response, Maples as Ursula ad libs, "It must have been an earthquake." Verdon stays in character as Charity in her spotlight as she listens at the door to the dialogue between Vittorio and Ursula. She swigs the bottle of beer that Vittorio opens the door to give to her, and raises it to say "Up yours" when Ursula describes her as "that little nothing" he picked up. During Vittorio's song "Too Many Tomorrows" Verdon reprises the closet moment when she lights a cigarette and blows the smoke into a plastic clothes cover. She also reacts in pleasure when Vittorio hands her Ursula's white fur piece and Charity wears it.

Verdon gets a second line with "Talk about your foreign movies," and sings a sad reprise of "If My Friends Could See Me Now" in a solo spotlight. After a blackout, Vittorio helps her out of the closet when Ursala is asleep and tells him, "I enjoyed you in the movies, but in person...!" When he asks her if she watched, she gestures that she did. She says *ciao* as goodbye, hands him back Ursula's fur, and exits. Verdon joined the other Charitys– Chita Rivera, Donna McKechnie, Bebe Neuwirth and Debbie Allen—at the end of the show to take a bow. She is also summoned by Cy Coleman to join him center stage after the cast members have taken bows and she sings "If They Could See Me Now" with the rest of the company.

The evening was praised by Christopher Isherwood in *Variety* who wrote that Verdon's brief appearance "proved her comic chops are as ageless as the audience's affection for her, and she was met with the kind of heartfelt ovation that reminds you how perfunctory they can seem."

Verdon was credited as the artistic advisor on *Fosse*, a bookless three-act show celebration of the choreographer which presented a collection of recreations of his original musical numbers. The idea was conceived by director Richard Maltby, Jr., and choreographer Chet Walker and co-director Ann Reinking. Verdon was credited as co-choreographer for the Fosse recreations with Walker, with dance reconstructions by Brad Musgrove and Lainie Sakakura. Interviewed about the show, she said that Fosse knew that people basically were very erotic and very sensual even though they denied it. He pushed people's buttons and they were seemingly shocked but they loved it so Verdon felt that they weren't really shocked at all. With Fosse you knew you were going to get something different because his point of view was off-center. Verdon also felt that Fosse would have found all kinds of fault with the show but he would still be absolutely thrilled.

Verdon said that the idea for the show originally came from Walker in 1986 and together he and Verdon worked on it for years. They would find people who were terrific and teach them for free, her feeling it was almost like being on a scholarship. When Verdon and Walker felt they had the right people, they started doing workshops and teaching dance numbers. She was determined to get Ann Reinking involved because Reinking could choreograph the show and she (Verdon) could not. Reinking came aboard in 1994; she and Verdon worked very well together, Verdon knew how to take the material and create a Fosse world of dance language. Reinking praised Verdon, saying that her mind and her memory were like no one's she had ever known. Not only was she a fantastic teacher and director, but in looking through all the tapes of her movies and television work, Reinking saw that her technique and her performing ability then was better than anybody's today. Verdon said that Reinking understood Fosse's elegance and attention to detail.

1n 1996 the show was developed by Garth H. Drabinsky's Livent company in Toronto. Its basic content was reflected by selections from Walker and Verdon, although others, including Drabinsky, had some influence on it. Drabinsky approached Richard Maltby, Jr., who at first turned it down though he attended a workshop. Maltby then began to see that his judgment of Fosse's work was incorrect. Like most people, he thought it was all about the style, the fingers, turned-in knees, etc. Instead, he saw that it was about emotion being expressed in a style. Verdon said that there were many facets to the choreography and to its vocabulary of movement. It was funny, sexy, quick, romantic, and there was so much detail. And you had such a sense of accomplishment—when you were finally able to accomplish it.

The month of the show's world premiere at the Toronto Ford Center for the Performing Arts differs in sources. Some say it was in July 1998 and others August. Rachelle Rak joined the company in Toronto. When she showed up with big hair, a tan and a leopard leotard, she felt that Verdon looked at her in amazement. Despite this, she was cast and she was put in "Bye Bye Blackbird," "Big Spender" and "Sing Sing Sing." In Boston, Elizabeth Parkinson was featured in every number and it was decided that she needed a break from the three-and-a-half-hour show. Verdon had Rak audition to be in the ensemble of "Rich Man's Frug" and she was hired, which put her in four numbers. As time went on, Verdon saw something in Rak and allowed her to do an understudy rehearsal day. She decided to do "I Gotcha" and there was something about it that Verdon liked. Rak became the understudy for Shannon Lewis for "I Gotcha." The first time before she went on in New York, Verdon asked if Rak, whom she called "Rak," if she got the notes for the number. Rak had not, so Verdon demonstrated that she wanted her to do a hip roll and slap the floor. At the performance Rak saw Verdon sitting at the sound booth and she did the number and got through it. Afterwards the dance captain asked if she would like to get her notes from Verdon. He also told her how Verdon had been bouncing in her chair during Rak's performance and that she had said, "She's great. One hundred percent trash." Everyone in the company heard about Verdon's comment. When Rak came in the next day she saw that there had been t-shirts made with the same written on them and signed **Gwen Verdon**.

In September the show played at the Colonial Theatre in Boston. From October 9, 1997, to December 6, 1998, it was at the Ahmanson Theatre in Los Angeles. It had previews in New York at the Broadhurst Theatre from December 26, 1998, and opened on Broadway on January 14, 1999. A hit, it ran till August 5, 2001. Verdon also planned that the company would go to London and have a European tour.

The show and Verdon were both parodied in an off-Broadway revue created and written by Gerard Alessandrini, *Forbidden Broadway: 2001 A Spoof Odyssey*. The revue had opened at the Stardust Theatre on December 6, 2000. The original cast recording was released by DRG Records on February 13, 2001. In it Christine Pedi impersonated Verdon to the tune of "I'm a Brass Band" from *Sweet Charity*. She also introduced some of her pals from *Fosse* for a parody of "Steam Heat" from *The Pajama Game*. Pedi's Verdon asked that the audience not sneak out the back way the way they had during *New Girl in Town*.

Verdon guested on the Warner Bros. Television comic talk show *The Rosie O'Donnell Show* on January 7, 1999. Since Ann Reinking also appeared, they were presumably both there to publicize *Fosse* which was then in previews. When she wasn't rehearsing *Fosse*, Verdon would drive up to Vermont where Nicole lived with her husband and their sons Sean, Noah and Leif. The Vermont house was where she kept her four Tony Awards in a suitcase in storage, since she believed that it was work not honors that mattered. Verdon thought Nicole's husband Andreas "Andy" Greiner was a terrific guy. "Most mothers can't stand their son-in-law, but I keep thinking, if they ever had an argument, I'd be on *his* side." Her son Jimmy gave her two granddaughters. The younger one, Jennifer, was an actress living in New York. Jennifer had a sister, Lisa, who had a twelve-year-old son also named James. Verdon said that her great-grandson was really handsome and also interested in theater.

She was conspicuously absent from the *E! True Hollywood Story* on Fosse that was broadcast on February 3, 1999, although there is a muted shot from an interview with her. It also featured a grainy black and white film re-enactment of the scene of Fosse's final heart attack in Washington when Verdon was with him. Her double is only seen from the back. The scene is notably free of onlookers, which adds a lonely poignancy to it. Another point of interest in the special is that it shows the *Chicago* billboard that announced that Liza Minnelli was replacing Verdon in the performance.

Verdon, Reinking and Valarie Pettiford appeared on the PBS talk show *Charlie Rose* to discuss *Fosse* in an episode broadcast on March 9, 1999. It was filmed in New York, and Verdon wore a black suit with white gray-striped open shirt and high-necked sweater. Reinking said that her favorite dance of Fosse's was "Cool Hand Luke" because it was so lyric and gentle, and so few people thought of his choreography that way. On April 20, 1999, Verdon made her third and final appearance at the Easter Bonnet Competition which benefited Broadway Cares/Equity Fights AIDS at the New Amsterdam Theatre. This appearance was a surprise one as she danced across the stage during the performance of a number from the cast of *Fosse*.

Verdon returned for her second guest appearance on *Walker, Texas Ranger* on the episode "Mind Games." It was also to be her last appearance

14. Charity One Last Time and Fosse 231

on television. It was broadcast on May 8, 1999, and written by Robin Madden and directed by Michael Preece. Verdon was back as Maisie Whitman, whose son Brian (Robin Thomas) is murdered by his wife, Caroline (Roxane Hart) and her lover Peter (David Allen Brooks). Caroline schemes to get Maisie's trust fund by drugging her tea with Ecstasy so that she can be declared mentally incompetent. Maisie's friend C.D. (Noble Willingham) saves her. Verdon appears in ten scenes in a variety of costumes that all feature neck scarves. Maisie wearing more cardigans than jackets indicates her age. Verdon dances again with C.D. at the beginning of the episode at a country and western dance but her being a drugged victim allows the actress to play degrees of confusion. Her best moment is perhaps her reaction to being face-slapped by Caroline, a mix of shock and disapproval. Maisie having a son in the narrative disproves the theory of the previous show's episode, "Forgotten People," that she may have been a lesbian, and her being wealthy is something else not indicated in that episode. Her drugged visions are demonstrated by director Preece using distorted imagery for point of view.

On June 6, 1999, Verdon attended the 1999 Tony Awards with her granddaughter Jennifer. They were held at the Gershwin Theatre and broadcast live on CBS television. She is seen four times in the show. For the first, Verdon is in the audience clapping after being thanked by Ralph Burns, who won the Tony for Best Orchestration of a Musical with Douglas Besterman for *Fosse*. She wears the same black gown with white collar that she wore at the 1994 Tribute to Fosse and at the 1994 Tonys. There is a second cut to Verdon applauding Thomas Bridge, who won the Best Lighting Design award for *Fosse*, after he thanked Bob Fosse. Verdon is seen for the third time sitting next to Ann Reinking when the camera cuts to Reinking and Richard Maltby Jr., as they are announced as nominees for the award for Best Director of a Musical. Reinking and Maltby, Jr. lost to Matthew Bourne for *Swan Lake*. Verdon is seen for the fourth time as part of the show team that accepts the Award for Best Musical for *Fosse* with Roy Furman, Ann Reinking, Chet Walker, and Richard Maltby Jr. As Furman speaks for the team to accept the award, she stands beside him. We see that Verdon's outfit is the black jacket with white collar worn with a broach and black necklace, and black skirt with a split.

In June an extended version of the 1990 interview with Michael Buckley was published in the fall 1999 issue of *Show Music* magazine. She appeared on the *A&E Biography* episode on Fosse broadcast on August 24, 1999. Verdon wore a black blouse and jacket, and was interviewed sitting down, with some extreme closeups showing her milky gray–colored eyes.

Among the things she spoke about was working with Fosse on *Damn Yankees*.

In the fall of 1999 *Fosse* began its national company tour in Chicago under her artistic director eye. On October 25, 1999, Verdon was presented with a Career Transition for Dancers' Award by Jerry Orbach at "The Next Step," a gala benefit program at the Kaye Playhouse. The performance benefited an organization that provided counselling, education and scholarship programs to help dancers move successfully to new fields when they retired.

Verdon next appeared in the supporting role of Alora Swanson in the comic crime drama *Walking Across Egypt* (1999). Directed by Arthur Allan Seidelman, it was shot on location around Orlando, Florida, including Clermont, Ocoee, St. Cloud and Windermere. The screenplay by Paul Tamasy was based on the novel by Clyde Edgerton. It focused on the relationship between an elderly religious woman, Mattie Rigsbee (Ellen Burstyn), and an inmate of the Listre Young Man's Rehabilitation Center, 16-year-old Wesley Benfield (Jonathan Taylor Thomas). As Mattie's next door neighbour, Alora is a minor character in the narrative. Like the others she speaks with a Southern accent and Verdon's red hair here appears straight. Alora dresses in loud colors and wears large earrings which hint at an eccentricity that is not explored. Verdon has two good moments. The first is her reaction to the news that Wesley is going to commit suicide which she describes as "committing sideways." She expresses it physically as mayhem when she runs. The second is Alora's smile of apology to Mattie over Wesley being taken back to the Center. Verdon's clown face makes the smile comic and also shows character empathy.

The film was released on December 17, 1999, with the tagline "Doing the right thing can be as hard as ... *Walking Across Egypt*."

In 1999, Verdon played a supporting role in *Bruno* (2000), a comedy directed by Shirley MacLaine, which was to be her last film appearance. The film was shot on location in New York and in Wilmington and Raleigh, North Carolina. The screenplay by David Ciminello centered on the titular eight-year-year old boy (Alex D. Linz) who cross-dresses as a "free spirit" and is his school's hope in the national Catholic spelling competition. Verdon is only in one scene, in what amounts to a cameo. She is Mrs. Drago, dressed in black with long braided black hair. She owns a large dog that Bruno and his friend Shawniqua (Kiami Davael) walk and take to the park. Mrs. Drago's attire suggests that she has a backstory that the narrative does not explore, and the fact that she is a friend of Shawniqua adds nothing to the story of any consequence.

14. Charity One Last Time and Fosse

The film was first screened on April 16, 2000, at the Los Angeles Independent Film Festival with the taglines "The comedy that's long on originality and short on pants" and "Some people are a little individual." It didn't receive a wide release but rather was screened on cable television on December 1, 2000.

In April 2000 Verdon received the "Living Legend" cast bronze medallion with a fabric red, white and blue ribbon by the Library of Congress during its bicentennial celebration. The award was selected by the Library's curators and subject specialists to honor artists, writers, activists, filmmakers, physicians, entertainers, sports figures and public servants who have made significant contributions to America's diverse cultural, scientific and social heritage. It was said that the Legends had provided examples of personal excellence that had benefited others and enriched the nation in a variety of ways. Verdon was one of the speakers in the PBS *Biography* episode on Shirley MacLaine entitled "This Time Around" broadcast on May 14, 2000.

In the summer of 2000 Verdon was interviewed by Rick McKay in his New York apartment, in what would prove to be her last interview. What she told him was included in his documentary *Broadway: The Golden Age, By the Legends Who Were There* (2004). It covers the period of New York Theatre from the end of World War II to the beginning of the Vietnam War. Verdon was featured in the chapter entitled "Gwen Verdon and Bob Fosse." In it she comments that the only time dancing was truly fulfilling for her was in shows that Fosse directed and choreographed. This was because Fosse believed that you have to act to dance. Verdon says that Fosse gave her the image of Lola from *Damn Yankees* as a "little flirty fat girl," so that the actress never felt the character was sexy. He told her that life is an onion and as an actor and dancer he wanted her to keep peeling away the layers to get to the heart of the material. Footage is shown from TV's American Musical Theatre show of Verdon singing and dancing "Whatever Lola Wants." We also see a snippet of Verdon doing the same number in the trailer of the film version. McKay ends the chapter with a screen title which reads that they won 13 separate Tony Awards in their careers.

Verdon is also featured in other chapters of the film. In "The Journey Begins" she speaks about when she first came to New York in 1947. A blizzard had hit the city so there were no subway trains, buses or taxis running. However she could still see the theater marquees in Times Square through the snow, with the names of the big stars she had only heard of up in lights. Verdon says she stood there and just looked. She looked so long that the pigeons landed on her as if she was a statue. In "For A Song..." she is one of many talking about "second acting." This was a practice by actors of arriving at the theater at the first intermission and returning with the audience for the second act, as a way to see the show for free. In "Waiting in the Wings" there is a still of Verdon from *Can-Can*. Shirley MacLaine tells how she had planned to leave her chorus job in *The Pajama Game* in 1955 to become an understudy for Verdon. In "When the Curtain Goes Down" Verdon is shown photographed at Downey's Restaurant in 1962 with Fosse and Robert Morse.

In his audio commentary on the DVD, McKay says she told him that the director of the film version of *Damn Yankees* refused to shoot her in close-up because he said Verdon was "much too unattractive for film." Offended, she went back to New York Theatre and only later returned to films to play what she said was "everyone's grandmother." Verdon also remarked that some of McKay's questions had never been put to her before. Her interview was the first he did for the film and Verdon was early for her appointment because she said that dancers were always early. The film's budget could not accommodate a driver to take her home and he apologized, offering to get her a taxi. She said it wasn't necessary. Fifty years ago she couldn't walk down a New York street without being mobbed but now, if she was recognized at all, it was as one of the old ladies from the *Cocoon* movies. McKay felt this was a sad comment on the legacy of a woman who won four Tony Awards, was the muse and partner of Bob Fosse, and made theatrical history. McKay's commentary also includes his vocal impersonation of Verdon speaking.

The documentary was first screened in April 2003 at the Palm Beach International Film Festival, then October 9, 2003, at the Austin Film Festival and February 6, 2004, at the Santa Barbara Film Festival. It was given a wide release in New York on June 11, 2004, with the taglines "The largest collection in history of award-winning stars brought together in a single movie!" and "One filmmaker's search for a Broadway that was lost, and the 100 legends that he found...." The film was lauded by Peter Travers in *Rolling Stone*.

Verdon died in her sleep in the night of October 17–18, 2000, in Woodstock, Vermont, at the home of Nicole. She was 75. It was reported in the *New York Times* obituary by Robert Berkvist that at the time of death Verdon had homes in Bronxville and Quogue. She was described by Berkvist as widely regarded as the best dancer ever to brighten the Broadway stage, and also a highly capable actress adept at enriching the characters she played with heart. The League of American Theatres and

Producers had the lights of Broadway's marquees dimmed in her memory on October 19.

A memorial was held for Verdon at the Broadhurst Theatre on February 20, 2001. It was organized by Ann Reinking and others, though a scheduling problem meant Reinking was unable to attend. More than 1,100 people did attend the hour-long tribute, including her friends and colleagues who came to speak and perform. These included Cy Coleman, Fred Ebb, Herb Gardner, John Kander, Bebe Neuwirth, Chita Rivera, Ben Vereen, Ethel Wyll, Ethel Martin, Elizabeth Parkinson, Keith Roberts, Byron Easley, Dana Moore, Mary MacLeod, Belle Calaway, and Nicole Fosse Greiner. Verdon's granddaughter Jennifer Henaghan brought a message from Verdon's son Jimmy.

Cy Coleman said that he always thought of Verdon as fun, family, warmth and caring. These qualities would always shine through her flawless dancing, her intelligent interpretation of a song, her immaculate timing and her exquisite sense of comedy—all this combined in the perfectly formed body of a beautiful woman. That's what he called a big star, which he felt she was. Coleman said Verdon loved jazz waltzes, and that's why he played and sang "You Should See Yourself." Chita Rivera held up the top hat she wore in *Chicago* and told the audience that when she danced with Verdon it was like two dancing as one and who wouldn't want to be identical to her? She remembered saying for the longest time: "I'm kickin' up my heels with Gwen Verdon, and having a ball being naughty, bad and just plain unprofessional!" Rivera continued that she had never seen anything like her. She was one of a kind and always would be in a class all her own. Rivera would remember her class, her style, her voice, her magic and laugh. "The skies are brighter and my life is fuller having known Gwen. It's impossible to think she's not here, but she is! And I'll always hear that laugh and that voice. My God, Gwen, how you could dance!"

Former Jack Cole dancer Ethel Martin reflected that you could be the best dancer in the world and a wonderful performer, but to be star you had to have something indefinable, something that makes the world love you. Verdon had that. Jennifer Henaghan commented that she was a better person than she was a dancer. Herb Gardner sent a written tribute which was read by the lighting designer, Jules Fisher. Cy Feuer said that he attended out of respect for her and Fosse, and also because he had cast Nicole in *A Chorus Line*. He reported that he watched the best he could, then slipped out without saying a word to anyone.

Performers at the memorial included Cy Coleman who sang "You Should See Yourself" from *Sweet Charity*, Vereen who sang "Life Is Just a

Bowl of Cherries," Elizabeth Parkinson, and Keith Roberts Byron Easley who danced "Cool Hand Luke," and John Kander and Fred Ebb who sang "Nowadays" from *Chicago* with counterpoint dancing provided by Dana Moore, Mary MacLeod and *Chicago* dancers Bebe Neuwirth and Belle Calaway. There were also reminiscences by old friends and a video tribute which had voiceovers from Verdon about her career, and film clips from her television, film and stage work. There was footage of her dancing in *Can-Can, Damn Yankees, Redhead, Sweet Charity* and *Chicago.* The entire crowd rose to give Verdon a final hand.

Most who attended the memorial were invited but the event was also open to the public. Some 500 seats were filled by people who had begun lining up along 44th Street three hours before the ceremonies began. The audience had its share of grayhairs, but many others were children, or were not even born, when Verdon last appeared on Broadway in 1975 in *Chicago.* Yet she touched their spirit, some of them said, reaffirming the ageless truth that young people were often molded by forces far removed from their lives. It was no coincidence that the memorial took place at the Broadhurst Theatre. This was where *Fosse* was playing, and next door was the Shubert Theatre where the revival of *Chicago* played. Cynics might comment that this provided for hype, but Broadway and the theater could always be self-referential and self-promoting. Perhaps no one would have appreciated the fact more than Verdon herself.

In the years that followed Verdon's death, several of her co-workers also passed on and their *New York Times* obituaries made mention of her relationship to them. These included Ray Walston, Albert Hague, Cy Coleman, Cy Feuer, Sidney Sheldon, Gretchen Wyler, David Shaw, Michael Kidd, Richard Adler, and Martin Richards. Beyoncé's "Single Ladies" music video (2008) returned Verdon's name briefly to popular culture, as did the release of the 2002 film *Chicago*, the revival of the stage shows *Chicago, Can-Can, Sweet Charity, Damn Yankees, New Girl in Town,* and the Jack Cole Project *Heat Wave.*

On November 20, 2013, Sam Wasson's biography of Fosse was published by Eamon Dolan/Houghton Mifflin Harcourt. Wasson chose his subject too late to talk to Verdon but he quotes one friend of hers who describes Verdon's way of dancing and cooking. When she made clam sauce for spaghetti, she did it "interrupting stirs with pliés." Verdon kept spices high in a cupboard, doing arabesques as she reached for them. Wasson also provides an artful description of Verdon as "a luscious lollipop person with a voice she said sounded like a 78 r.p.m. record with a wobble in it."

Appendix

Performances on Stage, Film, Television and Record

Stage Appearances

Season dates are for Gwen Verdon's run and not the show's entire run.

Show Boat (May 4, 1940). Los Angeles Auditorium Theatre. Director: Zeke Colvan. Part: Broadbent Dancer.

Bonanza Bound! (December 26, 1947, to January 3, 1948). Shubert Theatre, Philadelphia. Director: Charles Friedman. Part: Gypsy.

Magdalena (July 26, 1948, August 16, 1948, September 20 to December 4, 1948). Los Angeles Civic Light Opera, San Francisco Curran Theatre (San Francisco Light Opera), Ziegfeld Theatre. Director: Jules Dassin. Verdon was the assistant choreographer.

Alive and Kicking (January 17 to February 25, 1950). Winter Garden Theater. Director: Robert H. Gordon. Part: Abou's Wife.

Can-Can (May 7, 1953, to September 6, 1954). Shubert Theatre. Director: Abe Burrows. Parts: Claudine/Eve in "The Garden of Eden."

Damn Yankees (May 5, 1955, to November 24, 1956). 46th Street Theater. Director: George Abbott. Part: Lola.

New Girl in Town (May 14, 1957, to March 22, 1958). 46th Street Theater. Director: George Abbott. Part: Anna.

Redhead (February 5, 1959, to March 19, 1960). 46th Street Theater. Director: Bob Fosse. Part: Essie Whimple.

Sweet Charity (January 29, 1966, to June 30, 1967). Palace Theater. Director: Bob Fosse. Part: Charity.

Children! Children! (March 7, 1972). Ritz Theater. Director: Joseph Hardy. Part: Helen Giles.

Damn Yankees (revival) (March 26 to April 14, 1974). Arie Crown Music Theatre, Chicago. Director: Ray Walston. Part: Lola.

Chicago (January 3, 1975, to February 6, 1977). 46th Street Theater. Director: Bob Fosse. Part: Roxie Hart.

Sweet Charity (revival) (April 27, 1986, to March 15, 1987). Minskoff Theatre. Director: Bob Fosse. Verdon was director Fosse's assistant.

The 10th Man (December 10, 1989, to January 14, 1990). Vivian Beaumont Theatre. Director: Ulu Grosbard. Verdon was the dance consultant.

Love Letters (June 26 to July 1, 1990). Canon Theatre, Beverly Hills. Director: Unknown. Part: Melissa Gardner.

Sweet Charity: The Concert (June 15, 1998). Avery Fisher Hall, Lincoln Centre. Director: John Bowab. Part: Verdon also did the musical staging. Charity.

Fosse (January 14, 1999, to August 25, 2001). Broadhurst Theatre. Director:

Richard Maltby, Jr./Ann Reinking. Verdon was the artistic advisor.

Films

The King Steps Out (1936) aka *Sissy* and *Poor Sister*.
Presenting Lily Mars (1943) (DVD released by Warner Archives Collection on August 20, 2013).
Blonde from Brooklyn (1945).
Easter Parade (1948) (DVD released by Warner Home Video on February 8, 2011).
On the Riviera (1951) (DVD released by 20th Century Fox on May 22, 2007).
David and Bathsheba (1951) (DVD released by 20th Century Fox on March 14, 2006).
Meet Me After the Show (1951) aka *Don't Fence Me In* (DVD released by 20th Century Fox on April 16, 2013).
Dreamboat (1952) (DVD released by 20th Century Fox on December 11, 2012).
Singin' in the Rain (1952). (DVD released by MGM on June 6, 2000. Two-Disc Special Edition released by Warner Home Video on September 24, 2002. 60th Anniversary Edition released by Warner Home Video on October 2, 2012).
The Merry Widow (1952). MGM. (Only released on video by MGM (Warner) on February 24, 1995).
The Mississippi Gambler (1953). (DVD released on PAL by Universal but release date unknown).
The I Don't Care Girl (1953) (DVD released by 20th Century Fox Film Corporation on April 16, 2013).
The Farmer Takes a Wife (1953) (Only available on video. Released by 20th Century Fox on May 25, 1989).
Gentlemen Prefer Blondes (1953) (DVD released by 20th Century Fox on May 22, 2006).
Gentlemen Marry Brunettes (1955) (Only released on video by MGM date unknown).
Damn Yankees (1958) aka *Whatever Lola Wants*. DVD released by Warner Home Video on October 12, 2004).
Sgt. Pepper's Lonely Hearts Club Band (1978) (DVD released by Universal Studios on August 12, 2003).
The Cotton Club (1984) (DVD released by MGM (Video & DVD) on July 10, 2001).
Cocoon (1985) (DVD released by 20th Century Fox on June 1, 2004).
Nadine (1987) (DVD released by Sony Pictures Home Entertainment on July 5, 2005.
Cocoon: The Return (1988) aka *Cocoon II* (DVD released by 20th Century Fox on June 1, 2004).
Alice (1990) (DVD released by MGM (Video & DVD) on June 5, 2001 individually and in *The Woody Allen Collection*, Set 2, and *The Woody Allen Collection*, Sets 1–3, released by MGM on March 25, 2008).
Marvin's Room (1996) (DVD released by Miramax on February 9, 1999).
Walking Across Egypt (1999) (DVD released by Alumination on June 14, 2005).
Bruno (2000) aka *The Dress Code* (DVD released by MGM (Video & DVD) on September 25, 2001).
Broadway: The Golden Age. By The Legends Who Were There (2004) (DVD released by RCA Victor Broadway on November 9, 2004).

Television Shows

Ed Sullivan Hosts "Talk of the Town" (October 11, 1953).
Goodyear Television Playhouse (March 28, 1954). "Native Dancer."
Once Upon an Eastertime (April 18, 1954).
The Colgate Comedy Hour (July 10, 1955).
The Colgate Comedy Hour (December 11, 1955).
The Dinah Shore Chevy Show (September 21, 1958).

Performances on Stage, Film, Television and Record 239

The Dinah Shore Chevy Show (October 5, 1958).
The Dinah Shore Chevy Show (October 4, 1959). (DVD unavailable but "Erbie Fitch's Twitch" is viewable on You Tube.com).
Person to Person (January 29, 1960).
Perry Como's Kraft Music Hall (January 18, 1961).
The Garry Moore Show (October 31, 1961). CBS.
Perry Como's Kraft Music Hall (November 22 and 26, 1961).
The Garry Moore Show (December 19, 1961). (DVD released as *The Gary Moore Show presents A Carol Burnett Christmas* by Entertainment One on unknown date).
The Garry Moore Show (January 30, 1962).
The Garry Moore Show (February 27, 1962).
The Garry Moore Show (March 20, 1962).
American Musical Theatre (April 1, 1962).
The Garry Moore Show (June 5, 1962). (DVD in its entirety unavailable but "I Wanna Be a Dancin' Man" is available for viewing on YouTube).
The Garry Moore Show (January 1, 1963).
The Garry Moore Show (May 21, 1963).
The Garry Moore Show (November 5, 1963).
The Danny Kaye Show (November 20, 1963). (DVD of show unavailable but Kaye's closing monologue can be viewed on the Library of Congress website).
The Garry Moore Show (January 7, 1964).
The Garry Moore Show (April 14, 1964).
The Danny Kaye Show (September 23, 1964). (DVD of show unavailable but the "Jerome the Bachelor" skit which features Danny Kaye, Harvey Korman, Joyce Van Patten, and Gwen Verdon can be viewed on the Library of Congress website).
The Danny Kaye Show (November 25, 1963).

The Danny Kaye Show (December 23, 1964).
The Danny Kaye Show (February 10, 1965).
The Danny Kaye Show (December 1, 1965).
The Merv Griffin Show (March 29, 1966).
What's My Line? (May 15, 1966).
The Ed Sullivan Show (October 2, 1966). (DVD of show unavailable but "I'm a Brass Band" is available on the DVD *The Best of Broadway Musicals: Original Cast Performances from The Ed Sullivan Show* which was released by Sofa Home Entertainment on July 22, 2003).
The Merv Griffin Show (October 13, 1966).
The Merv Griffin Show (November 22, 1966).
The Ed Sullivan Show (March 5, 1967). (DVD of show unavailable but "If My Friends Could See Me Now" viewable on YouTube. Also part of "If My Friends Could See Me Now" is on the DVD *The Very Best of the Ed Sullivan Show. The Greatest Entertainers* released by Sofia Home Entertainment on January 6, 2004. The DVD also features Verdon talking about the show).
The Merv Griffin Show (July 20, 1967). (DVD of show unavailable but Verdon can be seen among the guests for the interview with West and Ward on YouTube, although it is dated at September 1, 1966).
The Carol Burnett Show (October 16, 1967).
The Ed Sullivan Show (December 10, 1967). (DVD of show unavailable but "Nothing Can Stop Me Now" viewable on YouTube).
The Joey Bishop Show (August 30, 1968).
The Jonathan Winters Show (September 25, 1968).
The Bob Hope Special (October 14, 1968). (DVD of show unavailable but "Cool Hand Luke" and "The Tijuana (Mexican) Shuffle" viewable on You Tube).

The Jackie Gleason Show (November 16, 1968).
The Mike Douglas Show (January 13–17, 1969).
The Ed Sullivan Show (March 2, 1969).
The 1969 Annual Tony Awards (April 20, 1969).
The Ed Sullivan Show (June 1, 1969). (DVD of show unavailable but "Mexican Breakfast" viewable on YouTube).
The Joan Rivers Show (June 22, 1969).
The Dick Cavett Show (July 7, 1969).
The Hollywood Palace (October 11, 1969). (DVD of show unavailable but the Beatles Medley is viewable on You Tube).
The Carol Burnett Show (November 3, 1969).
The Merv Griffin Show (January 6, 1970).
The Ed Sullivan Show (February 1, 1970)
The Dick Cavett Show (February 9, 1970).
The Merv Griffin Show (April 27, 1970).
The Mike Douglas Show (May 4–8, 1970).
NET Playhouse (July 14, 1970). "Actor's Choice."
Girl Talk (August 24, 1970).
The Don Knotts Show (January 26, 1971).
The 1971 Tony Awards (March 28, 1971). (DVD of show unavailable but Verdon's performance can be seen in the DVD *Broadway's Lost Treasures III. The Best of the Tony Awards* released by Acorn Media on September 27, 2005).
The 1972 Tony Awards (April 23, 1972).
Love, American Style (September 29, 1972). "Love and the New Act."
Ed Sullivan's Broadway (March 16, 1973). (DVD of show unavailable but "Who's Got The Pain" viewable on YouTube).
The 1973 Tony Awards (March 25, 1973).
Deadly Visitor aka *The Deadly Visitor* (July 3, 1973).
Captain Kangaroo (March 5, 1975).
The Today Show (July 22, 1975).
Captain Kangaroo (October 22, 1975).
Saturday Night Live with Howard Cosell (November 8, 1975).
Dinah! (November 19, 1975).
The Mike Douglas Show (June 14, 1976). (DVD of show unavailable but "Nowadays/Honey Rag" and the Verdon/Rivera interview are viewable on YouTube.com).
The Dick Cavett Show (December 5, 1977).
The American Dance Machine: A Celebration of Broadway Dance (1981). (Video released by MGM/CBS in 1981 but out of print).
*M*A*S*H* (October 26, 1981). "That's Showbiz." (DVD released by 20th Century Fox Home Entertainment on May 23, 2006).
Fame (March 11, 1982). "Come One, Come All." (DVD released by MGM (Video & DVD) on November 1, 2005).
Strippers (March 23, 1983). (Video out of print).
Parade of Stars (May 22, 1983).
The Jerk, Too (January 6, 1984). (DVD only available on PAL and released with *The Jerk* by Uca Catalogue on May 7, 2007).
Gimme a Break! (April 19, 1984). "The Center." (DVD unavailable but episode viewable on YouTube).
The 1984 Tony Awards (June 3, 1984). (DVD of show unavailable but "All That Jazz" by Chita Rivera and "Nowadays" by Rivera and Verdon available on the DVD *Broadway's Lost Treasures* released by Acorn Media on October 28, 2003).
Trapper John, M.D. (March 31, 1985). "All the King's Horses..." (DVD unavailable but viewable on YouTube).
Magnum, P.I. (October 31, 1985). "Going Home." (DVD released by Universal Studios on February 27, 2007).
Webster (January 1, 1986). "Hello, I Must Be Going." (DVD released by Shout! Factory on August 9, 2011.
The Equalizer (February 12, 1986). "Unnatural Causes." (DVD released by Universal Studios on February 12, 2008).
Webster (March 14, 1986). "There Goes the Bride." (DVD released by Shout! Factory on August 9, 2011).
All Is Forgiven (May 29, 1986). "I Can't Say No."
Magnum, P.I. (February 11, 1987). "Forty."

Performances on Stage, Film, Television and Record 241

(DVD released by Universal Studios on October 30, 2007).
Hotel (May 20, 1987). "Second Thoughts."
The 1987 Tony Awards (June 7, 1987).
Magnum, P.I. (October 7, 1987). "Infinity and Jelly Doughnuts." (DVD released by Universal Studios on March 4, 2008).
Best Friends for Life (January 18, 1988).
Magnum P.I. (May 1, 1988). "Resolutions: Part I and II." (DVD released by Universal Studios on March 4, 2008).
Webster (November 4, 1988). "Take My Cousin, Please."
Dear John (March 9, 1989). "The Second Time Around." (DVD unavailable but viewable on YouTube).
The 1989 Tony Awards (June 4, 1989).
Sanford Meisner: The Theater's Best Kept Secret (August 27, 1990). (DVD unavailable but viewable on YouTube).
Great Performances: Dance in America. (1990). *Bob Fosse: Steam Heat.*
Dream On (June 20, 1992). "For Peter's Sake."
Homicide: Life on the Street (February 3, 1993) "A Ghost of a Chance." (DVD released by New Video on May 27, 2003).
Key West (1993)."Gimme Shelter." (DVD unavailable but viewable on YouTube.com).
Oldest Living Confederate Widow Tells All (May 1, 1994). (DVD released by Allumination on September 7, 2004).
The New Dramatists Life Achievement Award to Neil Simon (May 19, 1994).
The 1994 Tony Awards (June 12, 1994). CBS.
The Cosby Mysteries (September 28, 1994). "Our Lady of Cement."
The Cosby Mysteries (October 5, 1994). "Self Defense."
In Cold Blood (November 24, 1996). (DVD released by RHI Entertainment on February 8, 2005, and Mill Creek Entertainment on October 15, 2013).
Touched By an Angel (April 13, 1997).
(DVD released by Paramount on November 28, 2006).
Walker, Texas Ranger (October 25, 1997). "Forgotten People." (DVD released by Paramount on July 1, 2008).
Promised Land (March 26, 1998). "Undercover Granny."
The Rosie O'Donnell Show (January 7, 1999).
Charlie Rose (March 9, 1999). (DVD released by Charlie Rose Inc. on December 21, 2006).
Walker Texas Ranger (May 8, 1999). "Mind Games." (DVD released by Paramount on January 13, 2009).
A&E Biography (August 24, 1999). "Bob Fosse: Dancing on the Edge." (Video released by New Video Group in 1999 and A&E Home Video on February 7, 2000).
Biography (May 14, 2000). *Shirley MacLaine: This Time Around.*

Recordings

Can-Can. Original Broadway Cast Recording. Capitol, 1953.
Damn Yankees. Original Broadway Cast Recording. RCA Victor, 1955.
The Girl I Left Home For. Joe Reisman and His Orchestra. RCA Victor, 1956.
New Girl in Town. Original Broadway Cast Recording. RCA Victor, 1957.
Damn Yankees. Original Motion Picture Soundtrack. RCA Victor, 1958.
Redhead. Original Broadway Cast Recording. RCA Victor, 1959.
Sweet Charity. Original Broadway Cast Recording. Columbia, 1966.
Lyle Lyle Crocodile and Other Adventures of Lyle, read by Gwen Verdon. Caedmon, 1969.
Chicago. A Musical Vaudeville. Original Cast Recording. Arista Spart, 1975.
The Velveteen Rabbit, read by Gwen Verdon. Vocalise conducted by Don Heckman. Caedmon, 1984.

Bibliography

Adler, Richard. "Warming Up 'Damn Yankees' for the Opening." *New York Times*, June 28, 1981. Retrieved September 9, 2014, from http://www.nytimes.com.

Alexander, Ron. "After Opening at Majestic, the Gala at the Beacon." *New York Times*, January 27, 1988. Retrieved September 11, 2014, from http://www.nytimes.com.

Aloff, Mindy. *Dance Anecdotes: Stories from the Worlds of Ballet, Broadway, the Ballroom, and Modern Dance.* New York: Oxford University Press, 2006.

_____. "The New Season/Theater: A Loving Celebration of All That's Fosse." *New York Times*, September 13, 1998. Retrieved September 13, 2014, from http://www.nytimes.com.

Als, Hilton. "The Lives They Lived: 01-07-01: Gwen Verdon, b. 1925: One of the Boys." *New York Times*, January 7, 2001. Retrieved August 27, 2014, from http://www.nytimes.com.

Anderson, Jack. "Dance Review: For the Day When the Feet Become Still." *New York Times*, October 27, 1999. Retrieved September 13, 2014, from http://www.nytimes.com.

Anderson, Lisa. "'Vogueing' Done to the Tune of $400,000 for Aids." *Chicago Tribune*, May 11, 1989. Retrieved March 19, 2014, from http://articles.chicagotribune.com.

Arnold, Jeremy. *Cocoon*. 1985. *Turner Classic Movies*. Retrieved January 16, 2014, from http://www.tcm.com.

Atkinson, Brooks. "At the Theatre: Charles Laughton Opens Experimental Theatre Season in Brecht's 'Galileo.'" *New York Times*, December 8, 1947. Retrived May 19, 2014, from http://www.nytimes.com.

_____. "At the Theatre: Heitor Villa-Lobos, Brazilian Composer, Has Written the Musical Score for 'Magdalena.'" *New York Times*, September 21, 1948. Retrieved April 11, 2014.

_____. "First Night at the Theatre." *New York Times*, May 8, 1953. Retrieved December 31, 2013, from http://www.nytimes.com.

_____. "Fun and Games. Two Examples of the George Abbott Formula for Musical Comedies." *New York Times*, May 26, 1957. Retrieved August 21, 2014, from http://www.nytimes.com.

_____. "Regarding 'Can-Can.'" *New York Times*, May 17, 1953. Retrieved December 31, 2013, from http://www.nytimes.com.

_____. "The Theatre: 'Redhead.'" *New York Times*, February 6, 1959. Retrieved June 3, 2014, from http://www.nytimes.com.

_____. "The Theatre: Singing Anna Christie; 'New Girl in Town' Opens at 46th St." *New York Times*, May 15, 1957. Retrieved April 27, 2014, from http://www.nytimes.com.

Bales, Melanie, and Karen Eliot. *Dance on Its Own Terms: Histories and Methodologies.* New York: Oxford University Press, 2013.

Banner, Lois. *Marilyn: The Passion and the Paradox.* New York: Bloomsbury, 2012.

Barnes, Clive. "'Dance' Broadway Style." *New York Times*, February 25, 1966. Retrieved September 8, 2014, from http://www.nytimes.com.
_____. "The Dance: Gala 'Aurora's Wedding' Aids National Ballet." *New York Times*, November 12, 1973. Retrieved October 4, 2014, from http://www.nytimes.com.
_____. "Dance: The New American Machine." *New York Times*, August 26, 1976. Retrieved October 31, 2014, from http://www.nytimes.com.
_____. "Dance: They Won't Joke, Don't Ask Them." *New York Times*, December 19, 1971. Retrieved October 3, 2014, from http://www.nytimes.com.
_____. "Liza Minnelli Lends Talents to 'Chicago.'" *New York Times*, August 15, 1975. Retrieved October 5, 2014, from http://www.nytimes.com.
_____. "Stage: 'Chicago,' Musical Vaudeville." *New York Times*, June 4, 1975. Retrieved October 5, 2014, from http://www.nytimes.com.
_____. "Stars Shine for Benefit of Library." *New York Times*, May 11, 1976. Retrieved October 30, 2014, from http://www.nytimes.com.
_____. "Theater: A Non-Thriller." *New York Times*, March 8, 1972. Retrieved September 10, 2014, from http://www.nytimes.com.
Basinger, Jeanine. *Lana Turner*. Pyramid Illustrated History of the Movies. New York: Pyramid, 1976.
Baxter, Joan. *Television Musicals: Plots, Criticisms, Casts and Credits for 222 Shows, 1944–1996*. Jefferson, NC: McFarland, 1997.
Baxter, John. *Hollywood in the Sixties*. London, New York: Tantivy, A.S. Barnes, 1972.
_____. *Von Sternberg*. Lexington: University Press of Kentucky, 2010.
Beddow, Margery. *Bob Fosse's Broadway*. Portsmouth, NH: Heinemann, 1996.
Behar, Henri. "Meryl Streep on Marvin's Room." *Film Scouts* Interviews. December 22, 1996. Retrieved March 28, 2014, from http://www.filmscouts.com.
Behlmer, Rudy. *Memo from Darryl F. Zanuck: The Golden Years at Twentieth Century-Fox*. New York: Grove, 1995.
Bellison, Lillian. "Future Events: Fringe Benefits." *New York Times*, October 12, 1980. Retrieved November 1, 2014, from http://ww.nytimes.com.
Bergan, Ronald. *The United Artists Story*. London: Octopus, 1986.
Berkvist, Robert. "Gwen Verdon, Redhead Who High-Kicked Her Way to Stardom, Dies at 75." *New York Times*, October 19, 2000. Retrieved June 3, 2014, from http://www.nytimes.com.
_____. "Theater Notes: Is Off-Broadway Finished? Footlights." *New York Times*, April 27, 1975. Retrieved October 4, 2014, from http://www.nytimes.com.
Bertolini, Diane. "The Lost Musicals: Redhead." *New York Public Library*. November 13, 2012. Retreved June 3, 2014, from http://www.nypl.org.
Billman, Larry. *Betty Grable: A Bio-Bibliography* (Bio-Bibliographies in the Performing Arts, no. 40). Westport, CT; London: Greenwood, 1993.
_____. *Film Choreographers and Dance Directors: An Illustrated Biographical Encyclopedia, with a History and Filmographies, 1893 Through 1995*. Jefferson, NC: McFarland, 1997.
Blau, Eleanor. "Capezio Awards Given to Four in Dance World." *New York Times*, May 5, 1987. Retrieved September 11, 2014, from http://www.nytimes.com.
Bordman, Gerald Martin. *American Musical Theatre: A Chronicle*. New York: Oxford University Press, 2010.
Boross, Bob. "Jack Cole." Jazz Dance History in America. 2010. Retrieved January 6, 2014, from http://www.bobboross.com.
Bosworth, Patricia. "The Drama Behind the Tony Awards." *New York Times*, June 5, 1977. Retrieved October 31, 2014, from http://www.nytimes.com.
Brannigan, Erin. *Dancefilm: Choreogra-

phy and the Moving Image. New York: Oxford University Press, 2011.

Brantley, Ben. "Theatre Review: An Album of Fosse." *New York Times*, January 15, 1999. Retrieved August 23, 2014, from http://www.nytimes.com.

Briley, Ron. *The Baseball Film in Postwar America: A Critical Study, 1948–1962*. Jefferson, NC: McFarland, 2011.

Brogdon, William. "Review: 'Gentlemen Prefer Blondes.'" *Variety*, July 1, 1953. Retrieved January 26, 2014, from http://www.variety.com.

Brown, Les. "TV Weekend." *New York Times*, June 11, 1976. Retrieved October 30, 2014, from http://www.nytimes.com.

Bryer, Jackson R., and Richard Allen Davison. *The Art of the American Musical: Conversations with the Creators*. New Brunswick, NJ: Rutgers University Press, 2005.

Buckley, Michael. "Gwen Verdon ... and All That Jazz." *Theater Week* 3, no. 52 (1990): 14–19.

———. "Gwen Verdon: Gypsy Emeritus." *Show Music* 15, no. 3 (1999): 23–28, 68.

Buckley, Tom. "At the Movies. Ann Reinking Plays Herself in 'All That Jazz.'" *New York Times*, January 4, 1980. Retrieved November 4, 2014, from http://www.nytimes.com.

Burke, Tom. "The Gallagher Who Gives 'Nanette' Its Sheen." *New York Times*, February 21, 1971. Retrieved October 2, 2014, from http://www.nytimes.com.

Caesar, Sid, with Eddy Friedfeld. *Caesar's Hours: My Life in Comedy, with Love and Laughter*. New York: PublicAffairs, 2003.

Calta, Louis. "Continues in Role." *New York Times*, May 6, 1954. Retrieved August 17, 2014, from http://www.nytimes.com.

———. "'Damn Yankees' at Bat Tonight." *New York Times*, May 5, 1955. Retrieved August 17, 2014, from http://www.nytimes.com.

———. "Four Producers Join in Stage and Film Company." *New York Times*, December 19, 1964. Retrieved September 7, 2014, from http://www.nytimes.com.

———. "Gwen Verdon Is Cast in Drama by Corrigan Opening March 7." *New York Times*, January 13, 1972. Retrieved October 3, 2014, from http://www.nytimes.com.

———. "Gwen Verdon Sought." *New York Times*, January 22, 1955. Retrieved August 17, 2014, from http://www.nytimes.com.

———. "Gwen Verdon to Star in Musical Revival of 'Chicago.'" *New York Times*, December 6, 1972. Retrieved October 3, 2014, from http://www.nytimes.com.

———. "Jottings from Broadway." *New York Times*, January 30, 1960. Retrieved September 6, 2014, from http://www.nytimes.com.

———. "News of the Stage: Musical 'Chicago' Due on Broadway." *New York Times*, July 28, 1973. Retrieved October 4, 2014, from http://www.nytimes.com.

———. "Ritz Theater Makes Broadway Return." *New York Times*, February 17, 1972. Retrieved October 3, 2014, from http://www.nytimes.com.

———. "Simon Gets Book Credit." *New York Times*, November 30, 1965. Retrieved September 8, 2014, from http://www.nytimes.com.

———. "Tall Story." *New York Times*, September 24, 1958. Retrieved September 6, 2014, from http://www.nytimes.com.

———. "Theatre for 'New Girl.'" *New York Times*, February 16, 1957. Retrieved August 19, 2014, from http://www.nytimes.com.

———. "Theatre Notes." *New York Times*, December 10, 1955. Retrieved August 18, 2014, from http://www.nytimes.com.

———. "Theatre Notes." *New York Times*, December 15, 1955. Retrieved August 18, 2014, from http://www.nytimes.com.

Canby, Vincent. "Film: Basinger and Bridges in 'Nadine.'" *New York Times*,

August 7, 1987. Retrieved January 21, 2014, from http://www.nytimes.com.
____. "Helen Gallagher in 'Charity' Lead." *New York Times*, July 1, 1967. Retrieved October 2, 2014, from http://www.nytimes.com.
____. "Is the Cost of 'Charity' Too High?" *New York Times*, April 6, 1969. Retrieved October 2, 2014, from http://www.nytimes.com.
____. "The Palace from Ed Wynn to Gwen Verdon." *New York Times*, January 23, 1966. Retrieved September 8, 2014, from http://www.nytimes.com.
____. "Palace Returns: That's Show Biz; Gwen Verdon Now Reigns at Vaudeville's Shrine." *New York Times*, January 30, 1966. Retrieved August 8, 2014, from http://www.nytimes.com.
____. "Review/Film: Woody Allen's Magical Realism Has an Herb for Every Plaint." *New York Times*, December 25, 1990. Retrieved March 11, 2014, from http://www.nytimes.com.
____. "Screen: A Blow-Up of 'Sweet Charity.'" *New York Times*, April 2, 1969. Retrieved August 24, 2014, from http://www.nytimes.com.
____. "Screen: Coppola's 'Cotton Club.'" *New York Times*, December 14, 1984. Retrieved February 11, 2014, from http://www.nytimes.com.
____. "The Screen: Roy Scheider Stars in 'All That Jazz': Peter Pan Syndrome." *New York Times*, December 20, 1979. Retrieved November 11, 2014, from http://www.nytimes.com.
Carroll, Maurice. "Rose Kennedy Helps Stage Rally Here for McGovern." *New York Times*, October 28, 1972. Retrieved October 3, 2014, from http://www.nytimes.com.
Chance, Norman. *Who Was Who on TV*, vol. 2. Philadelphia: Xlibris, 2011.
Chase, Chris. "Fosse, from Tony to Oscar to Emmy?" *New York Times*, April 29, 1973. Retrieved October 3, 2014, from http://www.nytimes.com.
Chetwynd, Lionel. "Except for Bob Fosse." *Penthouse*, January 1974: 89–93.

Chiu, Tony. "Gwen Verdon Keeps Them 'Dancin.'" *New York Times*, July 24, 1979. Retrieved October 31, 2014, from http://www.nytimes.com.
Clarity, James F. "Notes on People." *New York Times*, August 15, 1972. Retrieved October 3, 2014, from http://www.nytimes.com.
Coleman, Emily. "The Dance Man Leaps to the Top." *New York Times*, April 19, 1959. Retrieved September 6, 2014, from http://www.nytimes.com.
Collins, Glenn. "Festival of Arts Lowers Its Sights." *New York Times*, February 27, 1991. Retrieved September 13, 2014, from http://www.nytimes.com.
____. "A Male Bastion Bows, in Gracious Greeting." *New York Times*, April 22, 1989. Retrieved September 11, 2014, from http://www.nytimes.com.
____. "Walking the Tightrope that is 'Marvin's Room.'" *New York Times*, December 12, 1991. Retrieved March 26, 2014, from http://www.nytimes.com.
Corry, John. "Broadway." *New York Times*, November 24, 1978. Retrieved October 31, 2014, from http://www.nytimes.com.
____. "Rich and Beautiful Help to Raise Funds at Dalton School Auction." *New York Times*, December 6, 1972. Retrieved October 3, 2014, from http://www.nytimes.com.
Costantinou, Marianne. "Soap Opera Fans Are Seeing Stars." *New York Times*, February 7, 1982. Retrieved September 9, 2014, from http://www.nytimes.com.
Crivello, Kirk. *Fallen Angels: The Lives and Untimely Deaths of 14 Hollywood Beauties*. Secaucus, NJ: Citadel, 1988.
Crowther, Bosley. "Four New Films Arrive: Marilyn Monroe vs. Scenery at Roxy; Science-Fiction Drama Bows at Paramount." *New York Times*, May 1, 1954. Retrieved April 14, 2014, from http://www.nytimes.com.
____. "Movie Review: Betty Grable Has Prim, Folksy Role in 'The Farmer Takes a Wife,' Globe Newcomer." *New

York Times, June 13, 1953. Retrieved March 19, 2014, from http://www.nytimes.com.
____. "Movie Review: Danny Kaye 'On the Riviera,' With Gene Tierney, Arrives at the Roxy Theatre." New York Times, May 24, 1951. Retrieved February 2, 2014, from http://www.nytimes.com.
____. "Movie Review: 'The Merry Widow,' with Lana Turner and Fernando Lamas, Opens at Loew's State." New York Times, September 25, 1952. Retrieved January 19, 2014, from http://www.nytimes.com.
____. "Screen: 'Damn Yankees.'" New York Times, September 27, 1958. Retrieved May 29, 2014, from http://www.nytimes.com.
____. "A Season Come to Life." New York Times, October 5, 1958. Retrieved September 6, 2014, from http://www.nytimes.com.
____. "The Screen in Review: Clifton Webb Sneers His Best at Television in 'Dreamboat,' New Feature at the Roxy." New York Times, July 26, 1952. Retrieved February 23, 2014, from http://www.nytimes.com.
____. "The Screen in Review: 'Gentlemen Prefer Blondes' at Roxy, with Marilyn Monroe and Jane Russell." New York Times, July 16, 1953. Retrieved January 27, 2014, from http://www.nytimes.com.
Cullen, Frank. *Vaudeville, Old and New: An Encyclopedia of Variety Performers in America*, vol. 1. New York: Psychology, 2004.
Curtis, Charlotte. "American Fashions Take the Stage to Aid the Ballet Theatre." New York Times, September 26, 1966. Retrieved September 10, 2014, from http://www.nytimes.com.
____. "Billie Holiday Fans Turn Out for Film Premiere and Benefit Fete. Promotes Another Benefit." New York Times, October 19, 1972. Retrieved October 3, 2014, from http://www.nytimes.com.
____. "Weather Fails to Dampen Parties.... Building Unfinished." New York Times, April 23, 1964. Retrieved September 7, 2014, from http://www.nytimes.com.
Curtis, Houston. *Jimmy Dean: The Road to Restoration*. Bob Banner Associates and Hollywood Direct, 2013. Viewed July 13, 2014, on YouTube.
Daley, Suzanne. "Stepping into Her New Shoes." New York Times, May 17, 1981. Retrieved September 9, 2014, from http://www.nytimes.com.
Daly, Michael. "The Making of 'The Cotton Club': A True Tale of Hollywood." New York, May 7, 1984: 40–62.
Darlington, W.A. "London Letter." New York Times, April 14, 1957. Retrieved August 19, 2014, from http://www.nytimes.com.
Delatiner, Barbara. "Gwen Verdon Likes Being 'Just Folks' in East Hampton." New York Times, July 22, 1973. Retrieved October 4, 2014, from http://www.nytimes.com.
____. "The Lively Arts: Gwen Verdon Stages 'Nutcracker.'" New York Times, December 21, 1980. Retrieved November 2, 2014, from http://www.nytimes.com.
____. "On the Isle: Philharmonic Reprise." New York Times, August 2, 1981. Retrieved September 9, 2014, from http://www.nytimes.com.
____. "What the Film Doesn't Say, the Music Does." New York Times, August 24, 1980. Retrieved November 1, 2014, from http://www.nytimes.com.
Denisoff, R. Serge, and William D. Romanowski. *Risky Business: Rock in Film*. New Brunswick, NJ: Transaction, 1991.
DeVito, John and Frank Tropea. *Epic Television Miniseries: A Critical History*. Jefferson, NC: McFarland, 2010.
Dick, Bernard F. *Columbia Pictures: Portrait of a Studio*. Lexington: University Press of Kentucky, 1992.
Didinger, Ray and Glen Macnow. *The Ultimate Book of Sports Movies: Featuring the 100 Greatest Sports Films of All Time*. Philadelphia: Running, 2009.
Dietz, Dan. *The Complete Book of 1960s*

Broadway Musicals. Lanham, MD: Rowan & Littlefield, 2014.
Diffrient, David Scott. *M*A*S*H*. Detroit: Wayne State University Press, 2008.
Donalson, Melvin. *Black Directors in Hollywood*. Austin: University of Texas, 2010.
Dougherty, Philip H. "Advertising ... Written by the Stars." *New York Times*, April 12, 1976. Retrieved October 30, 1976 from http://www.nytimes.com.
_____. "At This Show, There's No Business ... Like Textiles: Jobs Down from 1,500, No Lessening of Interest." *New York Times*, May 31, 1973. Retrieved July 21, 2014, from http://www.nytimes.com.
Drew, Bernard. "Life as a Long Rehearsal." *American Film*, November, 1979: 26 – 31, 75, 77.
Dunning, Jennifer. "Ballet: New York Medalists." *New York Times*, July 4, 1984. Retrieved September 11, 2014, from http://www.nytimes.com.
Eames, John Douglas. *The MGM Story: The Complete History of Fifty Roaring Years*. London: Octopus, 1975.
Ebert, Roger. "Alice." *Chicago Sun-Times*, December 25, 1990. Retrieved March 11, 2014, from http://www.rogerebert.com.
_____. "Cocoon: The Return." *Chicago Sun-Times*, November 23, 1988. Retrieved January 26, 2014, from http://www.rogerebert.com.
_____. "The Cotton Club." *Chicago Sun-Times*, January 1, 1984. Retrieved February 11, 2014, from http://www.rogerebert.com.
_____. "Marvin's Room." *Chicago Sun-Times*, January 10, 1997. Retrieved March 27, 2014, from http://www.rogerebert.com.
_____. "Nadine." *Chicago Sun-Times*, August 7, 1987. Retrieved January 29, 2014, from http://www.rogerebert.com.
Edginton, K., Thomas Erskine and James M. Welsh. *Encyclopedia of Sports Films*. Lanham, MD: Scarecrow, 2010.
Edwards, Russell. "Future Social Events: Achieving Trio." *New York Times*, November 9, 1975. Retrieved October 5, 2014, from http://www.nytimes.com.
_____. "Future Social Events: A Capital Performance." *New York Times*, November 4, 1973. Retrieved October 4, 2014, from http://www.nytimes.com.
_____. "Future Social Events: East Hampton's Annual Art Happening." *New York Times*, July 7, 1974. Retrieved October 4, 2014, from http://www.nytimes.com.
_____. "Future Social Events": Kicks and Kudos." *New York Times*, June 1, 1975. Retrieved October 4, 2014, from http://www.nytimes.com.
_____. "Future Social Events: Take It Away, Terpsichore!" *New York Times*, July 22, 1973. Retrieved October 3, 2014, from http://www.nytimes.com.
_____. "Future Social Events: Want to Get Going?" *New York Times*, December 2, 1973. Retrieved October 4, 2014, from http://www.nytimes.com.
Elborough, Travis. *The Long-Player Goodbye: The Album from Vinyl to iPod and Back Again*. London: Hachette UK, 2009.
Elley, Derek. *The Epic Film: Myth and History*. London, Boston: Routledge, 2013.
Eskine, Thomas L., et al. *Video Versions: Film Adaptations of Plays on Video*. Westport, CT: Greenwood, 2000.
Esterow, Milton. "Old Palace Theater Prepares for a Musical." *New York Times*, January 14, 1966. Retrieved September 8, 2014, from http://www.nytimes.com.
Evans, Harvey. "Gwen Verdon #2: The Featured Movie Years." May 30, 2011. Viewed March 20, 2014, on YouTube.
_____. "Gwen Verdon #3: Recognition for Fosse and Cole—and from Beyonce." May 30, 2011. Viewed March 21, 2014, on YouTube.
_____. "Gwen Verdon #4: Special Guest Paul Phillips, Gwen's SM and Friend. Viewed August 29, 2014, on YouTube.
_____. "Gwen Verdon #5: The Can-Can Story, Pony Dance & New Girl in

Town." Viewed August 30, 2014, on YouTube.

____. "Gwen Verdon #6: New Version of Who's Got the Pain: DO40 introduces the Audience of Gypsy Stars." Viewed August 30, 2014, on YouTube.com.

____. "Gwen Verdon #7: Act II with Harvey, Lee Roy and Donna McKechnie." Viewed August 30, 2014, on YouTube.

____. "Gwen Verdon #9: Tony Stevens and Rachelle Rak—from Chicago to Fosse." Viewed September 1, 2014, on YouTube.

____. "Gwen Verdon #10: Gwen on Musical Theatre Acting ... and not being Lola." Viewed September 1, 2014, on YouTube.

____ with Gwen Verdon. "Who's Got the Pain." *The Ed Sullivan Show*. Viewed April 21, 2014, on YouTube.

____ with Lee Roy Reams. "Gwen Verdon #1: The Early Years, with Guest Marge Champion." May 30, 2011. Viewed March 20, 2014, on YouTube.

Faris, Jocelyn. *Ginger Rogers: A Bio-bibliography*. Westport, Connecticut: Greenwood Publishing, 1994.

Feldman, Gene. *Hollywood Collection - Shirley MacLaine: Kicking Up Her Heels*. Wombat Productions/Janson Associates, 1996.

Fellini, Federico. *Giulietta degli spiriti*. Rizzoli Film/Francoriz Production, 1965.

____. *La Notti Di Cabiria*. Dino de Laurentiis/Cinematografica Les Films Marceau, 1957.

Ferretti, Fred. "United New York Rally Draws Only a Sparse Crowd." *New York Times*, November 25, 1975. Retrieved October 30, 2014, from http://www.nytimes.com.

Feuer, Cy and Gross, Ken. *I Got the Show Right Here: The Amazing True Story of How an Obscure Brooklyn Horn Player Became the Last Great Broadway Showman*. New York: Applause Theatre and Cinema Books, 2005.

Fitzgerald, Peter. *What a Glorious Feeling. The Making of "Singin' in the Rain."* Turner Entertainment/Warner Home Video/Fitzfilm Inc, 2002.

Fleming, Michael. "Carrey, Gyllenhaal do 'Yankees.'" *Variety*, February 26, 2009. Retrieved September 15, 2014, from http://www.variety.com.

Fordin, Hugh. *M-G-M's Greatest Musicals: The Arthur Freed Unit*. Da Capo, 1996.

Fosse, Bob. *All That Jazz*. 20th Century Fox/Columbia Pictures, 1979.

____, ____. *Cabaret*. ABC Pictures/Allied Artists/Feuer & Martin, 1972.

____, ____. *Liza with a Z*. Showtime/Singer/Bob Fosse and Fred Ebb Productions/Flora, Inc., 1972.

Fraser, C. Gerald. "Benefit Review May 9 Set By Arts Research Center ." *New York Times*, March 29, 1976. Retrieved October 30, 2014, from http://www.nytimes.com.

____. "Going Out Guide. Street Fair." *New York Times*, June 8, 1974. Retrieved October 4, 2014, from http://www.nytimes.com.

____. "Television Week." *New York Times*, May 1, 1983. Retrieved September 10, 2014, from http://www.nytimes.com.

Friedler, Sharon E., and Glazer, Susan. *Dancing Female: Lives and Issues of Women in Contemporary Dance*. Amsterdam: Taylor & Francis, 1997.

Fristoe, Roger. Choreography by Jack Cole. *Turner Classic Movies*. Retrieved January 6, 2014, from http://www.tcm.com.

____. *The Merry Widow*. 1952. *Turner Classic Movies*. Retrieved January 20, 2014, from http://www/tcm.com.

Funke, Lewis. "Engaged in Mutual Support." *New York Times*, September 2, 1956. Retrieved August 18, 2014, from http://www.nytimes.com.

____. "News and Gossip Gathered from the Rialto: Round-Up." *New York Times*, September 5, 1954. Retrieved August 17, 2014, from http:///www.nytimes.com.

____. "News of the Rialto: Broadway's Hero." *New York Times*, January 30,

1966. Retrieved September 8, 2014, from http://www.nytimes.com.

———. "News of the Rialto: Change of Pace." *New York Times,* October 13, 1968. Retrieved October 2, 2014, from http://www.nytimes.com.

———. "News of the Rialto: "Chicago Saga." *New York Times,* January 28, 1973. Retrieved October 3, 2014, from http://www.nytimes.com.

———. "News of the Rialto: Firm at Work." *New York Times,* December 27, 1964. Retrieved September 7, 2014, from http://www.nytimes.com.

———. "News of the Rialto: Roundup." *New York Times,* October 25, 1970. Retrieved October 2, 2014, from http://www.nytimes.com.

———. "News of the Rialto: Sweet Charity Goes Abroad, and Hope She's Better." *The New York Times,* April 17, 1966. Retrieved September 8, 2014, from http://www.nytimes.com.

———. "Theatre: The Devil Tempts a Slugger: 'Damn Yankees' Tells Tale of Witchery." *New York Times,* May 6, 1955. Retrieved April 7, 2014, from http://www.nytimes.com.

Gamarekian, Barbara. "Kennedy Center Honors Five For Life Achievement in Arts." *New York Times,* December 2, 1979. Retrieved October 31, 2014, from http://www.nytimes.com.

Gardner, Paul. "Warming Up With Gwen." *New York Times,* February 7, 1965. Retrieved September 7, 2014, from http://www.nytimes.com.

———. "Whither The Dream Ballet?" *New York Times,* September 20, 1959. Retrieved September 6, 2014, from http://www.nytimes.com.

Gelb, Arthur. "Bob Fosse Quits 'Conquering Hero.'" *New York Times,* December 5, 1960. Retrieved June 18, 2014, from http://www.nytimes.com.

———. "The Devils and Their Disciples." *New York Times,* March 18, 1956. Retrieved August 18, 2014, from http://www.nytimes.com.

———. "Jottings." *New York Times,* July 16, 1955. Retrieved August 18, 2014, from http://www.nytimes.com.

———. "Jottings." *New York Times,* April 8, 1957. Retrieved August 19, 2014, from http://www.nytimes.com.

———. "Revisions for 'Redhead': Writer Is Assigned." *New York Times,* June 23, 1958. Retrieved September 8, 2014, from http://www.nytimes.com.

———. "Rights to Novel Acquired." *New York Times,* August 8, 1959. Retrieved September 6, 2014, from http://www.nytimes.com.

Gerard, Jeremy. "Review: 'In Cold Blood.'" *Variety,* November 17, 1996. Retrieved February 25, 2014, from http://www.variety.com.

Gilroy, Harry. "The Circus Is Here with 3 Rings of Razzle Dazzle." *New York Times,* April 6, 1966. Retrieved September 9, 2014, from http://www.nytimes.com.

Ginibre, Jean-Louis. *Ladies or Gentlemen: A Pictorial History of Male Cross-Dressing in the Movies.* New York: Filipacchi, 2005

Ginsberg, Merle, and Gary Baum. "Bob Fosse Biographer Unearths Lost 1961 ABC Special." *The Hollywood Reporter,* November 7, 2013. Retrieved June 28, 2014, from http://www.hollywoodreporter.com.

Godbout, Oscar. "Mime From Israel in TV Fairy Tale." *New York Times,* January 9, 1958. Retrieved August 21, 2014, from http://www.nytimes.com.

Goldberger, Paul. "Puerto Rican Dancers' Ten Years." *New York Times,* April 26, 1980. Retrieved November 1, 2014, from http://www.nytimes.com.

Good, Howard. *Diamonds in the Dark: America, Baseball, and the Movies.* Lanham, MD: Scarecrow, 1997.

Gottfried, Martin. *All His Jazz: The Life & Death of Bob Fosse.* Cambridge, MA: Da Capo, 1990.

———. *Nobody's Fool: The Lives of Danny Kaye.* New York: Simon and Schuster, 1994.

Gould, Jack. "Television: Fancy Footwork." *New York Times,* October 13,

1968. Retrieved October 2, 2014, from http://www.nytimes.com.

_____. "TV: Top Hat, Etc." *New York Times*, February 11, 1965. Retrieved September 7, 2014, from http://www.nytimes.com.

Gow, Gordon, *Hollywood in the Fifties: The International Film Guide Series*. New York: A.S. Barnes, and London: A. Zwemmer, 1971.

Gray, Beverly. *Ron Howard: From Mayberry to the Moon ... and Beyond*. Nashville, TN: Thomas Nelson, 2003.

Green, Harris. "Is the Broadway Musical Changing Its Tune?" *New York Times*, July 20, 1975. Retrieved October 5, 2014, from http://www.nytimes.com.

Green, Michelle. "Nightmare of 100 Stars." *People*, March 4, 1985. Retrieved May 15, 2014, from http://www.people.com.

Green, Stanley. *Encyclopedia of the Musical Theatre*. New York: Da Capo, 2009.

_____. *Hollywood Musicals Year by Year*. Milwaukee, WI: Hal Leonard, 1999.

Gross, Ken. "It's De-Movie Star." *New York Times*, June 20, 2004. Retrieved September 15, 2014, from http://www.nytimes.com.

Grubb, Kevin Boyd. *Razzle Dazzle: The Life and Work of Bob Fosse*. New York: St. Martin's, 1989.

Gruen, John. "Remember That Great Dance in...?" *New York Times*, May 23, 1976. Retrieved October 30, 2014, from http://www.nytimes.com.

Gussow, Mel. "Abbott Is Remembered in the Colorful Spirit of Broadway." *New York Times*, June 6, 1995. Retrieved September 13, 2014, from http://www.nytimes.com.

_____. "Broadway, Despite Inflation, Starts Off with a Full House: Music, Music, Music." *New York Times*, September 18, 1974. Retrieved October 4, 2014, from http://www.nytimes.com.

_____. "Walkout Stirs Fear over Forthcoming Musical Productions." *New York Times*, September 20, 1975. Retrieved October 5, 2014, from http://www.nytimes.com.

Haas, Nancy. "Two Decades Later, Just Right for the Role." *New York Times*, November 10, 1996. Retrieved September 13, 2014, from http://www.nytimes.com.

Haberman, Clyde. "NYC: Standing, a Last Time, for a Dancer." *New York Times*, February 21, 2001. Retrieved September 14, 2014, from http://www.nytimes.com.

Harding, Les. *They Knew Marilyn Monroe: Famous Persons in the Life of the Hollywood Icon*. Jefferson, NC: McFarland, 2012.

Harris, Roy. *Eight Women of the American Stage Talking About Acting*. Portsmouth, NH: Heinemann, 1997.

Hawkins, William. "Something about Gwen Verdon." *Dance Magazine*, August 1956: 26–27.

Heim, Alan. *All That Jazz*. DVD audio commentary. 20th Century Fox/Columbia Pictures, 1979.

Heitz, Dan. *The Complete Book of 1950s Broadway Musicals*. Lanham, MD: Rowman and Littlefield, 2014.

Hess, Earl J., and Pratibha A. Dabholkar. *Singin' in the Rain: The Making of an American Masterpiece*. Lawrence: University Press of Kansas, 2009.

Hewitt, Jean. "Organic Flood Fanciers Go to Great Lengths for the Real Thing." *New York Times*, September 7, 1970. Retrieved October 2, 2014, from http://www.nytimes.com.

Hewlett, Roger S. "Theater: The Devil's Disciple." *Time*, vol. 65, no. 24 (1955): 62–64.

Higham, Charles, and Joel Greenberg. *Hollywood in the Forties*. London: A. Zwemmer; New York: A.S. Barnes, 1968.

Hill, Constance Valis. "From Bharata Natyam to Bop: Jack Cole's 'Modern' Jazz Dance," in Julie Malnig, ed., *Ballroom, Boogie, Shimmy Sham, Shake: A Social and Popular Dance Reader*. Urbana: University of Illinois Press, 2009.

_____. *Tap Dancing America: A Cultural History*. New York: Oxford University Press, 2009.
Hirsch, Foster. *Harold Prince and the American Musical Theater*. Cambridge, England, and New York: Cambridge University Press, 1989.
Hirschhorn, Clive. *The Columbia Story*. London: Pyramid, 1989
_____. *The Universal Story*. London: Octopus, 1983.
_____. *The Warner Bros. Story*. London, Octopus, 1979.
Hischak, Thomas S. *American Literature on Stage and Screen: 525 Works and Their Adaptations*. Jefferson, NC: McFarland, 2012.
_____. *Boy Loses Girl: Broadway's Librettists*. Lanham, MD: Scarecrow, 2002.
_____. *The Oxford Companion to the American Musical: Theatre, Film, and Television*. Oxford and New York: Oxford University Press, 2008.
_____. *Through the Screen Door: What Happened to the Broadway Musical When it Went to Hollywood*. Lanham, MD: Scarecrow, 2004.
Hochswender, Woody. "Vogueing Against AIDS: A Quest for 'Overness.'" *New York Times*, May 12, 1989. Retrieved March 19, 2014, from http://www.nytimes.com.
Hodgson, Moira. "When Bob Fosse's Life Imitates Art, It's Just 'All That Jazz.'" *New York Times*, December 30, 1979. Retrieved November 1, 2014, from http://www.nytimes.com.
Hoey, Michael A. *Inside Fame on Television: A Behind-the-Scenes History*. Jefferson, NC: McFarland, 2010.
Holden, Stephen. "Cabaret Review: Singer-Dancer's Imperative: He's Gotta Get to Broadway." *New York Times*, December 21, 1998. Retrieved September 13, 2014, from http://www.nytimes.com.
_____. "Film Review: Legends and Lore Dished Up With After-Theater Panache." *New York Times*, June 11, 2004. Retrieved December 30, 2013, from http://www.nytimes.com.

_____. "A Lush Musical by Villa-Lobos." *New York Times*, November 19, 1987. Retrieved January 29, 2014, from http://www.nytimes.com.
_____. "Revue: 'Parade of Stars' for Actors' Fund Benefit." *New York Times*, May 4, 1983. Retrieved September 10, 2014, from http://www.nytimes.com.
Horn, David. *The Music of Kander and Ebb: Razzle Dazzle*. Great Performances/Thirteen/WNET/Educational Broadcasting Corp., 1997.
Howard. Ron. *Cocoon*, DVD audio commentary. 20th Century Fox, 2004.
Howe, Matt. "Funny Girl: On Broadway." *Barbra Archives*. Retrieved August 6, 2014, from http://www.barbra-archives.com.
Hughes, Andrew Mon. *The Bee Gees: Tales of the Brothers Gibb*. London and New York: Music Sales Group, 2009.
Hunter, Tab, with Eddie Muller. *Tab Hunter Confidential: The Making of a Movie Star*. New York: Algonquin, 2006.
Hurst, Richard M. *Republic Studios: Between Poverty Row and the Majors*. Metuchen, NJ: Scarecrow, 2007.
Ilson, Carol. *Harold Prince: A Director's Journey*. New York: Limelight, 2000.
Ingham, Chris. *The Rough Guide to the Beatles*. London: Rough Guides, 2003.
Isherwood, Charles. "Review: Sweet Charity: The Concert." *Variety*, June 15, 1998. Retrieved August 31, 2014, from http://www.variety.com.
Itzkoff, Dave. "ArtsBeat: Gyllenhaal, Carrey Suit Up for 'Damn Yankees' Remake." *New York Times*, February 27, 2009. Retrieved September 15, 2014, from http://www.nytimes.com.
Johnston, Laurie. "Library Racing Deadline to Raise Half a Million." *New York Times*, May 26, 1972. Retrieved October 3, 2014, from http://www.nytimes.com.
_____. "Theater Turns to a Rich Past to Aid Library." *New York Times*, October 20, 1980. Retrieved November 1, 2014, from http://www.nytimes.com.
Jones, Clark. "A New Pair of Shoes."

Night of 100 Stars II. Bentwood Television Productions/ABC. Viewed May 13, 2014, on YouTube.

Jones, Kenneth. "Verdon, Dench, 'Von Trapp' Kids Bring Magic to 'Easter Bonnet': More Than $2 Mil Reaped." *Playbill*, April 21, 1999. Retrieved July 30, 2014, from http://www.playbill.com.

____ and Robert Simonson. "Coleman, Rivera and Others Recall Gwen Verdon's Gifts at Feb. 20 Memorial." *Playbill*, February 20, 2011. Retrieved September 2, 2014, from http://www.playbill.com.

Jowitt, Deborah. "Dance Makes the Musicals Go 'Round." *New York Times*, November 23, 1975. Retrieved October 30, 2014, from http://www.nytimes.com.

____. *Jerome Robbins: His Life, His Theater, His Dance*. New York: Simon and Schuster, 2004.

Kael, Pauline. *5001 Nights at the Movies*. New York: Holt, Rinehart and Winston, 1984.

____. *Hooked*. New York: E.P. Dutton, 1989.

____. *State Of The Art*. New York: E.P. Dutton, 1985.

Kalat, David P. *Homicide: Life on the Streets: The Unofficial Companion*. Los Angeles: Renaissance, 1998.

Kauffmann, Stanley. "Theater: Show That Wants to Be Loved: 'Sweet Charity' Opens at Refurbished Palace." *New York Times*, January 31, 1966. Retrieved August 8, 2014, from http://www.nytimes.com.

Kaufman, George S. "Musical Comedy—Or Musical Serious?" *New York Times*, November 3, 1957. Retrieved August 21, 2014, from http://www.nytimes.com.

Kehr, Dave. "On Video: Dusting Off Items in Fox's Attic." *New York Times*, May 17, 2013. Retrieved February 8, 2014, from http://www.nytimes.com.

Kellow, Brian. *The Bennetts: An Acting Family*. Lexington: University Press of Kentucky, 2004.

Kelly, Gene, and Stanley Donen. *Singin' in the Rain*. MGM, 1952.

Kemnitz, Robert. "Film: Sgt. Pepper's Lonely Hearts Club Band." *Orange Coast Magazine*, October 1978: 70.

Kempley, Rita. "Cocoon: The Return." *Washington Post*, November 23, 1988. Retrieved January 26, 2014, from http://www.washingtonpost.com.

Kerr, Walter. "Stage View: 'Chicago' Comes on Like Doomsday." *New York Times*, June 8, 1975. Retrieved October 5, 2014, from http://www.nytimes.com.

Keyser, Les. *Hollywood in the Seventies*. New York: A. S. Barnes; London: Tantivy, 1981.

Kinberg, Judy. "Bob Fosse: Steam Heat." *Great Performances: Dance in America*. WNET/Thrirteen/PBS, 1990.

Kisselgoff, Anna. "Dance: Gala by a Junior Dance Troupe." *New York Times*, January 13, 1983. Retrieved September 10, 2014, from http://www.nytimes.com.

____. "Dance: Paul Taylor's Comic Strip America." *New York Times*, April 15, 1981. Retrieved September 9, 2014, from http://www.nytimes.com.

____. "Houston Ballet, Gwen Verdon (!)." *New York Times*, March 4, 1978. Retrieved October 31, 2014, from http://www.nytimes.com.

____. "Jack Cole Is Dead: A Choreographer." *New York Times*, February 20, 1974. Retrieved October 4, 2014, from http://www.nytimes.com.

____. "Review/Dance: Recalling an Innovator of Film Choreography." *New York Times*, February 7, 1994. Retrieved September 13, 2014, from http://www.nytimes.com.

Klein, Alvin. "The Lively Arts: Novel Casts Light on the Unglorified." *New York Times*, May 17, 1981. Retrieved September 9, 2014, from http://www.nytimes.com.

____. "Theater: Benefit to Reunite 2 Broadway Stars." *New York Times*, April 21, 1985. Retrieved September 11, 2014, from http://www.nytimes.com.

_____. "Theater: 'Damn Yankees' in Darien." *New York Times*, April 16, 1989. Retrieved September 11, 2014, from http://www.nytimes.com.

_____. "Theater: From When Musicals Were Musical." *New York Times*, March 27, 1983. Retrieved September 11, 2014, from http://www.nytimes.com.

_____. "Theater: Musicals Fare Well." *New York Times*, May 27, 1984. Retrieved September 11, 2014, from http://www.nytimes.com.

Klemesrud, Judy. "500 First-Nighters Go A-Partyin.'" *New York Times*, March 29, 1978. Retrieved October 31, 2014, from http://www.nytimes.com.

Kobal, John. *People Will Talk: Personal Conversations with the Legends of Hollywood*. London: Aurum, 1986.

Koehler, Robert. "Review: 'Walking Across Egypt.'" *Variety*, February 13, 2000. Retrieved April 14, 2014, from http://www.variety.com.

Kozak, Roman. "Lotsa Laughs in 'Sgt. Pepper.'" *Billboard*, July 29, 1978: 73.

Kuchwara, Michael. "Actors' Fund Gets $838,985 for 'Night of 100 Stars II.'" Associated Press, February 20, 1985. Retrieved May 15, 2014, from http://www.apnewsarchive.com.

_____. "'Fame' Star Comes Back to Broadway." *The Day*, April 30, 1986. Retrieved February 19, 2014, from http://www.news.google.com/newspapers.

Landazuri, Margarita. *Gentlemen Prefer Blondes*. 1953. *Turner Classic Movies*. Retrieved January 27, 2014, from http://www.tcm.com.

Laurie, Piper. *Learning to Live Out Loud: A Memoir*. New York: Random House, 2011.

Lawler, Sylvia. "Night of 100 Stars II." *The Morning Call*, March 10, 1985. Retrieved May 15, 2014, from http://www.articles.mcall.com.

Lawson, Carol. "Broadway: Event that Haunted Jung Inspires Play by Morris West." *New York Times*, February 8, 1982. Retrieved September 9, 2014, from http://www.nytimes.com.

Leonard, John. "Television: Ole Miss." *New York Magazine*, May 2, 1994: 83.

_____. "Television: Teens and Sympathy." *New York Magazine*, January 25, 1993: 56.

_____. "Television: True Grit." *New York Magazine*, November 25, 1996: 80–81.

_____. "Television: Wild about Barry." *New York Magazine*, February 1, 1993: 55.

Levine, Debra. "American Master Choreographer Jack Cole Feted at Jacob's Pillow." *Huffington Post*. August 19, 2010. Retrieved January 5, 2014, from http://www.huffingtonpost.com.

_____. "Jack Cole." Dance Heritage Coalition. 2012. Retrieved January 5, 2014.

_____. "Jack Cole Made Marilyn Monroe Move." *Los Angeles Times*, August 9, 2009. Retrieved January 5, 2014, from http://www.latimes.com.

___. "Why the Recent Interest in Choreographer Jack Cole?" *Huffington Post*, August 28, 2012. Retrieved January 6, 2014, from http://www.huffingtonpost.com.

Levy, Emmanuel. "Review: 'Marvin's Room.'" *Variety*, December 14, 1996. Retrieved March 27, 2014, from http://www.variety.com.

Lichtenstein, Grace. "Women Protest Prices." *New York Times*, June 22, 1971. Retrieved October 3, 2014, from http://www.nytimes.com.

Limnander, Armand. "Women's Fashion: Is Beyoncé the New Willi Ninja?" *New York Times*, February 18, 2009. Retrieved September 15, 2014, from http://www.nytimes.com.

Livingstone, Jennie. *Paris Is Burning*. Off White Productions, 1990.

Loewenstein, Lael. "Film Review: 'Bruno.'" *Variety*, June 13, 2000. Retrieved March 5, 2014, from http://variety.com.

Loney, Glenn. *Unsung Genius: The Passion of Dancer-Choreographer Jack Cole*. New York, London, Toronto, Sydney: Franklin Watts, 1984.

Loos, Anita, and Cari Beauchamp. *Anita Loos Rediscovered: Film Treatments and Fiction*. Berkeley: University of California Press, 2003.

Lyons, Warren. "No More Crying the 'Blue Leaves' Blues." *New York Times*, July 25, 1971. Retrieved October 3, 2014, from http://www.nytimes.com.

MacDonald, Annette. "Jack Cole: Jazz." Viewed on YouTube, January 6, 2014,.

MacLaine, Shirley. *Sage-ing While Ageing*. New York: Simon and Schuster, 2008.

Mailer, Norman. *Marilyn: A Biography*. New York: Random House, 2012.

Mandelbaum, Ken. *Not Since Carrie: Forty Years of Broadway Musical Flops*. New York: Macmillan, 1992.

Mann, William J. *Hello, Gorgeous: Becoming Barbra Streisand*. New York: Harcourt, 2012.

Marks, Peter. "Two Wrenching Dramas Find Unexpected New Lives." *New York Times*, December 8, 1996. Retrieved March 26, 2014, from http://www.nytimes.com.

Marks, Robert W. "Gwen Verdon: The Anatomy of Glamour." *Esquire* 41, no. 2 (1954): 73, 75, 111–114.

Marshall, Rob. *Chicago*. Miramax Films/Producer Circle Co./Zadan/Meron Productions/Kalis Productions, 2002.

_____ and Bill Condon. *Chicago*, DVD audio commentary. DVD Diamond Edition. Miramax Films/Producer Circle Co./Zadan/Meron Productions/Kalis Productions, 2002.

Martin, John. "The Dance" in the Broadway Musical Sector." *New York Times*, February 26, 1950. Retrieved August 17, 2014, from http://www.nytimes.com.

_____. "Dance Magazine Awards." *New York Times*, February 25, 1962. Retrieved September 7, 2014, from http://www.nytimes.com.

_____. "The Dance: Theatre." *New York Times*, June 15, 1957. Retrieved August 21, 2014, from http://www.nytimes.com.

Martin, Len D. *The Republic Pictures Checklist: Features, Serials, Cartoons, Short Subjects and Training Films of Republic Pictures Corporation, 1935–1959*. Jefferson, NC: McFarland, 2006.

Maslin, Janet. "Books of the Times: A Showman Whose Dazzle Hid Darkness. 'Fosse,' a Biography by Sam Wasson." *New York Times*, November 6, 2013. Retrieved September 15, 2014, from http://www.nytimes.com.

_____. "Movie Review: Bittersweet Lessons as a Family Reunites." *New York Times*, December 18, 1996. Retrieved March 27, 2014, from http://www.nytimes.com.

_____. "Reviews/Film: At Issue: Is it Better to Have a Lot of Trouble and Die, or Not?" *New York Times*, November 23, 1988. Retrieved January 25, 2014, from http://www.nytimes.com.

_____. "Screen: 'Cocoon' Opens." *New York Times*, June 21, 1985. Retrieved January 16, 2014, from http://www.nytimes.com.

_____. "Screen: Son of 'Sgt. Pepper': Many Forms Involved." *New York Times*, July 21, 1978. Retrieved March 3, 2014, from http://www.nytimes.com.

McBrien, William. *Cole Porter*. New York: Vintage, 2000.

McDonald, Frank. *Hoosier Holiday*. Republic Pictures, 1943.

McDonough, Dick. *Highlights of a Quarter of a Century of Bob Hope on Television*. NBC/Texaco, 1975.

McFadden, Robert D. "Bob Fosse Exits with Tip of Hat to Friends." *New York Times*, October 4, 1987. Retrieved September 11, 2014, from http://www.nytimes.com.

McGrath, Ed. "Milliken Breakfast Show: The Best of Broadway." *Spartanburg Herald-Journal*, July 1, 1973. Retrieved July 20, 2014, from http://www.google.com/newspapers.

McKechnie, Donna, with Greg Lawrence. *Time Steps: My Musical Comedy Life*. New York: Simon and Schuster, 2006.

McLaughlin, Mark. *Hollywood Singing and Dancing: The 1970s*. Great Musical Treasures, 2008; DVD released May 19, 2009.

McLean, Adrienne L. "The Thousand Ways There Are to Move: Camp and Oriental Dance in the Hollywood Musicals of Jack Cole," in Matthew Bernstein and Gaylin Studlar, eds., *Visions of the East: Orientalism in Film*. New Brunswick, NJ: Rutgers University Press, 1997.

McWhorter, John. "Razzle Dazzle: Sam Wasson's 'Fosse.'" *New York Times*, December 6, 2013. Retrieved September 15, 2014, from http://www.nytimes.com.

Mellen, Joan. *Marilyn Monroe*. Pyramid Illustrated History of the Movies. New York: Pyramid, 1973.

Meyer, David N. *The Bee Gees: The Biography*. New York: Da Capo, 2013.

Miletich, Leo N. *Broadway's Prize-winning Musicals: An Annotated Guide for Libraries and Audio Collectors*. New York: Psychology, 1993.

Miller, Frank. *Gentlemen Marry Brunettes*. 1955. Turner Classic Movies. Retrieved March 31, 2014, from http://www.tcm.com.

Mitchell, Elvis. "Bare Legs and All, Now on Film." *New York Times*, December 27, 2002. Retrieved April 11, 2014, from http://www.nytimes.com.

Molotsky, Irvin. "Bob Fosse, Director and Choreographer, Dies." *New York Times*, September 24, 1987. Retrieved September 11, 2014, from http://www.nytimes.com.

Morgan, Michelle. *Marilyn Monroe: Private and Confidential*. New York: Skyhorse, 2013.

Mordden, Ethan. *Anything Goes: A History of American Musical Theatre*. New York: Oxford University Press, 2013

_____. *Broadway Babies*. New York: Oxford University Press, 1983.

_____. *Coming Up Roses: The Broadway Musical in the 1950s*. New York: Oxford University Press, 2000.

Morgan, Michelle. *Marilyn Monroe: Private and Undisclosed*. New York: Constable and Robinson, 2012.

Morgan, Thomas. "Debbie Allen's 'Charity': Coached by the Original." *New York Times*, May 28, 1986. Retrieved September 11, 2014, from http://www.nytimes.com.

Morris, Bernadine. "A Master of the Draped Dress Won't Rest on His Laurels." *New York Times*, June 21, 1976. Retrieved October 30, 2014, from http://www.nytimes.com.

Nachman, Gerald. *Right Here on Our Stage Tonight! Ed Sullivan's America*. Berkeley: University of California Press, 2009.

Naden, Corinne J. *The Golden Age of American Musical Theatre: 1943–1965*. Lanham, MD: Scarecrow, 2011.

Nelson, Murry R. *American Sports: A History of Icons, Idols, and Ideas: A History of Icons, Idols, and Ideas*. 4 vols. Santa Barbara, CA: Greenwood, 2013.

Nemy, Enid. "Party on L.I. Assists Attica Defense." *New York Times*, August 21, 1972. Retrieved October 3, 2014, from http://www.nytimes.com.

_____. "A Popular Setting for Philanthropy: The Store Fashion Show." *New York Times*, October 10, 1971. Retrieved October 3, 2014, from http://www.nytimes.com.

_____. "Salute to Ballet Theater Puts Seventh Ave. on Its Toes." *New York Times*, September 8, 1966. Retrieved September 12, 2014, from http://www.nytimes.com.

_____. "A Too-Long Night of 100-Plus Stars." *New York Times*, February 19, 1985. Retrieved May 15, 2014, from http://www.nytimes.com.

Nichols. Louis. "Gwen Verdon—The Town's New Girl." *New York Times*, May 26, 1957. Retrieved August 20, 2014, from http://www.nytimes.com.

Nixon, Rob. *The King Steps Out*. 1936. Turner Classic Movies. Retrieved January 2, 2014, from http://www.tcm.com.

Nugent, Frank. "Grace Moore's First Operetta, 'The King Steps Out,' Opens at the Music Hall—'Florida Special' at the Rialto." *New York Times*, May 29, 1936. Retrieved January 2, 2014, from http://www.nytimes.com.

O'Conne, Patricia. "Review: 'Oldest Living Confederate Widow Tells All.'" *Variety*, May 2, 1994. Retrieved May 26, 2014, from http://www.variety.com.

O'Connor, John J. "The 38th Tony Awards." *New York Times*, June 5, 1984. Retrieved September 11, 2014, from http://www.nytimes.com.

____. "TV: A Case of Pollution." *New York Times*, May 23, 1983. Retrieved September 10, 2014, from http://www.nytimes.com.

____. "TV: 'Legs,' a Story about Being a Rockette." *New York Times*, May 2, 1983. Retrieved September 10, 2014, from http://www.nytimes.com.

____. "TV Review. Tony Awards Pleasant Enough on ABC." *New York Times*, March 27, 1973. Retrieved October 3, 2014, from http://www.nytimes.com.

____. "TV Weekend: How a Confederate Widow Became the Oldest." *New York Times*, April 29, 1994. Retrieved May 26, 2014, from http://www.nytimes.com.

Osbourne, Robert, and Debra Levine. *Choreography by Jack Cole*. Turner Classic Movies. September 10, 2012. Viewed on YouTube.com on January 4, 2014.

Parish, James Robert. *Fiasco: A History of Hollywood's Iconic Flops*. Hoboken, NJ: Wiley, 2007.

Peck, Seymour. "'Anna Christie' Sings." *New York Times*, May 12, 1957. Retrieved August 19, 2014, from http://www.nytimes.com.

____. "'Can-Can' From Old Montmartre." *New York Times*, May 3, 1953. Retrieved August 17, 2014, from http://www.nytimes.com.

____. "Hit on Stage—Hit on Screen?" *New York Times*, June 15, 1958. Retrieved September 6, 2014, from http://www.nytimes.com.

____. "A Musical in the Making." *New York Times*, April 14, 1957. Retrieved August 19, 2014, from http://www.nytimes.com.

Perlmutter, Emanuel. "Musicians' Strike Still at Impasse." *New York Times*, September 28, 1975. Retrieved October 5, 2014, from http://www.nytimes.com.

Picano, Felice. "Tab Talks." *The Advocate*, October 11, 2005: 70–72.

Prideaux, Tom. "Theater: Gwen Knocks 'Em in the Aisles." *Life* 46, no.8 (1959): 81–84.

Pryor, Thomas M. "Britain's Censors Bar Movie Dance." *New York Times*, June 6, 1955. Retrieved August 17, 2014, from http://www.nytimes.com.

____. "Gets Feminine Lead." *New York Times*, March 25, 1958. Retrieved August 21, 2014, from http://www.nytimes.com.

Rabin, Nathan. *My Year of Flops: The A.V. Club Presents One Man's Journey Deep into the Heart of Cinematic Failure*. New York: Simon and Schuster, 2010.

Reed, Rex. "I Never Wanted to Be Special." *New York Times*, February 6, 1966. Retrieved September 8, 2014, from http://www.nytimes.com.

Reid, John. *CinemaScope Two: 20th Century-Fox*. Morrisville, NC: Lulu, 2005.

____. *Films Famous, Fanciful, Frolicsome and Fantastic*. Morrisville, NC: Lulu, 2006.

____. *Memorable Films of the Forties*. Lulu, 2004.

____. *These Movies Won No Hollywood Awards*. Morrisville, NC: Lulu, 2005.

Reid, John Howard. *Hollywood Movie Musicals: Great, Good and Glamorous*. Morrisville, NC: Lulu, 2006.

Reiner, Carl. *The Jerk*. Aspen Film Society/Universal Pictures, 1979.

Reynolds, Debbie, et al. *Singin' in the Rain*, DVD audio commentary. Warner Home Video, 2002.

Rich, Frank. "Review: Chayefksy's View of the Power of Faith." *New York Times*, December 11, 1989. Retrieved October 26, 2014, from *http://www.nytimes.com*.

____. "Review/Theater: A Woman's Power to Banish Defeat with Goodness." *New York Times*, December 6,

1991. Retrieved March 26, 2014, from http://www.nytimes.com.
_____. "Stage: 'Sweet Charity,' a Bob Fosse Revival." *New York Times,* April 28, 1986. Retrieved February 19, 2014, from http://www.nytimes.com.
Richter, Simon. *Women, Pleasure, Film: What Lolas Want.* New York: Palgrave Macmillan, 2013.
Ridley, Jim. *Walking Across Egypt.* Film Vault. *Nashville Scene.* April 10, 2000. Retrieved April 14, 2014, from http://www.filmvault.com.
Roberts. Jerry. *Encyclopedia of Television Film Directors.* New York: Scarecrow, 2009.
Robinson, Louie. "Michael Schultz: A Rising Star behind The Camera." *Ebony Magazine,* September 1978: 94–96, 98, 100, 102.
Rogers, Ginger. *Ginger: My Story.* New York: It, 2008.
Rogers, Joe. "Metropolitan Diary." *New York Times,* May 31, 2004. Retrieved September 15, 2014, from http://www.nytimes.com.
Rosenberg, Howard. "Television: A Chilling Retelling of 'Cold Blood.'" *Los Angeles Times.* November 22, 1996. Retrieved February 25, 2014, from http://www.articles.latimes.com.
Rothstein, Mervyn. "'Phantom of the Opera' Wins Seven Tonys; Best Play: 'Butterfly.'" *New York Times,* June 6, 1988. Retrieved September 11, 2014, from http://www.nytimes.com.
Sagola, Lisa Jo. *The Girl Who Fell Down: A Biography of Joan McCracken.* Boston: Northeastern University, 2003.
Salamon, Julie. "Television Review: On a New Limb with Shirley MacLaine." *New York Times,* December 1, 2000. Retrieved March 5, 2014, from http://www.nytimes.com.
Salman, Sandra. "'Cotton Club' Is Neither a Smash nor a Disaster." *New York Times,* December 20, 1984. Retrieved February 11, 2014, from http://www.nytimes.com.
Saule, Louise. "Teachers Moving to Verdon Steps." *New York Times,* April 1, 1973. Retrieved October 4, 2014, from http://www.nytimes.com.
Scheib, Richard. "Cocoon: The Return." *Moria: Science Fiction, Horror and Fantasy Review.* Retrieved January 26, 2014, from http://www.moria.co.nz.
Scheider, Roy. *All That Jazz,* DVD audio commentary. Columbia Pictures/20th Century Fox, 1979.
Schumach, Murray. "Baseball Movies Not U.S. Pastime." *New York Times,* April 14, 1959. Retrieved September 6, 2014, from http://www.nytimes.com.
_____. "'Can-Can Dancer Gwen Verdon Says Ballet and Burlesque Contributed to Her Current Role." *New York Times,* May 31, 1953. Retrieved August 17, 2014, from http://www.nytimes.com.
_____. "Devil Damns Yankees." *New York Times,* May 1, 1955. Retrieved August 17, 2014, from http://www.nytimes.com.
Schwartz, Charles. *Cole Porter: A Biography.* New York: Da Capo, 1979.
Schwarz, Ted. *Marilyn Revealed: The Ambitious Life of an American Icon.* Lanham, MD: Taylor, 2008.
Scott, Tony. "Key West." *Variety,* Janaury 19, 1993. Retrieved March 15, 2014, from http://www.books.google.com.au.
Seibert, Brian. "Theater Review: Following in the Footsteps of Gwen Verdon and Ann Miller, 'Heat Wave' Revue at Queens Theater in the Park." *New York Times,* May 9, 2012. Retrieved on March 8, 2014, from http://www.nytimes.com.
Shanley, John P. "Television: Dinah Shore in Bright Seasonal Debut." *New York Times,* October 6, 1958. Retrieved September 6, 2014, from http://www.nytimes.com.
Shapiro, Eddie. *Nothing Like a Dame: Conversations with the Great Women of Musical Theater.* New York: Oxford University Press, 2014.
Shelley, Peter. *Jules Dassin. The Life and Films.* Jefferson, NC: McFarland, 2011.

Shepard, Richard. "Going Out Guide: On The Hoof." *New York Times,* March 18, 1981. Retrieved November 2, 2014, from http://www.nytimes.com.

Shepard, Richard F. "Going Out Guide: Showbiz." *New York Times,* November 17, 1973. Retrieved October 4, 2014, from http://www.nytimes.com.

Shewey, Don. "The New Season/Movies: It Ought to Be a Movie, They Said, and Said." *New York Times,* September 8, 2002. Retrieved September 13, 2014, from http://www.nytimes.com.

Shirley, Don. "Obituaries: Gwen Verdon: Dancer, Actress Won 4 Tony Awards in 6 Years." *Los Angeles Times,* October 19, 2000. Retrieved September 4, 2014, from http://www.articles.latimes.com.

Simon, Neil. *Rewrites: A Memoir.* New York: Simon and Schuster, 1996.

Simonson, Robert. "Channeling Fosse: Beyoncé and Beyond." *Playbill,* February 10, 2009. Retrieved July 23, 2014, from http://www.playbill.com.

Smith, Cecil A., and Glenn Litton. *Musical Comedy in America: From the Black Crook to South Pacific, from The King and I to Sweeney Todd.* New York: Routledge, 2013.

Solomon, Aubrey. *Twentieth Century-Fox: A Corporate and Financial History.* Metuchen, NJ: Rowman and Littlefield, 2002.

Sonneborn, Liz. *A to Z of American Women in the Performing Arts.* New York: Infobase, 2002.

Spoto. Donald. *Marilyn Monroe: The Biography.* New York: Rowman and Littlefield, 1993.

Stackpole, Peter. "Making of a Musical: The Trials and Talent that Went into 'Damn Yankees.'" *Life* 38, no. 20 (1955): 163–171.

Stanley, John. *Creature Features: The Science Fiction, Fantasy and Horror Movie Guide.* New York: Boulevard, 1997.

Stein, Ruthe. "Broadway: The Golden Age." *San Francisco Chronicle,* July 9, 2004. Retrieved December 30, 2013, from http://www.sfgate.com.

Steinberg, Jay S. *On the Riviera.* 1951. *Turner Classic Movies.* Retrieved February 2, 2014, from http://www.tcm.com.

Sterritt, David. *Gentlemen Prefer Blondes.* 1953. *Turner Classic Movies.* Retrieved January 27, 2014, from http://www.tcm.com.

Steyn, Mark. *Broadway Babies Say Goodnight: Musicals Then and Now.* New York: Routledge, 1999.

Suskin, Steven. *Broadway Yearbook 2000–2001: A Relevant and Irreverent Record.* New York: Oxford University Press, 2002.

_____. *Show Tunes: The Songs, Shows, and Careers of Broadway's Major Composers.* New York: Oxford University Press, 2000.

Taurog, Norman. *Presenting Lily Mars.* MGM, 1943.

Taylor, Clarke. "Gwen Verdon and 'Chicago': The Reincarnation of Roxie Hart." *After Dark* 8, no. 2 (1975): 43–45.

_____. "On Stage: Separated but Still Mated Professionally, Gwen Verdon Hoofs Again for Her Ex." *People Weekly,* no. 24 (1975): 60–61.

Terrace, Vincent. *Encyclopedia of Television Shows, 1925 through 2010.* Jefferson, NC: McFarland, 2008.

_____. *Television Specials: 5,336 Entertainment Programs, 1936–2012.* Jefferson, NC: McFarland, 2013.

Thomas, Tony, and Aubrey Solomon. *The Films of 20th Century Fox: A Pictorial History.* Secaucus: NJ: Citadel, 1979.

Thompson, David. *Musicals, Great Musicals: The Arthur Freed Unit at MGM.* Alternate Current/NHK/Thirteen/WNET/Turner Entertainment Company/BBC Television/La Sept ARTE, 1996.

Thompson, Howard. "Going Out Guide: Take Your Pick." *New York Times,* November 1, 1975. Retrieved October 5, 2014, from http://www.nytimes.com.

_____. "Sullivan on Broadway." *New York Times,* March 16, 1973. Retrieved October 3, 2014, from http://www.nytimes.com.

Thompson, Thomas. "Theater: Gwen Verdon All Aglow." *Life* 60, no. 12 (1966): 99–102.

Thomson, David. *The New Biographical Dictionary of Film*, 5th ed. London: Hachette, 2010.

Traubner, Richard. *Operetta: A Theatrical History*. New York: Routledge, 2003.

Travers, Peter. "Alice." *Rolling Stone*, January 10, 1990. Retrieved March 11, 2014, from http://www.rollingstone.com.

———. "Broadway: The Golden Age." *Rolling Stone*, June 2, 2004. Retrieved December 30, 2013 from http://www.rollingstone.com.

Van Eyssen, Lisa. *The Jack of Clubs: The Choreography of Jack Cole*. 20th Century Fox Film Corporation, 2007.

Van Leer, David. *The Queening of America*. New York: Routledge, 2012.

Verdon, Gwen. "Musical Comedy: The Theatre's Awkward Adolescent." *Theatre Arts* 40, no. 4 (1956): 26–27, 88–89.

Viagas, Robert. *I'm the Greatest Star: Broadway's Top Musical Legends from 1900 to Today*. New York: Applause Theatre and Cinema, 2000.

Voorhees, John. "'In Cold Blood': Acting Is Good: Film a Bit Long." *The Seattle Times*, November 24, 1996. Retrieved on February 25, 2014, from http://www.community.seattletimes.nwsource.com.

W., A. "Movie Review: The Mississippi Gambler." *New York Times*, January 30, 1953. Retrieved February 27, 2014, from http://www.nytimes.com.

Walters, Charles. *Easter Parade*. MGM, 1948. DVD released by Warner Home Video on February 8, 2011. Two-disc special edition DVD released by Warner Home Video on March 15, 2005.

Warren, Virginia Lee. "A Cooperative Fights High Cost of Organic Food." *New York Times*, May 16, 1972. Retrieved October 3, 2014, from http://www.nytimes.com.

Wasson, Sam. *Fosse*. New York: Houghton Mifflin Harcourt, 2013.

Weiler, A. H. "By Way of Report: Back to Films." *New York Times*, June 13, 1954. Retrieved August 17, 2014, from http://www.nytimes.com.

———. "Of People and Pictures: Sales Report." *New York Times*, May 15, 1955. Retrieved August 17, 2014, from http://www.nytimes.com.

———. "Screen: Charleston Era: Mayfair Has 'Gentlemen Marry Brunettes.'" *New York Times*, October 31, 1955. Retrieved March 31, 2014, from http://www.nytimes.com.

Wilson, Earl. "The Girl Who Showed 'Em How." *Silver Screen* 24, no. 4 (1954): 24–25, 56.

Wilson, John S. "Comediennes on LP." *New York Times*, February 19, 1956. Retrieved August 18, 2014, from http://www.nytimes.com.

———. "A Famous 'Redhead.'" *New York Times*, May 10, 1959. Retrieved September 5, 2014, from http://www.nytimes.com.

———. "Recordings View: Musicals to Be Seen, Not Heard." *New York Times*, August 31, 1975. Retrieved October 5, 2014, from http://www.nytimes.com.

———. "31 Songwriters Inducted into Music's Hall of Fame: One for Cosmetician." *New York Times*, May 17, 1972. Retrieved October 3, 2014, from http://www.nytimes.com.

———. "Whatever Verdon Sings." *New York Times*, February 27, 1966. Retrieved September 8, 2014, from http://www.nytimes.com.

Winchell, Walter. *Daytona Beach Morning Journal*, December 28, 1949. Retrieved January 30, 2014, from http://www.google.newspapers.com.

Wittibois, James. H. *Watching M*A*S*H, Watching America: A Social History of the 1972–1983 Television Series*. Jefferson, NC: McFarland, 2003.

Wollman, Elizabeth L. *The Theater Will Rock: A History of the Rock Musical, from Hair to Hedwig*. Ann Arbor: University of Michigan Press, 2006.

Woollcott, Alexander. "'Anna Christie':

Second Thoughts on First Nights." *New York Times*, November 13, 1921. Retrieved May 7, 2014, from http://www.nytimes.com.

Wooten, Frank. "'In Cold Blood' Triggers a Chillier Reaction Now." *The Post and Courier*, November 21, 1996. Retrieved February 25, 2014, from http://www.news.google.com.

Yarrow, Andrew L. "Stars Gather in Tribute to George Abbott at 100." *New York Times*, June 23, 1987. Retrieved July 1, 2014, from http://www.nytimes.com.

Zinsser, William K. "Far Out on Long Island." *Horizon* 5, no. 5 (1963): 4–27.

Zolotow, Sam. "Adieu to Gwen Verdon." *New York Times*, April 21, 1958. Retrieved August 21, 2014, from http://www.nytimes.com.

_____. "Cast of 'La Plume,' French Hit, Gets Special Tony." *New York Times*, April 13, 1959. Retrieved September 6, 2014, from http://www.nytimes.com.

_____. "'Christine,' Musical, Booked." *New York Times*, January 1, 1960. Retrieved September 6, 2014, from http://www.nytimes.com.

_____. "Fryer-Carr Ponder Show." *New York Times*, March 11, 1958. Retrieved August 21, 2014, from http://www.nytimes.com.

_____. "'Girls of Summer' Arriving Tonight." *New York Times*, November 19, 1956. Retrieved August 18, 2014, from http://www.nytimes.com.

_____. "Greer Garson Set to Star in 'Mame.'" *New York Times*, June 3, 1957. Retrieved August 19, 2014, from http://www.nytimes.com.

_____. "Gwen Verdon Injured." *New York Times*, August 12, 1959. Retrieved September 6, 2014, from http://www.nytimes.com.

_____. "Gwen Verdon to Do Movie." *New York Times*, August 27, 1954. Retrieved August 17, 2014, from http://www.nytimes.com.

_____. "Gwen Verdon Returns." *New York Times*, May 17, 1966. Retrieved September 8, 2014, from http://www.nytimes.com.

_____. "'Hello, Dolly!' Wins Half of Theater Wing's 20 Tonys." *New York Times*, May 25, 1964. Retrieved July 13, 2014, from http://www.nytimes.com.

_____. "Japanese Movie to Be Stage Play." *New York Times*, June 10, 1957. Retrieved August 19, 2014, from http://www.nytimes.com.

_____. "Judith Anderson Weighs New Role." *New York Times*, February 19, 1958. Retrieved August 21, 2014, from http://www.nytimes.com.

_____. "Lerner Musical Accounts for Largest Pre-Offering Sale." *New York Times*, October 15, 1965. Retrieved September 8, 2014, from http://www.nytimes.com.

_____. "Lillian Hellman Forms Stage Firm." *New York Times*, May 30, 1957. Retrieved August 19, 2014, from http://www.nytimes.com.

_____. "Max Wilk Comedy Finds A Producer." *New York Times*, June 7, 1957. Retrieved August 19, 2014, from http://www.nytimes.com.

_____. "Miller Theater Brings $500,000: Producer's Wife Is Selling it to Detroit Chain." *New York Times*, November 1, 1966. Retrieved August 16, 2014, from http://www.nytimes.com.

_____. "Musical Planned For Gwen Verdon: Bob Fosse, Her Husband, to Try Show He Conceived." *New York Times*, April 26, 1963. Retrieved September 7, 2014, from http://www.nytimes.com.

_____. "Musical Postponed." *New York Times*, October 8, 1958. Retrieved September 6, 2014, from http://www.nytimes.com.

_____. "Musical to Rely on Fellini Movie." *New York Times*, July 8, 1965. Retrieved September 8, 2014, from http://www.nytimes.com.

_____. "Notes on the Theatre." *New York Times*, October 30, 1959. Retrieved September 6, 2014, from http://www.nytimes.com.

_____. "Opening Dates Exchanged." *New*

York Times, January 17, 1966. Retrieved September 8, 2014, from http://www.nytimes.com.

_____. "Palace Premiere Postponed." *New York Times,* August 28, 1965. Retrieved September 8, 2014, from http://www.nytimes.com.

_____. "Palace Seating Capacity Cut." *New York Times,* August 11, 1965. Retrieved September 8, 2014, from http://www.nytimes.com.

_____. "'Redhead' Is Going on Tour of West." *New York Times,* January 26, 1960. Retrieved September 6, 2014, from http://www.nytimes.com.

_____. "'Sea Gull' To Open At 4th St. Tonight." *New York Times,* October 22, 1956. Retrieved August 18, 2014, from http://www.nytimes.com.

_____. "Summer Measures." *New York Times,* July 6, 1966. Retrieved September 9, 2014, from http://www.nytimes.com.

_____. "'Sweet Charity' Arrives Dec. 28 as 'New' Palace's First Show." *New York Times,* July 22, 1965. Retrieved September 8, 2014, from http://www.nytimes.com.

_____. "Sweet Stardom." *New York Times,* June 30, 1967. Retrieved October 2, 2014, from http://www.nytimes.com.

_____. "Theatre Wings 'Tony' Awards Presented at Dinner Here." *New York Times,* April 2, 1956. Retrieved August 18, 2014, from http://www.nytimes.com.

_____. "Vacation." *New York Times,* April 29, 1966. Retrieved September 8, 2014, from http://www.nytimes.com.

_____. "A Year Old and Growing." *New York Times,* January 27, 1967. Retrieved October 2, 2014, from http://www.nytimes.com.

Index

Numbers in **_bold italics_** indicate pages with illustrations.

A&E Biography 231–232
Abbott, George 42, 46, 47, 49, 51, 52, 55, 56, 58, 59, 60, 62, 63, 65, 66, 76, 121, 201, 214, 219, 221
Alice 211–***212***, 222
Alive and Kicking ***17***, 18–19, 167, 190
All Is Forgiven 198
All That Jazz 142, 167, 169–171, 172–***174***, 175, 203, 214
Allen, Debbie 182, 183, ***184***, 191, 193–194, 197, 198, 200, 202, 213, 226–227
Allen, Woody 211–212
Ameche, Don 189, 190, 209
American Dance Machine 166–167, 179–180, 181, 193, 198

Bancroft, Anne 217, 218
Beddow, Margery 3, 79, 81, 82, 113, 223
Best Friends for Life 207
Big Deal 191, 197, 198, 204
Blonde from Brooklyn 12, 13
The Bob Hope Show 126–128
Bonanza Bound! 16
Breakfast at Tiffany's (stage) 93, 96, 97–98, 102
Broadway: The Golden Age, By the Legends Who Were There 233–234
Bruno 232–233
Burnett, Carol 87, 88, 90, 91, 181
Burrows, Abe 33, 34, 102

Cabaret (film) 132, 133, 135–137, 165
Can-Can (film) 43, 121
Can-Can (stage) 2, 11, 15, 32, 35–36, ***37***, 38, 39, 40, 42, 43, 51, 58, 62, 78, 84, 102, 129, 134, 143, 153, 170, 212, 225, 234, 236
Capote, Truman 93, 97, 98, 223

Captain Kangaroo 157, 164
The Carol Burnett Show 124, 132
Cavett, Dick 27, 33
Champion, Marge 7, 8
Channing, Carol 2, 218
Charlie Rose 175, 230
Charnin, Martin 95, 114
Chicago (film) 162, 163, 236
Chicago (stage) 42, 78, 93, 94, 143, 150, 151, 152, 153–154, 157–***159***, 160–163, 164, 165, 166, 168, 172, 188, 193, 212, 223, 225, 230, 235, 236
Children! Children! 2, 138–139, ***140***, 168
Cocoon 189–190, 209, 234
Cocoon: The Return 209, 234
Cole, Jack 1, 2, 12, 13, 14, 15, 16, 17, 18, 19, 20, 21, 22, 23, 24, 25, 26, 27, 28, 29, 31, 32, 34, 35, 39, 43, 45, 57, 59, 123, 149–150, 155, 166, 169, 170, 183, 190, 217, 223, 235, 236
Coleman, Cy 90, 95, 99, 111, 128, 130, 149, 191, 213, 217, 227, 235, 236
Coppola, Francis Ford 179, 186
The Cosby Mysteries 219–220
The Cotton Club 179, 186–187, 222
Cronyn, Hume 221, 222

Damn Yankees (film) 1, 2, 61, 63, 64, 65–***68***, 69–70, 91, 121, 144, 177, 213, 214, 233, 234
Damn Yankees (stage) 12, 45, 46–***50***, 51, 52, 53, 54, 55, 57, 61, 78, 83, 88, 89, 91, 116, 123, 127, 134, 139, 150, 170, 201, 210, 219, 225, 232, 233, 236
Dancin' 172, 175–176, 193, 213
The Danny Kaye Show 96, 98, 99, ***100***, 101, 107

David and Bathsheba 23, **24**
Davis, Sammy, Jr. 33, 118, 123, 125
Deadly Visitor 3, 147, **148**
Dear John 209–210
The Dick Cavett Show 132, 133, 134, 169–171
The Dinah Shore Chevy Shore 70, 71, 78–79
Donen, Stanley 27, 63, 65, 66, 113, 157, 206
Douglass, Stephen 49, **50**, 51, 53, 65
Dream On 215–216
Dreamboat 27

E! True Hollywood Story 203, 207, 230
Easter Parade 16–17
Ebb, Fred 143, 151, 153, 155, 157, 158, 160, 162, 173, 188, 191, 193, 217, 224, 235, 236
The Ed Sullivan Show 19, 40, 119, 122, 124–125, 130–131, 133, 214
Ed Sullivan's Broadway 143–144, **145**, 150
The Equalizer 195

Fame (TV show) 182–183, **184**, 191
The Farmer Takes a Wife 29–30, 34
Fields, Dorothy 63, 71, 75, 91, 95, 99, 111, 133
Fosse (stage) 128, 228–229, 230, 231, 232, 236
Fosse, Bob 1, 2, 3, 6, 14, 15, 16, 18, 34, 35, 42, 45, 46–47, 48, 51, 52, 54, 55, 56, 57, 58, 59, 60, 61, 62, 63, 65, 66, 67, 71, 72, 74, 75, 76, 77, 78, 79, 80, 81, 84, 85, 88, 89, 90, 91, 92, 93, 94, 95, 96, 97, 99, 102, 103, 104, 105, 106, 107, 108, 109, 111, 112, 113, 114, 115, 116, 117, 118, 120, 121, 122, 123, 124, 125, 126, 128, 130, 131, 132, 133, 134, 135, 136, 137, 141, 142, 143, 144, 146, 147, 150, 151, 152, 153, 154, 155, 156, 157, 158, 159, 160, 161, 162, 163, 166, 167, 168, 169, 170, 171, 172, 173, 174, 175, 176, 177, 179, 183, 187, 190, 191, 193, 194, 197, 200, 201, 202, 203, 204, 205, 206, 207, 208, 212–213, 214, 216, 218, 222, 223, 228, 230, 231, 232, 233, 234, 235, 236
Fosse, Nicole 91, 92, 96, 99, 102, 105, 106, 112, 116, 117, 122, 123, 128, 129, 130, 133, 135, 136, 137, 138, 141, 142, 146, 147, 148, 151, 152, 155, 156, 157, 161, 163, 165, 167, 169, 173, 175, 176, 177, 178, 179, 183, 204, 205, 207, 213, 214, 215, 230, 234, 235
Funny Girl (stage) 95–96

Garbo, Greta 5–6, 56
Garland, Judy 10
The Gary Moore Show 85, 87–88, 89–90, 91, 96, 97, 214
Gaynor, Mitzi 25, 26, 45, 70, 223
Gentlemen Marry Brunettes 43–45, 54
Gentlemen Prefer Blondes 31, 34, 44
Gimme a Break! 187–188
Goodyear Television Playhouse 40
Gottfried, Martin 3, 22, 213–214
Grable, Betty 24, 25, **26**, 29, 33, 52, 217
Great Performances: Dance in America 214, *215*
Grubb, Kevin Boyd 3, 212–213

Hague, Albert 63, 71, 74, 75, 182, 236
Haney, Carol 11, 14, 27, 45, 47, 98
Happy Birthday Mr. Abbott! / The Night of 100 Years 201
Harris, Roy 2–3, 225
Hayworth, Rita 13, 33
Henaghan, Jimmy 11, 31, 32, 37, 51, 55, 61, 63, 65, 70, 97, 106, 148, 163, 230, 235
Homicide: Life on the Street 216
Hotel (TV show) 200–201
Howard, Ron 189, 209
Hunter, Tab 65, 66, 70

The I Don't Care Girl 25–26
In Cold Blood 223

The Jerk, Too 187

Kander, John 143, 151, 153, 157, 160, 162, 188, 191, 193, 217, 224, 235, 236
Kaye, Danny 20, 21, 22, 33, 72, 96, 98, 99, **100**, 101, 107
Keaton, Diane 221, 222
Kelly, Gene 14, 27, 149
Key West 216–217
Kidd, Michael 32, 33, 34, 35, 36, 37, 38, 54, 170, 236
Kiley, Richard 72, 73, 75, 76, 79, 123, 125, 134
The King Steps Out 9

Lanning, Jerry 70, 150, 152, 163, 167
Laurie, Piper 30, 31
Legs 185

Lilo 35–36, 38
Loney, Glenn 3, 190
Love Letters (stage) 213

MacLaine, Shirley 43, 111, 121, 122, 123, 125, 126, 166, 172–173, 232, 234
Magdalena 17, 167
Magnum, P.I. 194, 199–200, 205–206, 207–208
Marvin's Room 218, 221–222
*M*A*S*H* (TV show) 180–181, 191, 198
May, Elaine 95, 99, 102, 103
McCracken, Joan 16, 54, 63, 80, 85, 86
McKechnie, Donna 85, 144, 165–166, 202, 205, 227
McMartin, John 106, 111, 113, 122
Meet Me After the Show 19, 24–25, **26**, 52
Meisner, Sanford 48, 56, 57, 101, 213
Merman, Ethel 2, 37, 71, 144
The Merry Widow **28**–29, 34, 213
The Merv Griffin Show 118, 119, 120, 133
The Mike Douglas Show 128–130, 133, 139, 167–168
Minnelli, Liza 135, 141, 161–162, 165, 193, 223, 225, 230
The Mississippi Gambler **30**, 129
Monroe, Marilyn 31, 32, 33, 43, 45, 56, 70

Nadine 198–**199**
Neuwirth, Bebe 197, 217, 218, 227, 235, 236
New Girl in Town 48, 55–**62**, 63, 78, 89, 95, 129, 139, 170, 212, 214, 225, 230, 236
Night of 100 Stars II 190–191
Nights of Cabiria 93, 94, 95, 96, 99, 102, 105–106
The Nutcracker 177–178, 179

Oldest Living Confederate Widow Tells All 217–218
On the Riviera 20, **21**, 23, 34
Once Upon an Eastertime 40, **41**

The Pajama Game 43, 45, 46, 48, 52, 89, 91, 230, 234
Palmer, Leland 142, 172, 173, **174**
Parade of Stars 185–186
Paris Is Burning 210–211
Perry Como's Kraft Music Hall 83–84, 86–87

Porter, Cole 33, 36, 38, 143
Power, Tyrone 25, 30
Presenting Lily Mars 10
Prince, Harold 45, 46, 49, 55, 56, 58, 59, 60, 62, 83, 132, 137, 144
Promised Land 226

Redhead (film) 78, 79
Redhead (stage) 2, 63, 64, 71–76, 77, 78, 79, 80, 88, 89, 91, 92, 93, 95, 101, 102, 111, 116, 117, 123, 134, 139, 182, 212, 214, 225, 236
Reinking, Ann 86, 146–147, 151–152, 155, 156, 157, 160, 161, 162–163, 169, 174, 175, 178, 183, 190, 191, 200, 202, 206, 207, 223, 224, 228, 230, 231, 235
Ritter, Thelma 55, 59, 61, 214
Rivera, Chita 118, 123, 126, 141, 143, 153, 154, 155, 157, 158, **159**, 160, 161, 162, 163, 164, 165, 166, 167, 168, 188, 192, 193, 202, 217, 224, 225, 226, 235
Robbins, Jerome 54, 170, 211
Rogers, Ginger 27, 42
The Rosie O'Donnell Show 230
Russell, Jane 31, 32, 44, 149

St. Leon, Kim 156, 206
Sanford Meisner: The American Theatre's Best Kept Secret 213
Scheider, Roy 172, 173, **174**, 175, 203, 206
Selleck, Tom 194, 200, 205, 206, 207
Sgt. Pepper's Lonely Hearts Club Band (film) 171
Sheldon, Sidney 63, 71, 72
Simon, Neil 76, 90, 103–104, 105, 113, 132, 137, 208, 210, 215, 218
Sinatra, Frank 43, 52–53
Singin' in the Rain 27–28
Star 80 183, 187
Streep, Meryl 221, 222
Streisand, Barbra 95, 111–112
Sweet Charity (film) 120, 121–123, 124, 125–126, 130, 163, 170, 186, 191
Sweet Charity (stage) 1, 2, 40, 93, 94, 102, 103–105, 106–**110**, 111–118, 122, 124, 127, 129, 130, 133, 139, 141, 166, 170, 179, 185–186, 188, 191, 193–194, 197, 200, 202–203, 204, 206, 212, 213, 225, 226–228, 230, 235, 236

Toast of the Town see *The Ed Sullivan Show*

Touched by an Angel 224
Trapper John, M.D. 191–***192***

Ungerer, Phoebe 190, 202, 205, 206

Walker, Texas Ranger 225–226, 230–231

Walking Across Egypt 232
Walston, Ray 49, 51, 53, 66, 67, 134, 150, 188, 213, 236
Wasson, Sam 3, 236
Webster 194–195, 196–197, 208–209

www.ingramcontent.com/pod-product-compliance
Ingram Content Group UK Ltd.
Pitfield, Milton Keynes, MK11 3LW, UK
UKHW041932140426
5217IPUK00014B/432